Table of Contents

A Visual Approach to SPSS for Windows
A Guide to SPSS 17.0

Second Edition

Leonard D. Stern
Eastern Washington University

Allyn & Bacon

Boston   New York   San Francisco
Mexico City   Montreal   Toronto   London   Madrid   Munich   Paris
Hong Kong   Singapore   Tokyo   Cape Town   Sydney

TO BARBARA

Acquisitions Editor: *Michelle Limoges*
Editorial Assistant: *Paige Clunie*
Marketing Manager: *Nicole Kunzmann*
Production Assistant: *Maggie Brobeck*
Manufacturing Buyer: *JoAnne Sweeney*
Cover Administrator: Brenda Carmichael

10 9 8 7 6 5 4 3   15 14 13

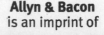
Allyn & Bacon
is an imprint of

ISBN 10: 0-205-00207-2
ISBN 13: 978-0-205-00207-8

Preface

When I began using *SPSS for Windows* several years ago, I already had considerable experience with the statistical package. However, my experience was with a version of the program that ran from lines of text usually typed into a file and submitted to a mainframe computer from a remote terminal. The *Windows* version was supposed to make running *SPSS* easier because it was based on pull-down menus rather than lines of commands that had to conform to rules of syntax. I thought that making the switch to the *Windows* version of the program would be easy. I was wrong. In my first attempt to use the *Windows* version, I managed to enter data for analysis using an *ANOVA*. However, I couldn't find a way to name the variables. I also had difficulty locating the menu from which to request the analysis, and when I did, and managed to run the analysis, I found I had made an error entering the data but was unable to find my way back to the data from the window that showed the results. My point here is that if you want to use your time efficiently, you'll need instructions for using the program.

Once I learned the basics of using *SPSS for Windows*, my next problem was how to teach it to others. The process of teaching the older version of *SPSS* was straightforward. To convey how to request an analysis, I showed students lines of text that I had recorded in my lecture notes and described (as well as demonstrated) what each line or series of lines did. Students, in turn, wrote the commands in their notes and used them to run their own analyses. Teaching the *Windows* version of the program was not so easy. I had difficulty recording in my lecture notes what needed to be done. Some sequences were easy to describe such as where to locate commands in the pull-down menus. Others were more difficult, such as the sequence of variables to transfer, buttons to click, windows that open, and options to select. To record the necessary information, I found it useful to make a quick sketch of each window that opened, and to attach a sequence of numbered instructions that pointed to locations that had to be acted on to request a procedure. This approach was the beginning of the technique I use in this guide, an approach I call visual sequencing.

Use of most *Windows* programs involves responding primarily to visual prompts—clicking on sub-menu items that become visible in pull-down menus, selecting buttons that become accessible in windows, typing characters using the keyboard into fields displayed in windows. Describing such processes with words is generally cumbersome and difficult for the listener to follow. It's much easier to point to something and say "click this" than to rely exclusively on words that describe the location of a button in a window and the action that must be taken. The visual approach used in this guide is intended to mirror the visually-based interactions required for running *SPSS for Windows*. Numbered instructions and arrows that are presented guide the reader through the sequences of actions needed to perform each task. The same approach is applied to assist the reader in inspecting the output of an analysis.

The guide is intended to be helpful to new users of *SPSS* who have (or are in the process of acquiring) basic knowledge of statistical procedures. In the first few chapters, fundamental information about the program is presented, such as how to start *SPSS*, and how to enter, modify, and save data. These chapters also introduce the basic components of the program such as the viewer and the data editor. The next few chapters cover ways to describe single distributions. The remaining chapters show how to conduct statistical analyses with *SPSS* that are most frequently covered in an introductory course such as *t*-tests, *ANOVA*s, regression analyses, chi-square tests, and other nonparametric tests. In addition, more advanced procedures—exploratory factor analysis and discriminant analysis—are described. In each chapter that presents an analytic procedure, I review underlying theory, including key formulas for the analysis and assumptions about the data, and give an example of how the outcome of each analysis is reported. Assignments at the end of each chapter draw on real-world data from various disciplines.

This second edition of the text incorporates several changes from what appeared in the previous edition. Most notably, use of the most recent version of the software, **SPSS Statistics 17.0** is described. The latest version of *SPSS* has a number of new features. Additions to the *Base* version include the ability to easily create a codebook that describes the dataset (see Appendix C), an improved graphing procedure (see Chapter 6), and an improved ability to export tables to *Microsoft Office*® products (e.g., *Microsoft Word*®, see Chapter 5). For more experienced users, version 17 has an enhanced syntax editor to facilitate preparation of syntax statements; it allows preparation of Window interfaces through the **Custom Dialog Builder** that enable less experienced users to easily implement specified procedures; and it has improved ways to deal with missing data. A summary of the new features of **SPSS Statistics 17** and a comparison of the features with previous versions is available at this web address:

http://www.spss.com/media/collateral/S17CMP-06081.pdf

A detailed list of the features available in **SPSS Statistics 17.0** *Base*, with new features highlighted, is available here:

http://www.spss.com/media/collateral/S17SPC-06081.pdf

Another key change in the second edition of this text is the availability of answers to odd-numbered end-of-chapter exercises.

I wish to thank all at Allyn & Bacon who have assisted with this project, especially Susan Hartman, Editor in Chief in Psychology and Michelle Limoges, Acquisitions Editor in Psychology for their encouragement, helpful advice, and trust in my ability to see this project to completion. I also want to thank my family, my children Drew, Chelsea, and Jennifer, for their support during the many months that I spent working on the book. I specially thank my daughter Chelsea for generously and willingly giving up many hours of her spring break from college to proofread some of the introductory chapters in the first edition. By catching and correcting numerous errors she considerably improved these chapters. I also thank my wife, Barbara, to whom I dedicate this book, for her encouragement and inspiration; without the motivation and support she provided, I never would have completed this guide.

Chapter 1: The Basics

Starting SPSS

If *SPSS Statistics 17* (or a previous version) is installed on a computer running under *Windows XP*, you can start *SPSS* either by finding an icon on the desktop that looks like the one shown below and double-clicking it;

or, if no such icon is available on your desktop, by following the sequence shown below:

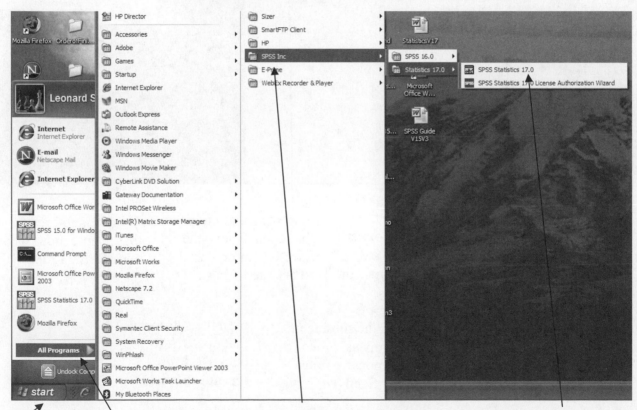

1. Move the mouse pointer over the **Start** button and click the left mouse button once.

2. Move the mouse pointer over the **All Programs** icon.

3. In the program list that opens, move the mouse pointer over the **SPSS Inc** listing.

4. In the sub-menu that opens, left-click **SPSS 17.0**.

Because it's easier to start *SPSS* by double-clicking an *SPSS* icon on the desktop, it is worthwhile taking time to create a desktop icon if one does not exist (and if you have permission to modify the desktop). To create such an icon, follow the procedure shown below which differs from that shown above only in that step 4 requires a single right-click of the mouse button before proceeding to the new steps 5 and 6.

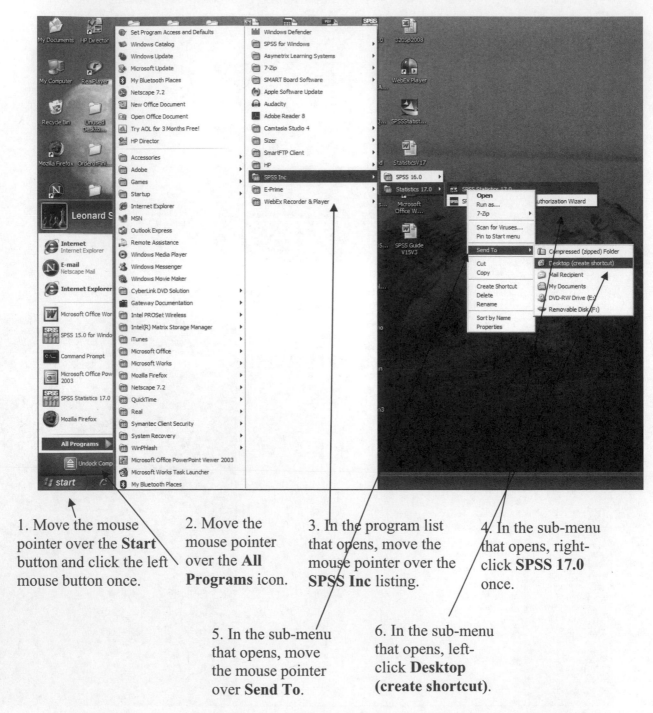

1. Move the mouse pointer over the **Start** button and click the left mouse button once.

2. Move the mouse pointer over the **All Programs** icon.

3. In the program list that opens, move the mouse pointer over the **SPSS Inc** listing.

4. In the sub-menu that opens, right-click **SPSS 17.0** once.

5. In the sub-menu that opens, move the mouse pointer over **Send To**.

6. In the sub-menu that opens, left-click **Desktop (create shortcut)**.

Note that from now on, the instruction to click with the mouse will mean to click the left button on the mouse; if the right mouse button is to be clicked, the instruction will be to right-click the mouse.

Exiting SPSS

As with most *Windows* programs, you can close *SPSS* by selecting **Exit** from the **File** menu or by clicking on the close box in the *SPSS* window that is active:

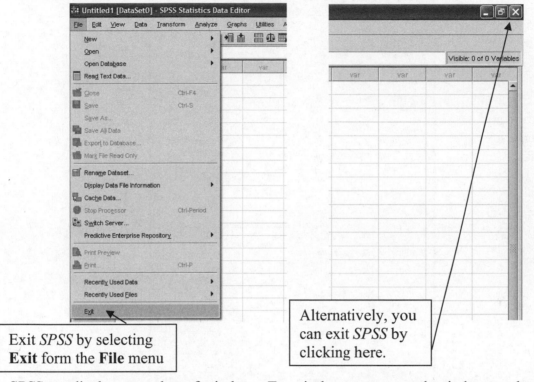

Exit *SPSS* by selecting **Exit** form the **File** menu

Alternatively, you can exit *SPSS* by clicking here.

SPSS can display a number of windows. To exit the program, each window can be closed using the procedure described above. If the window contains modified data, (for example, if you have entered new data into the **Data Editor** spreadsheet) a dialog box is presented asking if you want to save the contents in a file. If you click the **No** button, the window will close without saving the contents. Information about saving *SPSS* data files will be presented later in Chapter 2.

Using the Tutorial for More Information

There is a tutorial available in *SPSS* that gives more information about features of *SPSS*. To access the tutorial, use one of these procedures:

    1) Use the **Help** menu on the **Toolbar**.

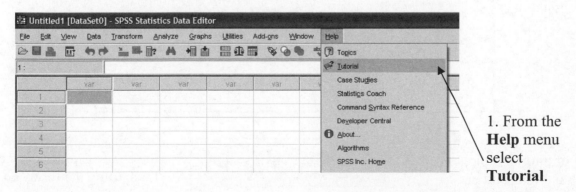

1. From the **Help** menu select **Tutorial**.

2) Alternatively, if the program begins by displaying a window such as the one shown below that asks what you would like to do, select the option **Run the tutorial** and click the button marked **OK**.

1. Click this option and then click **OK**.

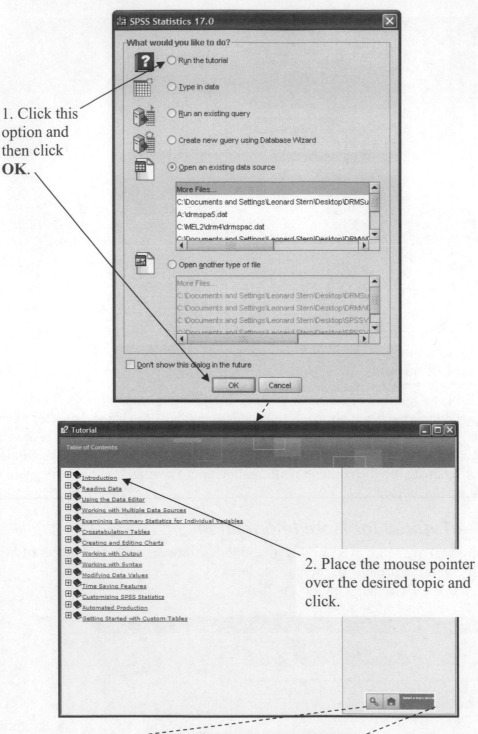

2. Place the mouse pointer over the desired topic and click.

4. You can return to the list of tutorial topics by pressing this button.

3. You can proceed through the contents of the selected topic using the forward (or reverse) arrows.

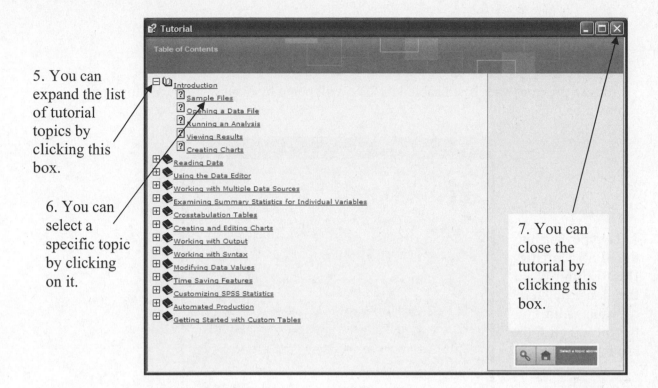

5. You can expand the list of tutorial topics by clicking this box.

6. You can select a specific topic by clicking on it.

7. You can close the tutorial by clicking this box.

Exercises for Chapter 1

Exercise 1.1

If *SPSS* is installed on your computer, start the program. If a window opens that presents the question "What would you like to do?" click the button labeled **Cancel.** Explore the contents of the menus shown in the toolbar. Exit the program. If you have entered data into the spreadsheet, do not save it.

Exercise 1.2

Start *SPSS*. Start the tutorial. Expand the *Introduction* in the Table of Contents and read the topic *Sample Files* (it's just a single page). Exit the program when you've finished.

Chapter 2: Entering and Saving Data

Entering Data Using the Keyboard

Unless a previous user has disabled it, *SPSS* will begin by displaying the dialog box shown below:

1. To type data into the **SPSS Statistics Data Editor**, place the mouse pointer over this radio button and click the left mouse button.

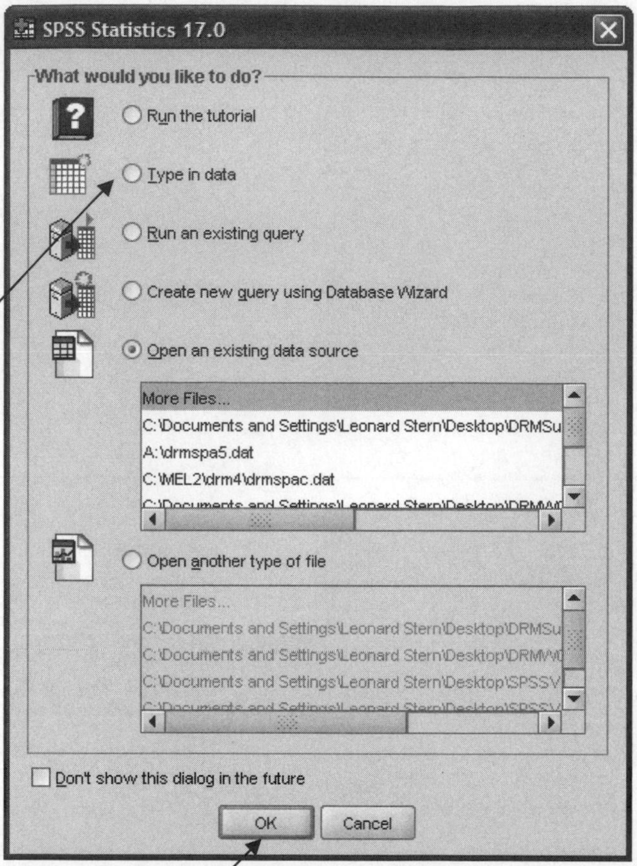

2. Click **OK**.

Making the selections shown above takes you to the **SPSS Statistics Data Editor**. You now can type in numeric data that *SPSS* can subsequently analyze.

The process of typing data into the **SPSS Statistics Data Editor** will be illustrated with a small data set. The data shown below represent the number of arguments occurring during the interval between therapy sessions one and two reported by each of 20 hypothetical couples receiving marriage counseling:

2 4 5 9 0 10 1 2 8 4 3 1 7 8 3 2 3 2 5 2

The data can be entered into the **SPSS Statistics Data Editor** using the procedure outlined below:

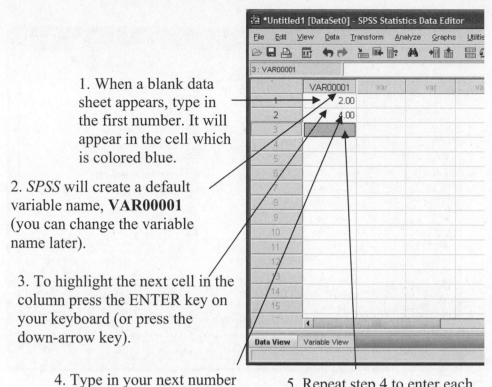

1. When a blank data sheet appears, type in the first number. It will appear in the cell which is colored blue.

2. *SPSS* will create a default variable name, **VAR00001** (you can change the variable name later).

3. To highlight the next cell in the column press the ENTER key on your keyboard (or press the down-arrow key).

4. Type in your next number then press the ENTER key

5. Repeat step 4 to enter each number into the spreadsheet.

Entering Data from an SPSS Data File

Data saved in an *SPSS* data file will have the extension *.sav*. For example, if the file named *demo* that was created previously has been saved as an *SPSS* file, it will have the name *demo.sav*. To open an *SPSS* file stored in or accessible from your computer do the following:

If the data editor is showing   If this dialog box is showing

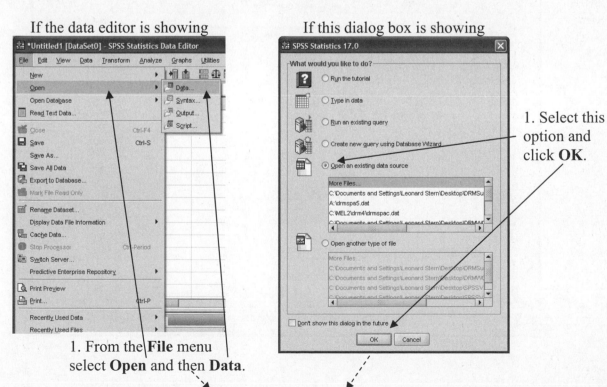

1. Select this option and click **OK**.

1. From the **File** menu select **Open** and then **Data**.

2. Select the location of the *SPSS* file by clicking on an icon in this panel or by using this drop-down list.

3. Use the drop-down menu to select *.sav* as the file type if *.sav* is not already showing.

4. Position the mouse over the desired *SPSS* file and give it a single click to place the file name in the **File name** box.

5. Click here to open the file.

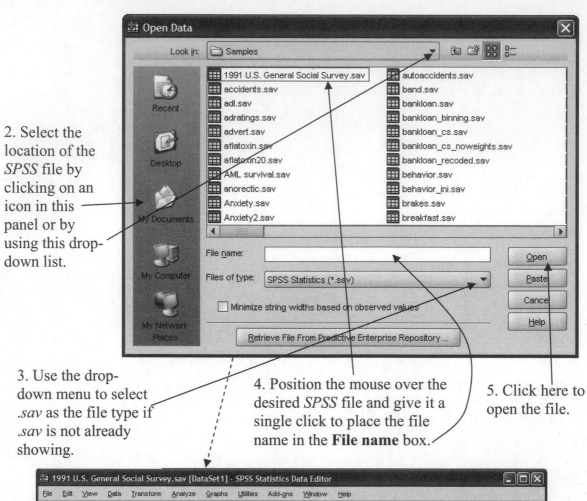

Entering Data from a Microsoft Excel® *File*

Data that has been stored in a *Microsoft Excel®* file can easily be imported into *SPSS*. Starting with the **SPSS Statistics Data Editor** showing, do the following:

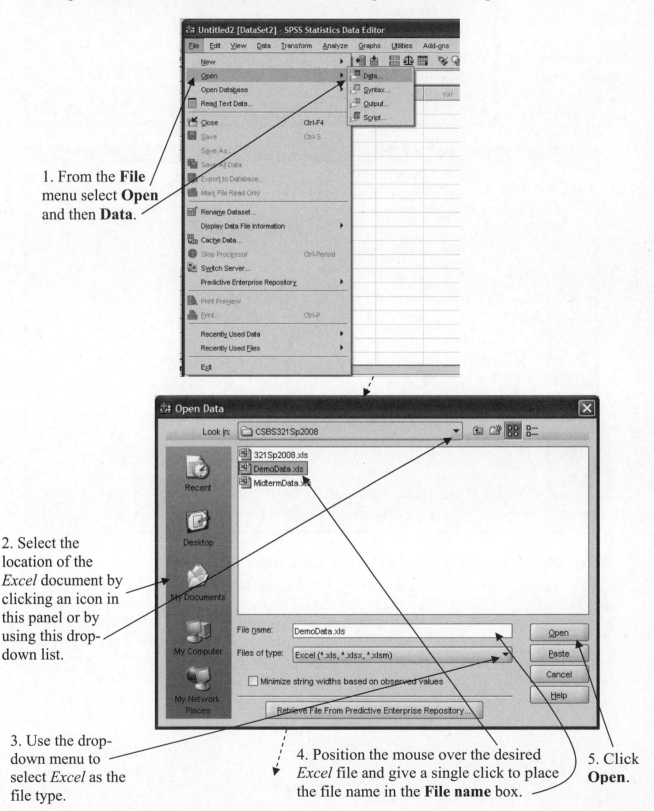

1. From the **File** menu select **Open** and then **Data**.

2. Select the location of the *Excel* document by clicking an icon in this panel or by using this drop-down list.

3. Use the drop-down menu to select *Excel* as the file type.

4. Position the mouse over the desired *Excel* file and give a single click to place the file name in the **File name** box.

5. Click **Open**.

6. Select this option if the file has variable names in row 1.

7. Click **OK** to import the data

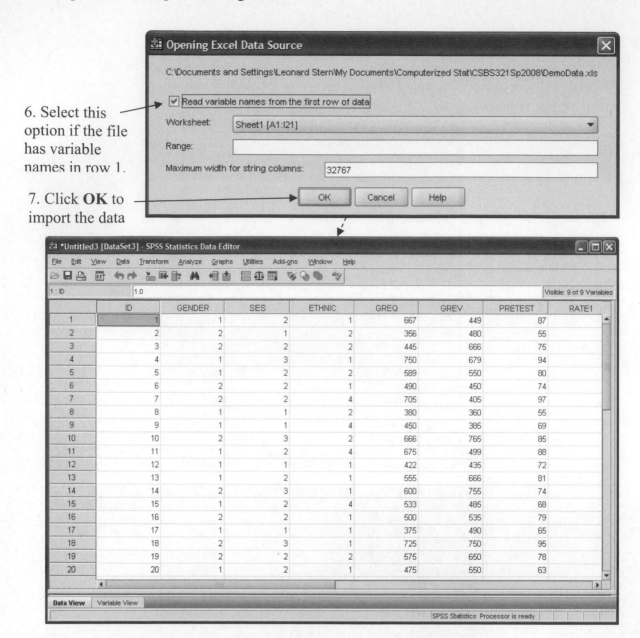

Entering Data from a Text (.txt) or Data (.dat) File

Data files that have the extension *.txt* or *.dat* represent information in a format that is distinct from *SPSS* and *Microsoft Excel*® data files (those given the extension *.sav* and *.xls*, respectively). The sequence shown below illustrates the process of reading a data file into *SPSS* that was created with a word-processing program such as *Notepad* and given the extension *.dat*. In the data file, values are separated by a space.

1. From the **File** menu select **Read Text Data**.

2. Select the location of the *.dat* or *.txt* file by clicking an icon in this panel or by using this drop-down list.

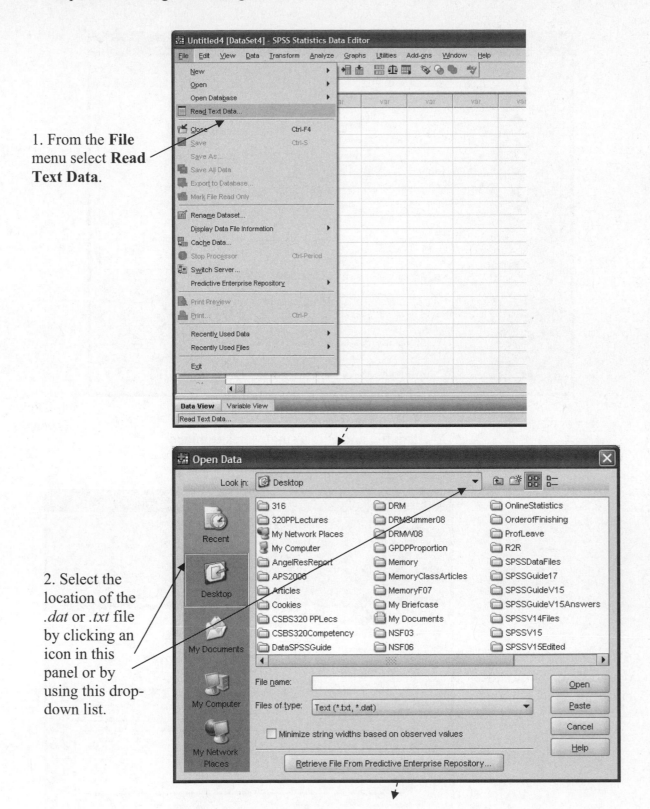

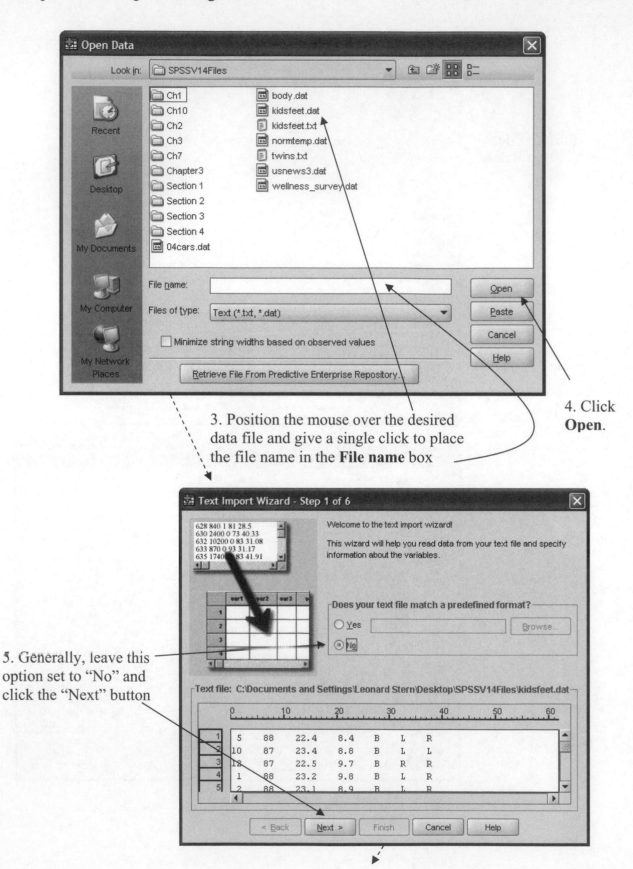

3. Position the mouse over the desired data file and give a single click to place the file name in the **File name** box

4. Click **Open**.

5. Generally, leave this option set to "No" and click the "Next" button

6. Because the data are separated by spaces (rather than having assigned columns) leave the option selected to "Delimited."

7. Because no variable names are listed on the first line of this data file, leave this option set to "No."

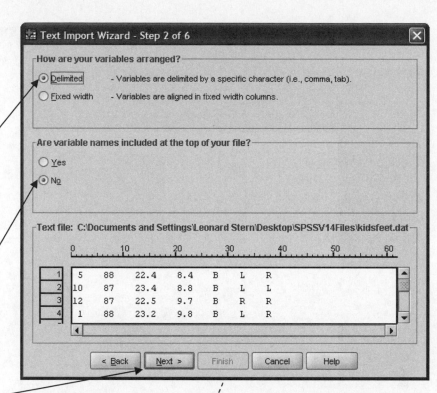

8. Click **Next**.

9. No variable names are listed on the first line of the data file, and the first case begins on line 1. Therefore leave this value set to "1."

10. Data for each case begins on a separate line. Leave this option selected.

11. To import data for all cases, leave this option selected.

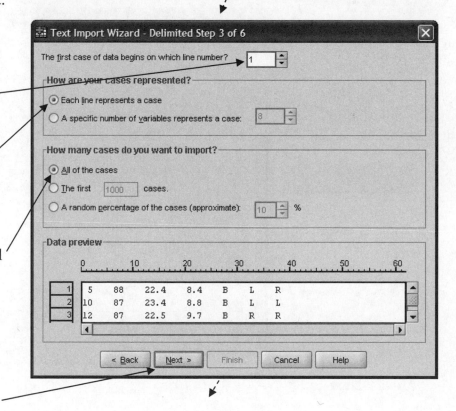

12. Click **Next**.

13. The wizard has detected that values in the file are separated by a space. If the data showing in the **Data preview** window look correct, leave this option selected.

14. Click **Next**.

15. If you wish, you can highlight a variable name that *SPSS* has created by placing the mouse pointer over the variable name and single- or double-clicking.

16. The variable name and data format appears. Each can be changed from the default value if necessary.

17. Click **Next**.

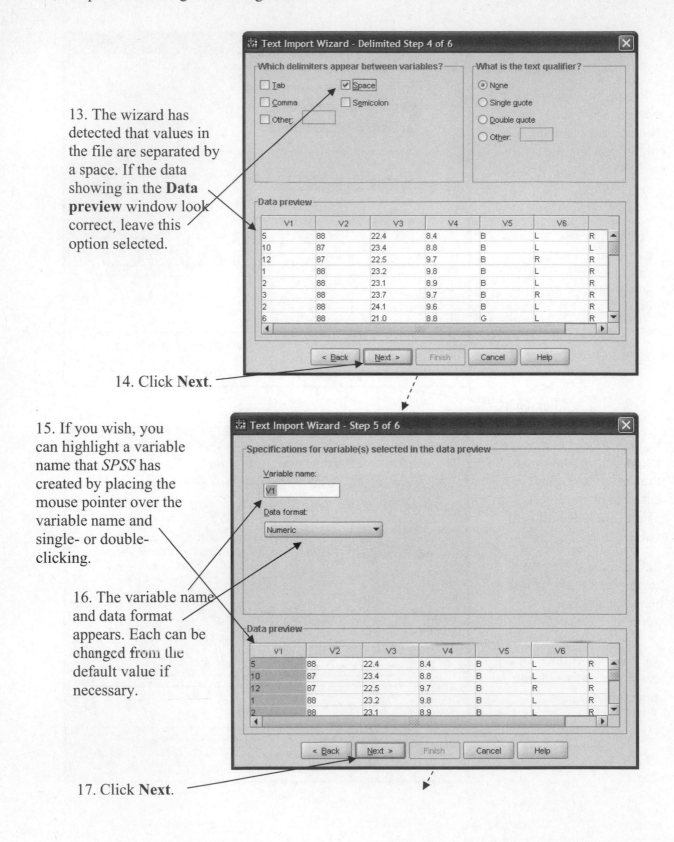

18. Click
Finish.

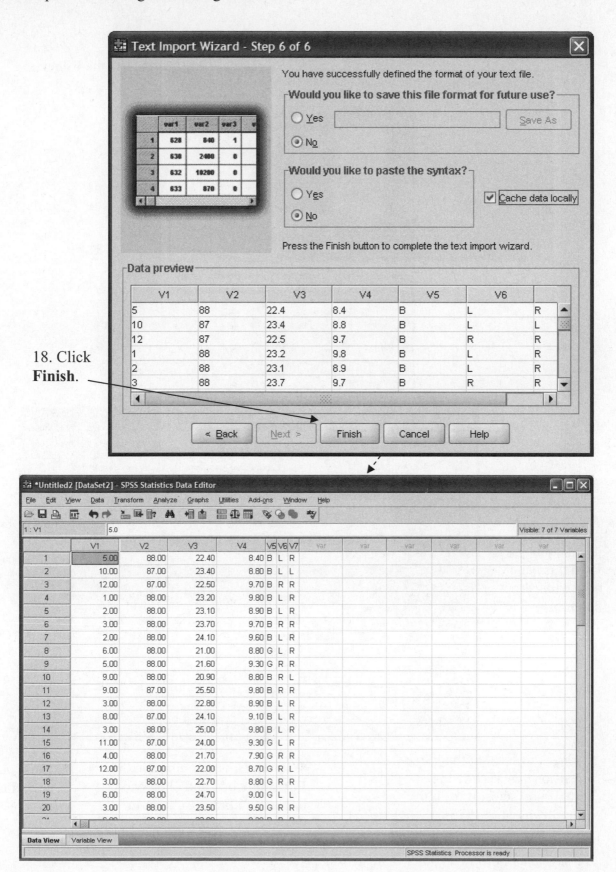

Saving Data

To save a data set that is displayed on the **SPSS Statistics Data Editor**, use the **File** menu on the menu bar.

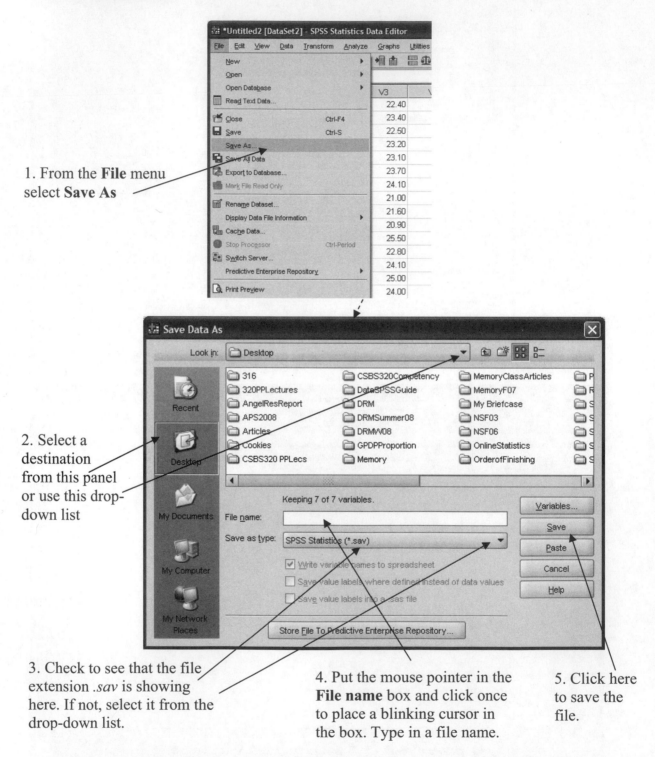

1. From the **File** menu select **Save As**

2. Select a destination from this panel or use this drop-down list

3. Check to see that the file extension *.sav* is showing here. If not, select it from the drop-down list.

4. Put the mouse pointer in the **File name** box and click once to place a blinking cursor in the box. Type in a file name.

5. Click here to save the file.

To save data in formats other than an *SPSS* system file (e.g., *Microsoft Excel*®), select another file type from the drop-down list in step 3 shown above.

Exercises for Chapter 2

Exercise 2.1

1. Type the data shown in the picture below into the **SPSS Statistics Data Editor**:

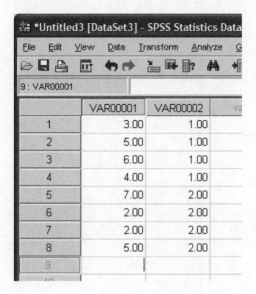

2. Save the data to your desktop as *Ex2.1.sav*

Exercise 2.2

Read the file *EX22.sav* into the **SPSS Statistics Data Editor**. The data file is available on the publisher's website for this text at the address http://www.pearsonhighered.com/stern2e.

Exercise 2.3

Read the file *EX23.xls* into the **SPSS Statistics Data Editor**. The data file is available on the publisher's website for this text at the address http://www.pearsonhighered.com/stern2e.
Note that the variable names are contained in the *Microsoft Excel*® file.

Exercise 2.4

Read the file *EX24.txt* into the **SPSS Statistics Data Editor**. The data file is available on the publisher's website for this text at the address http://www.pearsonhighered.com/stern2e. The file has the following properties: variable names in the first line; the first case begins on line 2; each case begins on a separate line; the values are separated by a space; all the variables are numeric.

Exercise 2.5

At the beginning of this chapter in the section titled **Entering Data Using the Keyboard**, an example data set presented the number of arguments reported by 20 couples. Type these 20 numbers into the first column of the **SPSS Statistics Data Editor**. Save the data file to your desktop (or some other convenient location) using the name *Ex25.sav*.

Exercise 2.6

1. In **Exercise 2.5** the file *Ex25.sav* was created. Read the data from *Ex25.sav* into the **SPSS Statistics Data Editor**.
2. Type in a second column of data that consists of the number 1 for the first 10 cases and the number 2 for the next 10 cases. The results should look as follows:

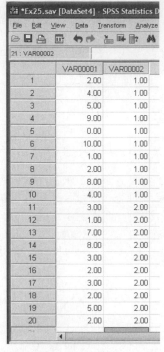

3. Save the data as a tab-delimited data (*.dat*) file name *Ex26.dat*. After you save the data file, *SPSS* presents a message about the file saving process in a new window. To get back to the **SPSS Statistics Data Editor,** close the window and respond to the question about saving the output file by pressing the **No** button.
4. After exiting *SPSS*, open file *Ex26.dat* using *WordPad*® or *Notepad*® (to find these programs, use the **Start** menu to highlight **All Programs** and then **Accessories**). Were the file names included in the *.dat* file?

Exercise 2.7

In Exercise 2.6 the file *Ex26.dat* was saved. Use the Text Import Wizard to read the data from *Ex26.dat* into *SPSS*.

Exercise 2.8

It is possible to have more than one data source open in SPSS. In this exercise, data from two *.sav* files will be opened.

1. Start *SPSS* and read in the file *Ex21demo.sav* created in exercise 2.1.
2. Open a new **Data Editor** window. Do this using the **File** menu to select **Open**, then **Data**. Specify the file name *Ex25.sav* as the file name.
3. Move between the windows of **SPSS Statistics Data Editor** by clicking in any visible part of the window that is obscured, by clicking the icon for the data set in the *Windows* taskbar, or by using the keyboard key combination **Alt-Tab**.

Chapter 3: Modifying Data in the *Data Editor*

Data entered into the **SPSS Statistics Data Editor** will not always be in a form suitable for an analysis. When typing in data, for example, incorrect information may be entered; or, entire variables may be missing. These circumstances require modifying the data. Some commonly required data modification procedures are described in this chapter.

Changing the Content of a Data Cell

If, after entering data, you notice an error in a data cell, you can replace existing data by doing the following:

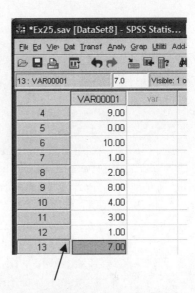

1. To change the number in this cell, put the mouse pointer on the cell and click it once to highlight the cell.

2. To insert a new number, type the new number using the number keys on the keyboard

3. Press the **Enter** key to finish the process. The number in the cell will be changed to the predefined format (it will change to 1.00) and the cell below will be highlighted.

Inserting a Variable

Consider this situation: you're entering into the **SPSS Statistics Data Editor** five quiz scores for each student in a class, and, by mistake, you omit the scores for quiz 2. The left panel of Figure 3.1 shows the data you intended to enter; the data you actually entered is pictured in the right panel:

Figure 3.1. The panel on the left shows the quiz data intended to be entered into the **SPSS Statistics Data Editor**. In the panel on the right the scores for the second quiz have been omitted.

Smith	77	76	80	90	81
Harris	98	99	100	100	90
Jones	69	71	80	81	88
Fraser	99	89	90	90	99
Barker	100	99	99	100	100

What's needed is to insert scores for quiz 2 in a newly-created third column in the **SPSS Statistics Data Editor**. Here's how to do this:

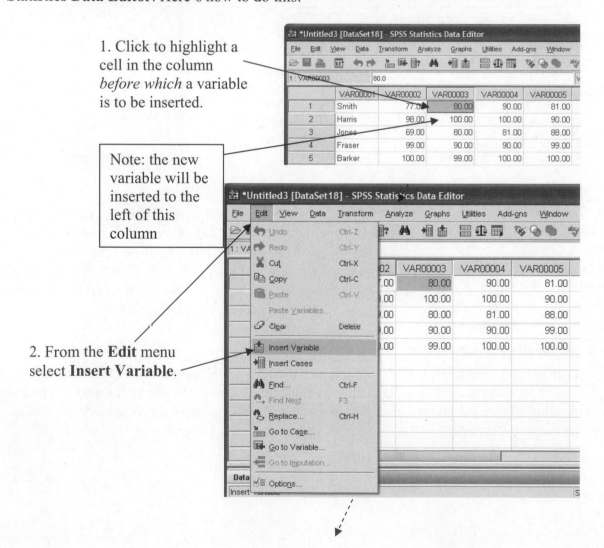

1. Click to highlight a cell in the column *before which* a variable is to be inserted.

Note: the new variable will be inserted to the left of this column

2. From the **Edit** menu select **Insert Variable**.

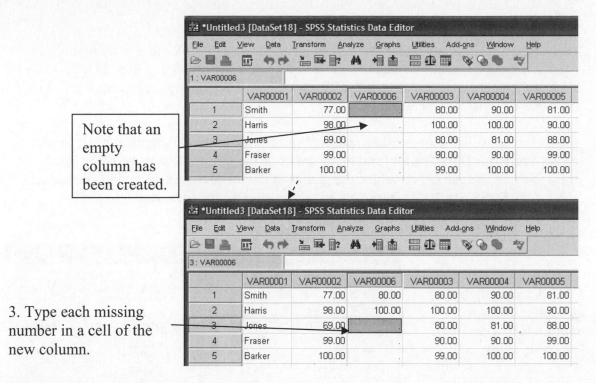

Note that an empty column has been created.

3. Type each missing number in a cell of the new column.

Removing a Variable

To remove all the data including the variable name, highlight the column containing the variable's values as shown below and select **Cut** from the **Edit** menu.

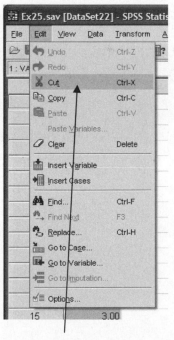

1. Move the mouse pointer over the variable name and click once.

2. The column will be highlighted.

3. Use the mouse pointer to highlight **Cut** from the **Edit** menu and click once to delete the column.

Inserting a case

In the **SPSS Statistics Data Editor**, columns represent variables and rows represent cases. Thus, if a teacher wishes to record student quiz scores so that a mean quiz score for each student can be calculated, the different quiz scores will each represent a variable and each student will represent a case.

Consider, now, that a teacher has recorded student names in alphabetical order in the **SPSS Statistics Data Editor**, and that a new student with the last name of Munoz transfers into the class. To include the grades of the transfer student in the appropriate row of the **SPSS Statistics Data Editor**, a new case must be inserted into the spreadsheet. Here's how to do this:

1. Click to highlight any cell in the row *above which* a case is to be inserted.

Note: the new case will be inserted above this row.

2. From the **Edit** menu select **Insert Cases**.

Note that an empty row has been created.

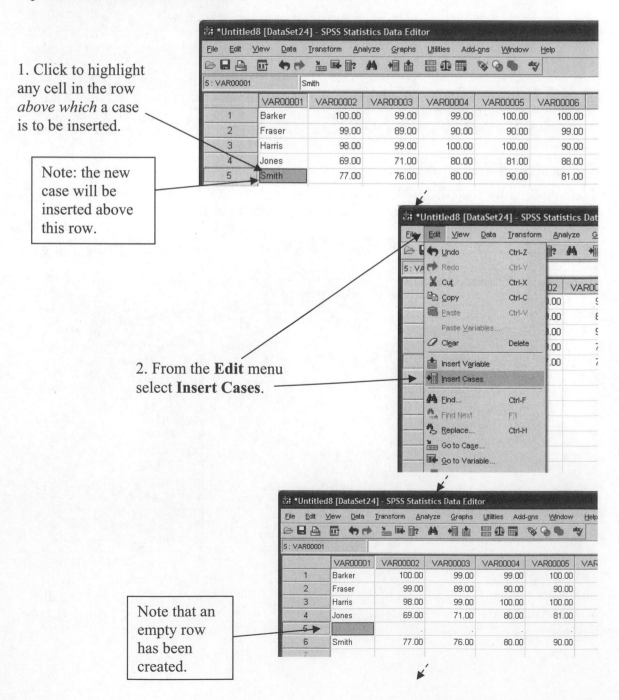

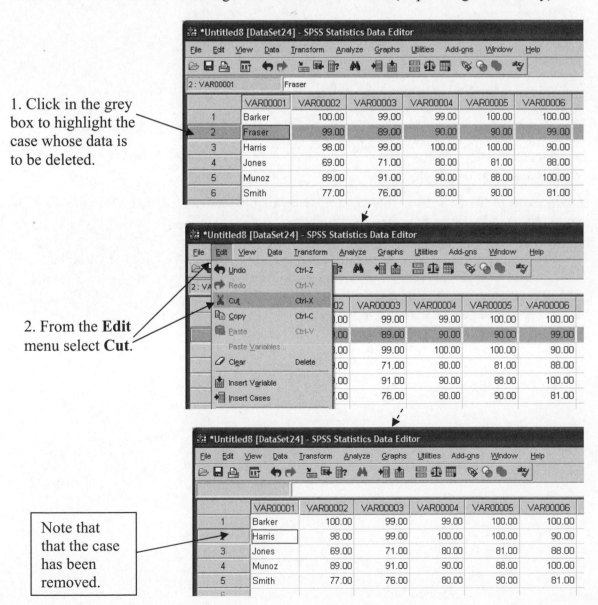

3. Type each new value in a cell of the new row.

Removing a Case

A case may be removed from the **SPSS Statistics Data Editor** by highlighting the data that is to be removed and selecting **Cut** from the **Edit** menu (or pressing the **Del** key).

1. Click in the grey box to highlight the case whose data is to be deleted.

2. From the **Edit** menu select **Cut**.

Note that that the case has been removed.

Exercises for Chapter 3

Exercise 3.1

Open the data file *Ex2.1.sav* that you previously created in Exercise 2.1. (If you did not previously create such a file, do it now.)

1. Create a new variable in the third column to produce a data set that is shown in the table below:

VAR00001	VAR00002	VAR00003
3.00	1.00	1.00
5.00	1.00	1.00
6.00	1.00	2.00
4.00	1.00	2.00
7.00	2.00	1.00
2.00	2.00	1.00
2.00	2.00	2.00
7.00	2.00	2.00

2. Insert a variable between **VAR00001** and **VAR00002**.
3. Delete the variable **VAR00003**.
4. Type in the values of **VAR00003** into the newly-created variable in column 2.
5. Save the data file using the name *Ex2.1.2.sav*.

Exercise 3.2

Open the data file *Ex3.2.sav*. The data file is available on the publisher's website for this text at the address http://www.pearsonhighered.com/stern2e.

1. For case 12, change the value of **GREQ** from 659 to 695.
2. Insert a new case 2 that has the values 2, 512, 490, 3.0, and 82 for the variables **Gender**, **GREV**, **GREQ**, **GPA**, and **FinalExam**, respectively.
3. Remove the case that is now case 15.
4. Save the file as *Ex3.2new.sav*.

Chapter 4: Defining Variables' Properties

Naming Variables and Declaring Their Types

In the **SPSS Statistics Data Editor**, rows in the spreadsheet represent cases and columns represent variables. Thus, if a marriage counselor has 20 couples as clients and wishes to record for each couple the number of arguments reported during the week between sessions 1 and 2, whether the couple is married or not (1 = married, 2 = not married), and the code name provided by each couple to identify their information for record-keeping purposes, an *SPSS* data file will consist of 20 cases (each couple represents a case) and three variables (columns). The data displayed in Table 4.1 shows values of each of these variables for the 20 couples. Note that the cell representing the marital status of couple 11 is blank to represent that the couple has failed to provide a response to the question.

Table 4.1. Data for each of 20 couples that shows the number of arguments per week between counseling sessions 1 and 2, whether the couple is currently married (represented by the value 1) or not (2), and a code name provided by each couple.

Couple Number	Number of Arguments	Married?	ID Code
1	2	1	Jones7
2	4	1	HiHo
3	5	1	9827HJ
4	9	2	2Bornot2B
5	0	1	Jack&Jill
6	10	2	Help01
7	1	1	Frey2
8	2	2	Tempr
9	8	1	2P909
10	4	1	Kay2006
11	3		Boomers
12	1	2	JJY5
13	7	1	LHY502
14	8	1	348901
15	3	1	BBG
16	2	2	2US
17	3	1	HeyU2
18	2	1	CouldBU
19	5	1	YNot
20	2	1	29&30

It is important to notice that the spreadsheet shown in the **SPSS Statistics Data Editor** has two small tabs at the bottom (see picture below). One tab is labeled **Data View** and the other is labeled **Variable View**. When the spreadsheet is in the **Data View**, data can be entered into the spreadsheet. When the spreadsheet is in the **Variable View**, properties of the variables (including the assignment of variable names) and formatting of the spreadsheet can be manipulated.

It is sometimes necessary to set properties of variables in the **Variable View** before typing in data in the **Data View.** For example, to enter data such as those shown in Table 4.1, three variable names together with their properties could first be specified using the **Variable View** of the **SPSS Statistics Data Editor**. The steps shown below accomplish this. Note that the variable in column 3, because it contains letters and other non-numeric characters, is what is known as a string variable (as opposed to a numeric variable) and so must be declared as such in column 2 of the **Variable View** spreadsheet.

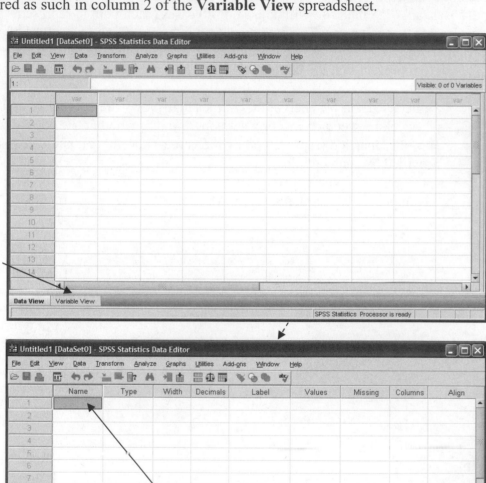

1. Move the mouse pointer over the **Variable View** tab and click once.

2. In the **Variable View** spreadsheet that appears, you can start by providing a name for each variable.

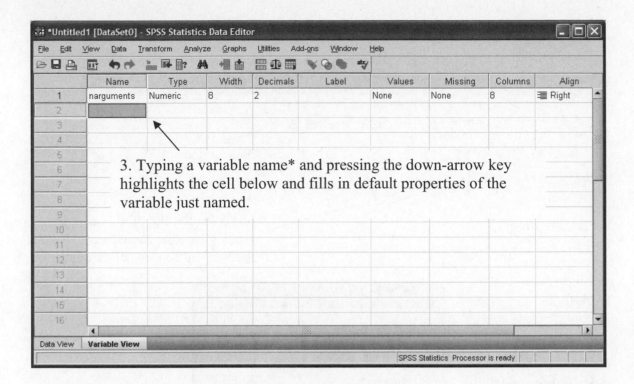

3. Typing a variable name* and pressing the down-arrow key highlights the cell below and fills in default properties of the variable just named.

* Variable names must begin with a letter, can be up to 64 characters long, can contain upper and lower case letters, can contain numbers and symbols such as a period, or @, #, _, or $, but should not end with a period. Reserved words (ALL, AND, BY, EQ, GE, GT, LE, LT, NE, NOT, OR, TO, WITH) should not be used nor should special symbols such as blanks, ?, *, ‘, or !.

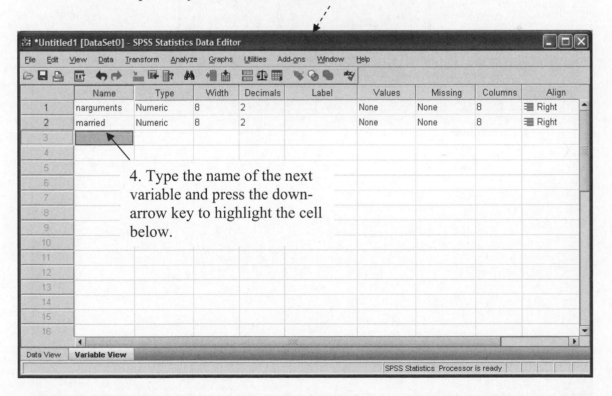

4. Type the name of the next variable and press the down-arrow key to highlight the cell below.

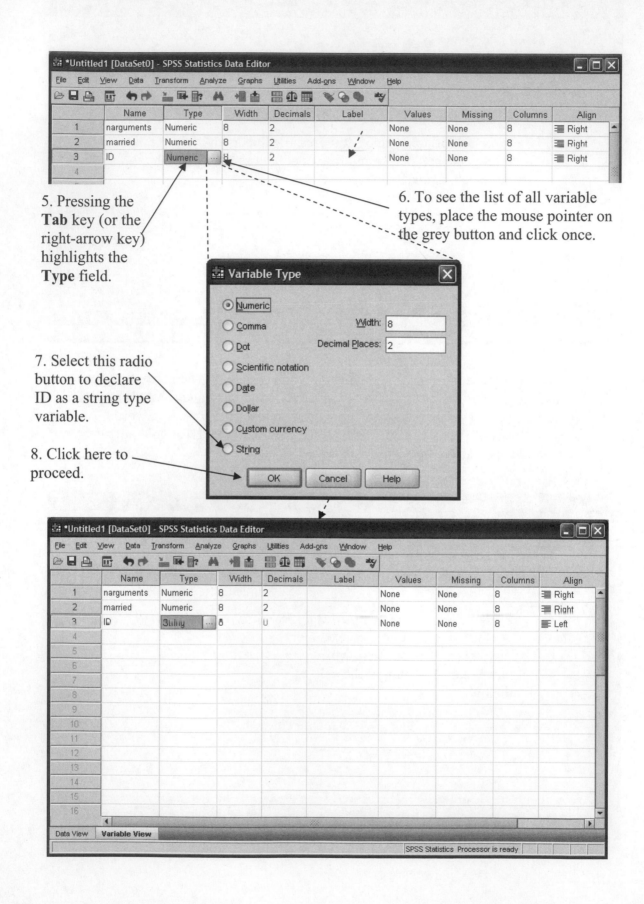

5. Pressing the **Tab** key (or the right-arrow key) highlights the **Type** field.

6. To see the list of all variable types, place the mouse pointer on the grey button and click once.

7. Select this radio button to declare ID as a string type variable.

8. Click here to proceed.

Labeling Variables

Variable labels are optional. They are useful, however, because, as their name implies, they provide a means for identifying variables with labels that can be more extensive than the variable name (variable labels can be up to 256 characters in length and can contain special characters and reserved words prohibited in variable names). For the data shown in Table 4.1, it might be helpful to label the variable **arguments** as "Number of arguments reported by couples between sessions 1 and 2," and to label **married** as "Is the couple married or not" and to label **ID** as "Code to identify each couple." As shown below, this is accomplished by highlighting each cell in the **Label** column and typing the appropriate label in the highlighted cell.

1. Move the mouse pointer over the variable's **Label** box and click once to highlight.

2. Type the label in the highlighted cell. Dragging here expands the column to accept the text.

3. Press the down-arrow key to highlight the **Label** cell for the next variable and type in its information.

4. Type in the label for the last variable.

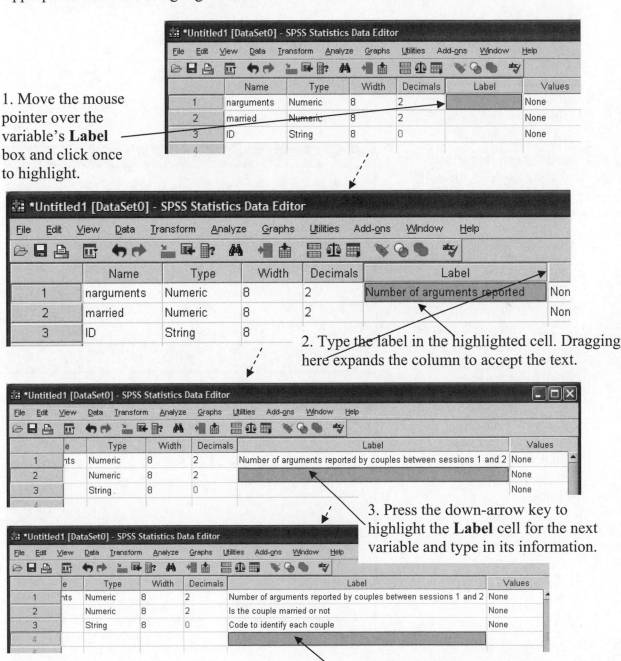

Assigning Value Labels for Categorical Numeric Variables

Categorical variables such as **married** that are coded numerically but whose values refer to labels such as married or not married, benefit from having values defined in the **Values** column of the **SPSS Statistics Data Editor's Variable View**. The following sequence illustrates labeling values of the variable **married**.

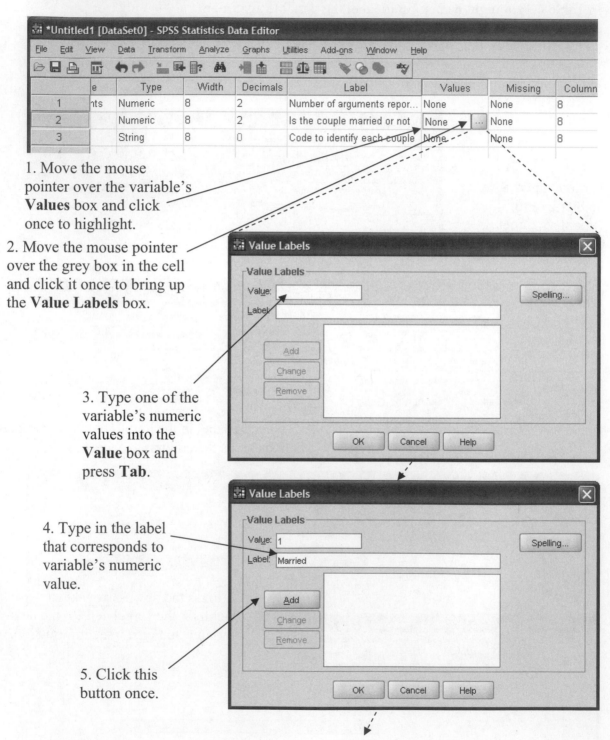

1. Move the mouse pointer over the variable's **Values** box and click once to highlight.

2. Move the mouse pointer over the grey box in the cell and click it once to bring up the **Value Labels** box.

3. Type one of the variable's numeric values into the **Value** box and press **Tab**.

4. Type in the label that corresponds to variable's numeric value.

5. Click this button once.

6. Move the mouse pointer over the variable's **Value** field and click once to insert blinking cursor.

7. Type another of the variable's numeric values into the **Value** field and press **Tab**.

8. Type the label that corresponds to variable's numeric value and press **Tab**.

9. Click this button once. This adds the information to the display list.

10. Click here to proceed.

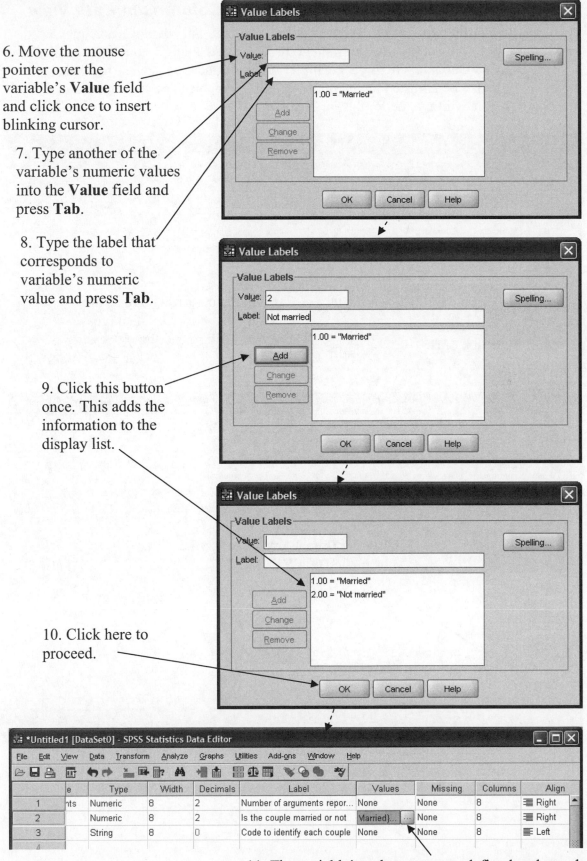

11. The variable's values are now defined and may be viewed (or modified) by clicking this grey button once.

Adjusting Column Width and Number of Columns in Data View

The default column width for numeric and string data is 8. That default value may need to be adjusted. For example, the data in the ID column of Table 4.1 contains strings that are longer than 8 characters (e.g., Jack&Jill). To avoid truncating such strings, the column width may be adjusted in the **Width** cell of a variable. The sequence shown below adjusts the width value for the variable **ID** to 10.

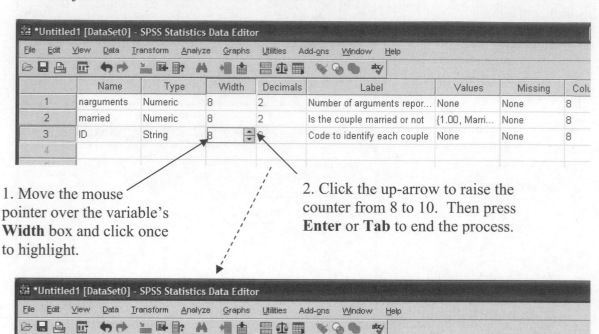

1. Move the mouse pointer over the variable's **Width** box and click once to highlight.

2. Click the up-arrow to raise the counter from 8 to 10. Then press **Enter** or **Tab** to end the process.

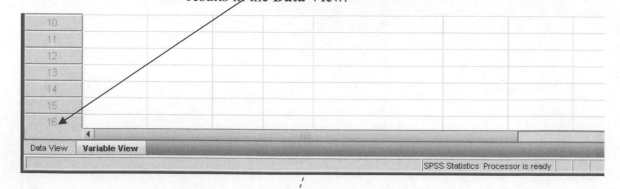

3. Click the **Data View** tab to see the results in the **Data View**.

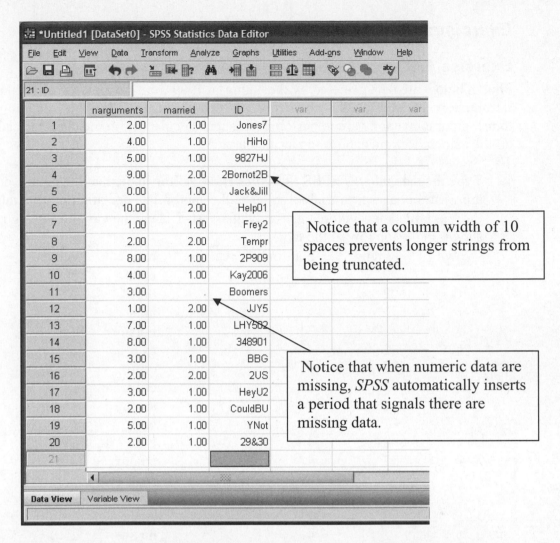

Notice that a column width of 10 spaces prevents longer strings from being truncated.

Notice that when numeric data are missing, *SPSS* automatically inserts a period that signals there are missing data.

Note that the column width shown in the **Data View** is actually 10 spaces wide, (even though the default width in the **Columns** cell of the **Variable View** is set to 8). For strings longer than 10 characters, the **Columns** value for the variable in **Variable View** would need to be adjusted using a similar process to that shown above in order to make all the characters visible:

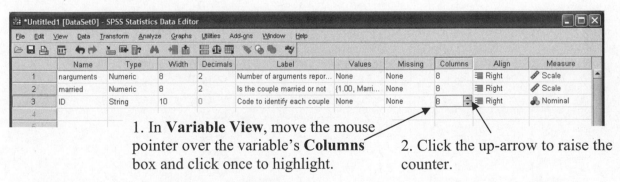

1. In **Variable View**, move the mouse pointer over the variable's **Columns** box and click once to highlight.

2. Click the up-arrow to raise the counter.

As described in Appendix C, the **Codebook** procedure provides a useful way to obtain a summary of how each variable in an *SPSS* data file has been defined (as well as to obtain some descriptive statistics for the variables' values).

Exercises for Chapter 4

Exercise 4.1

Shown below are data gathered by the author in 1999 from students enrolled in an introductory statistics class. The intent of the survey was to assess the reaction of students to using computer software to perform statistical calculations in the class instead of doing all the calculations by hand using a calculator.

1. Type the data into the **SPSS Statistics Data Editor**. Note that the data in column 5 are values of a string variable, so make the appropriate declaration of variable type in the **Variable View** before entering values. Also, name the variables using names shown in the top row of the table.

own	brand	comfort	reaction	major	gender
1	2	4	3	nurs	2
1	2	4	4	biol	1
1	2	4	5	nurs	2
1	2	3	4	nurs	2
1	2	4	4	exer	2
1	2	5	5	crim	1
1	2	5	5	crim	1
1	1	3	3	smed	2
1	2	4	4	crim	1
1	2	4	3	crim	2
1	2	4	3	comm	2
1	2	4	3	psyc	1
1	2	5	5	crim	2
1	2	1	4	smed	1
1	2	4	3	nurs	2
1	2	4	4	exer	1
1	2	4	4	nurs	2
1	1	5	5	psyc	2
1	2	4	4	nurs	2
1	2	4	1	spch	2
1	1	4	4	crim	-1
1	2	4	5	nurs	2
1	2	4	4	heal	2
1	2	2	5	nurs	2
1	2	2	1	comm	2
1	1	3	3	crim	2
1	2	3	3	exer	2
1	2	4	2	cedp	2
1	2	5	5	psyc	1
1	2	4	5	ched	2
1	2	4	4	psyc	2
1	2	5	4	exer	2
1	2	4	5	psyc	1

2. Use the information in the column labeled **Meaning** in the table shown below to make suitable variable labels for the data. Then create value labels using the information in the column labeled Values.

Column #	Variable Name	Meaning	Values
1	own	Do you own a computer?	1=yes 0=no
2	brand	What kind of computer?	1=Mac 2=PC
3	comfort	Comfort with using computers	1=very uncomfortable 2=fairly uncomfortable 3=neutral 4=fairly comfortable 5=very comfortable
4	reaction	Reaction to using computers for statistics	1=strongly disfavor 2=slightly disfavor 3=neutral 4=slightly favor 5=strongly favor
5	major	Major in college	biol=biology nurs=nursing exer=exercise science crim=criminal justice psyc=psychology ched=community health education comm=communitations cepd=counseling/educational spch=speech therapy smed=sports medicine
6	gender	Gender of respondent:	1=male 2=female -1=missing data

3. Save the data file to your desktop (or some other convenient location) as an *SPSS* (i.e., *.sav*) file named *ComputeSurvey*.

Exercise 4.2

The data for this exercise are from Shoemaker (1996). The data set for this exercise is available from http://www.amstat.org/publications/jse/jse_data_archive.html
The file is given the name *normtemp.dat* or *normtemp.txt*.

1. Download the article from the address shown above and save it on the desktop (or some other convenient location).
2. Read the data from your saved file into *SPSS* using the data wizard.
3. Create variable names and labels for the variables. The table below shows the correspondence between the order in which the variables are listed and their identity. Use the text in the column labeled **Description** as the variable label.

Variable Number	Description	Value Labels
1	Body temperature (degrees Fahrenheit)	None
2	Gender	1=male, 2=female
3	Heart rate (beats per minute)	None

4. Make value labels for the variable named **Gender**.
5. If the first line of data in the **SPSS Statistics Data Editor** is blank, remove the case.
6. Change the number of decimal places for variable 1 to 1, and for variable 3 to 0.
7. Save the data file to your desktop (or some other convenient location) as an *SPSS* file named *bodytemp.sav*.

Exercise 4.3

The data for this exercise are based on analysis of magnetic resonance images of brains of 10 identical twins (Tramo, Loftus, Green, Stukel, Weaver, and Gazzaniga, 1998). The data are available at **Statlib** at this web address:
http://lib.stat.cmu.edu/datasets/
The file can be found by following the link labeled *IQ Brain Size*.

1. The data can be copied and pasted into the **SPSS Statistics Data Editor**. To paste the data, when a new blank window in the **Data View** of the **SPSS Statistics Data Editor** is requested and the top left cell in the spreadsheet is highlighted, use the keyboard command **control-v** (i.e., hold down the control key and press the letter v). The data should appear.
2. Use the information in the table below to make suitable variable names and labels for the data. Make suitable value labels for the variable sex.

Variable Name	Description
CCMIDSA	Collasum Surface Area (cm2)
FIQ	Full-Scale IQ
HC	Head Circumference (cm)
ORDER	Birth Order
PAIR	Pair ID (Genotype)
SEX	Sex (1=Male 2=Female)
TOTSA	Total Surface Area (cm2)
TOTVOL	Total Brain Volume (cm3)
WEIGHT	Body Weight (kg)

3. Save the data as *IQBrainSize.sav*

Chapter 5: The *SPSS Statistics Viewer*

Producing and Working with Output

The results of an *SPSS* analysis are shown in the **SPSS Statistics Viewer**. The **Viewer** becomes visible after an analysis has been run. To get a better sense of the process, observe what happens when a frequency distribution is requested for the variable **medhouse** (the median price of owner-occupied houses in 2000) in the data set shown below:

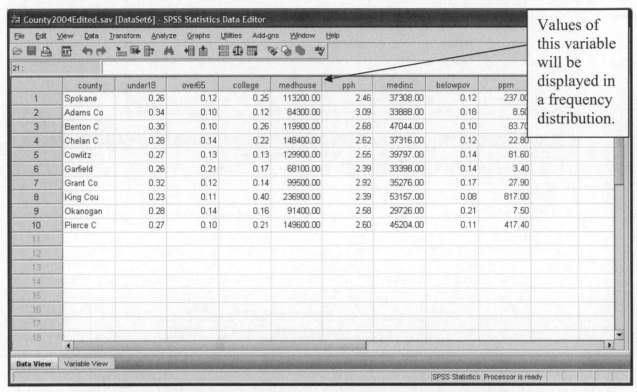

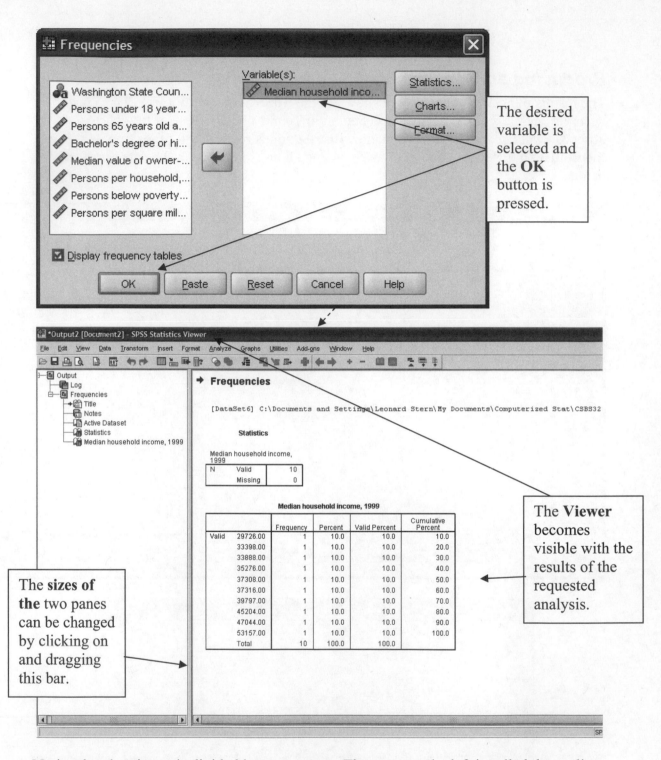

The desired variable is selected and the **OK** button is pressed.

The **Viewer** becomes visible with the results of the requested analysis.

The **sizes of the** two panes can be changed by clicking on and dragging this bar.

Notice that the viewer is divided into two panes. The pane on the left is called the outline pane; that on the right is the contents pane. The sizes of the panes can be changed by clicking and dragging the bar that separates the two panes.

Working with Data in the Outline Pane

As its name indicates, the outline pane represents the components of the output in outline form. There are several ways to manipulate the data that appear in the contents pane using information that appears in the outline pane.

Making output disappear/reappear. Notice that in the outline pane, there are icons in the form of books under the name of the procedure that has run. Notice also, that some of the icons show books that are either open or closed.

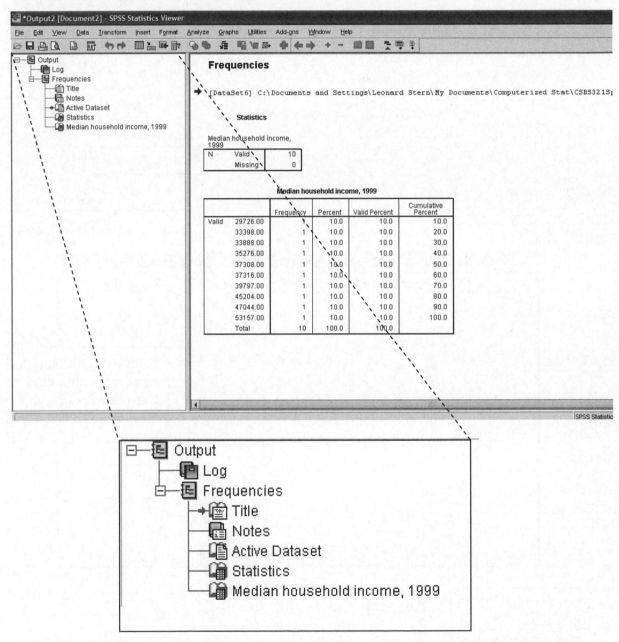

Double-clicking on an open book makes the book close. When a book closes, the output that corresponds to the title of the book will disappear in the contents pane. For example, double-clicking on the **Title** book icon in the outline pane will close the book and cause the title information in the contents pane to disappear. Double-clicking on a closed book in the outline pane has the opposite effect: the book will open and its associated content will re-appear in the contents pane.

Another way to control the display of information in the contents pane is to click on an icon in the outline pane that contains a minus symbol. The result is shown below:

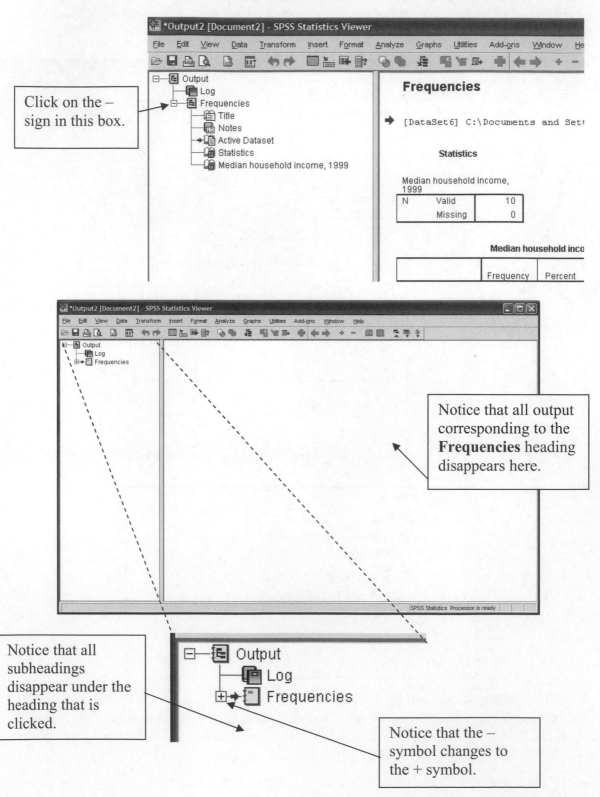

To make all the information re-appear, you can click on the icon showing a + symbol in the outline pane.

Changing the order of information displayed in the two panes. There are two ways to change the order of information shown in the panes of the viewer. Both require selecting the output to be moved by clicking on it and dragging it to the desired location. One method is to apply these operations to data in the outline pane; the other is to apply them to data in the contents pane. In both methods, as the selected information is dragged to a new location, the red arrow in each pane will move in the direction the selected information is dragged. As soon as the mouse button is released, the selected information will appear *below* the location marked by the red arrow:

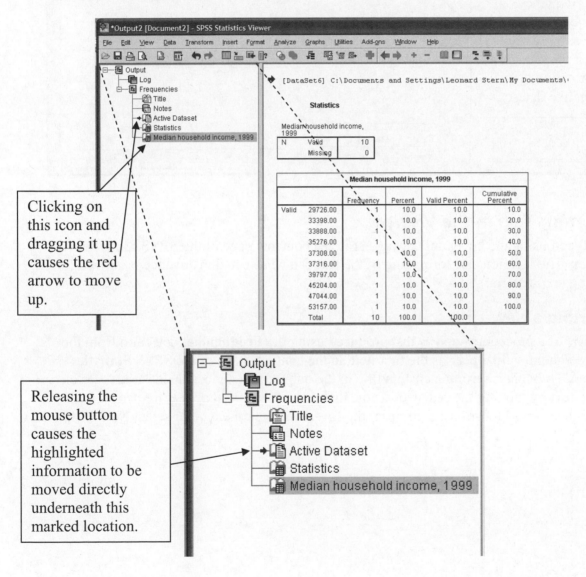

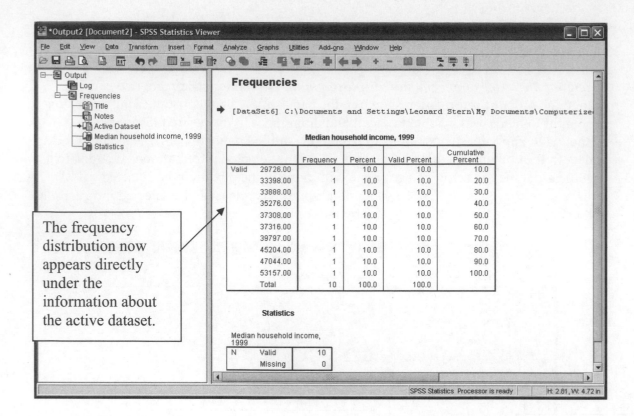

Inserting Text in the Viewer

Text typed using the keyboard can appear in the contents pane of the **SPSS Statistics Viewer**. The location and formatting of the text can be selected in advance or altered for existing text material.

Inserting a New Title

The title of a procedure such as that produced using the **Frequencies** selection from the **Analyze** menu will appear as the first item in the contents pane of the **SPSS Statistics Viewer**. To begin inserting a custom title in the output, first choose the desired location for the text by moving the red arrow (note that the new title will appear immediately below the marked location); then, from the **Insert** menu in the toolbar select **New Title**.

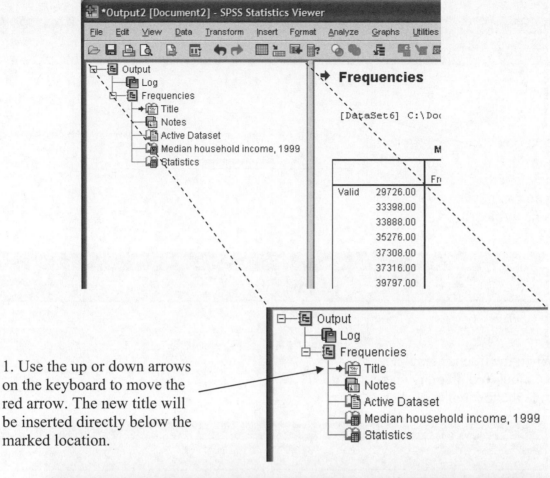

1. Use the up or down arrows on the keyboard to move the red arrow. The new title will be inserted directly below the marked location.

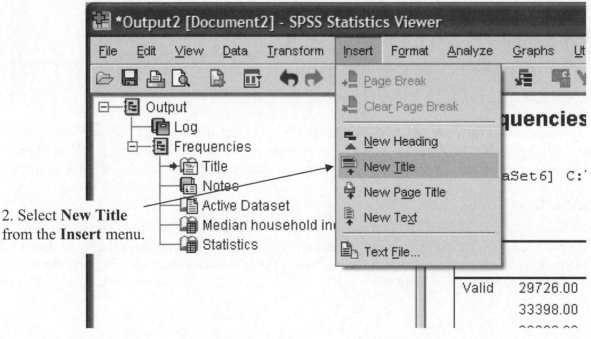

2. Select **New Title** from the **Insert** menu.

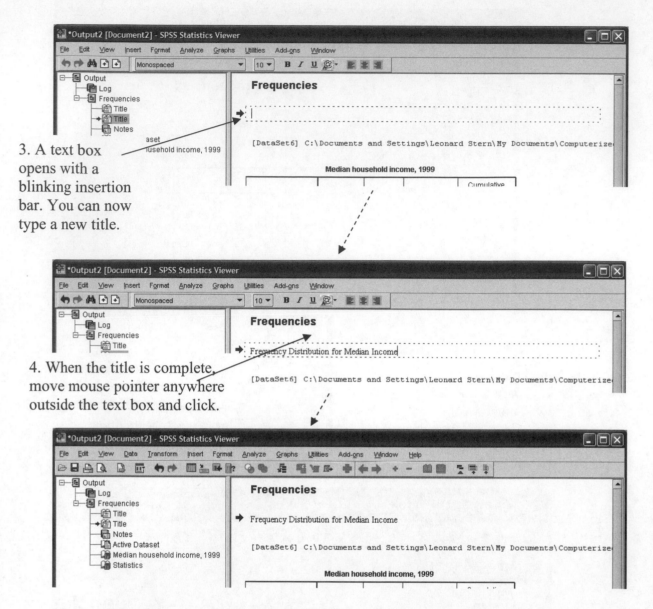

3. A text box opens with a blinking insertion bar. You can now type a new title.

4. When the title is complete, move mouse pointer anywhere outside the text box and click.

The location of the new title may be changed by clicking on its name in the outline pane then dragging it to a desired location. The new (or old) title can be deleted by clicking on its name in the outline pane so that the red arrow points to it, and pressing the **delete** key.

Inserting Text

New text can be inserted in much the same way as a new title is inserted: The location for the new text is selected by moving the red arrow in the outline pane with the up or down arrow keys. Then from the **Insert** menu, **New Text** is selected. A blank text box opens into which new text can be typed.

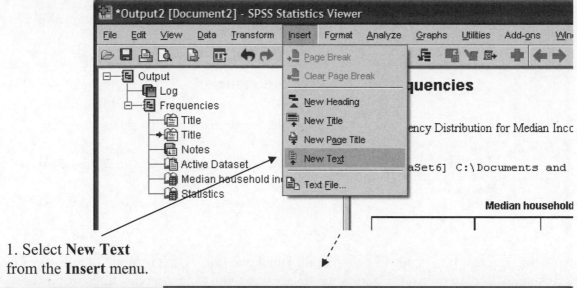

1. Select **New Text**
from the **Insert** menu.

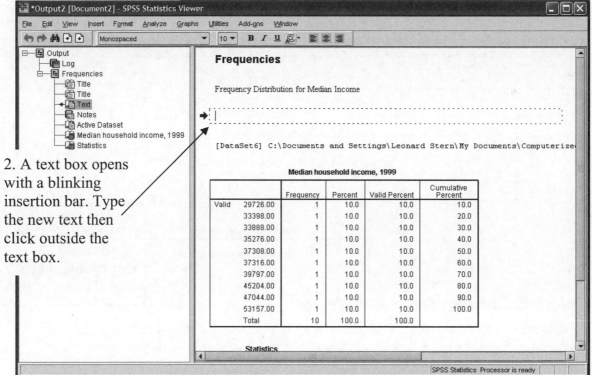

2. A text box opens
with a blinking
insertion bar. Type
the new text then
click outside the
text box.

Editing Text

To edit text, click on it in the contents pane to select it (a box composed of a single line will surround the text when it is selected). Then double-click inside the box to enter edit mode (the single line surrounding the text will change to a dotted line). Text in the box can be selected by dragging across it with the mouse. The format of the selected text can be changed using various boxes and buttons on the formatting toolbar that appears:

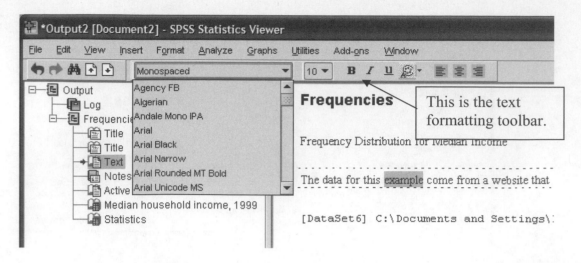

Note that if a text box needs to contain more than one line of text, pressing the **Enter** key will size the box to reveal the additional lines of text you type. Increasing the font size also adjusts the size of the text box:

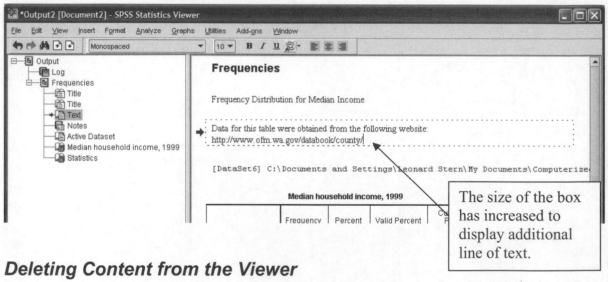

Deleting Content from the Viewer

To remove content from the **SPSS Statistics Viewer** the content must be selected. Content may be selected either by clicking on it in the contents or outline pane.

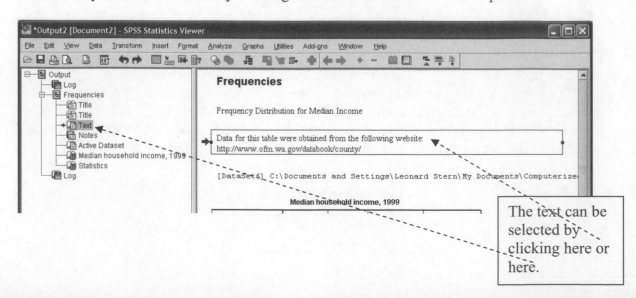

Multiple, noncontiguous output can be selected by holding down the **Ctrl** key on the keyboard and clicking on the output or its name in the outline pane.

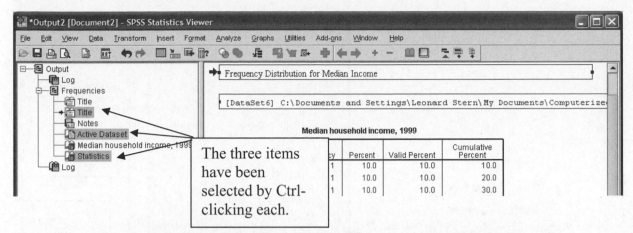

The selected output can then be deleted by selecting **Delete** from the **Edit** menu or by pressing the **Delete** key on the keyboard.

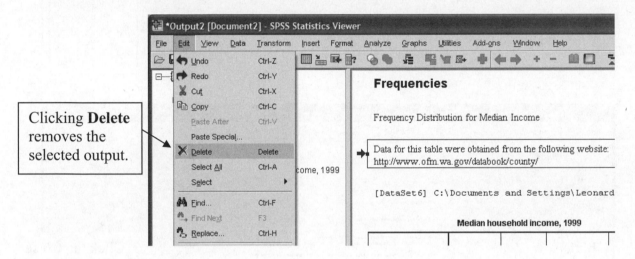

Printing the Output Visible in the Contents Pane

Printing the Output

There are two ways to print the output that appears in the contents pane of the **SPSS Statistics Viewer**. One is to use the **Print** command from the **File** menu. Another is to first use the **Print Preview** command from the **File** menu and then to use the **Print** button in the window that appears. The second method is recommended because it helps avoid printing information that was not intended to be printed.

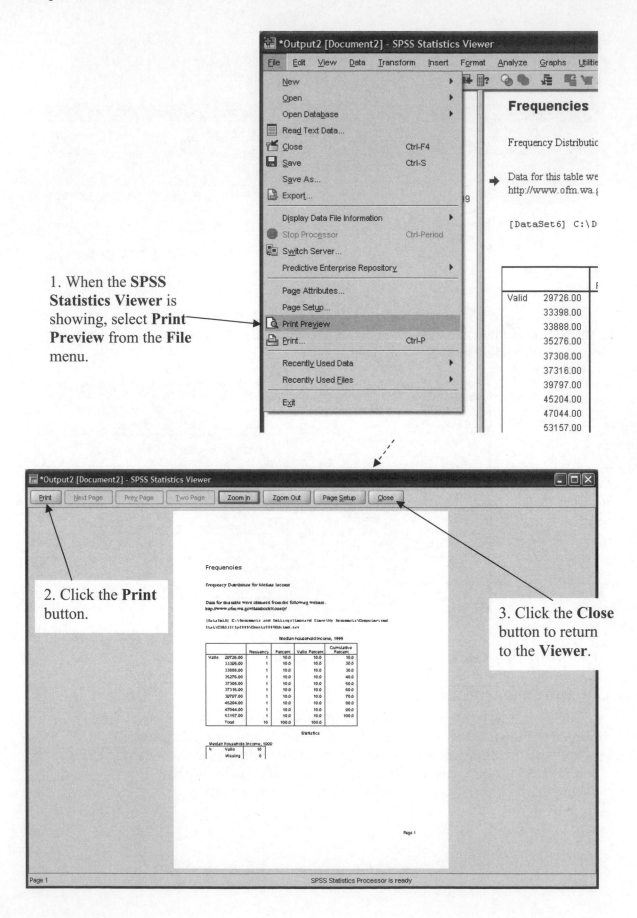

1. When the **SPSS Statistics Viewer** is showing, select **Print Preview** from the **File** menu.

2. Click the **Print** button.

3. Click the **Close** button to return to the **Viewer**.

Printing a Portion of the Output

To print a single item from the contents pane, select it by clicking on it once in the contents pane or the outline pane. A box will appear around the selected information. Then use the **Print Preview** screen to inspect the intended printout. Click the **Print** button to print the selection.

To select more than one item to be printed, you can hold down the **Ctrl** key on the keyboard and click one-at-a-time on the name of each item in the outline pane to select it. The multiple selections should then appear when the **Print Preview** screen is viewed.

Copying Information to Microsoft Word® *Documents*

Individual tables and charts that appear in the output viewer can be embedded in a word processing document. One way to do this is to select the table or chart in the viewer by clicking on it once, then use the **Copy** key in *SPSS* and **Paste** key in the word-processor to insert the item into the destination document.

1. Select the table or chart to be copied by clicking on it once.

2. From the **Edit** menu select **Copy**.

3. From the **Edit** menu in the word processor select **Paste**.

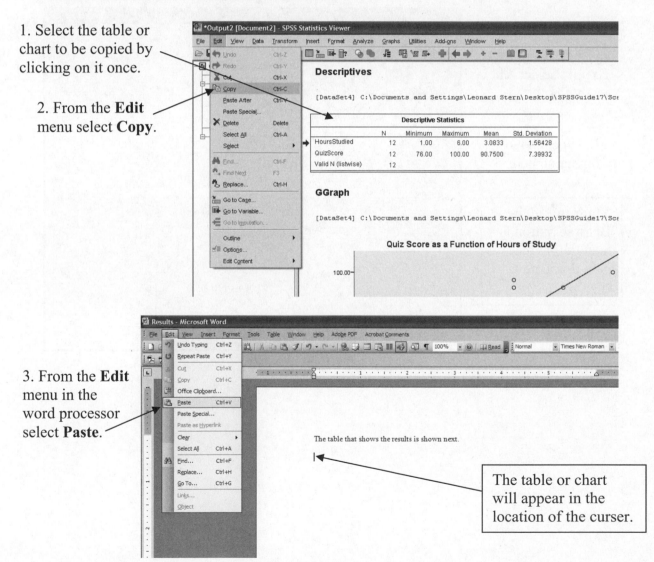

The table or chart will appear in the location of the curser.

Exporting All Output

You can copy all the output visible in the **SPSS Statistics Viewer** to a new *Microsoft Word®* file by using the **Export** procedure as illustrated below.

1. When the **SPSS Statistics Viewer** is showing, select **Export** from the **File** menu.

2. Under **Objects to Export** select **All visible**.

3. Type a new file name here.

You can use the **Browse** button to help define the path to the new file.

4. Click **OK**.

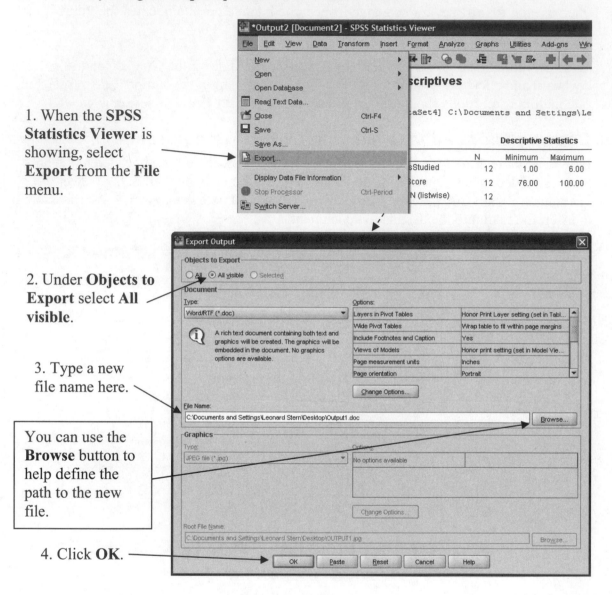

A portion of the file that is created is shown below:

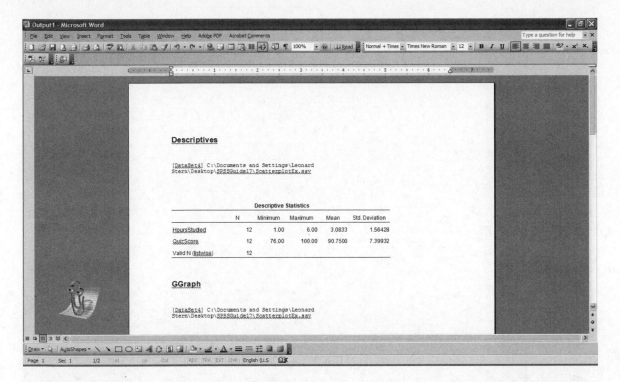

Note that exporting output to an existing file will replace all the information in the file.

Exporting Wide Tables to Fit a Page

It is possible to shrink wide tables so they fit onto a page in a word processing document without wrapping. You can begin the process by clicking on the wide table in the **SPSS Statistics Viewer** to select it, then select **Export** from the **File** menu, or use the shortcut shown below:

1. When the **SPSS Statistics Viewer** is showing, give a single right-click to the wide table and select **Export** from the menu that appears.

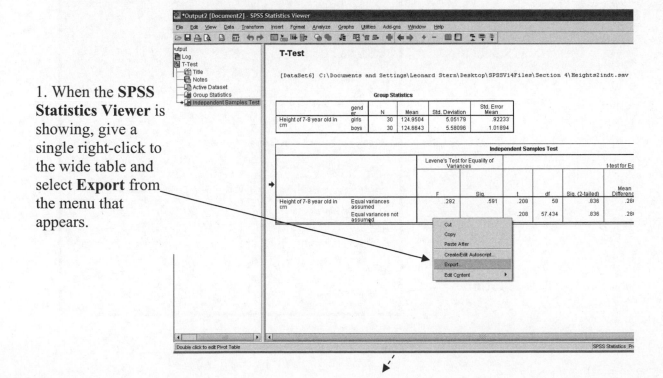

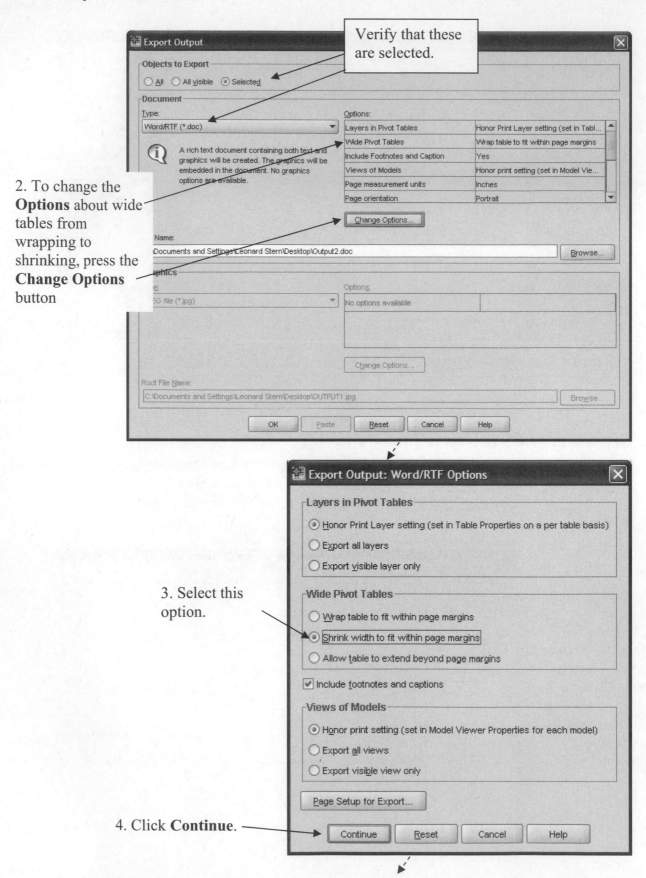

2. To change the **Options** about wide tables from wrapping to shrinking, press the **Change Options** button

Verify that these are selected.

3. Select this option.

4. Click **Continue**.

5. Type a new file name here.

6. Click OK

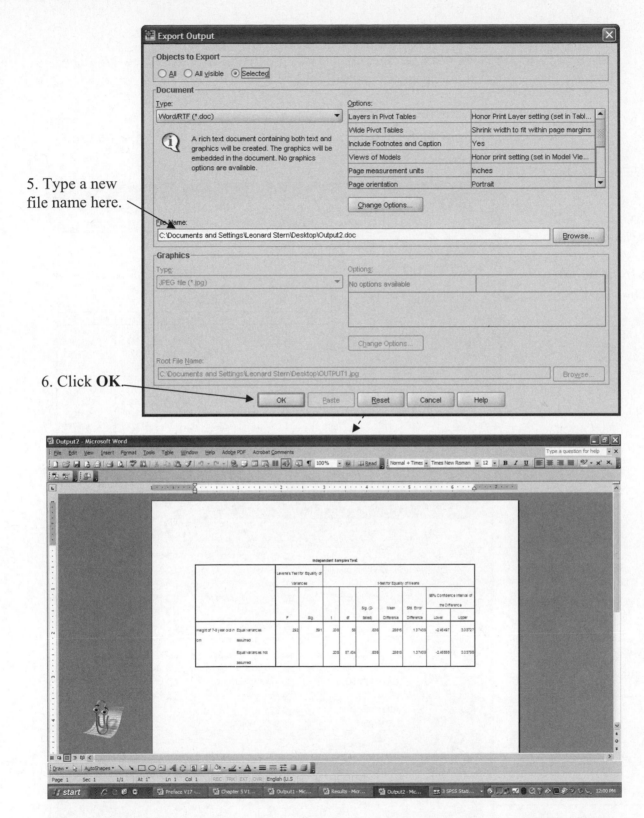

Note again that exporting output to an existing file will replace all the information in the file. However, you can copy and insert the shrunken table into another, existing word processing document.

Saving Information Contained in the Viewer

The contents of the viewer can be saved in an *SPSS* file that has the extension *.spv*. The file can subsequently be opened and viewed from *SPSS*.

Saving to an Output File

The contents of the viewer can be saved to a new output file by selecting **Save As** from the **File** menu when the **SPSS Statistics Viewer** is showing:

1. When the **SPSS Statistics Viewer** is showing, select **Save As** from the **File** menu.

2. Select the location for the output file and type the file name here.

3. Click **Save**.

Note that the file extension *.spv* will be added to the file name.

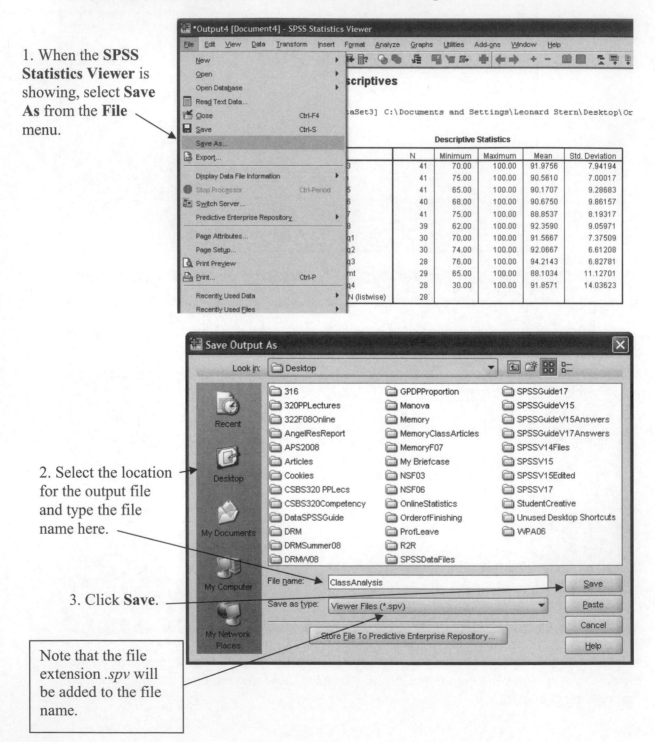

Opening an Existing Output File

To open an exiting output file, you can either double-click the icon of the output file (an example of such an icon is shown below)

or, if *SPSS* is running, you can use the **Open** selection from the **File** menu to select **Output** as the type of data file to be opened:

1. Select **Open** then **Output** from the **File** menu.

2. Select the location for the *.spv* file and type the file name here or click on its icon.

3. Click **Open**.

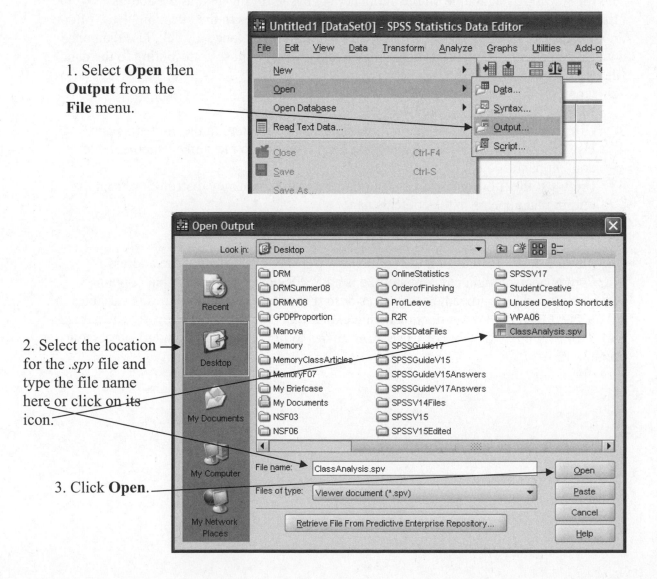

Exercises for Chapter 5

Exercise 5.1

The data in the file *TV.sav* available on the publisher's website for this text at the address http://www.pearsonhighered.com/stern2e, shows the number of hours of TV watched per day reported by randomly selected adults aged 18-65 who were contacted by the National Opinion Research Center between 1993-1998.

1. Open the file *TV.sav* in *SPSS*.
2. Make a frequency distribution of the variable **tvhrs**.
3. In the viewer's contents pane, change the title of the *Frequencies* output to *Frequency Distribution of the Number of Hours of TV Watched*.
4. Move the frequency distribution table directly underneath the revised title.
5. Paste the title and the frequency distribution into a word-processing document.

Exercise 5.2

The file *Radio.sav* available on the publisher's website for this text at the address http://www.pearsonhighered.com/stern2e contains responses to the question "How often do you read the newspaper—every day, a few times a week, once a week, less than once a week, or never?" obtained from the same respondents as those contributing to the data file used in exercise 5.1.

1. Open the file *Radio.sav* in *SPSS*.
2. Make a frequency distribution of the variable **newsfreq**.
3. Create a new title consisting of your name as the first item in the contents pane.
4. Use the outline pane to close the book corresponding to the statistics table in the content pane.
5. Print just the title consisting of your name and the frequency distribution from the output that appears in the contents pane.

Exercise 5.3

The file *Ex5.3.spv* available on the publisher's website for this text at the address http://www.pearsonhighered.com/stern2e is an *SPSS* viewer document that contains tables produced by a procedure that gives descriptive information for various variables in a data file. Open the viewer document and export all contents to a *Microsoft*® file named *Ex5.3*. Shrink the wide table of **Case Summaries** to fit the page of the word-processing document.

Chapter 6: Graphing Data with the *Chart Builder*

There are a number of ways to prepare graphs using **SPSS Statistics**. Some procedures that perform statistical analyses such as a chi square test of independence or a one-way analysis of variance also provide the option of graphing the data being analyzed. Alternatively, three stand-alone graphing procedures are available from the **Graphs** menu. As shown below, these are the **Chart Builder**, the **Graphboard Template Chooser**, and **Legacy Dialogs**.

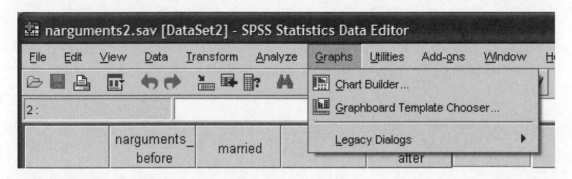

Preparing the Data for Graphing

In this chapter, use of the **Chart Builder** will be described. Later chapters will illustrate use of **Legacy Dialogs**. However, regardless of which procedure is utilized, data that are included in a graph should first be properly labeled and categorized in the **Data Editor**'s **Variable View**. Of particular importance is specification of a variable's level of measurement (i.e. nominal, ordinal, scale). Consider, for example, a data file that lists the number of arguments reported by each of 20 couples, the couple's marital status (1 = married, 2 = not married), and each couple's self-chosen identification label. In the portion of the data file shown below, this information is represented by the variables named **narguments**, **married**, and **ID**.

narguments.sav [DataSet1] - SPSS Statistics Data Editor					
File Edit View Data Transform Analyze Graphs Utilities Add-ons Window Help					
1 : narguments	2.0				
	narguments	married	ID	var	var	va
1	2.00	1.00	Jones7		
2	4.00	1.00	HiHo		
3	5.00	1.00	9827HJ		
4	9.00	2.00	2Bornot2B		
5	0.00	1.00	Jack&Jill		
6	10.00	2.00	Help01		

To properly prepare the file for graphing the variables **narguments** and **married**, a suitable descriptive label for each variable should be placed in the **Label** column of the **Data Editor**'s **Variable View**. In addition, the level of measurement of each variable that will be included in the graph should be specified in the **Measure** column. Finally, for nominal- and ordinal-level variables whose values are represented numerically (e.g., if 1 = married and 2 = not married) these values should be defined in the **Values** column.

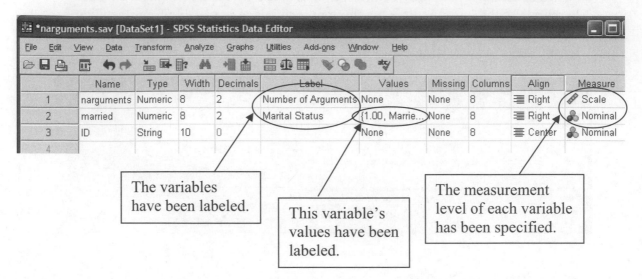

The variables have been labeled.

This variable's values have been labeled.

The measurement level of each variable has been specified.

Various types of graphs can be prepared with the **Chart Builder**. Important determiners in choosing the type of graph prepared are the number of variables represented and each variable's measurement level. Described below are graphs suitable for various combinations of numbers of variables depicted and the measurement level of each variable.

Graphs of One Variable

One nominal or one ordinal scale: bar charts.

Classification of a person's eye color into the values blue, brown, green, or hazel forms a nominal scale. A person's preference for a political candidate (strongly supports, weakly supports, undecided, weakly disfavors, strongly disfavors) is an example of a variable measured on an ordinal scale. The distribution of values of such variables can be graphed with a bar chart. The example below shows how to use the **Chart Builder** to graph values of the variable **married** represented in the data set shown above. Each bar in the graph represents a count of the number of cases in each category of the variable.

1. From the **Graphs** menu select **Chart Builder**.

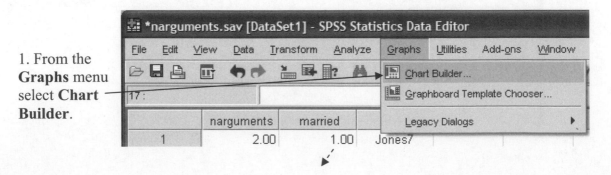

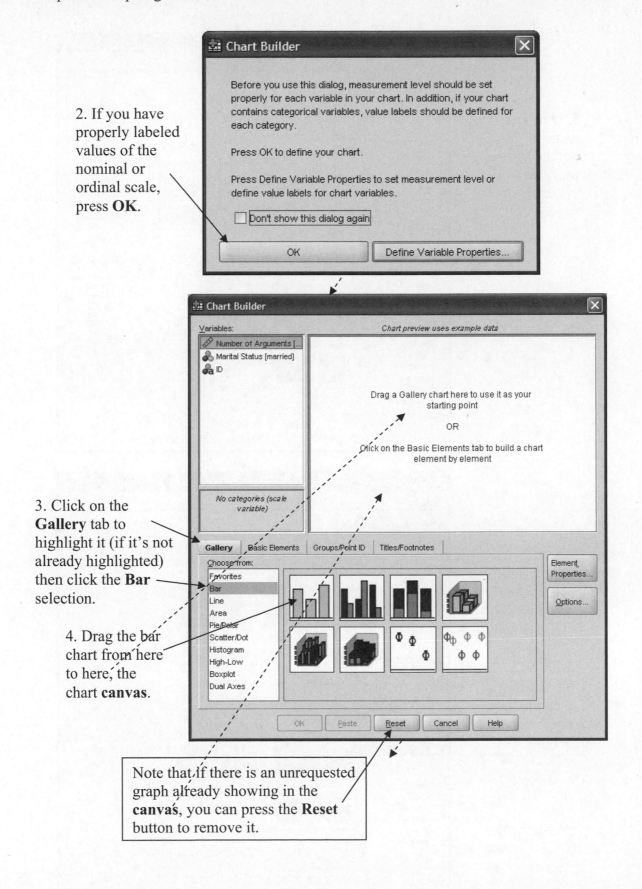

2. If you have properly labeled values of the nominal or ordinal scale, press **OK**.

3. Click on the **Gallery** tab to highlight it (if it's not already highlighted) then click the **Bar** selection.

4. Drag the bar chart from here to here, the chart **canvas**.

Note that if there is an unrequested graph already showing in the **canvas**, you can press the **Reset** button to remove it.

5. Drag the name of the nominal scale **married** to the x-axis **drop zone**.

Notice that the label on the y-axis changes to **Count**.

The heights of these bars are not their actual heights.

6. Click **OK**.

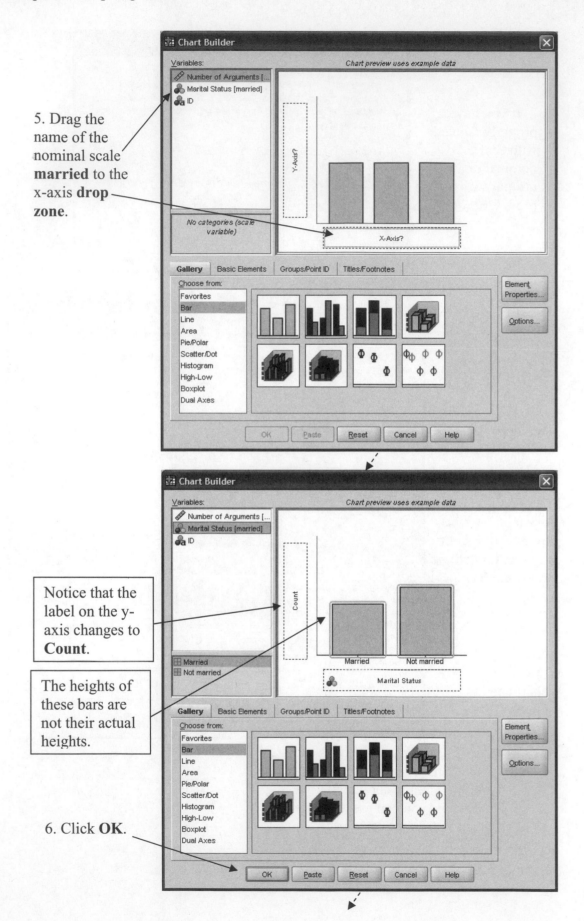

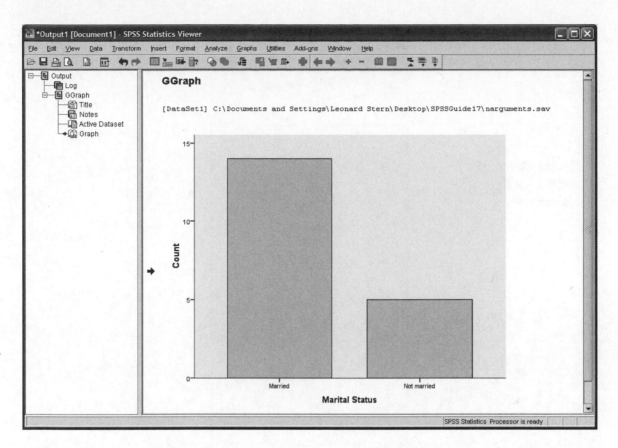

If you prefer to show the percent of total cases in each category on the y-axis (instead of a count), then, before clicking **OK** in step 6 above, use the **Element Properties** window as shown below.

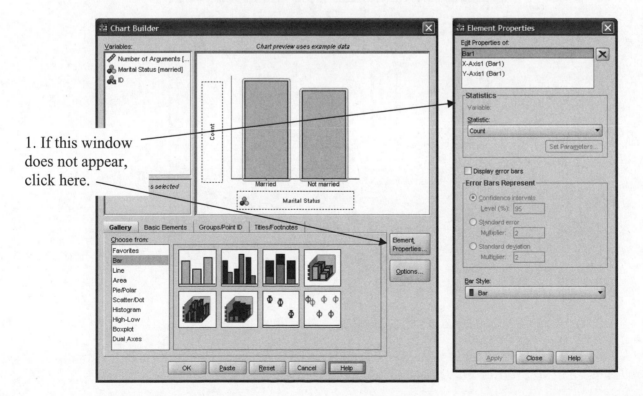

1. If this window does not appear, click here.

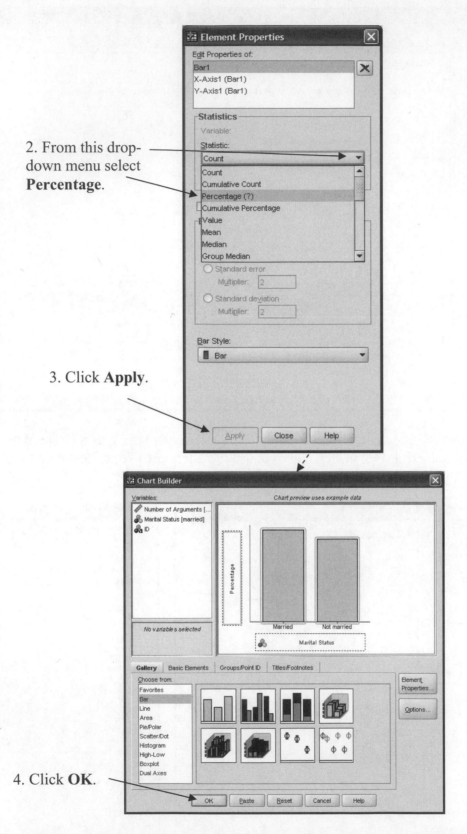

2. From this drop-down menu select **Percentage**.

3. Click **Apply**.

4. Click **OK**.

To insert a title for the graph as well as other notation, before clicking **OK** in the final step, select the **Titles/Footnotes** tab as shown below:

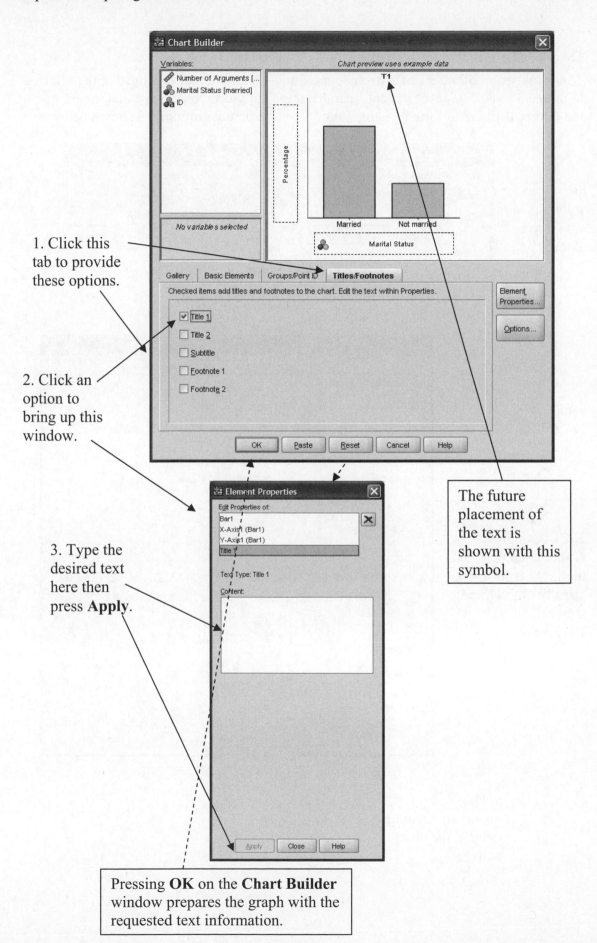

1. Click this tab to provide these options.

2. Click an option to bring up this window.

3. Type the desired text here then press **Apply**.

The future placement of the text is shown with this symbol.

Pressing **OK** on the **Chart Builder** window prepares the graph with the requested text information.

One scale variable: histograms.

The distribution of values of a variable measured on an interval or a ratio scale, referred to in *SPSS* as a scale-level variable, can be graphically depicted with a histogram. Use of the **Chart Builder** to form a histogram of the variable **narguments** is shown below.

1. From the **Graphs** menu select **Chart Builder**.

2. Click on the **Gallery** tab to highlight it (if it's not already highlighted) then select **Histogram**.

3. Drag the histogram from here to here; the chart **canvas**.

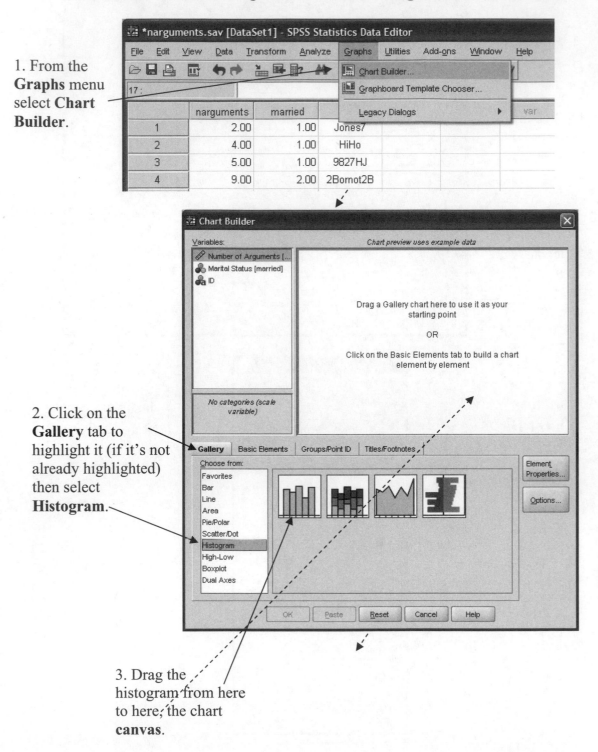

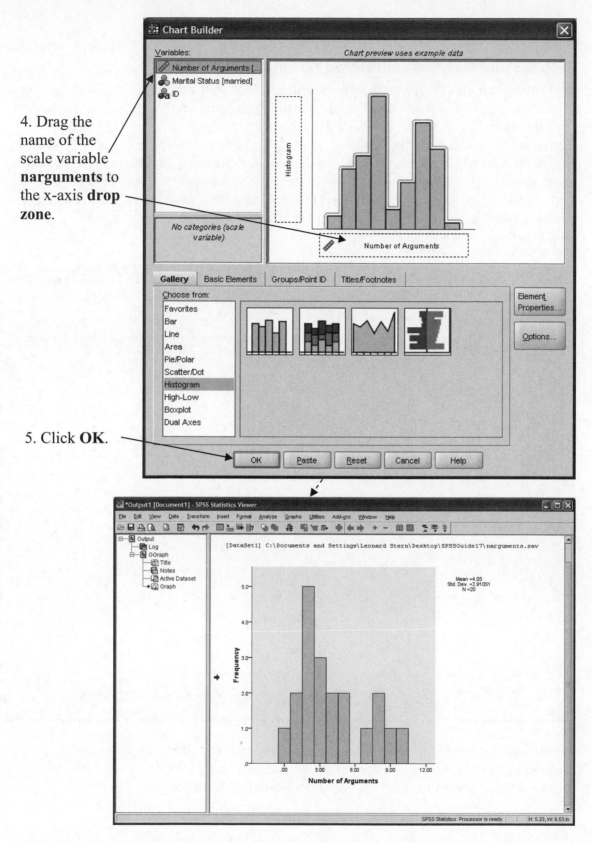

4. Drag the name of the scale variable **narguments** to the x-axis **drop zone**.

5. Click **OK**.

You can change the measure shown on the y-axis to percent and add text to the histogram using similar procedures to those described for the bar chart.

Graphs of Two Variables

Two nominal scales: clustered bar chart.

A clustered bar chart displays the number of cases (or their percentage) in each category of one nominal- or ordinal-scale variable further broken down by categories of a second such variable. For example, if 20 couples who are either married or not married are further distinguished into those whose relationship is short-term (6 months or less) or long-term (more than 6 months), we can display in a clustered bar chart counts of married couples in short- and long-term relationships and non-married couples in short- and long-term relationships. The new variable **term** in the data file shown below uses the numeric values 1 and 2 to represent couples whose relationship is long- or short-term, respectively.

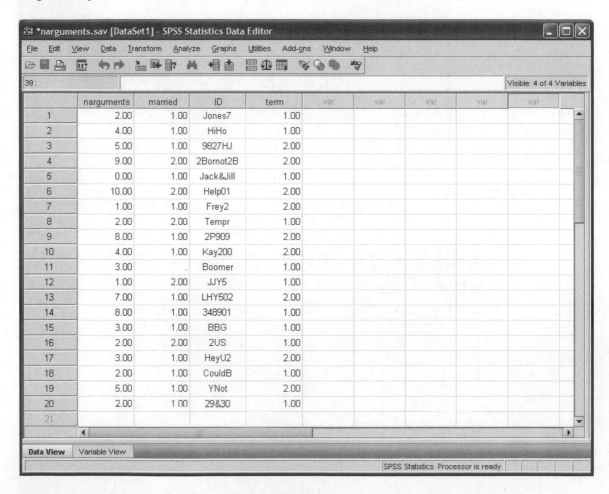

Before using **Chart Builder** to form a clustered bar chart, information about the measurement level of the variable **term**, its label, and labels for its values, must be included in the **Variable View** of the **SPSS Statistics Data Editor**.

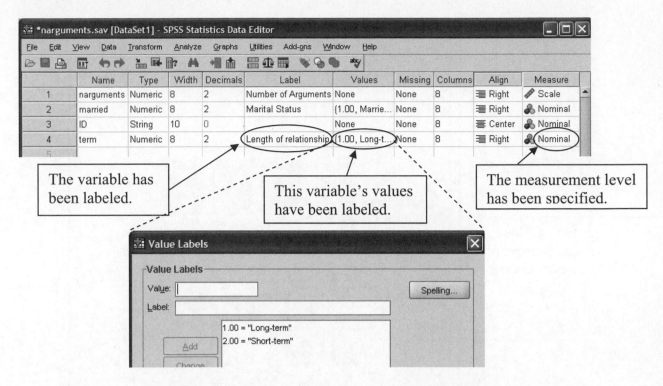

The variable has been labeled.

This variable's values have been labeled.

The measurement level has been specified.

The following selections form a clustered bar chart showing the number of married and not married couples broken down by duration of their relationship.

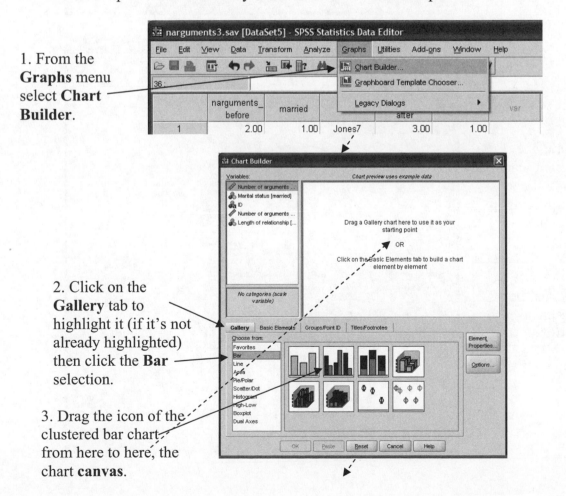

1. From the **Graphs** menu select **Chart Builder**.

2. Click on the **Gallery** tab to highlight it (if it's not already highlighted) then click the **Bar** selection.

3. Drag the icon of the clustered bar chart from here to here, the chart **canvas**.

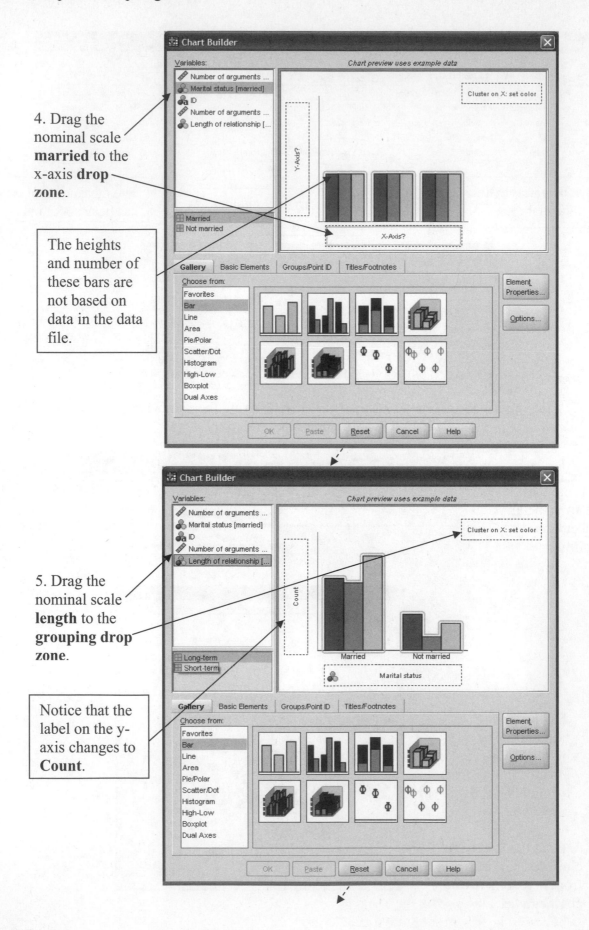

4. Drag the nominal scale **married** to the x-axis **drop zone**.

The heights and number of these bars are not based on data in the data file.

5. Drag the nominal scale **length** to the **grouping drop zone**.

Notice that the label on the y-axis changes to **Count**.

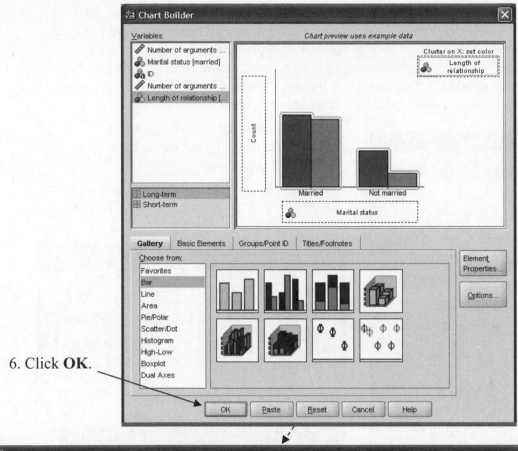

6. Click **OK**.

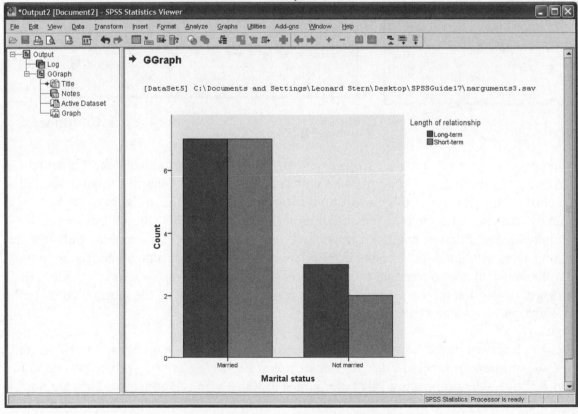

Displaying percents on the y-axis of a clustered bar chart. Care must be taken in choosing a proper denominator for calculating percent whenever percent of cases rather than count of cases is displayed on the y-axis of a clustered bar chart. As shown below, selecting **Percentage ( )** from the **Statistic** field in the **Element Properties** window makes available the **Set Parameters** window which gives three choices of a denominator for calculating percent:

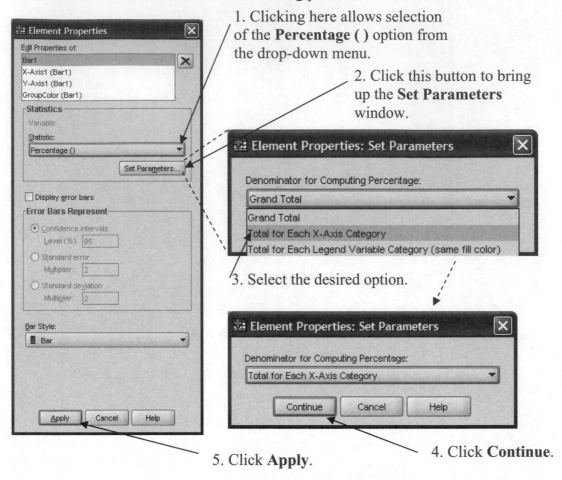

1. Clicking here allows selection of the **Percentage ( )** option from the drop-down menu.

2. Click this button to bring up the **Set Parameters** window.

3. Select the desired option.

5. Click **Apply**.

4. Click **Continue**.

Selecting *Total for each X-Axis Category* in step 3 above will produce a chart in which percentages sum to 100 among the bars within each cluster. The graph shown in the left panel of Figure 6.1, formed by selecting this option, indicates that of couples in the example data set who are married, 50% are in short-term and 50% are in long-term relationships and that of couples who are not married, 40% are in short-term and 60% are in long-term relationships. This choice of denominator is appropriate when it's important that the reader not be distracted by differences in the numbers of cases among values of the variable plotted on the x-axis, that is, in our example, between the numbers of couples who are married vs. not married.

The graph shown in the right panel of Figure 6.1 uses the same data set but bases percent on the denominator labeled *Total for each Legend Variable Category (same fill color)* in step 3 above. The graph shows that of couples in short-term relationships, 20% are not married and 80% are married, and of couples in long-term relationships, 30% are not

Figure 6.1. Clustered bar charts using different denominators to calculate percents. The chart in the left panel uses the option *Total for each X-Axis Category* and that in the right panel uses *Total for each Legend Variable Category (same fill color)*

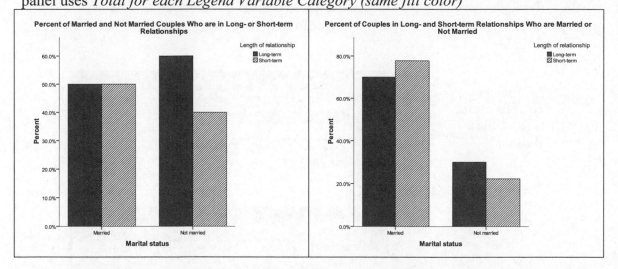

married and 70% are married. This choice is appropriate when the reader should not be distracted by differences in the numbers of cases among values of the variable represented by different bar colors (and/or textures). As another example, consider the data shown in the left panel of Figure 6.2 which displays the number of males and females who respond correctly or incorrectly to a question that involves abstract reasoning. To prevent a reader from being distracted by the very different number of males and females in the data set, the percent of males and percent of females answering the question correctly or incorrectly could be displayed on the y-axis by choosing *Total for each Legend Variable Category (same fill color)*. The resulting graph, shown in the right panel of Figure 6.2, makes it clear that males and females show a similar pattern of answers to the question. With percent on the y-axis, care should be taken in titling the graph.

Figure 6.2. The chart in the left panel displays the number of males and females answering a question correctly or incorrectly. The chart in the right panel uses the option *Total for each Legend Variable Category (same fill color)* to display the percentages.

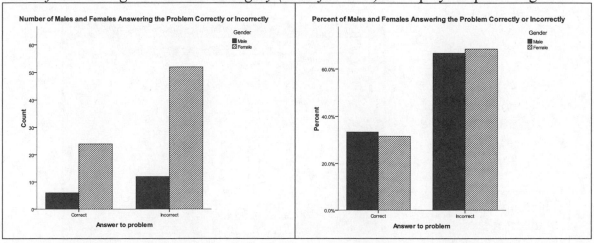

One nominal scale, one scale variable: bar chart.

A bar chart can display a summary statistic (e.g., mean, median, standard deviation) of a scale variable for each category of a nominal- or ordinal-scale variable. The steps outlined below produce a bar chart of the mean number of arguments of married vs. not married couples.

1. From the **Graphs** menu select **Chart Builder**.

2. Click on the **Gallery** tab to highlight it (if it's not already highlighted) then click the **Bar** selection.

3. Drag the icon of the bar chart from here to here, the chart **canvas**.

4. Drag the nominal scale **married** to the x-axis **drop zone**.

The heights and number of these bars are not based on data in the data file.

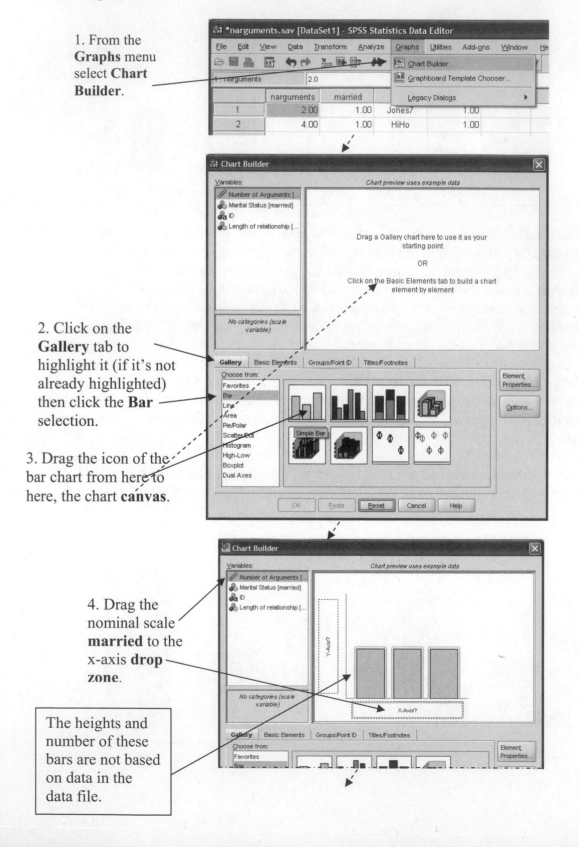

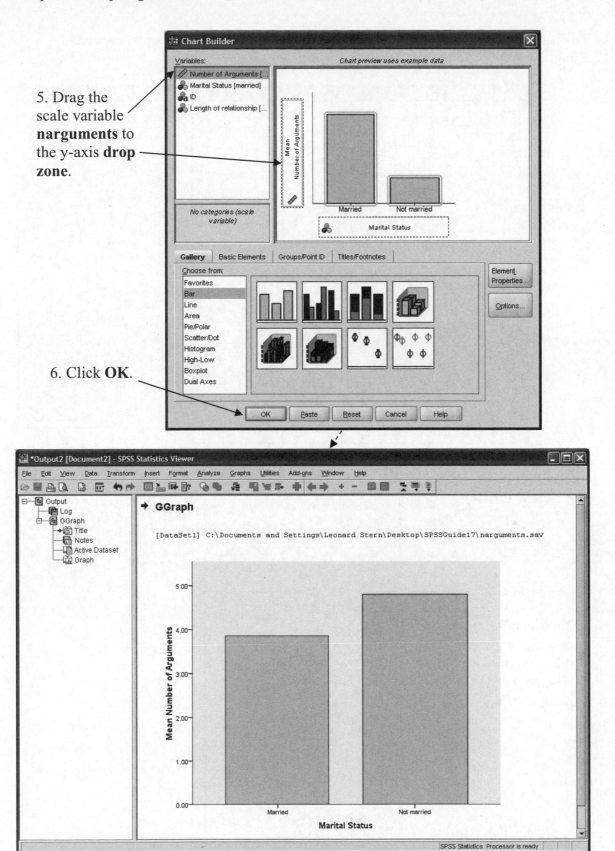

5. Drag the scale variable **narguments** to the y-axis **drop zone**.

6. Click **OK**.

To change the summary statistic shown on the y-axis, use the **Element Properties** window:

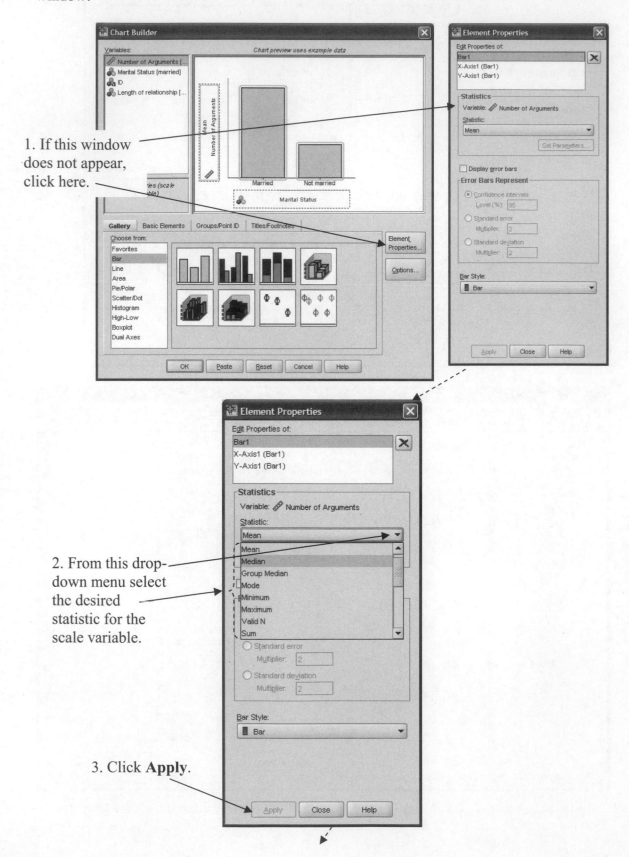

1. If this window does not appear, click here.

2. From this drop-down menu select the desired statistic for the scale variable.

3. Click **Apply**.

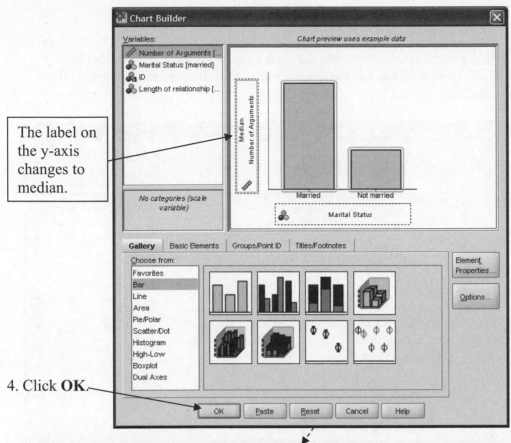

The label on the y-axis changes to median.

4. Click **OK**.

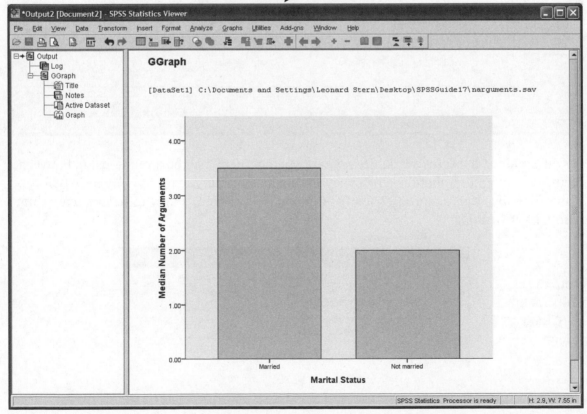

Two scale variables: scatterplot.

A scatterplot shows the relation between two scale variables. Consider, for example, that 20 couples record the number of arguments they have per week both before and after entering counseling. The variables **narguments_before** and **narguments_after** in the file below show the data:

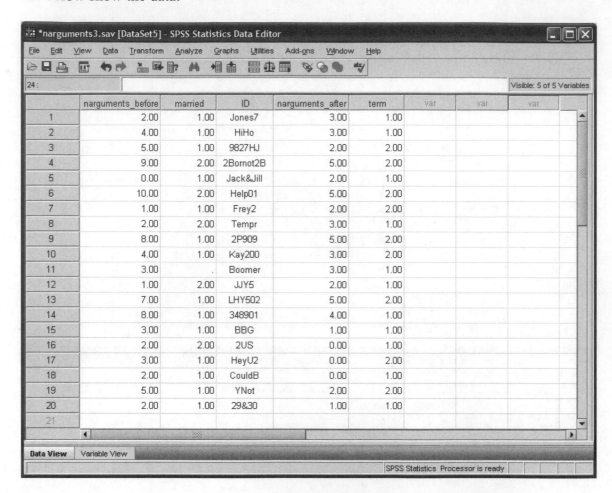

A scatterplot of these two variables reveals whether there may be a relationship between them, for example, if there is a tendency for couples who argue more frequently before counseling also argue more frequently after counseling. Here's how to form a scatterplot with **Chart Builder**.

1. From the **Graphs** menu select **Chart Builder**.

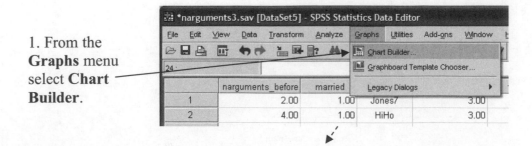

2. Click on the **Gallery** tab to highlight it (if it's not already highlighted) then click the **Scatter/Dot** selection.

3. Drag the icon of the simple scatterplot from here to here.

4. Drag one scale variable to the x-axis **drop zone**.

5. Drag the other scale variable to the y-axis **drop zone**.

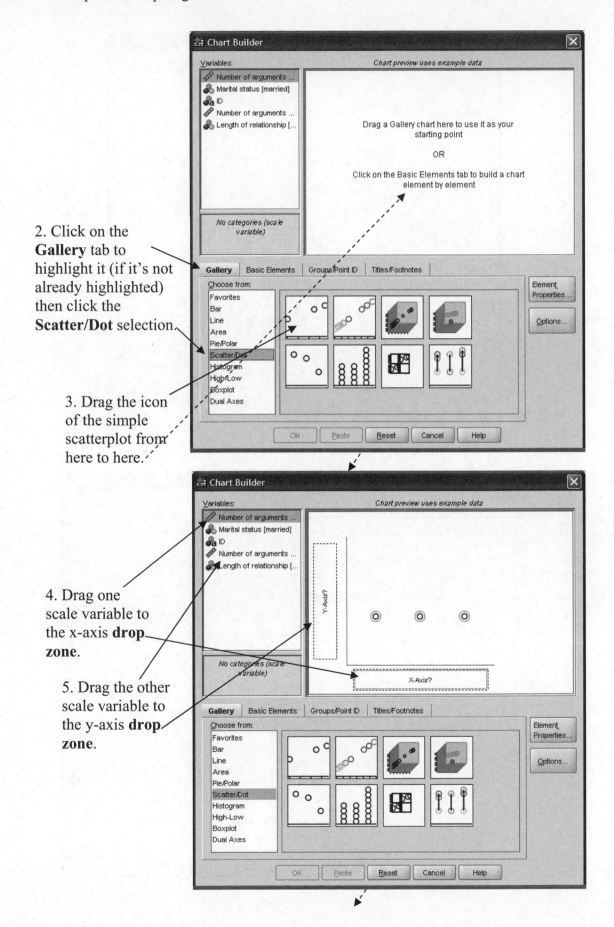

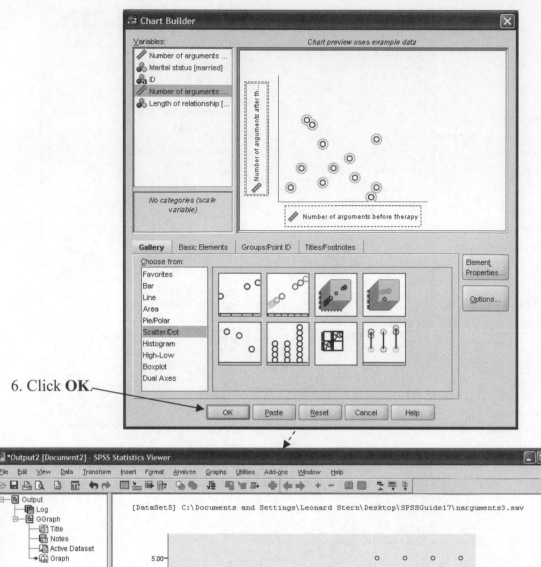

6. Click **OK**.

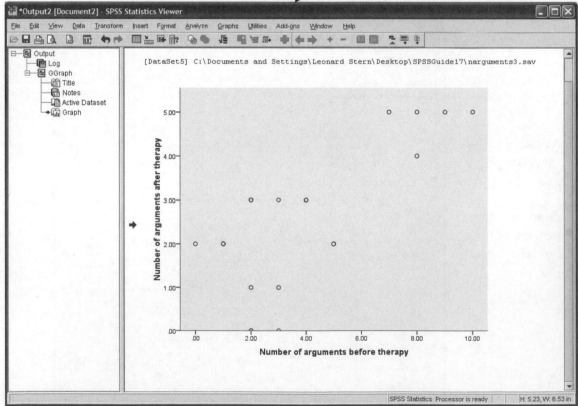

Graphs of Three Variables

Two nominal scales, one scale variable: multiple line plot.

Imagine that one wishes to graph the possible effect of length of a relationship (6 months or less, more than 6 months) and marital status (married, not married) on the mean number of arguments that couples have per week. This exemplifies the inclusion of two nominal scales (functioning as independent variables) and one scale variable (serving as the dependent variable) and can be represented as a multiple line plot. Here's how the data in our example data file can be plotted:

1. From the **Graphs** menu select **Chart Builder**.

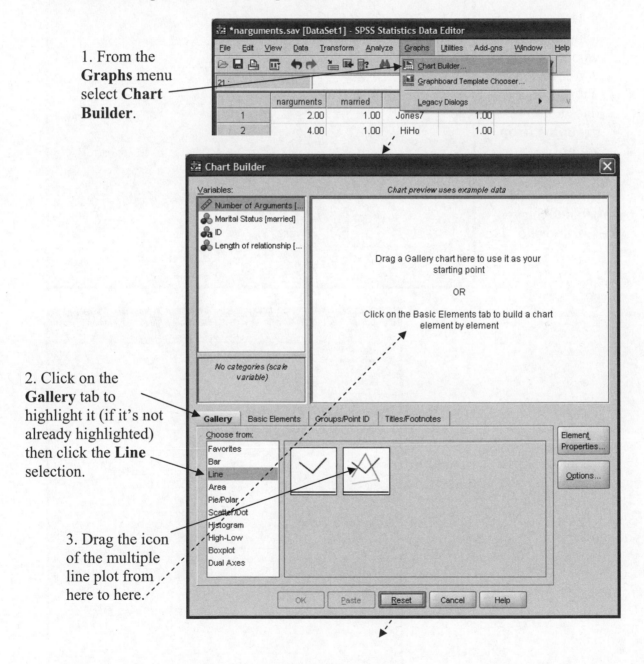

2. Click on the **Gallery** tab to highlight it (if it's not already highlighted) then click the **Line** selection.

3. Drag the icon of the multiple line plot from here to here.

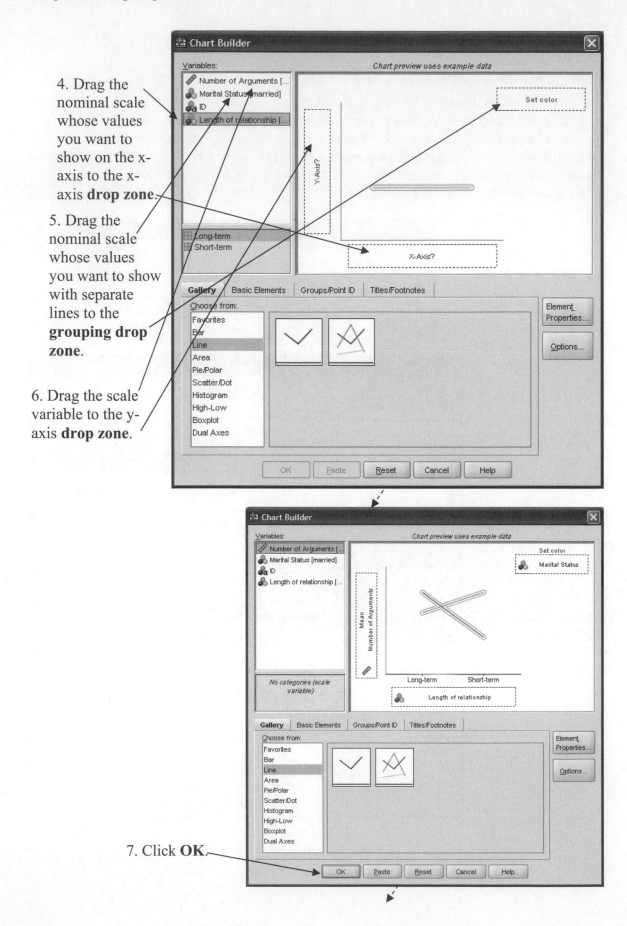

4. Drag the nominal scale whose values you want to show on the x-axis to the x-axis **drop zone**.

5. Drag the nominal scale whose values you want to show with separate lines to the **grouping drop zone**.

6. Drag the scale variable to the y-axis **drop zone**.

7. Click **OK**.

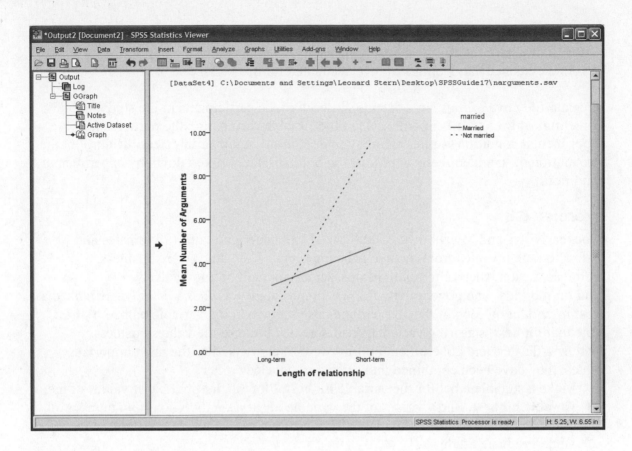

Exercises for Chapter 6

Exercise 6.1

Male and female volunteers are asked to solve a problem while given either a distracting or no distracting task to perform. The time it takes each person to solve the problem is recorded. The data file *Problem.sav* available on the publisher's website for this text at the address http://www.pearsonhighered.com/stern2e shows, for each participant, the time to solve the problem, whether the person is given a distracting task or not, and the person's gender in the variables **dv**, **condition**, and **gender**, respectively. Prepare a graph showing mean problem solving time as a function of distraction condition (displayed on the x-axis) and gender.

Exercise 6.2

To help understand why people who write a few sentences about why a value is most important to them (e.g., religion, social relationships, the pursuit of knowledge) become less defensive about information that may be threatening to them, Crocker, Niiya, and Mischkowski (2008) had 102 participants rank six values from most to least important then either write for 10 minutes about why their highest ranked value was most important to them (the values affirmation condition) or why their lowest ranked value may be most important to others (the control condition). Participants then rated how strongly they experienced various feelings, including love, on a 1-5 scale (1 = not at all and 5 = extremely) while writing their essay. Participants in the values affirmation who were smokers were found to be more accepting of a research article that claimed to find new evidence of a harmful effect on health than smokers in the control condition. Crocker et al. found evidence that feelings of love accounted for this change.

The data file *LoveRatings.sav* contains, for each of the participants in the study, a rating of feelings of love on a 1-5 point scale in the variable **rating,** and the participant's experimental condition (values affirmation or control) in the variable **condition**. Plot the distribution of the rated feelings of love (an ordinal scale) broken down by experimental condition.

Exercise 6.3

Crocker, Niiya, and Mischkowsi (2008) asked 139 undergraduates (99 females and 61 males) to rank 6 values from most to least important. The values were business, art/music/theater, social life/relationships, science/pursuit of knowledge, religion/morality, and government/politics. In the data file *Values.sav* the value ranked as most important by each of the 139 participants is shown in the variable named **highest**. Note that **highest** is a string variable. Also note that because the values business, art/music/theater, and government/politics were rarely ranked as the most important values, they have been combined into a category labeled "other."

a.   Make a suitable label for the variable **highest**. Plot the distribution of values of the variable **highest**. Show values of the variable **highest** on the x-axis and number of cases on the y-axis. Title the graph "Highest Ranked Values Selected by Undergraduate Students."

b.   The variable **gender** contains the values 1 and 2 to represent females and males, respectively. After making a suitable label for the variable **gender**, plot the distribution of values of the variable **highest** on the x-axis broken down by females and males. Show percent of cases on the y-axis using a denominator that causes the different numbers of males and females in the study to not be apparent and thus distract a person inspecting the graph. Again, title the graph appropriately.

Exercise 6.4

The number of remembered dreams from the previous night reported by randomly selected adult males and females is shown in the table below:

Number of Dreams	Gender	Number of Dreams	Gender	Number of Dreams	Gender
3	F	0	F	0	M
0	M	1	M	0	M
1	M	3	F	2	F
1	F	4	F	0	M
0	M	2	M	0	F
2	M	1	F	1	M
1	F	1	M	1	M
0	M	2	F	2	F

a. Enter the data into an *SPSS* data file. In the **Data Editor**'s **Variable View**, provide
    suitable variable labels for the two variables and label values of the variable that
    represents gender of the person. Also, specify each variable's level of measurement.
b. Graph the distribution of values of the variable that represents the number of dreams
    a person reports.
c. Graph the median number of dreams remembered broken down by gender.

Exercise 6.5

The file *Ex6.5.sav* available on the publisher's website for this text at the address
http://www.pearsonhighered.com/stern2e contains percent correct scores on a homework
assignment (the variable **Homework1**) and a quiz (the variable **Quiz1**) for students
enrolled in a statistics class. Make a scatterplot for the data showing homework scores on
the x-axis and quiz scores on the y-axis. Form a suitable title for the graph.

Chapter 7: Data Transformation and Case Selection

Recoding Data

Recoding to Form a New Variable

A variable will not always consist of values suitable for an analysis. Consider, for example, that a researcher wishes to determine whether the mean number of hours of sleep of children aged 9-12 differs from that of teens aged 14-17. To perform the analysis, the researcher may require that a data file contains values of two variables: one consisting of values of a categorical variable to represent a child's age, perhaps using the value 1 to signal the child is between the ages of 9-11, and the value 2 to signal the child is between 14-17, and the other consisting of the number of hours of sleep per night the child generally gets. Consider, now, the problem that arises if the researcher's data file has values of the variables **age** and **hoursleep**, as shown below:

	age	hoursleep
1	5.00	9.00
2	6.00	8.00
3	4.00	10.00
4	7.00	8.00
5	8.00	9.00
6	10.00	9.00
7	15.00	7.00
8	7.00	8.00
9	14.00	9.00
10	15.00	7.00

Given the data shown above, the researcher might find it appropriate to recode values of the continuous quantitative variable **age** into values of a categorical variable that represents ranges of age. The value 1 could represent ages 9-12, 2 could represent ages 14-17, and 3 could, perhaps, represent all other ages. These transformations can be accomplished using the recoding procedure shown below.

1. From the **Transform** menu select **Recode into Different Variables**.

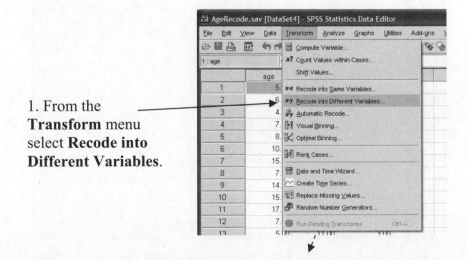

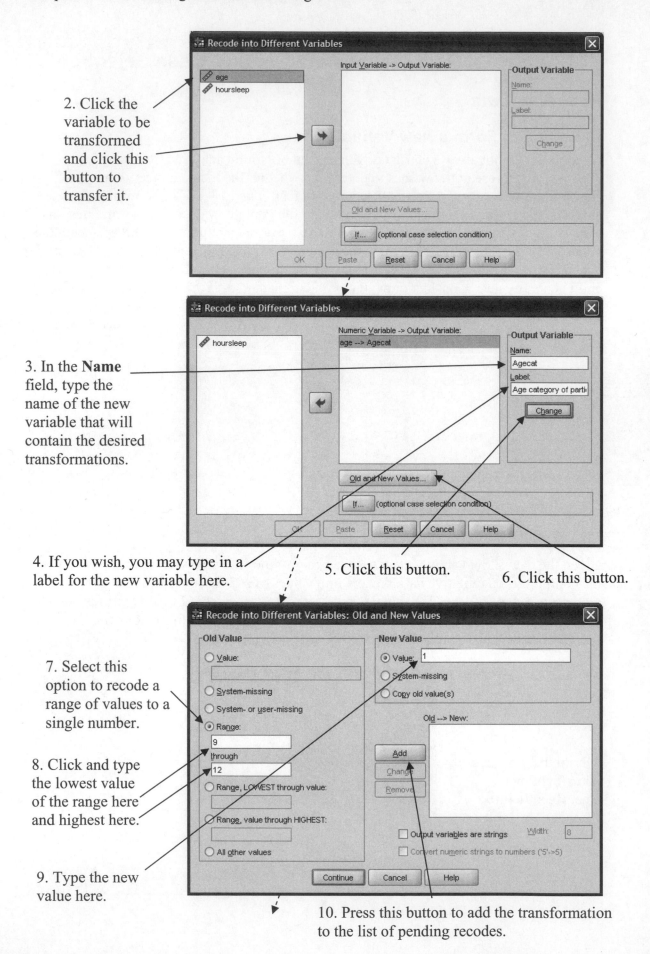

2. Click the variable to be transformed and click this button to transfer it.

3. In the **Name** field, type the name of the new variable that will contain the desired transformations.

4. If you wish, you may type in a label for the new variable here.

5. Click this button.

6. Click this button.

7. Select this option to recode a range of values to a single number.

8. Click and type the lowest value of the range here and highest here.

9. Type the new value here.

10. Press this button to add the transformation to the list of pending recodes.

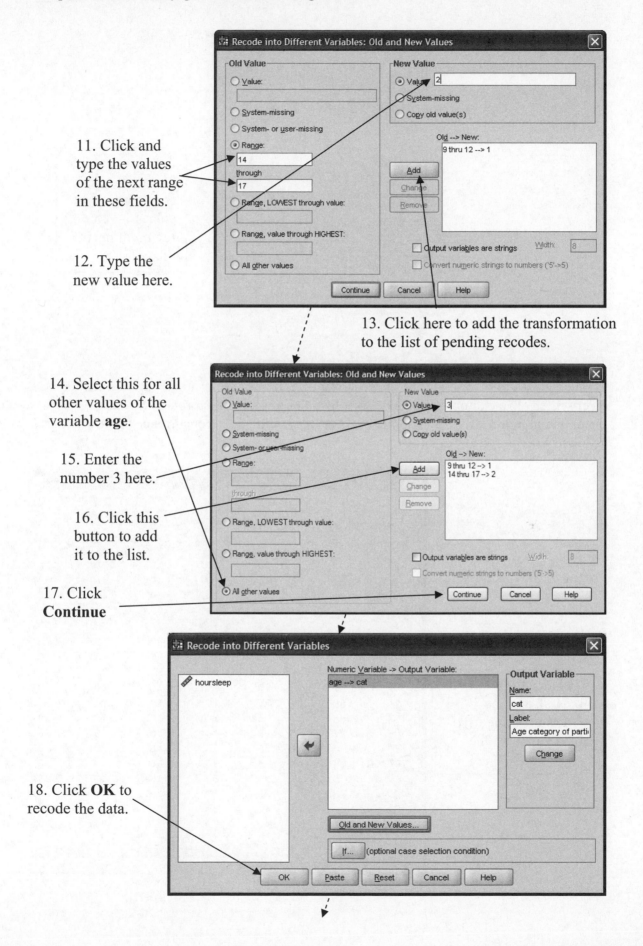

11. Click and type the values of the next range in these fields.

12. Type the new value here.

13. Click here to add the transformation to the list of pending recodes.

14. Select this for all other values of the variable **age**.

15. Enter the number 3 here.

16. Click this button to add it to the list.

17. Click **Continue**

18. Click **OK** to recode the data.

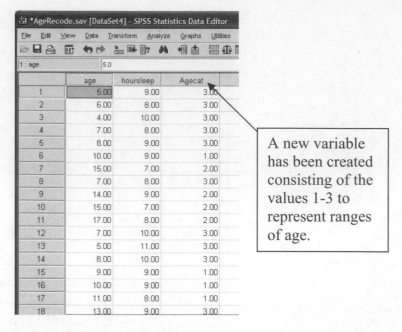

A new variable has been created consisting of the values 1-3 to represent ranges of age.

Recoding to the Same vs. Different Variables

If one chooses to recode into the same variable, values of the original variable will be overwritten. The example shown below illustrates applying the process to values of a string variable **major**. The example illustrates changing every occurrence of *psyc* to the value *psych*.

Notice the value *psych* and the desired value *psyc* both exist in the file.

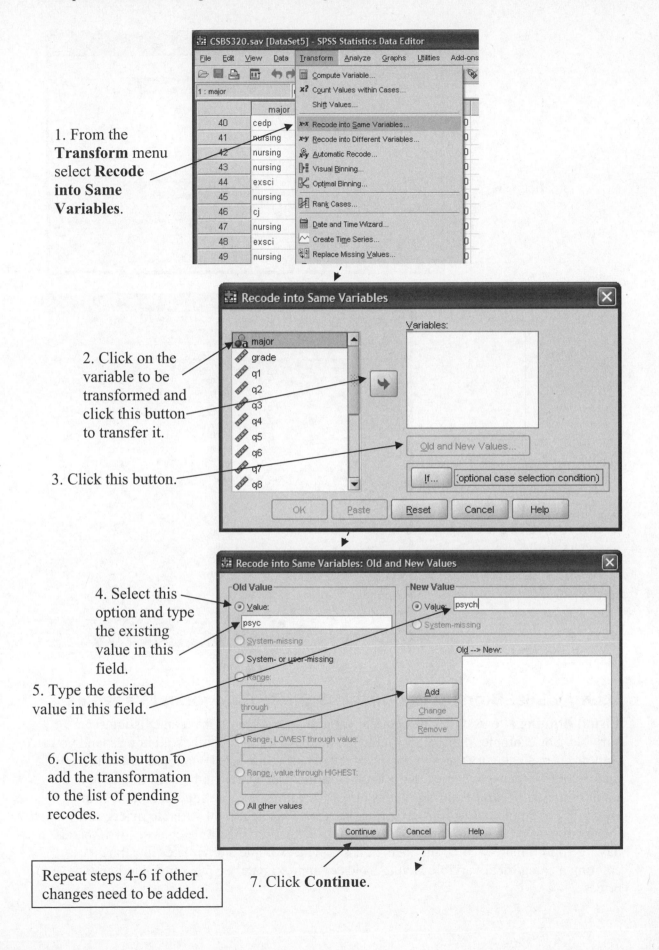

1. From the **Transform** menu select **Recode into Same Variables**.

2. Click on the variable to be transformed and click this button to transfer it.

3. Click this button.

4. Select this option and type the existing value in this field.

5. Type the desired value in this field.

6. Click this button to add the transformation to the list of pending recodes.

Repeat steps 4-6 if other changes need to be added.

7. Click **Continue**.

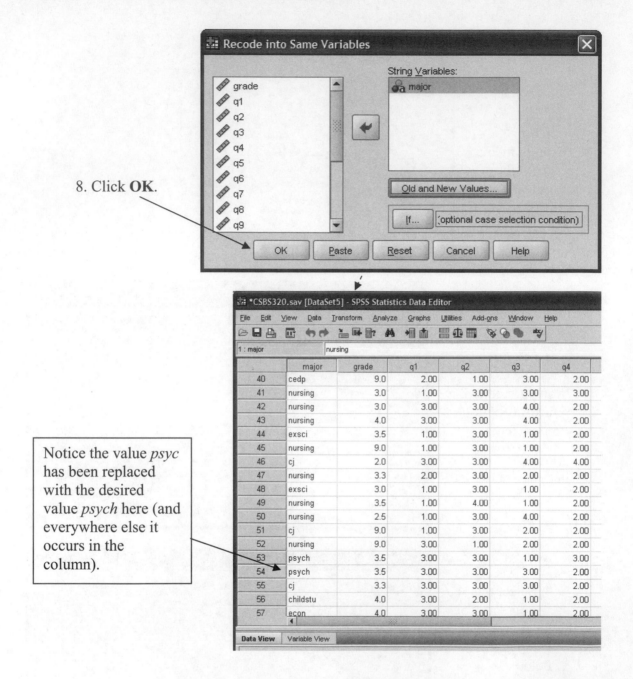

8. Click **OK**.

Notice the value *psyc* has been replaced with the desired value *psych* here (and everywhere else it occurs in the column).

Using Visual Binning *to Convert Scale to Categorical Variables*

Visual Binning allows a new categorical variable to be created from an existing scale variable. For example, if a scale variable shows the price of recently sold homes, and you want to form a category variable that uses the values 1 through 10 to represent ranges of increasingly-expensive homes, the **Visual Binning** procedure can be used to facilitate the transformation. **Visual Binning** allows ranges of values to be defined in a number of ways. The example below illustrates creating the new categorical variable **pricecat** from the existing scale variable **salepric** in which the categorical variable consists of 10 bands having approximately equal numbers of cases. The example shown later illustrates creating a categorical variable having bands of approximately equal ranges of home prices.

1. From the **Transform** menu select **Visual Binning**.

2. Click the variable to be transformed and click this button to transfer it to the **Variables to Bin** pane.

3. Click **Continue**.

4. Click on the name of the variable to be binned. Information about the variable appears in various fields.

5. Click **Make Cutpoints.**

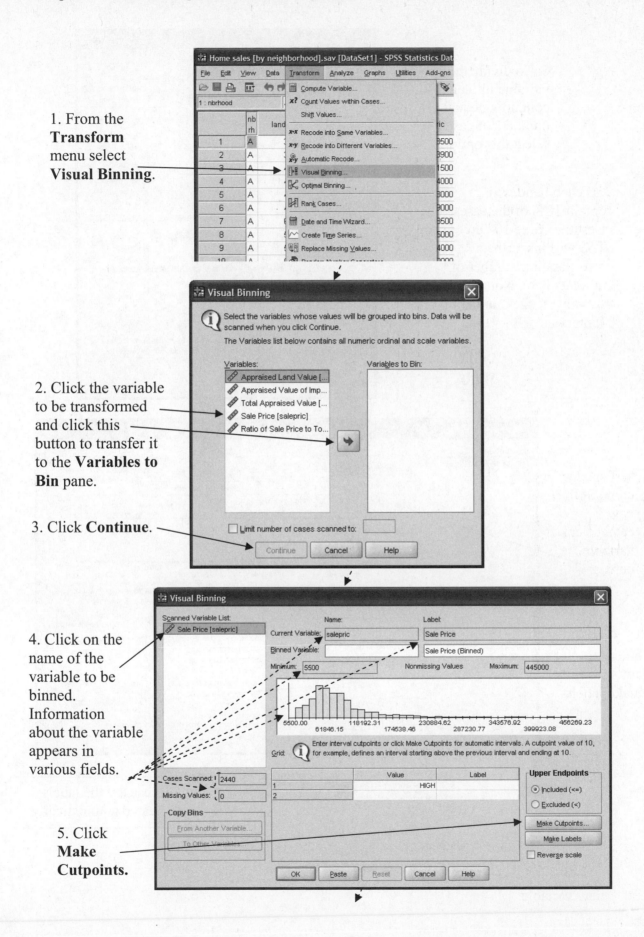

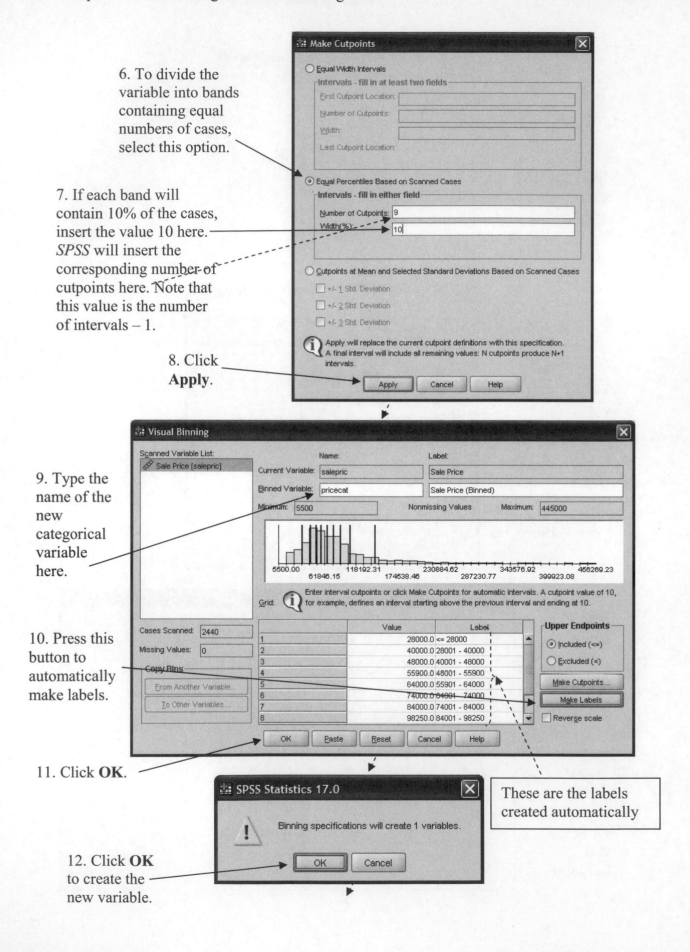

6. To divide the variable into bands containing equal numbers of cases, select this option.

7. If each band will contain 10% of the cases, insert the value 10 here. *SPSS* will insert the corresponding number of cutpoints here. Note that this value is the number of intervals – 1.

8. Click **Apply**.

9. Type the name of the new categorical variable here.

10. Press this button to automatically make labels.

11. Click **OK**.

12. Click **OK** to create the new variable.

These are the labels created automatically

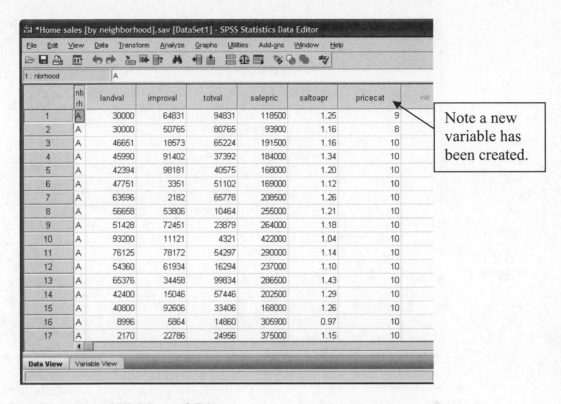

Options for Creating Widths of Bins

One option allows creating bins from equally-wide intervals of the scale variable. For example, to create 9 categories of newly sold home prices that each span intervals of $40,000 starting with the value $80,000 (prices less than $80,000 are given the category value 1), the following specifications on the **Make Cutpoints** window are suitable:

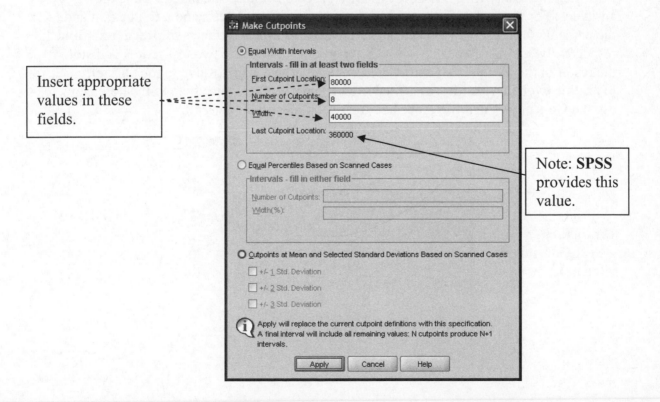

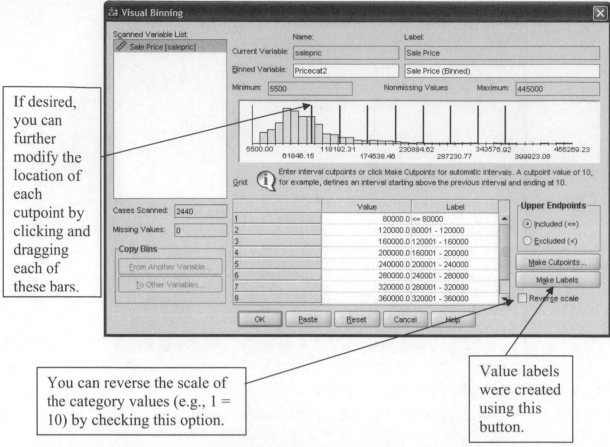

If desired, you can further modify the location of each cutpoint by clicking and dragging each of these bars.

You can reverse the scale of the category values (e.g., 1 = 10) by checking this option.

Value labels were created using this button.

Using **COMPUTE** *to Create New Variables*

It is often necessary to create new variables based on values calculated from existing variables. For example, if students in a class are given a midterm and a final exam and the percent correct score of each student is recorded in the variables **midterm** and **final**, respectively, an instructor may wish to obtain the mean of the two test scores and store the result in the variable **overall**. The formula used to assign a value to the variable **overall** is **overall** = (**midterm** + **final**) / 2. The procedure shown below illustrates how to use the **Compute Variable** procedure to create the variable **overall**.

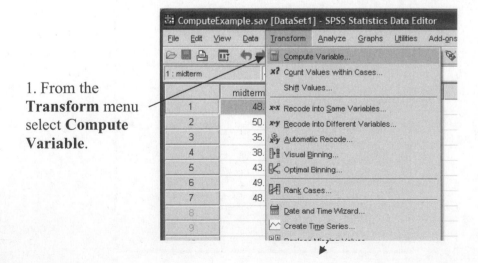

1. From the **Transform** menu select **Compute Variable**.

2. Type the name of the variable to be created (**overall**) in this field.

3. Using a combination of the variable names and the symbol keys, insert the desired equation into this field.

4. Press **OK**.

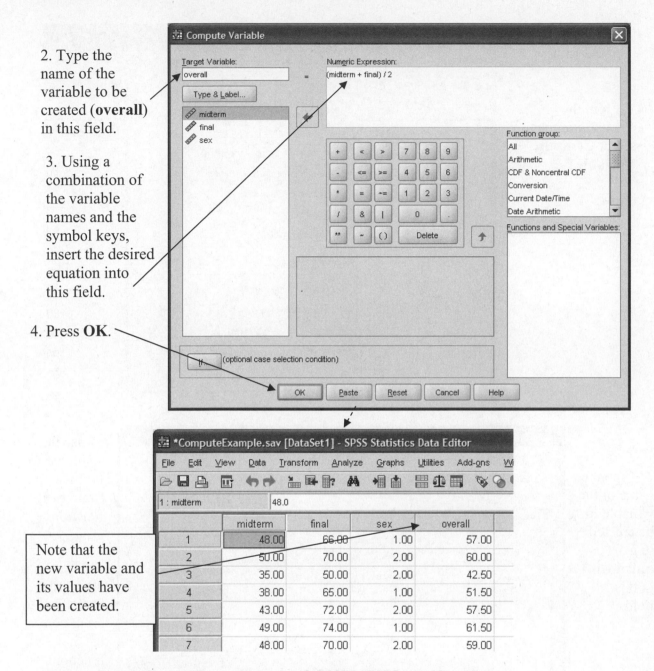

Note that the new variable and its values have been created.

Using Predefined Functions in *COMPUTE* Specifications

SPSS makes a number of predefined functions available for use in **COMPUTE** expressions. For example, if each case in a data file consists of several variables whose mean is desired, the function **Mean** can be used to facilitate the calculation. Although a mean could be obtained by entering an algebraic expression as shown in the example above, using the **Mean** function is generally easier. In the example shown below, the data consist of a percent correct score for each of five quizzes and the **Compute Variable** procedure uses the **Mean** function to obtain a mean quiz score.

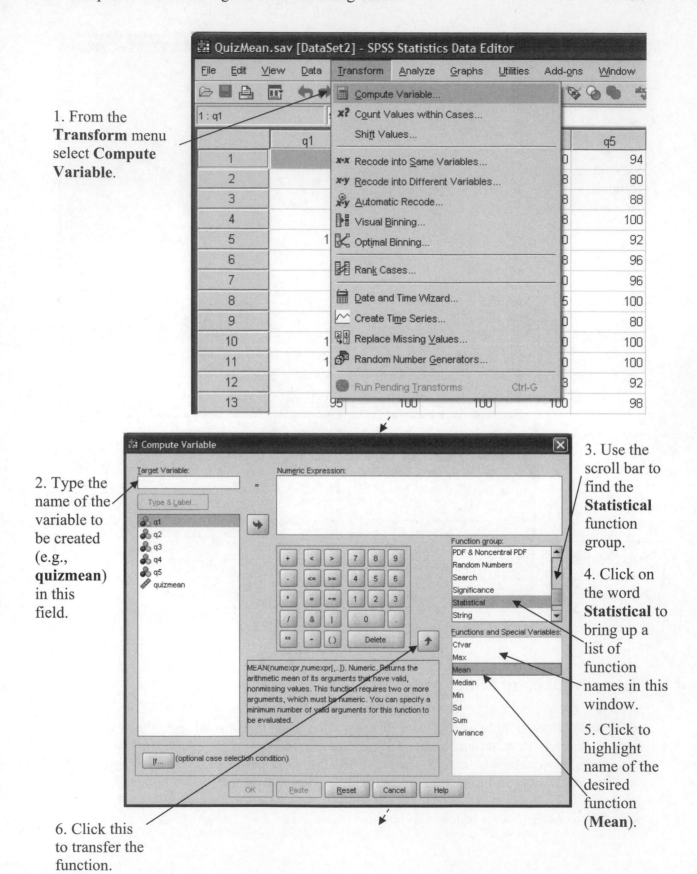

1. From the **Transform** menu select **Compute Variable**.

2. Type the name of the variable to be created (e.g., **quizmean**) in this field.

3. Use the scroll bar to find the **Statistical** function group.

4. Click on the word **Statistical** to bring up a list of function names in this window.

5. Click to highlight name of the desired function (**Mean**).

6. Click this to transfer the function.

7. Click the name of the first variable in the list then click this to transfer it into the function.

8. Use the mouse to highlight the next question mark in the expression.

9. Click the name of the next variable in the list then transfer it into the function.

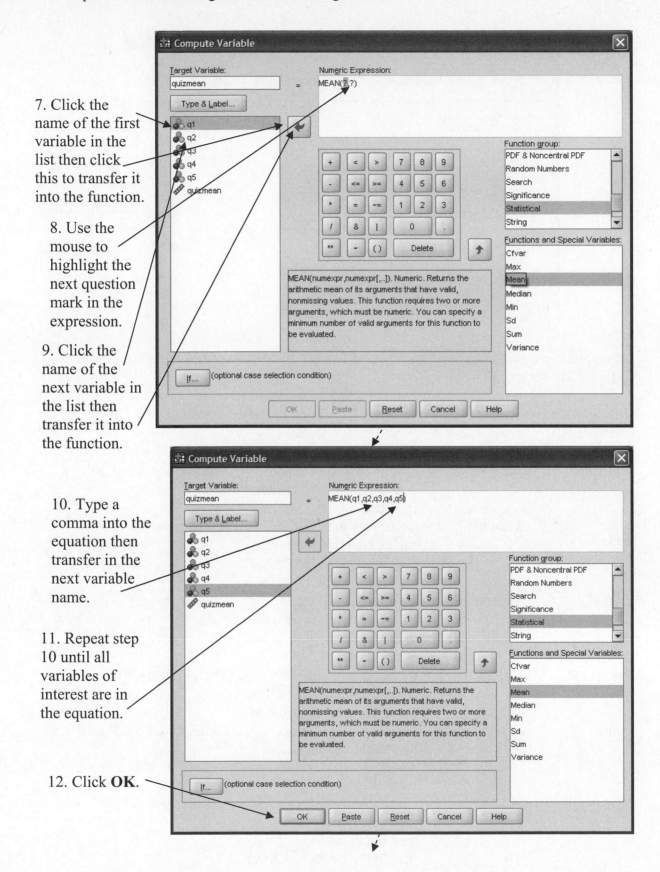

10. Type a comma into the equation then transfer in the next variable name.

11. Repeat step 10 until all variables of interest are in the equation.

12. Click **OK**.

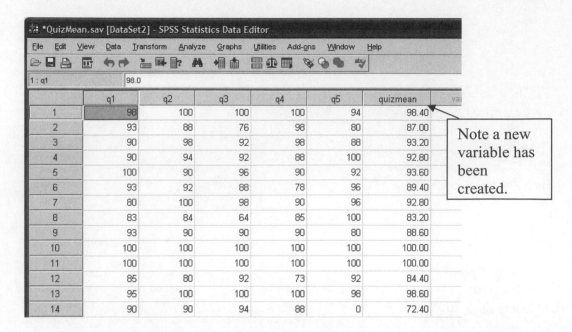

Some predefined functions are described in Table 7.1 and examples of their application to the quiz dataset are shown in Figure 7.1 below.

Table 7.1. Some functions available in the **Compute Variable** procedure.

Function Name	Function Group Name	Purpose	Example
Variance	Statistical	Calculates the variance of a set of numeric variables specified.	Variance(q1,q2,q3,q4,q5)
Sqrt	Arithmetic	Calculates the positive square root of a positive number in a named numeric variable.	Sqrt(quizvar)
Rnd(1)	Arithmetic	Rounds the value of a specified numeric variable to the nearest whole number.	Rnd(quizmean)
Trunc(1)	Arithmetic	Removes any decimal value from the value of the numeric variable specified	Trunc(quizmean)
Nmiss	Missing Values	Gives a count of the number of missing values among the numeric variables specified	Nmiss(q1,q2,q3,q4,q5)
$Casenum	Miscellaneous	Creates a variable that has the value corresponding to the ordinal position of the case in the **SPSS Statistics Data Editor**	$Casenum

Figure 7.1. Variables created by applying the functions listed in Table 7.1 (in the order shown in the table) to the quiz dataset. The variable names shown in the data file were specified in the **Target Variable** pane of the **Compute Variable** window.

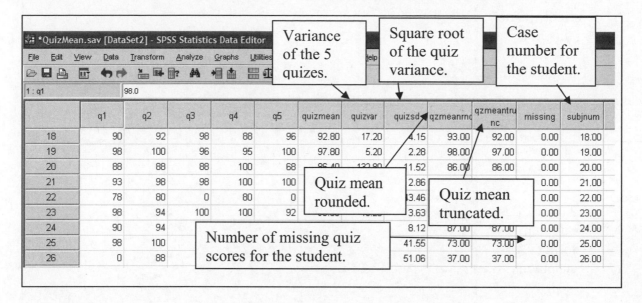

Prefacing *COMPUTE* specifications with *IF* statements

By pairing a **COMPUTE** statement with an **IF** statement, it is possible to create a variable with computed values only when certain conditions prevail. For example, one might wish to flag students in a class who have taken five quizzes if any quiz score is zero. The steps shown below demonstrate how to create the numeric variable **zeroscore** that has the value 1 only if one or more quiz score has the value zero. In the **IF** statement for this example, the predefined function **MIN** detects any occurrence of the value zero in the listed variables (i.e., the statement *MIN(q1,q2,q3,q4,q5)=0* has the value 'true' when the value of q1, q2, q3, q4, or q5 is 0).

1. From the **Transform** menu select **Compute Variable**.

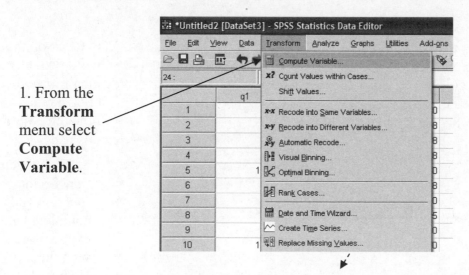

2. Type a variable name in this field and the value 1 in this field.

3. Click this button to form an IF statement.

4. Click this option.

5. Use the scroll bar to find the Search function group

6. Click on the word Search then find and click on the function Min in this pane.

7. Click this to transfer the function and complete the expression with the keyboard keys.

8. Click Continue.

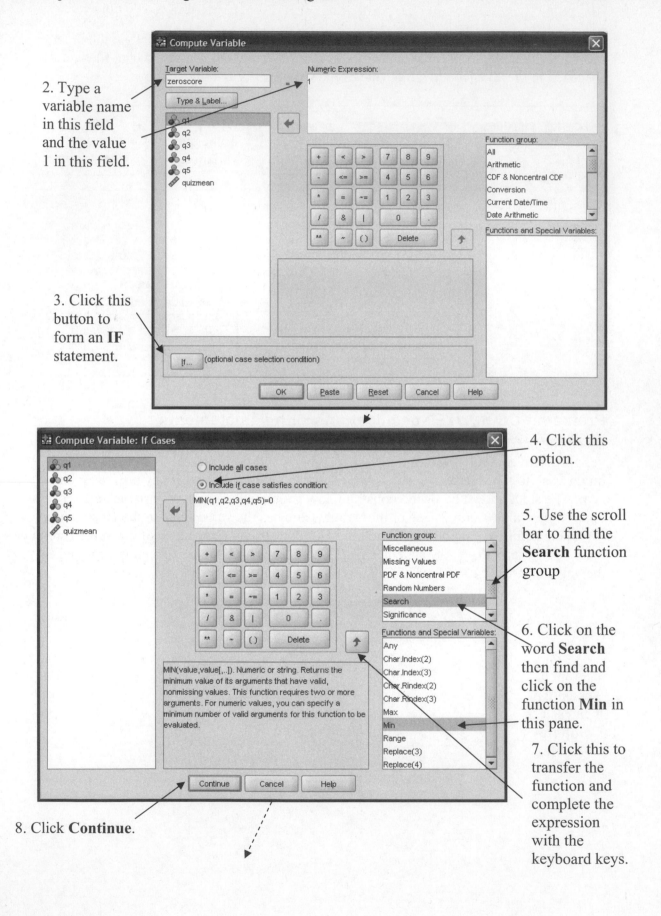

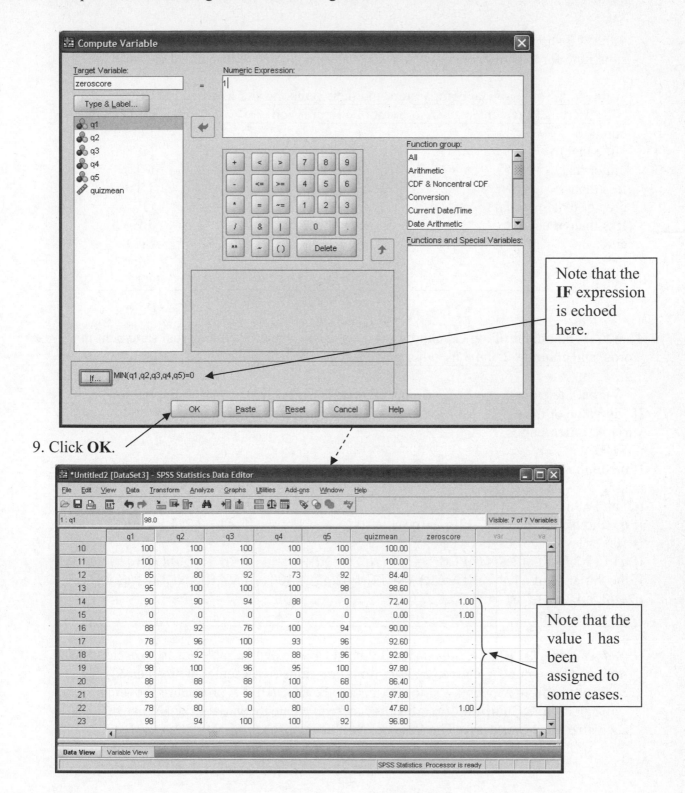

9. Click **OK**.

Note that the **IF** expression is echoed here.

Note that the value 1 has been assigned to some cases.

Table 7.3 shows other examples of **IF** statements. Note that *SPSS* accepts letter pairs as a substitute for logical operators (such as equal to, not equal to) as shown in Table 7.2.

Table 7.2. Some logical comparators and their symbolic and letter equivalents.

Verbal Statement	Symbolic Expression	Letter Equivalent
equal to	=	EQ
not equal to	~=	NE
grater than	>	GT
less than	<	LT
greater than or equal to	>=	GE
less than or equal to	<=	LE
and	&	AND
or	|	OR
not	~	NOT

Table 7.3. Examples of logical expressions. Column 1 expresses the logical statement in words, and columns 2 and 3 use alternative symbols acceptable to SPSS.

Verbal Statement	Logical Expression	Alternate form of Logical Expression
If any value of the variable **quizmean** is not 100	If quizmean ~= 100	If quizmean NE 100
If the highest score among the variables **q1, q2,** and **q3** is 100.	If MAX(q1,q2,q3) = 100	If MAX(q1,q2,q3) EQ 100
If **q1** and **q2** combined is 100 or less	If (q1 + q2) <= 100	If (q1 + q2) LE 100
If **q1** or **q2** is 50 or less	If (q1 <= 50) | (q2 <= 50)	If (q1 <= 50) OR (q2 <= 50)
If the variance of **q1, q2, q3, q4,** and **q5** is greater than 100	If VARIANCE(q1,q2,q3) > 100	If VARIANCE(q1,q2,q3) GT 100

Sequencing **COMPUTE** *Statements.* In the newly-created variable **zeroscore**, cases not assigned the value 1 are given a system-missing value (represented with a period). To prevent this from happening, prior to running the **COMPUTE** procedure shown above, you can use the **Compute Variable** procedure to create the variable **zeroscore** that has the value 0 for every case. The form below illustrates the process.

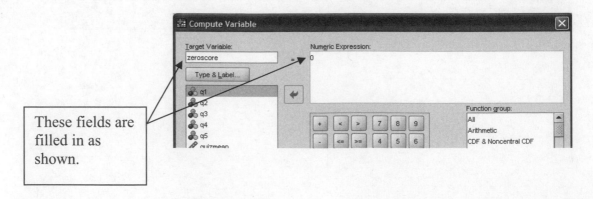

These fields are filled in as shown.

After the **Compute Variable** procedure is run, all cases will have the value 0. If the previously described **Compute Variable** procedure with the **IF** statement is run next, values of the variable **zeroscore** for cases having any quiz score of 0 will be set to 1. Note that before the second **Compute Variable** procedure runs, a dialog box will appear confirming that values of the variable are about to be changed. Click the **OK** button to allow the transformation.

Note that, as illustrated below, the function **ANY** is useful for producing these same results in a single step.

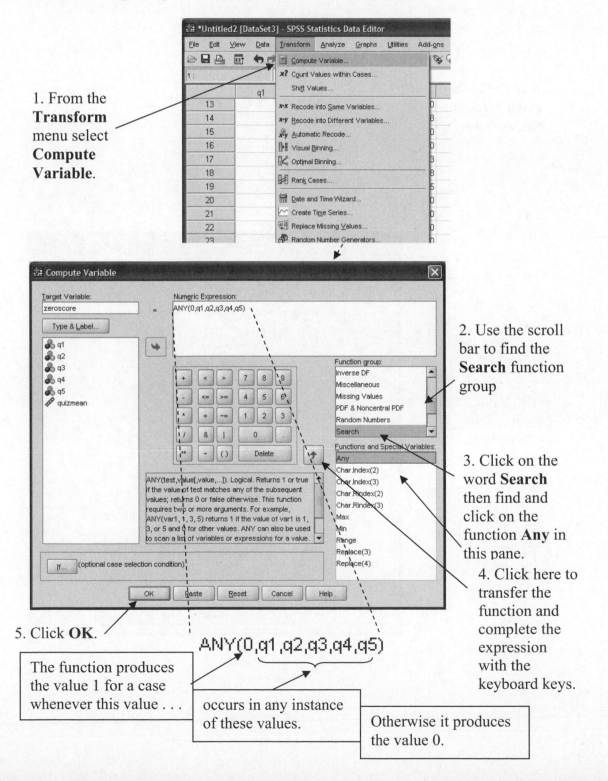

1. From the **Transform** menu select **Compute Variable**.

2. Use the scroll bar to find the **Search** function group

3. Click on the word **Search** then find and click on the function **Any** in this pane.

4. Click here to transfer the function and complete the expression with the keyboard keys.

5. Click **OK**.

ANY(0,q1,q2,q3,q4,q5)

The function produces the value 1 for a case whenever this value . . .

occurs in any instance of these values.

Otherwise it produces the value 0.

Selecting a Subset of Cases for Analysis

It is often appropriate to restrict an analysis to a subset of all cases in a data file. For example, an analysis may be desired for only participants within a particular age range. To analyze just some of the cases in a data file and ignore the others, use **Select Cases**. In the example below, cases are selected if the value of the variable **agecat** is 3.

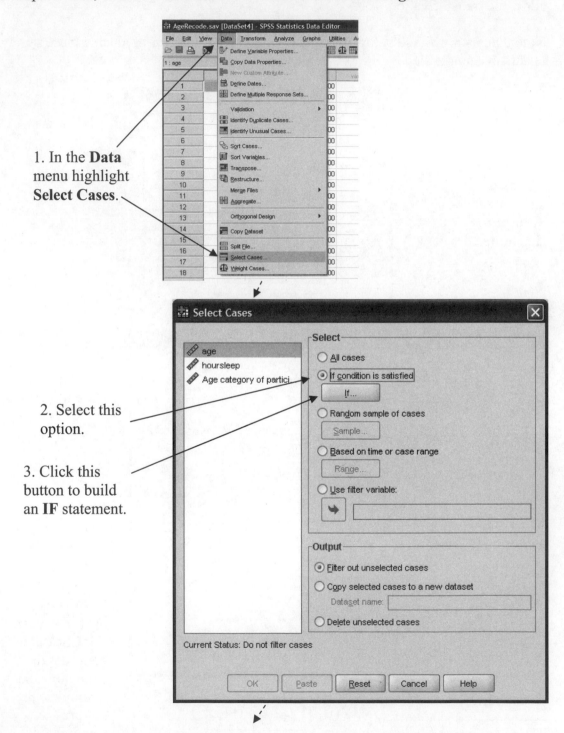

1. In the **Data** menu highlight **Select Cases**.

2. Select this option.

3. Click this button to build an **IF** statement.

4. Highlight the variable around which to build the **IF** statement.

5. Click to transfer the variable.

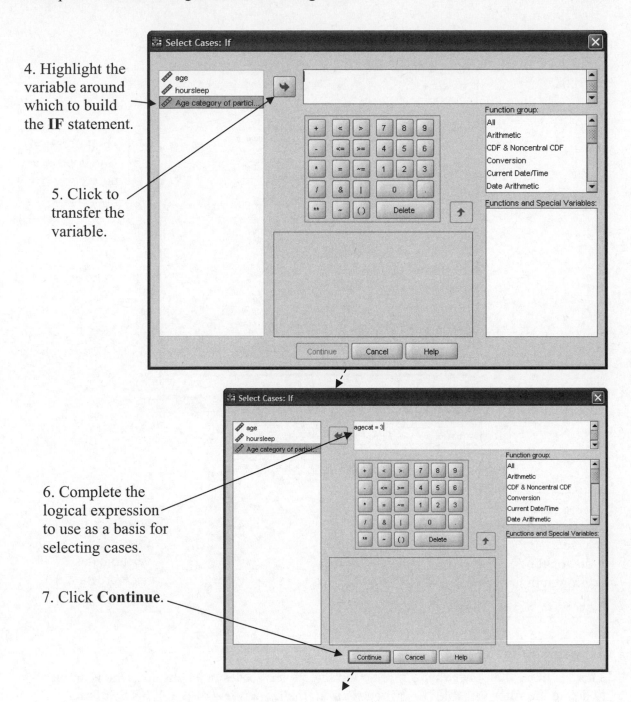

6. Complete the logical expression to use as a basis for selecting cases.

7. Click **Continue**.

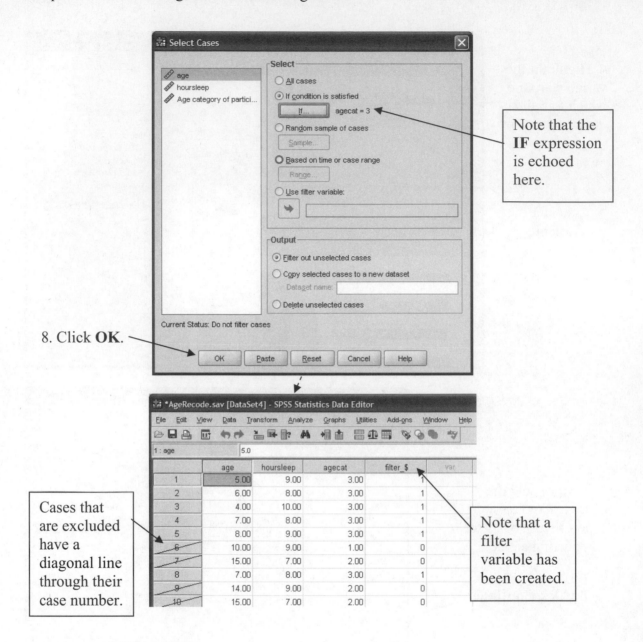

Note that the **IF** expression is echoed here.

8. Click **OK**.

Cases that are excluded have a diagonal line through their case number.

Note that a filter variable has been created.

Turning Filtering Off

There is more than one way to reverse the selection of cases in a data file. One is simply to delete the filter variable (i.e., **filter_$**) from the **Data View** of the **SPSS Statistics Data Editor**. To do this, highlight the variable by placing the mouse pointer in the filter variable name and clicking; then, when the column of variable values turns dark, pressing **delete** on the keyboard:

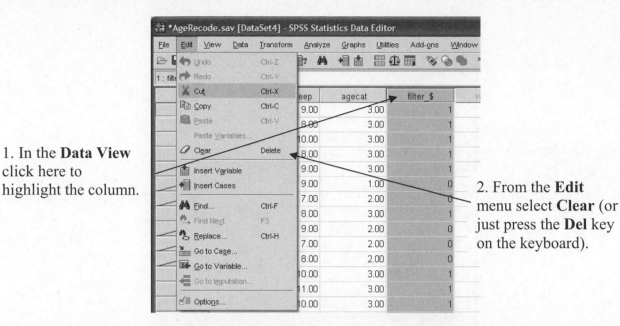

1. In the **Data View** click here to highlight the column.

2. From the **Edit** menu select **Clear** (or just press the **Del** key on the keyboard).

Another method is to use the **Select Cases** window to select **All cases**.

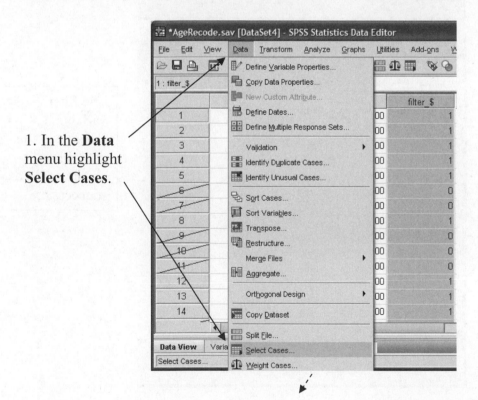

1. In the **Data** menu highlight **Select Cases**.

2. Click on
this option.

3. Click **OK**.

Notice that
the lines
through the
case numbers
have
disappeared.

The filter
variable
remains in the
data file so it
can be re-used,
if necessary.

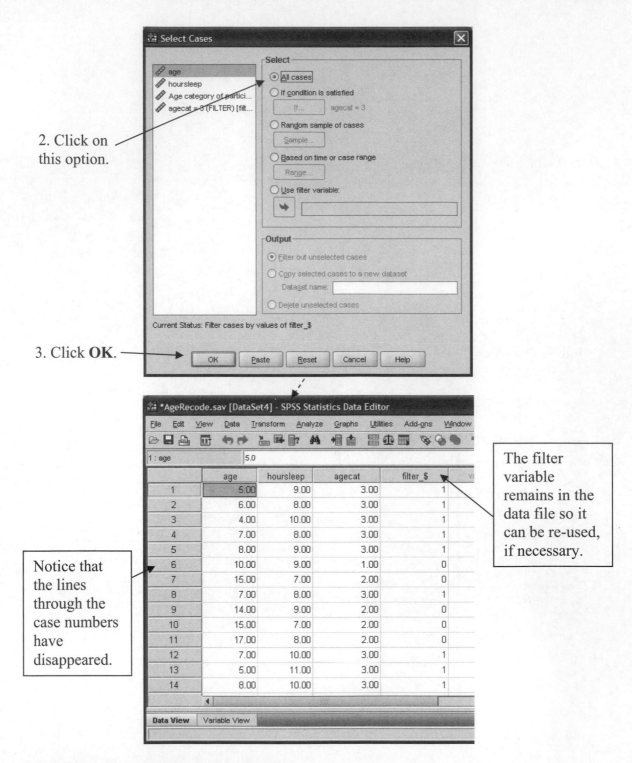

Other Bases for Selecting Cases

Random Sample. One can select a random sample consisting of either a specified percent of the cases in the data file or a specified number of cases. In both situations, the **Select Cases** procedure is requested from the **Data** menu, and the desired option chosen from the **Random sample of cases** option:

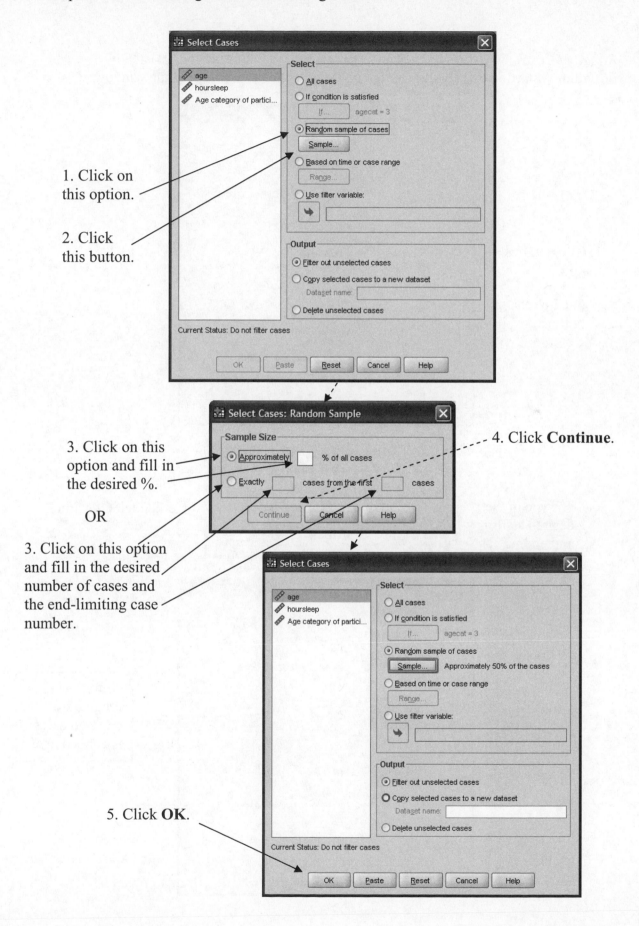

1. Click on
this option.

2. Click
this button.

3. Click on this
option and fill in
the desired %.

OR

3. Click on this option
and fill in the desired
number of cases and
the end-limiting case
number.

4. Click **Continue**.

5. Click **OK**.

Range of Cases. One can specify that a continuous range of cases be selected by providing a starting and ending case number on the **Select Cases: Range** window:

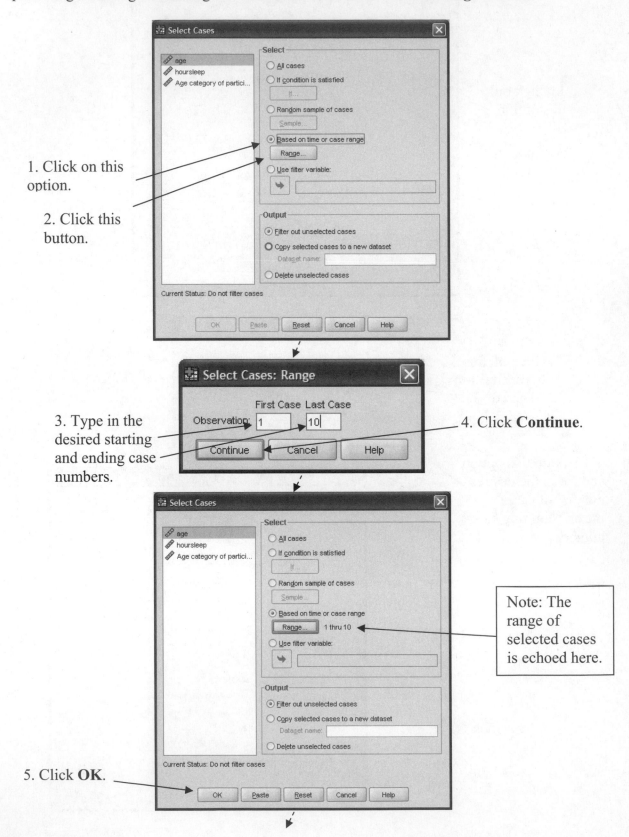

1. Click on this option.

2. Click this button.

3. Type in the desired starting and ending case numbers.

4. Click **Continue**.

Note: The range of selected cases is echoed here.

5. Click **OK**.

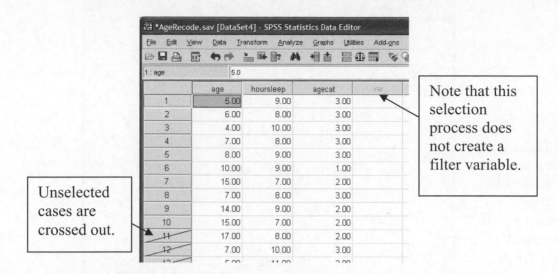

Note that this selection process does not create a filter variable.

Unselected cases are crossed out.

Using an Existing Variable as a Filter Variable. An existing variable can be used as a filter variable to select cases. Cases are selected when the filter variable has a value other than zero or system missing.

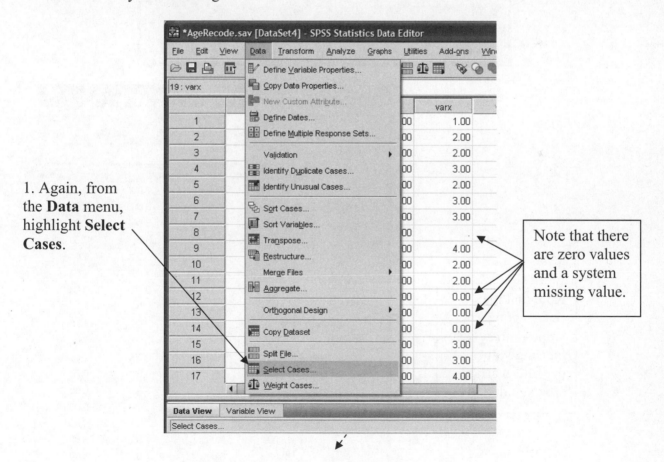

1. Again, from the **Data** menu, highlight **Select Cases**.

Note that there are zero values and a system missing value.

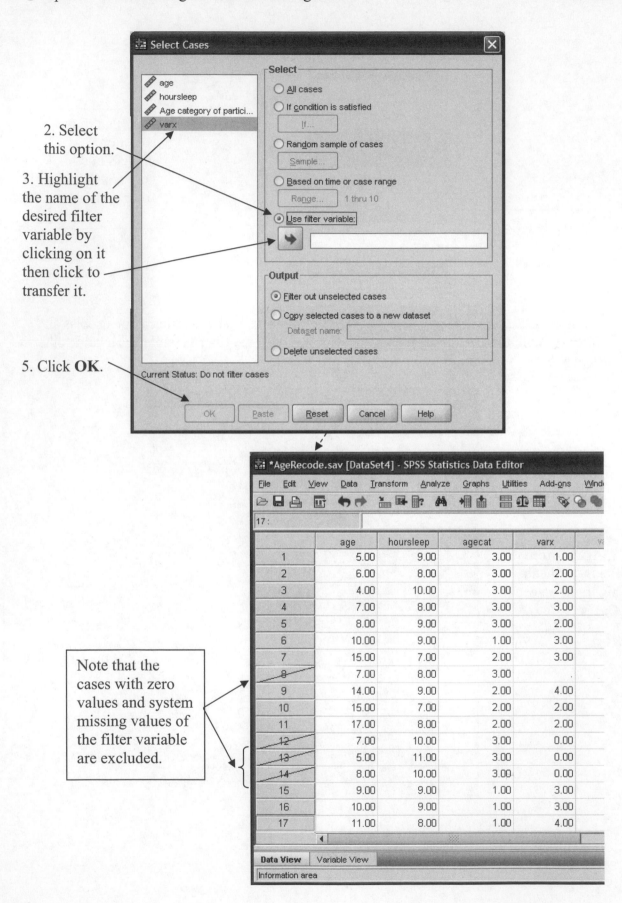

2. Select this option.

3. Highlight the name of the desired filter variable by clicking on it then click to transfer it.

5. Click **OK**.

Note that the cases with zero values and system missing values of the filter variable are excluded.

Exercises for Chapter 7

The data in the file *GSS92.sav* are from randomly selected adults aged 18-65 contacted by the National Opinion Research Center from 1993-1998. The data include two variables used in this chapter's exercises--**news** and **tvhrs**. The variable **news** is the response to the question "How often do you read the newspaper—every day, a few times a week, once a week, less than once a week, or never?" The variable **tvhrs** is the response to the question "On the average day, how many hours do you personally watch television?" The table below describes the variables and their values in the data file.

Variable #	Variable Name	Concept Measured	Value Identification
1	year	Year contacted	
2	id	Identification number of respondent	
3	news	How often newspaper read	0 = Not applicable
			1 = Every day
			2 = A few times a week
			3= Once a week
			4 = Less than once a week
			5 = Never
			8 = Don't know
			9 = No answer
4	tvhrs	Number of hours of TV per day	-1 = Not applicable
			98 = Don't know
			99 = No answer

Exercise 7.1

1. Recode the variable **news** into the variable **newsfreq** whose values have the following meaning:

news		newsfreq	
Variable Label	Value Labels	Variable Label	Value Labels
How often newspaper read	0 = Not applicable	How often newspaper read, ordinal values	0 = never
	1 = Every day		1 = Less than once a week
	2 = A few times a week		2 = Once a week
	3= Once a week		3 = A few times a week
	4 = Less than once a week		4 = Every day
	5 = Never		5 = All other responses
	8 = Don't know		
	9 = No answer		

2. Use **COMPUTE** to create the new variable **newsfreq1** whose values are one number higher than those of the variable **newsfreq**. That is, for **newsfreq1**, 1 = never, 2 = less than once a week, 3 = once a week, 4 = a few times a week, 5 = every day, and 6 = all other responses.

Exercise 7.2

Make a new variable, **tvhrsfreq**, from the variable **tvhrs** that categorizes the number of hours of TV watched per day into 5 intervals each having about 20% of the cases. For the variable **tvhrsfreq** use the value 1 to represent the lowest 20% of hours of TV watched per day, the number 2 to represent the next highest 20% of hours of TV watched per day, etc.

Exercise 7.3

1. Make up a new variable called **seqnum** that is the case number of each person in the survey.
2. Make up a new variable called **nocontact** that has the value 1 if a person both watches 1 or fewer hours of TV per day and never reads a newspaper, and has the value 0 otherwise.
3. Select the cases for which the variable **nocontact** has the value 1. Check your data file to see if the first three cases in which **nocontact** has the value 1 are case numbers 279, 293, and 347.

Chapter 8: The *Frequencies* Procedure

Information Obtained from a Frequency Distribution

One of the most useful ways for a researcher to get a sense of the overall characteristics of a data set is to examine its frequency distribution. A frequency distribution organizes values of a variable into a table whose rows represent single values of the variable (or, although the **Frequencies** procedure does not do this, ranges of values called class intervals) ordered by magnitude and, in an accompanying column, counts of the number of scores in the data set having the designated value (or values, if the data are arranged in class intervals). An example is shown in Table 8.1. Note that the frequency distribution shown in Table 8.1 also includes columns derived from values in the **frequency** column: one column shows the percent of scores in the data set with a particular value and the other, labeled **cumulative percent**, lists the percent of scores having values equal to or lower than a given score.

Table 8.1. A frequency distribution of the variable **number of words recalled** derived from the *SPSS* **Frequencies** procedure.

Number of words free-recalled				
	Frequency	Percent	Valid Percent	Cumulative Percent
21.00	1	4.3	4.3	4.3
25.00	2	8.7	8.7	13.0
26.00	1	4.3	4.3	17.4
27.00	2	8.7	8.7	26.1
28.00	2	8.7	8.7	34.8
29.00	1	4.3	4.3	39.1
30.00	2	8.7	8.7	47.8
31.00	1	4.3	4.3	52.2
32.00	1	4.3	4.3	56.5
33.00	3	13.0	13.0	69.6
34.00	4	17.4	17.4	87.0
36.00	1	4.3	4.3	91.3
37.00	1	4.3	4.3	95.7
39.00	1	4.3	4.3	100.0
Total	23	100.0	100.0	

There is considerable variation in the recommended format of a frequency distribution. For example, some authors of statistics textbooks recommend that score values in the first column be arranged in descending order starting at the top of the column, that missing scores within the range of scores listed in the table be included in the first column (for example in Table 8.1, the scores 22, 23, 24, 35, and 38 would be included in column 1), and that the first column of the table be given the title of the name of the variable.

Key Properties of Distributions

Inspecting the frequency distribution of a variable can provide useful information about a number of its key properties including central tendency, variability, and shape. Central tendency refers to the value of a distribution's most representative score; it can be described using numerical measures such as mean, median, and mode. Variability refers to the extent to which scores in a distribution deviate from central tendency. Measures such as range, inter-quartile range, standard deviation and variance are commonly used to describe a distribution's variability numerically. The shape of a distribution can be characterized using descriptive terms such as *normal distribution* or *positively skewed distribution*, and supplemented with numerical measures such as kurtosis and skewness. Table 8.2, 8.3, and 8.4 provide information about these measures and guidelines for selecting them, and Figure 8.1 illustrates some key terms used to describe a distribution's shape.

Figure 8.1. The top panels show normal distributions with different central tendencies and variances. The bottom panels show unimodal distributions that are positively skewed (left panel), symmetrical (center panel) or negatively skewed (right panel).

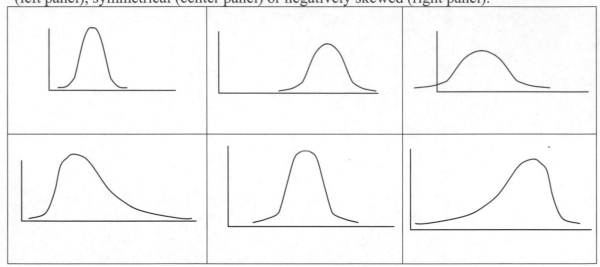

Visual inspection of a frequency distribution such as that shown in Table 8.1 makes apparent some values of the distribution's key properties. For the data shown in Table 8.1 it can be seen that the most frequent number of words recalled is 34, that the number of words recalled ranges between 21 and 39, and that the distribution has a single peak at 34 and a slight negative skew. To obtain a wider range of descriptive statistics, a procedure such as **Frequencies** can be run.

Table 8.2. Numerical measures of central tendency and guidelines for their use.

Name	Definition	Algebraic Formula	When to Use
Mode	The value of a distribution's most frequently-occurring score		To describe the location and number of peaks in the distribution of quantitative variables; to describe the central tendency of qualitative variables.
Median	If scores in a distribution are arranged in order of magnitude, the median is the value of the middle score.		To describe the central tendency of moderately or extremely skewed quantitative variables.
Mean	The "balance point" of a distribution	$\bar{x} = \dfrac{\Sigma x}{N}$	To describe the central tendency of symmetrically or approximately symmetrically distributed quantitative variables.

Table 8.3. Numerical measures of variability and guidelines for their use.

Name of Measure	Definition	Algebraic Formula	When to Use
Range	The difference between the distribution's highest and lowest score.		To give the reader information about how widely a distribution's scores vary.
Interquartile range	If scores in a distribution are arranged in order, it is the range covered by the middle 50% of the scores in the distribution.		To describe the variability of quantitative variables that are moderately or extremely skewed.
Variance (of a sample)	The mean squared deviation of scores from the distribution's mean, adjusted to be unbiased (i.e., accurate in the long run).	$s^2 = \dfrac{\sum \left(x_i - \bar{x}\right)^2}{N-1}$	To describe the variability of quantitative variables that are symmetrically or approximately symmetrically distributed.
Standard deviation (of a sample)	Square root of the sample variance	$s = \sqrt{\dfrac{\sum \left(x_i - \bar{x}\right)^2}{N-1}}$	See sample variance.

Table 8.4. Terms and measures for describing a distribution's shape and guidelines for their interpretation.

Term/Measure	Definition	Algebraic Formula*	Interpretation
Normal distribution	A unimodal, symmetrical, bell-shaped curve		
Skewness	The degree to which a distribution lacks symmetry.	$$\dfrac{\dfrac{\sum(x-\bar{x})^3}{N}}{\left(\sqrt{\dfrac{\sum(x-\bar{x})^2}{N}}\right)^3}$$	A value of 0 = symmetric; positive values = positively skewed; negative values = negatively skewed. When the skewness value is divided by its standard error, values ≤ 1 are not greatly skewed; values between 1 and 2 are becoming very skewed; values ≥ 2 are extremely skewed.
Kurtosis	The degree to which symmetric, unimodal distribution's scores are concentrated in its tails, center, or both (see DeCarlo, 1997).	$$\dfrac{\dfrac{\sum(x-\bar{x})^4}{N}}{\left(\dfrac{\sum(x-\bar{x})^2}{N}\right)^2} - 3$$	A value of 0 = *normal distribution*; positive values = too many scores in the tails, center, or both compared to a normal distribution; negative values = too few scores in the tails, center, or both compared to a normal distribution. When the kurtosis value is divided by its standard error, values ≤ 1 = not greatly different than *normal*; values between 1 and 2 = becoming very different than *normal*; values ≥ 2 = extremely different than *normal*.

*The formulas used in *SPSS* are slightly different. They are based on formulas described by Bliss (1967) that provide unbiased estimates of the population values.

Using the Frequencies *Procedure*

The steps shown below illustrate how to request the **Frequencies** procedure.

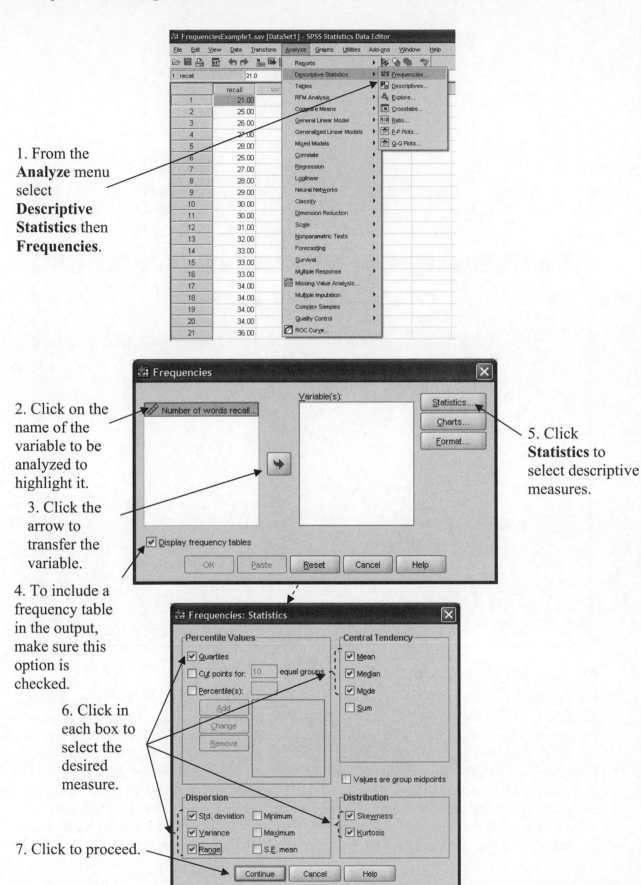

1. From the **Analyze** menu select **Descriptive Statistics** then **Frequencies**.

2. Click on the name of the variable to be analyzed to highlight it.

3. Click the arrow to transfer the variable.

4. To include a frequency table in the output, make sure this option is checked.

5. Click **Statistics** to select descriptive measures.

6. Click in each box to select the desired measure.

7. Click to proceed.

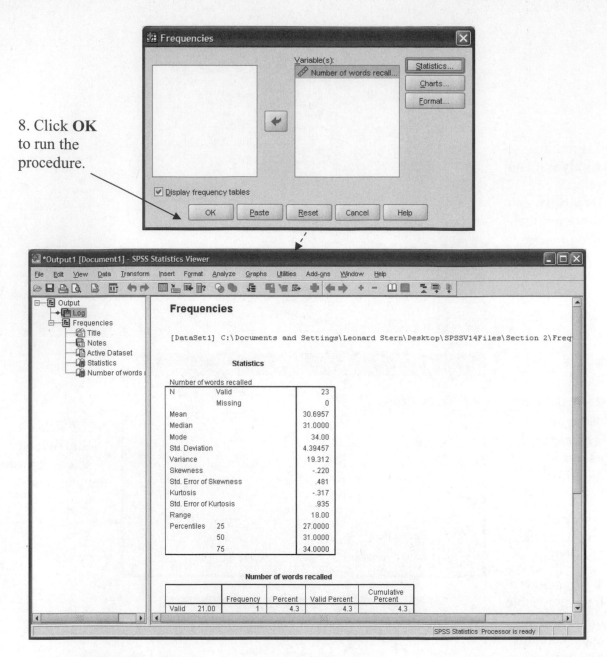

8. Click **OK** to run the procedure.

Interpreting the Output

The table of summary statistics and the frequency distribution output by the **Frequencies** procedure are shown below. The table of summary statistics includes information about the number of scores in the distribution and the number of missing values followed by values of requested measures of the distribution's central tendency, variability, and shape. Note that the **Frequencies** procedure does not directly provide a value of the distribution's interquartile range. However, the interquartile range may be calculated from the values of the distributions 25th and 75th percentiles. That is, by subtracting the value of the score that has a percentile rank of 25 from that having a percentile rank of 75, one obtains the range covered by the middle 50% of the scores in the distribution.

The negative value of the index of skewness indicates the distribution is negatively skewed. To interpret its magnitude, divide the value of the index of skewness by its standard error. A similar process can be applied to the kurtosis statistic. In both cases, the resulting value for our example is less than 1, indicating that the distribution does not differ substantially from *normal* in either skewness or kurtosis.

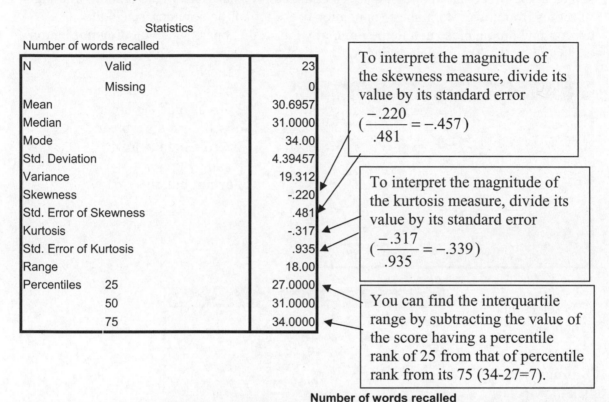

Statistics

Number of words recalled

N	Valid	23
	Missing	0
Mean		30.6957
Median		31.0000
Mode		34.00
Std. Deviation		4.39457
Variance		19.312
Skewness		-.220
Std. Error of Skewness		.481
Kurtosis		-.317
Std. Error of Kurtosis		.935
Range		18.00
Percentiles	25	27.0000
	50	31.0000
	75	34.0000

To interpret the magnitude of the skewness measure, divide its value by its standard error $(\frac{-.220}{.481} = -.457)$

To interpret the magnitude of the kurtosis measure, divide its value by its standard error $(\frac{-.317}{.935} = -.339)$

You can find the interquartile range by subtracting the value of the score having a percentile rank of 25 from that of percentile rank from its 75 (34-27=7).

Number of words recalled

		Frequency	Percent	Valid Percent	Cumulative Percent
Valid	21.00	1	4.3	4.3	4.3
	25.00	2	8.7	8.7	13.0
	26.00	1	4.3	4.3	17.4
	27.00	2	8.7	8.7	26.1
	28.00	2	8.7	8.7	34.8
	29.00	1	4.3	4.3	39.1
	30.00	2	8.7	8.7	47.8
	31.00	1	4.3	4.3	52.2
	32.00	1	4.3	4.3	56.5
	33.00	3	13.0	13.0	69.6
	34.00	4	17.4	17.4	87.0
	36.00	1	4.3	4.3	91.3
	37.00	1	4.3	4.3	95.7
	39.00	1	4.3	4.3	100.0
	Total	23	100.0	100.0	

Notice that the value of each score having a different value in the data set is listed in this table. If the data set contains many different scores, the table can be long.

Options for the Frequencies *Procedure*

Ascending vs. Descending Order of Scores.

One option that can be applied to a frequency distribution affects the order in which scores in the first column of the table are arranged. To change from the default ordering of scores from lowest to highest (in relation to the top of the column), select the appropriate option presented in the **Format** window that opens when the **Format** button is clicked on the **Frequencies** window:

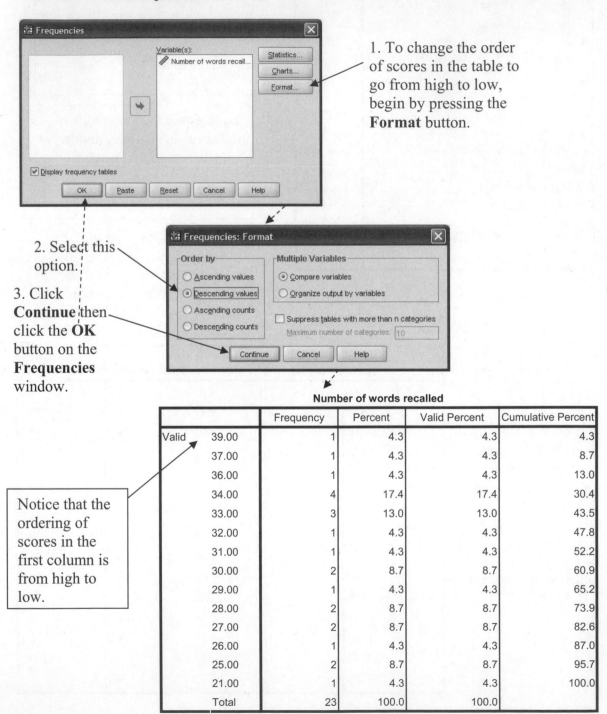

1. To change the order of scores in the table to go from high to low, begin by pressing the **Format** button.

2. Select this option.

3. Click **Continue** then click the **OK** button on the **Frequencies** window.

Notice that the ordering of scores in the first column is from high to low.

Number of words recalled

		Frequency	Percent	Valid Percent	Cumulative Percent
Valid	39.00	1	4.3	4.3	4.3
	37.00	1	4.3	4.3	8.7
	36.00	1	4.3	4.3	13.0
	34.00	4	17.4	17.4	30.4
	33.00	3	13.0	13.0	43.5
	32.00	1	4.3	4.3	47.8
	31.00	1	4.3	4.3	52.2
	30.00	2	8.7	8.7	60.9
	29.00	1	4.3	4.3	65.2
	28.00	2	8.7	8.7	73.9
	27.00	2	8.7	8.7	82.6
	26.00	1	4.3	4.3	87.0
	25.00	2	8.7	8.7	95.7
	21.00	1	4.3	4.3	100.0
	Total	23	100.0	100.0	

Multiple vs. Single Tables of Summary Statistics for Multiple Variables.

It is possible to apply the **Frequencies** procedure to more than a single variable. When applied to multiple variables, the summary statistics for all variables will by default be displayed in a single table; alternatively, if requested, a separate table of statistics for each variable can be displayed. The examples below illustrate these options.

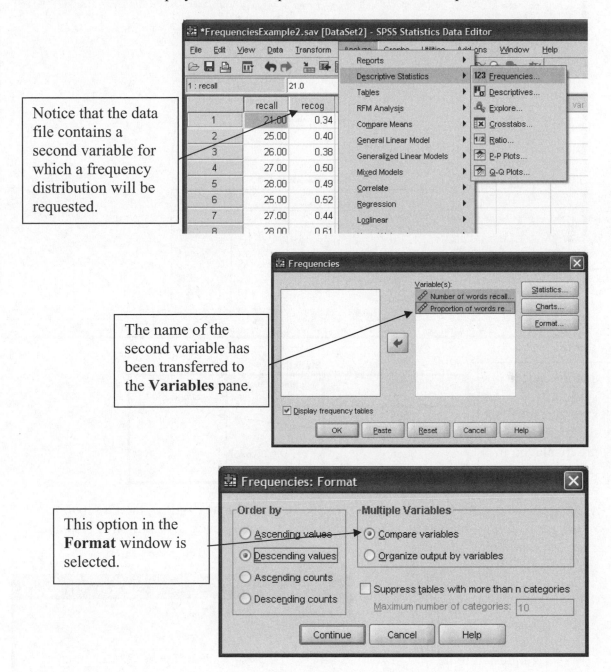

Notice that the data file contains a second variable for which a frequency distribution will be requested.

The name of the second variable has been transferred to the **Variables** pane.

This option in the **Format** window is selected.

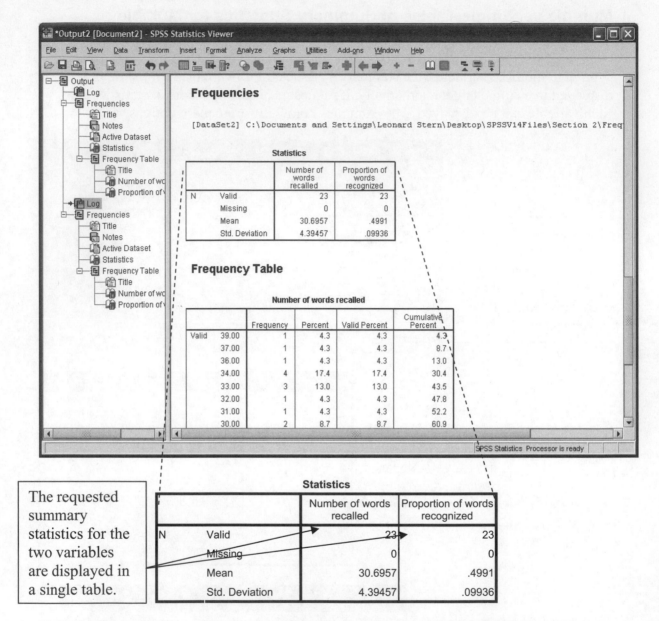

The requested summary statistics for the two variables are displayed in a single table.

Statistics

		Number of words recalled	Proportion of words recognized
N	Valid	23	23
	Missing	0	0
	Mean	30.6957	.4991
	Std. Deviation	4.39457	.09936

If **Organize output by variables** is selected in the **Format** window, then a separate summary table of requested statistics followed by a frequency distribution is displayed for each variable.

The output is requested to be organized by variables.

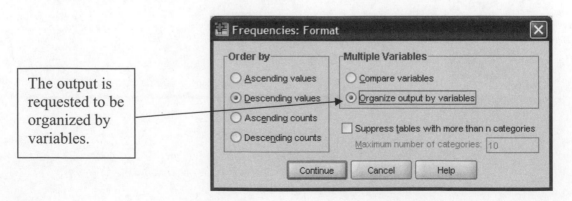

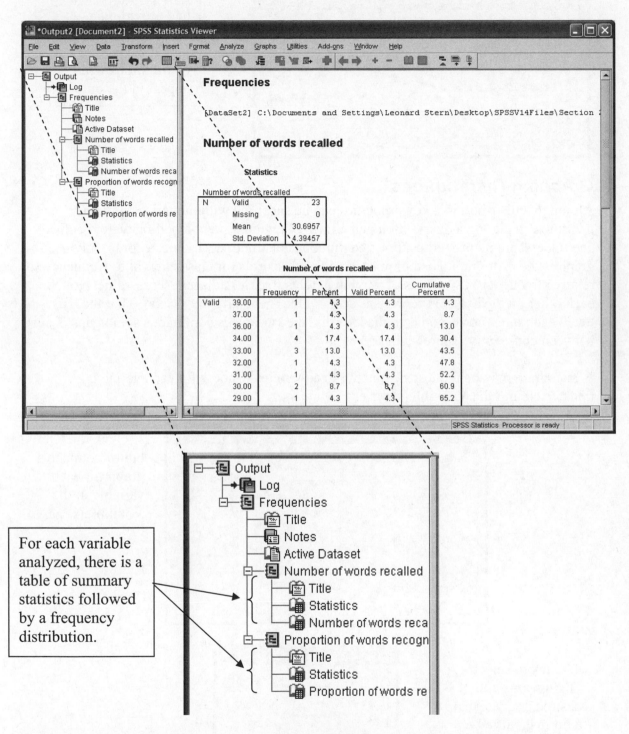

For each variable analyzed, there is a table of summary statistics followed by a frequency distribution.

Suppressing the output of long tables. The **Frequencies** procedure produces only ungrouped, not grouped frequency distributions. That is, in the first column of a frequency distribution, individual scores, not ranges of scores (i.e., class intervals), are listed. If there is a big range of scores in a data set with many different intermediate values, long tables can result. As shown below, an option available in the **Format** window prevents the display of tables longer than some user-specified number of lines.

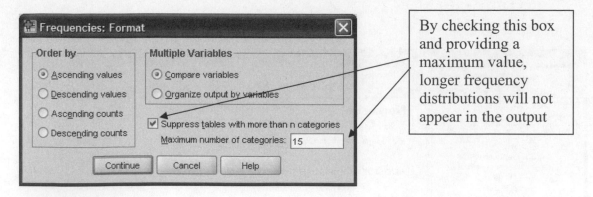

By checking this box and providing a maximum value, longer frequency distributions will not appear in the output

Graphing Distributions

Although a distribution's key properties can be specified with numerical summary measures, depicting a distribution in the form of a graph is a compelling way to convey and underscore its properties. For a continuous quantitative variable, a commonly used graph is the histogram. Histograms convey each score's (or class interval's) frequency (or relative frequency) using bars of varying heights that, for adjacent score values, touch each other on the axis that represents score value (generally the x-axis). That the bars touch each other corresponds to the idea that the variable is continuous so no gaps occur between consecutive score values.

A histogram may be requested from the **Frequencies** window for each variable transferred into the **Variable(s)** pane.

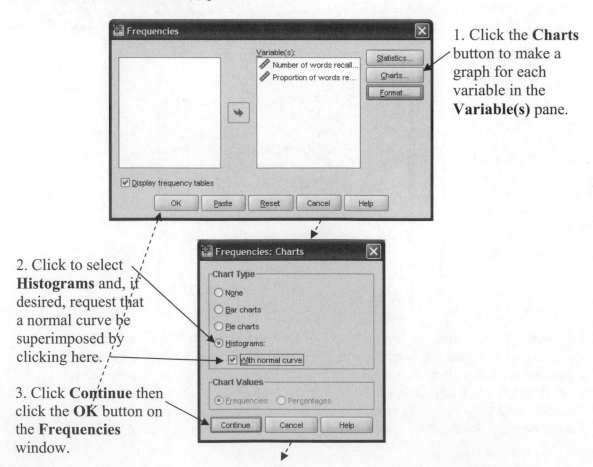

1. Click the **Charts** button to make a graph for each variable in the **Variable(s)** pane.

2. Click to select **Histograms** and, if desired, request that a normal curve be superimposed by clicking here.

3. Click **Continue** then click the **OK** button on the **Frequencies** window.

Histogram

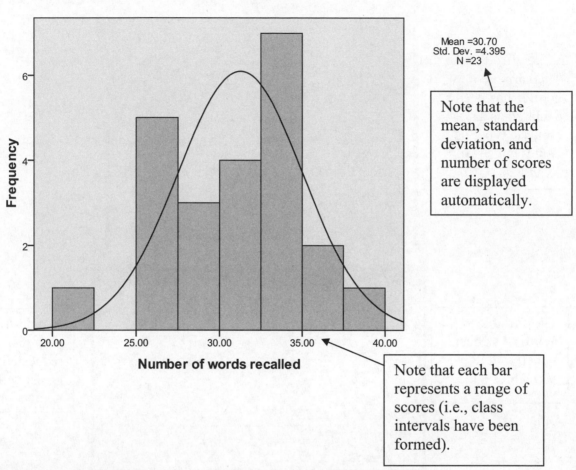

Note that the mean, standard deviation, and number of scores are displayed automatically.

Note that each bar represents a range of scores (i.e., class intervals have been formed).

Qualitative variables

Distributions of variables such as gender or ethnicity can be depicted with bar or pie charts. When a bar chart is requested from the **Frequencies** procedure, the scale on the y-axis can be selected to show either the frequency or percent of scores in the data set with each given value.

Presented below is a bar chart produced by the **Frequencies** procedure that displays the number of males and females in a data set. Note that a bar or pie chart can be requested for data entered in the **SPSS Statistics Data Editor** as either a string or numeric variable; in the example shown below, the variable **gender** has been declared a numeric variable and variable and value labels have been specified in the **Variable View** of the **SPSS Statistics Data Editor**. The value labels appear in the bar graph to identify each bar and the variable label appears as the label for the x-axis.

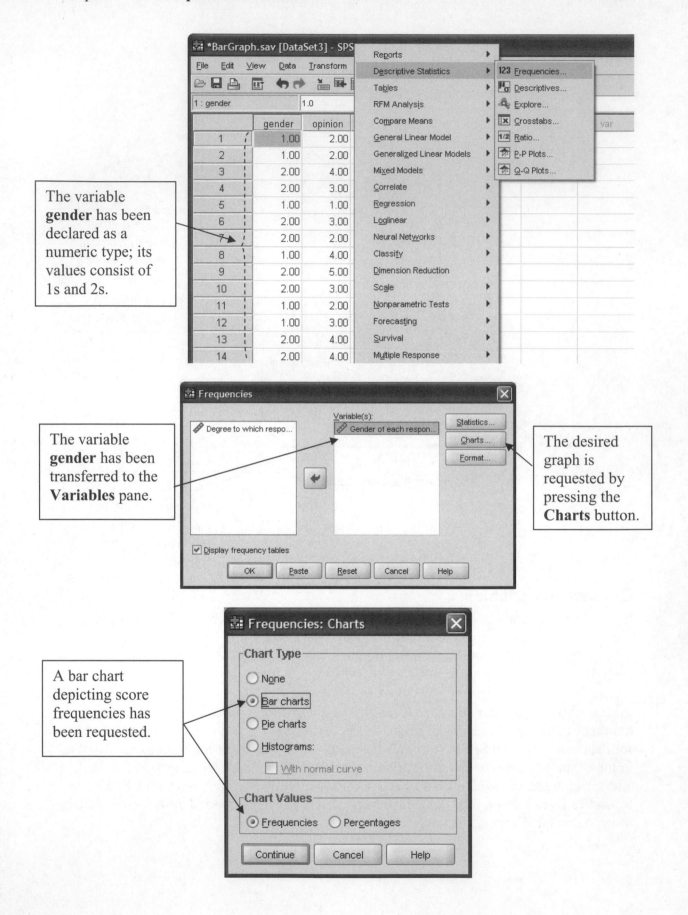

The variable **gender** has been declared as a numeric type; its values consist of 1s and 2s.

The variable **gender** has been transferred to the **Variables** pane.

The desired graph is requested by pressing the **Charts** button.

A bar chart depicting score frequencies has been requested.

The frequency distribution can list the value labels for the variable **gender**.

Gender of each respondent

		Frequency	Percent	Valid Percent	Cumulative Percent
Valid	male	6	42.9	42.9	42.9
	female	8	57.1	57.1	100.0
	Total	14	100.0	100.0	

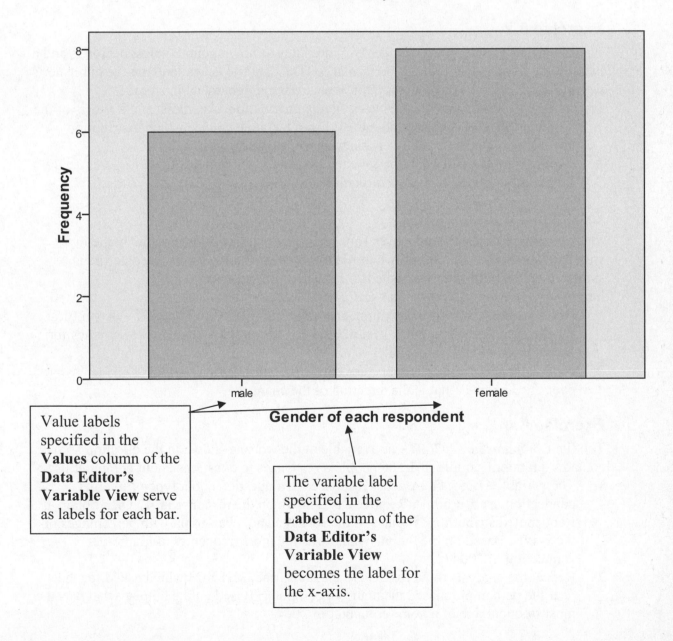

Gender of each respondent

Value labels specified in the **Values** column of the **Data Editor's Variable View** serve as labels for each bar.

The variable label specified in the **Label** column of the **Data Editor's Variable View** becomes the label for the x-axis.

Exercises for Chapter 8

Exercise 8.1

The file *Bodytemp.sav* was created in Exercise 4.2. The file contains values of body temperature for randomly selected males and females.
1. Form a frequency distribution of the variable **bodytemp**. Include a table that shows the mean and standard deviation, kurtosis and skewness, and value of the distribution's 25th, 50th and 75th percentiles. Plot the values of the variable using a histogram that has a normal distribution superimposed over it.
2. From the frequency distribution, determine the percentile rank of the body temperature 98.6 degrees.
3. Based on your output, is the distribution of the variable **bodytemp** approximately normal?

Exercise 8.2

The file *Hypnotizability.sav* includes two measures of how hypnotizable a person is and a measure of recognition memory performance. The data file is available on the publisher's website for this text at the address http://www.pearsonhighered.com/stern2e.
1. In a single table, provide the mean, standard deviation, skewness, and kurtosis of the variables **object**, **subject**, and **mem1**. From the table values, which distribution appears symmetrical, positively skewed, or negatively skewed?
2. Form a frequency distribution for each variable listed in question 1. List frequency distribution scores in descending order.

Exercise 8.3

Mean commute times of adults over 16 years of age who work outside the home in various cities of the U.S. are shown in file *Commute2001-2003.sav*. The data file is available on the publisher's website for this text at the address http://www.pearsonhighered.com/stern2e.
1. Obtain a mean, standard deviation, and values of the 25th, 50th and 75th percentiles for the variables **Mean2003**, **Mean2002**, and **Mean2001**. Display the statistics for each variable in the same table.
2. From an inspection of the table, determine if commute times appear to have changed over the 3 years. What is the direction of the change?

Exercise 8.4

The file *ComputerSurvey2004.sav*, available at the website shown in the question above, contains a random sample of 1,500 people's responses to questions about computer use.
1. The variable **HESINT2A** codes responses to a question about type of internet connection used at home. Remove cases in which the response is -1. Then obtain a frequency distribution of values of the variable and a bar graph with percentages on the y-axis. Based on the output, which was the most frequently used internet connection in 2004?
2. Repeat the analysis requested above for the variable **HESC3** which asked for the year the person purchased their current computer. Based on the output, what was the most frequent age of a home computer in 2004?

Chapter 9: Other Procedures for Obtaining Descriptive Measures: *Descriptives, Explore, Means*

In its earliest versions, *SPSS* provided descriptive measures primarily from the **Frequencies** procedure. More recently, other procedures have become available for providing such measures. In this chapter, some of the more recent procedures for describing distributions will be presented together with the features that distinguish each.

Descriptives

The **Descriptives** procedure provides a table of commonly-used statistics that summarize key properties of distributions of quantitative variables. The procedure can be applied to a single quantitative variable or to a set of quantitative variables whose values are intended to be compared. Use of the procedure is illustrated with a set of quiz scores for students in a statistics class.

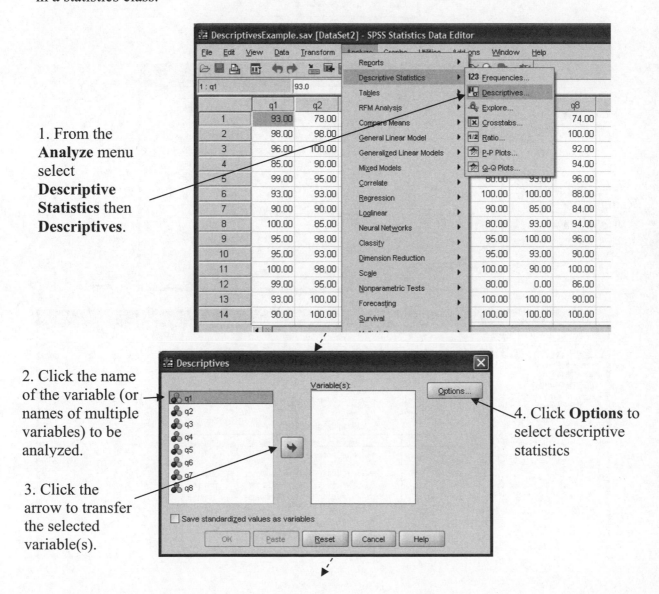

1. From the **Analyze** menu select **Descriptive Statistics** then **Descriptives**.

2. Click the name of the variable (or names of multiple variables) to be analyzed.

3. Click the arrow to transfer the selected variable(s).

4. Click **Options** to select descriptive statistics

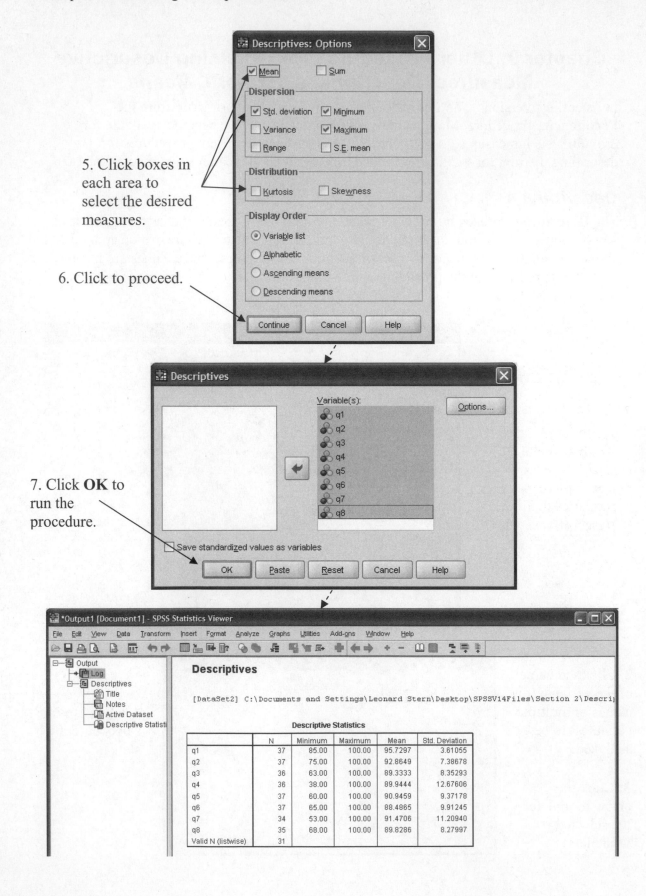

5. Click boxes in each area to select the desired measures.

6. Click to proceed.

7. Click **OK** to run the procedure.

An expanded view of the table produced by the **Descriptives** procedure is shown below. Note that in the data set used for this demonstration, some students missed a quiz which resulted in their being assigned a quiz score of zero. To avoid having scores of zero influencing the summary measures, for every quiz, the value zero was assigned as a missing score in the **Variables View** of the **SPSS Statistics Data Editor**. Thus, although there were grades for 38 students recorded in the class, the number of grades evaluated for each quiz ranged between 34 and 37.

Descriptive Statistics

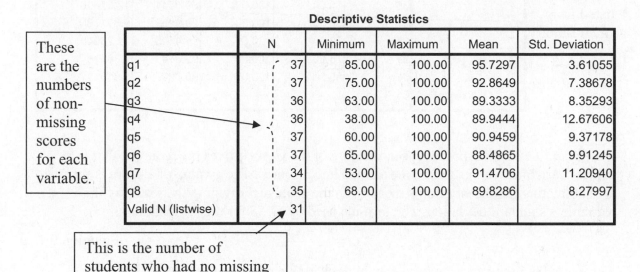

	N	Minimum	Maximum	Mean	Std. Deviation
q1	37	85.00	100.00	95.7297	3.61055
q2	37	75.00	100.00	92.8649	7.38678
q3	36	63.00	100.00	89.3333	8.35293
q4	36	38.00	100.00	89.9444	12.67606
q5	37	60.00	100.00	90.9459	9.37178
q6	37	65.00	100.00	88.4865	9.91245
q7	34	53.00	100.00	91.4706	11.20940
q8	35	68.00	100.00	89.8286	8.27997
Valid N (listwise)	31				

These are the numbers of non-missing scores for each variable.

This is the number of students who had no missing quiz scores for all quizzes.

Special Features of the Procedure

Reordering the rows of summary table information. One special feature of the **Descriptives** procedure is that it allows the order in which data are displayed in the summary table to easily be modified. In the table shown above, the data were arranged in the order in which variables were listed in the **Data Editor** (i.e., **q1**, **q2**, **q3**, etc.). Other possible orderings may be specified in the **Options** window:

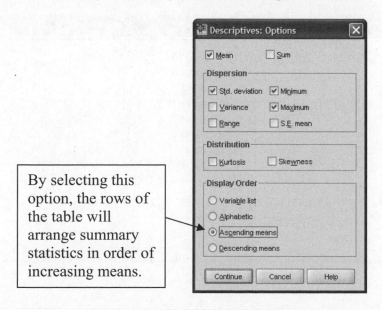

By selecting this option, the rows of the table will arrange summary statistics in order of increasing means.

Descriptive Statistics

	N	Minimum	Maximum	Mean	Std. Deviation
q6	37	65.00	100.00	88.4865	9.91245
q3	36	63.00	100.00	89.3333	8.35293
q8	35	68.00	100.00	89.8286	8.27997
q4	36	38.00	100.00	89.9444	12.67606
q5	37	60.00	100.00	90.9459	9.37178
q7	34	53.00	100.00	91.4706	11.20940
q2	37	75.00	100.00	92.8649	7.38678
q1	37	85.00	100.00	95.7297	3.61055
Valid N (listwise)	31				

Notice that means are listed from smallest to largest.

Producing z-scores. Another special feature of the **Descriptives** procedure is that it allows variables' values to be transformed into z-scores. The z-value of a score is formed by subtracting the distribution's mean from the score and dividing the result by the variable's standard deviation. The formula used by *SPSS* for this calculation is:

$$z = \frac{(x - \bar{x})}{s}$$

Equation 9.1

For example, in the data set used above, the variable **q6** has a mean of 88.49 and a standard deviation of 9.91. Thus, the score 100 in **q6** has a z-value $\frac{(100 - 88.49)}{9.91} = 1.16$.

Z-scores are useful in that, because they are a standardized measure (all z-distributions have a mean of zero and a standard deviation of 1), z-scores from different distributions can be meaningfully compared.

To transform a distribution of scores to z-values, check the appropriate box on the **Descriptives** window:

Check this box to obtain z-scores for the variables listed in the **Variables** pane.

Clicking **OK** creates the z-scores in the **Data Editor**.

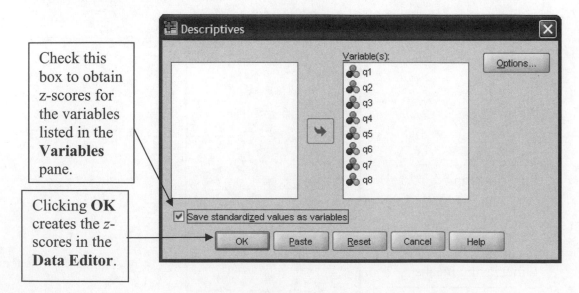

Notice that the names automatically created have a **Z** before the existing variable name.

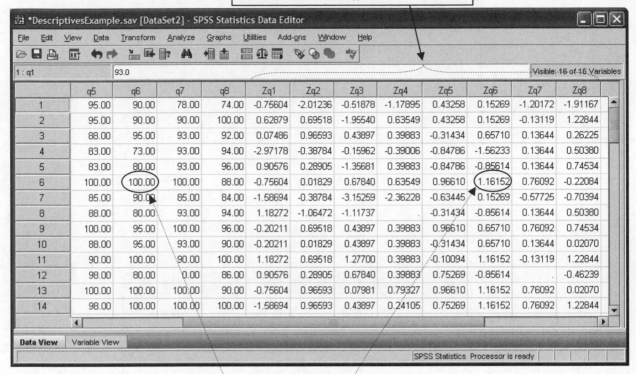

Notice that the score 100 for **q6** corresponds to a z-value of 1.16.

Explore

The **Explore** procedure provides a number of useful ways to inspect distributions of one or more continuous quantitative variables either as intact variables or broken down by values of categorical variables (entered in the **SPSS Statistics Data Editor** as numeric or string types). Thus, if values of the variable **temperature** are being analyzed, the distribution of all values of **temperature** may be described as a whole, or, if values of **temperature** are paired with values of a categorical variable such as **season**, **Explore** can analyze distributions of **temperature** separately for each different value of **season**. In the first demonstration shown below, the distribution of the continuous quantitative variable **meantemp** is examined.

Examining the Distribution of a Single Variable

In this demonstration, the distribution of values of the variable **meantemp** will be examined using **Explore**.

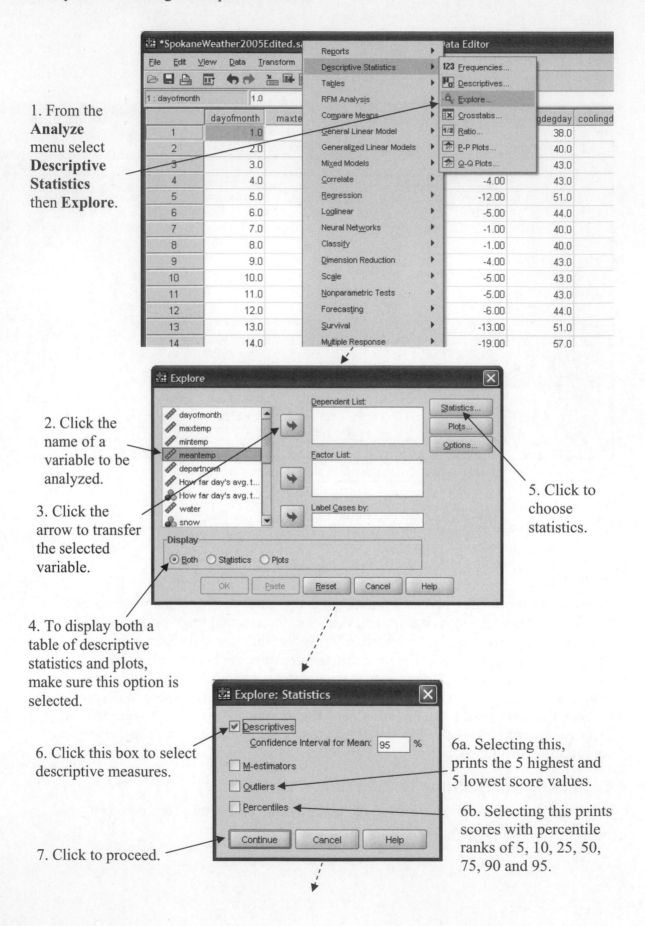

1. From the **Analyze** menu select **Descriptive Statistics** then **Explore**.

2. Click the name of a variable to be analyzed.

3. Click the arrow to transfer the selected variable.

4. To display both a table of descriptive statistics and plots, make sure this option is selected.

5. Click to choose statistics.

6. Click this box to select descriptive measures.

6a. Selecting this, prints the 5 highest and 5 lowest score values.

6b. Selecting this prints scores with percentile ranks of 5, 10, 25, 50, 75, 90 and 95.

7. Click to proceed.

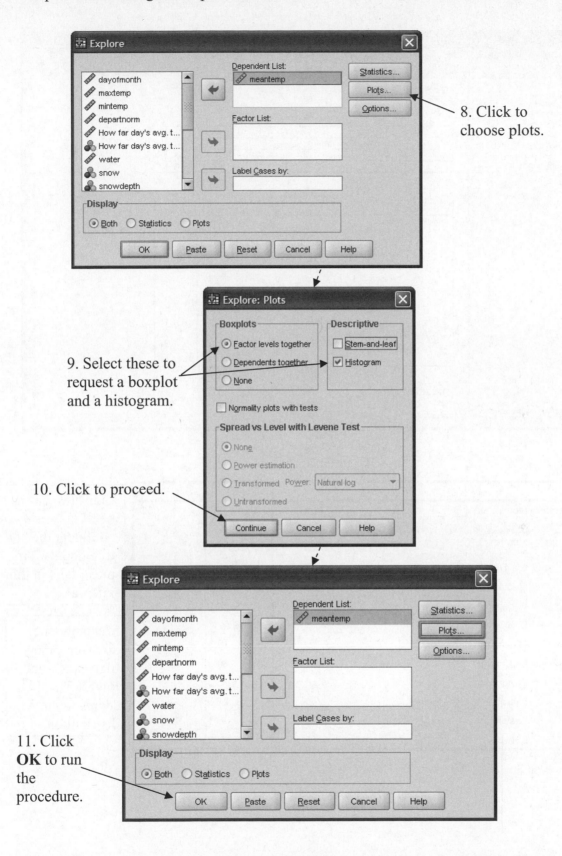

8. Click to choose plots.

9. Select these to request a boxplot and a histogram.

10. Click to proceed.

11. Click **OK** to run the procedure.

Shown below is some output produced by **Explore** followed by a copy of the table of descriptive statistics and the two requested plots.

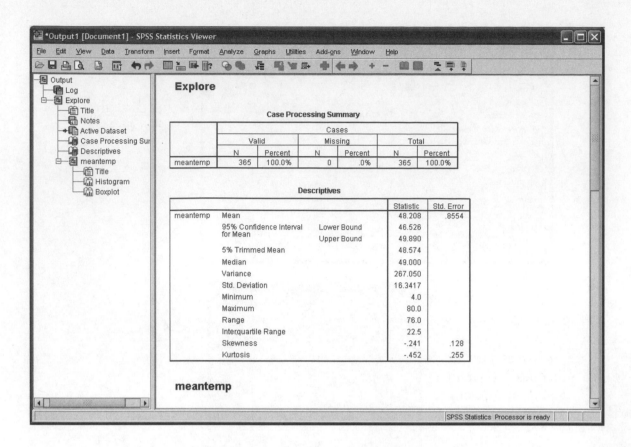

Descriptives

			Statistic	Std. Error
meantemp	Mean		48.208	.8554
	95% Confidence Interval for Mean	Lower Bound	46.526	
		Upper Bound	49.890	
	5% Trimmed Mean		48.574	
	Median		49.000	
	Variance		267.050	
	Std. Deviation		16.3417	
	Minimum		4.0	
	Maximum		80.0	
	Range		76.0	
	Interquartile Range		22.5	
	Skewness		-.241	.128
	Kurtosis		-.452	.255

Indicates we can be 95% confident the true population mean falls in this interval.

Mean obtained after removing highest 5% and lowest 5% of scores in the distribution.

Histogram

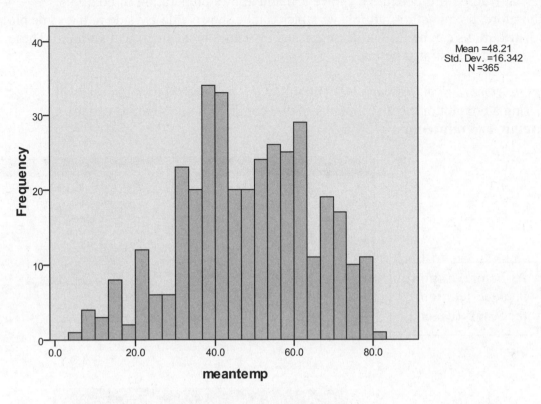

Mean =48.21
Std. Dev. =16.342
N =365

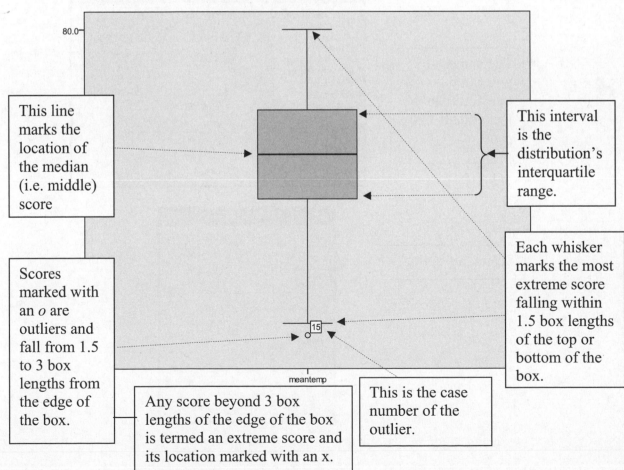

This line marks the location of the median (i.e. middle) score

This interval is the distribution's interquartile range.

Scores marked with an *o* are outliers and fall from 1.5 to 3 box lengths from the edge of the box.

Each whisker marks the most extreme score falling within 1.5 box lengths of the top or bottom of the box.

Any score beyond 3 box lengths of the edge of the box is termed an extreme score and its location marked with an x.

This is the case number of the outlier.

Special Features of *Explore*

A special feature of procedure **Explore** is that it allows preparation of boxplots. Furthermore, boxplots for multiple variables can be shown side-by-side in the same plot and distributions can be further distinguished by values of a categorical variable. These options are demonstrated below.

Boxplots of more than one variable. The following sequence shows key steps in preparing a boxplot of the distributions of two continuous quantitative variables, **maxtemp**, and **mintemp**.

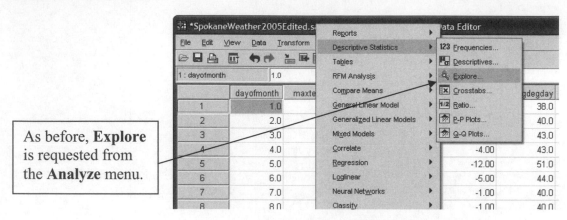

As before, **Explore** is requested from the **Analyze** menu.

The names of two variables are transferred to the **Dependent List** pane.

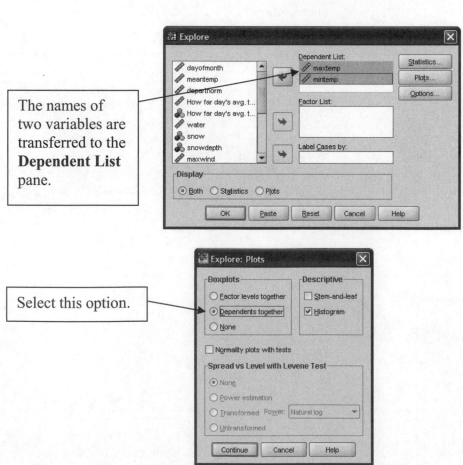

Select this option.

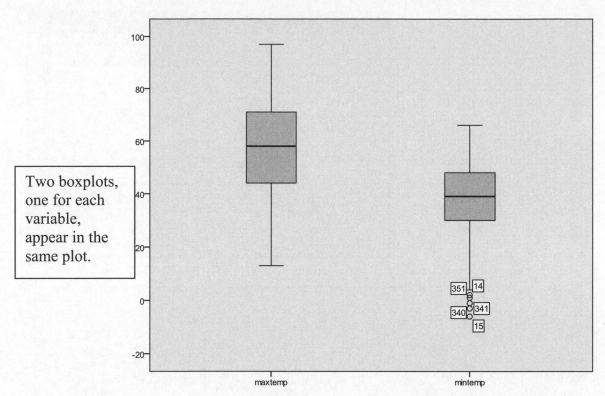

Two boxplots, one for each variable, appear in the same plot.

Boxplots of a variable broken down by values of a categorical variable. Using **Explore,** the distribution of a continuous quantitative variable such as **meantemp** can be examined separately for each value of a category variable such as **season**. Important steps in implementing such an analysis are shown below:

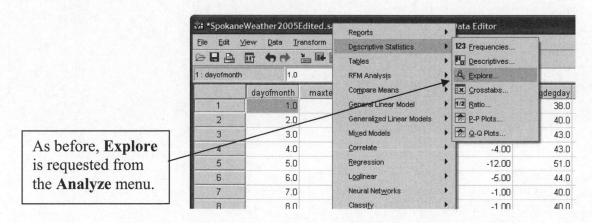

As before, **Explore** is requested from the **Analyze** menu.

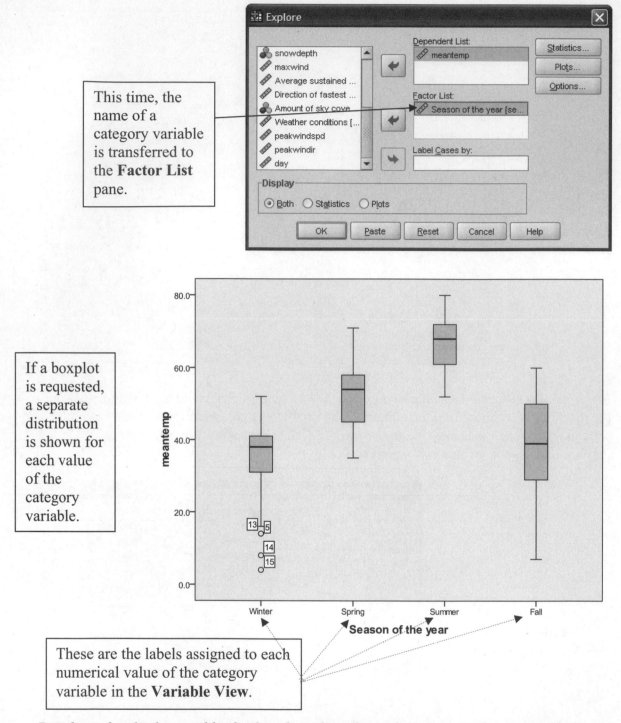

This time, the name of a category variable is transferred to the **Factor List** pane.

If a boxplot is requested, a separate distribution is shown for each value of the category variable.

These are the labels assigned to each numerical value of the category variable in the **Variable View**.

Boxplots of multiple variables broken down by values of a categorical variable. If multiple variable names are placed in the **Dependent List** pane of the **Explore** window and the name of a single categorical variable is placed in the **Factor List** pane, a request for boxplots can produce either separate plots for each dependent variable or a single plot with the variables side-by-side. As shown below, the format that is implemented depends on the option selected on the **Explore: Plots** window. In the first demonstration shown below, separate plots depict the distribution of each dependent variable (**maxtemp** or **mintemp**) broken down by levels of the categorical variable **season.**

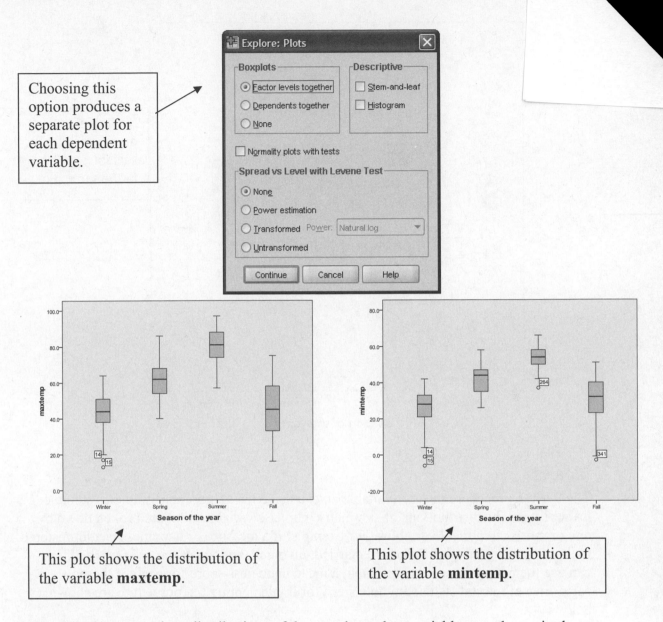

Choosing this option produces a separate plot for each dependent variable.

This plot shows the distribution of the variable **maxtemp**.

This plot shows the distribution of the variable **mintemp**.

In the next demonstration, distributions of the two dependent variables are shown in the same plot, each broken down by levels of the categorical variable **season.**

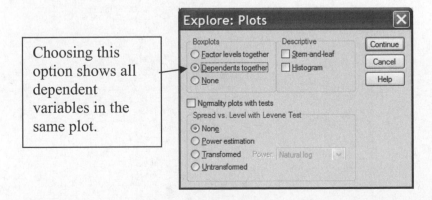

Choosing this option shows all dependent variables in the same plot.

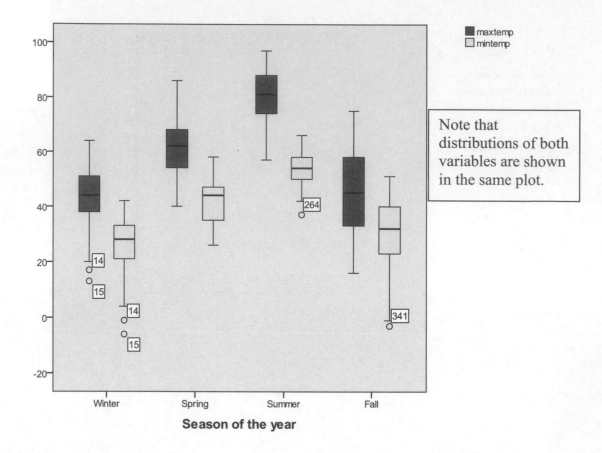

Note that distributions of both variables are shown in the same plot.

Means

The **Means** procedure makes available an extensive list of summary statistics suitable primarily for the distributions of symmetric numeric variables that are broken down by one or more categorical variables. For example, if a measure of happiness is administered to randomly chosen adults who are married, divorced, widowed, or never married, one can use the **Means** procedure to obtain a mean happiness score for each of these categories of marital status. Suitable steps for implementing the procedure are shown below:

1. From the **Analyze** menu select **Compare Means** then **Means**.

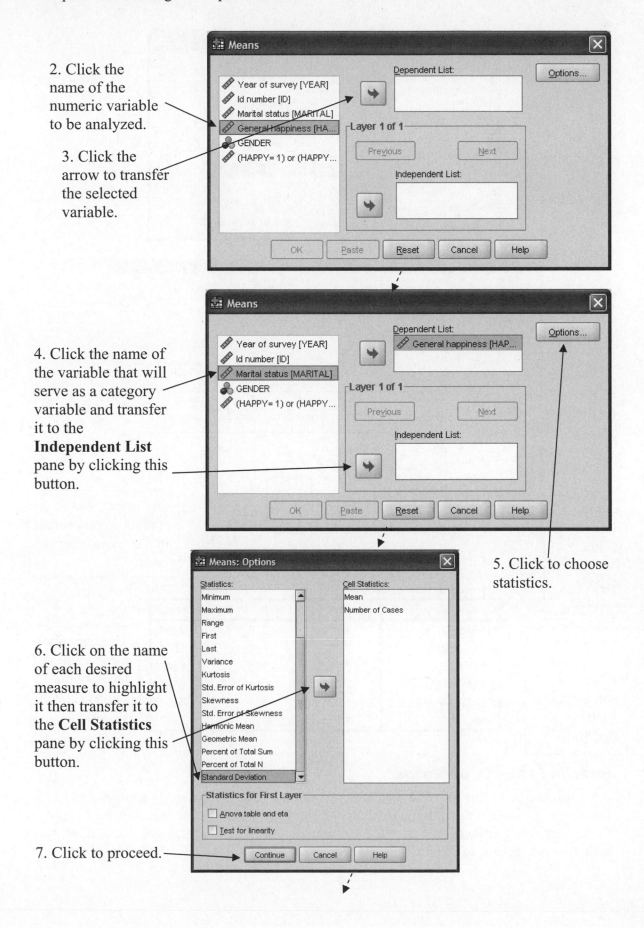

2. Click the name of the numeric variable to be analyzed.

3. Click the arrow to transfer the selected variable.

4. Click the name of the variable that will serve as a category variable and transfer it to the **Independent List** pane by clicking this button.

5. Click to choose statistics.

6. Click on the name of each desired measure to highlight it then transfer it to the **Cell Statistics** pane by clicking this button.

7. Click to proceed.

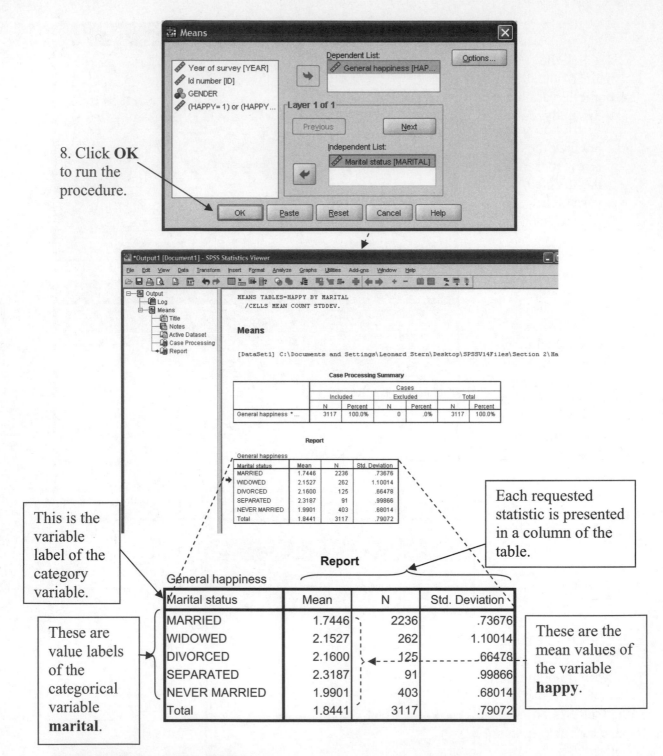

8. Click **OK** to run the procedure.

This is the variable label of the category variable.

Each requested statistic is presented in a column of the table.

These are value labels of the categorical variable **marital**.

These are the mean values of the variable **happy**.

Report

General happiness

Marital status	Mean	N	Std. Deviation
MARRIED	1.7446	2236	.73676
WIDOWED	2.1527	262	1.10014
DIVORCED	2.1600	125	.66478
SEPARATED	2.3187	91	.99866
NEVER MARRIED	1.9901	403	.68014
Total	1.8441	3117	.79072

Special Features of *Means*

A useful feature of this procedure is that it allows summary statistics for a dependent variable to be broken down by more than one category variable. For example, statistics for the variable **happy** can be reported as a function of both marital status and gender. As demonstrated below, to request a breakdown by a second category variable, the **Next**

To break down the dependent variable by a second category variable, press the **Next** button after the first category variable has been entered in the **Independent List**.

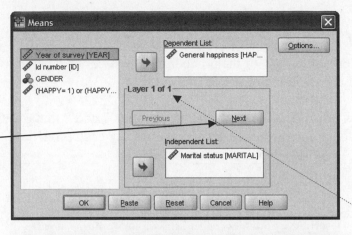

Notice that the **Layer** number of the **Independent List** originally is 1 and that after the **Next** button is pressed the value changes to 2.

The name of the second category variable has been transferred to the **Independent List** pane.

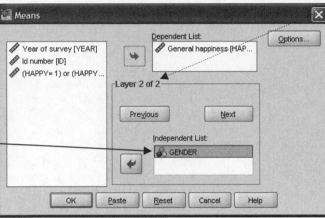

Report

General happiness

Marital status	GENDER	Mean	N	Std. Deviation
MARRIED	Male	1.7956	1135	.76092
	Female	1.6921	1101	.70751
	Total	1.7446	2236	.73676
WIDOWED	Male	2.1600	50	1.23487
	Female	2.1509	212	1.06910
	Total	2.1527	262	1.10014
DIVORCED	Male	2.1739	46	.70881
	Female	2.1519	79	.64228
	Total	2.1600	125	.66478
SEPARATED	Male	2.3871	31	1.43009
	Female	2.2833	60	.69115
	Total	2.3187	91	.99866
NEVER MARRIED	Male	2.0244	246	.54904
	Female	1.9363	157	.84491
	Total	1.9901	403	.68014
Total	Male	1.8687	1508	.78049
	Female	1.8210	1609	.79974
	Total	1.8441	3117	.79072

The table of statistics now breaks each marital status category into categories of gender before reporting summary statistics.

Summary of Procedures Providing Descriptive Measures

Table 9.1 provides a summary of the procedures discussed in Chapters 7 and 8 that provide descriptive measures for variables.

Table 9.1. Names of procedures described in chapters 7 and 8 that provide descriptive measures. Included are menu sequences for requesting each procedure, statistics available in the procedure, and plots that can be requested.

Procedure Name	Menu Sequence to Access	Statistics Available	Plots
Frequencies	**Analyze** **Descriptive Statistics** **Frequencies**	Ungrouped frequency distributions that list score frequency, percent, and cumulative percent; mean, median, mode, sum, standard deviation, variance, range, minimum and maximum values, standard error of the mean, skewness and kurtosis (both with standard errors), quartiles, user-specified percentiles.	Bar charts, pie charts, histograms.
Descriptives	**Analyze** **Descriptive Statistics** **Descriptives**	Mean, minimum, maximum, standard deviation, variance, range, sum, standard error of the mean, kurtosis and skewness with their standard errors.	
Explore	**Analyze** **Descriptive Statistics** **Explore**	Mean, median, 5% trimmed mean, standard error, variance, standard deviation, minimum, maximum, range, interquartile range, skewness and kurtosis and their standard errors, confidence interval for the mean (and specified confidence level), percentiles, highest and lowest five scores, robust maximum-likelihood estimators of central tendency.	Boxplots, stem-and-leaf plots, histograms, normality plots, and spread-versus-level plots.
Means	**Analyze** **Compare Means** **Means**	Sum, number of cases, mean, median, grouped median, standard error of the mean, minimum, maximum, range, variable value of the first category of the grouping variable, variable value of the last category of the grouping variable, standard deviation, variance, kurtosis, standard error of kurtosis, skewness, standard error of skewness, percentage of total sum, percentage of total N, percentage of sum in, percentage of N in, geometric, and harmonic means, one-way ANOVA with eta and eta squared, test of linear trend and deviation from linear trend.	

Exercises for Chapter 9

Exercise 9.1

1. Open the file *WaterUseSpokane.sav*. The variable **Changerate** shows the rate of change in gallons of water consumption per person of residents of the city of Spokane compared to the previous year. Make a histogram and a boxplot for this variable and obtain a table of descriptive statistics for the variable. Use the variable **Year** to label cases in the boxplot.
2. How would you describe the central tendency, variability, and shape of the distribution of the variable **Changerate**?
3. What year shows the highest rate of change? How would you describe the extremity of that year's change?
4. For the variable **Usageperc** make a histogram and a boxplot and obtain a table of descriptive statistics for the variable. Use the variable **Year** to label cases in the boxplot. How would you describe the central tendency, variability, and shape of the distribution of the variable **Usageperc**?

Exercise 9.2

The file *FalseRecognitionExp.sav* contains the proportion of words recognized in an experiment by participants who were tested on three categories of words: words that were not presented in lists of strong associates of the missing word (variable **preccnp**); words that were presented in lists of strong associates of the presented word (**preccpp**); or words that both were neither presented nor had any lists of strong associates presented (**preccnn**).

1. Prepare a table that shows the means of the three variables in descending order. Include in the table each variable's standard deviation, minimum, and maximum value.
2. Present a single boxplot of the three variables. Use the variable **name** to label cases. What does the plot reveal about the shape of the distribution of each variable and about the presence of unusual scores?

Exercise 9.3

The data for this exercise are in the file *Hurricanes.sav*. The data show the number of hurricanes during the Atlantic hurricane season (June 1-November 30) from 1944 to 2005. The data will be used here to examine the effect of transforming a distribution to z-scores.

1. Open the file *Hurricanes.sav* and convert the variable **Hurricanes** to z-scores.
2. Obtain a histogram and values of the mean and standard deviation of the distribution of the variable **Hurricanes**. Do the same for the distribution of z-scores formed for the variable **Hurricanes**. What do you notice about the shape of the two distributions?

Exercise 9.4

The file *Births1978.sav* shows the number of births in the U.S. on each day of 1978. The data were obtained from http://www.stat.ucla.edu/data/. Use the file *Births1978.sav* to answer the following questions:

1. Is the distribution of the variable **NumberBirth** approximately normally distributed?
2. Was the distribution of the variable **NumberBirth** approximately normal for each month of the year?
3. Produce a plot of the distribution of the variable **NumberBirth** for each day of the week (i.e., Sunday through Saturday) so that each day's distribution of the variable can be compared. Based on the plot, does there appear to be an effect of day of the week on number of births?
4. Perform the same analysis that was requested in question 3, this time using month as the factor. Does there appear to be any effect of month of the year on number of births?
5. Produce a table showing mean number of births and standard deviation of this variable broken down by the variables month of the year and day of the week.

Chapter 10: Bivariate Correlation and Regression

Overview

What is the relation between a person's height and their weight, between the mean expenditure per pupil a state provides and the mean achievement test score of students in the state, between a person's income and their rated happiness, or between the size of a city and the average commute time of workers in the city? All these questions concern relations between numeric variables and can be addressed using regression and correlation analyses.

In general, to describe the relation between a pair of numeric variables, two aspects of the relation should be assessed: one is a description of the ideal underlying form of the relation and the other is a description of the degree to which values of the variables conform to the ideal form; these two aspects are addressed using regression and correlation analyses, respectively.

Describing the Ideal Underlying Form of a Relation

A common assumption made in the social sciences is that if two numeric variables are related, their relation can best be described with a straight line. This and some other possible ideal forms that may underlie the relation between two numeric variables are shown in Figure 10.1.

Figure 10.1. Three possible ideal forms underlying the relation between two numeric variables. Panel *a* shows a linear relation, panel *b* a relation that has a quadratic form, and panel *c* a cubic form.

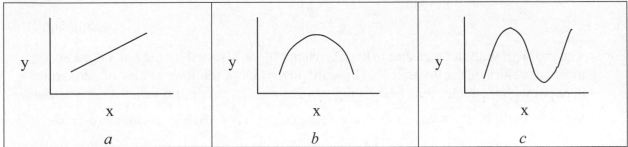

The assumption that a straight line is the ideal underlying form of a relation between two variables is incorporated in the statistical procedure known as linear regression analysis. One of its purposes is to provide a description of the ideal (also called a best-fitting, or regression) line. The description usually takes the form of an equation for a straight line:

$$\widetilde{Y} = bX + a \qquad \text{Equation 10.1}$$

where b is the slope of the best-fitting straight line, a is its y-intercept, and $\widetilde{Y}$ is the predicted value of the y-variable for a given value of the x-variable. Values of b and a are calculated so that the straight line is one for which the mean squared distances of data points from the straight line in the y-direction is a minimum. Figure 10.2 illustrates the distances involved in this requirement.

Figure 10.2. An illustration of the rule for determining the equation for a best-fitting straight line. The rule is that the line is the one for which the data points have a minimum variance in the y-direction.

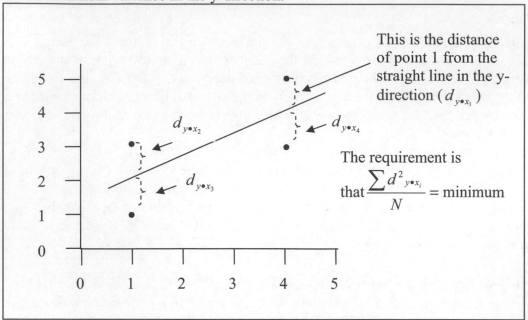

Describing the Extent to Which Data Conform to a Straight Line

It may seem that the variance measure presented in Figure 10.2 and identified below as the quantity $\sigma_{y \cdot x}^2$ would provide a good quantitative measure of the extent to which data conformed to a straight line.

$$\sigma_{y \cdot x}^2 = \frac{\sum d^2_{y \cdot x_i}}{N}$$ Equation 10.2

The problem with the measure is that its magnitude is affected by the units used to measure values of the y-variable. Thus, although it has a minimum value of zero when data points fall exactly on a best-fitting straight line, its maximum value is not invariant, but rather will be the same as σ_y^2 , the variance of the y-variable. To standardize $\sigma_{y \cdot x}^2$, it is divided by its maximum possible value (σ_y^2) and the result subtracted from 1 to produce the coefficient r^2 often referred to as the coefficient of determination. The operations underlying the calculation of r^2 are shown in Equation 10.3.

$$r^2 = 1 - \frac{\sigma_{y \cdot x}^2}{\sigma_y^2}$$ Equation 10.3

Unlike $\sigma_{y \cdot x}^2$, r^2 is a standardized coefficient with a range of 0 to 1; 1 indicates a perfect fit of the data points to a straight line and 0 indicates the worst possible fit. Scenarios corresponding to these extremes as well as an intermediate value are illustrated in Figure 10.3.

Figure 10.3. Three configurations of data points and best-fitting lines that correspond to r^2 values of 1 (panel *a*), 0 (panel *c*) and an intermediate value (panel *b*).

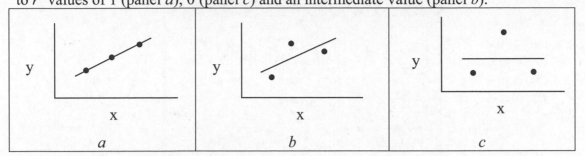

Assumptions About the Data

In addition to the assumption that the underlying form of the relation between two variables is linear, proper interpretation of the results of a linear regression analysis entails other assumptions. Some of these are that each observation is randomly selected from a population and independent of all other observations, outliers or extreme data points do not substantially affect the outcome of the analysis, the residuals (i.e., $d_{y \cdot x_i}$) are normally distributed, and the variance of these residuals is approximately the same across values of the x-variable (an assumption sometimes referred to as homoscedasticity).

Requesting a Scatterplot

Visual inspection of a scatterplot can provide insight into a number of aspects of a relation between two variables. One can assess whether the two variables are related, whether it is reasonable to assume that the relation between them is linear, how closely the data points conform to an underlying straight line, the possible presence of outliers, and whether the residuals appear to satisfy the assumptions of normality and homoscedasticity. Thus, forming a scatterplot is often the first step in analyzing the relation between two variables. The procedure will be illustrated for the variables **HoursStudied** and **QuizScore** which measure, respectively, the hours studied for a statistics quiz reported by randomly selected students in a statistics class and percent correct score on the quiz.

1. From the **Graphs** menu select **Legacy Dialogs** then **Scatter/Dot**.

Notice that each case consists of a variable that identifies the case (**StudentId**, it's optional) and a value of each of the numeric variables whose relation will be assessed.

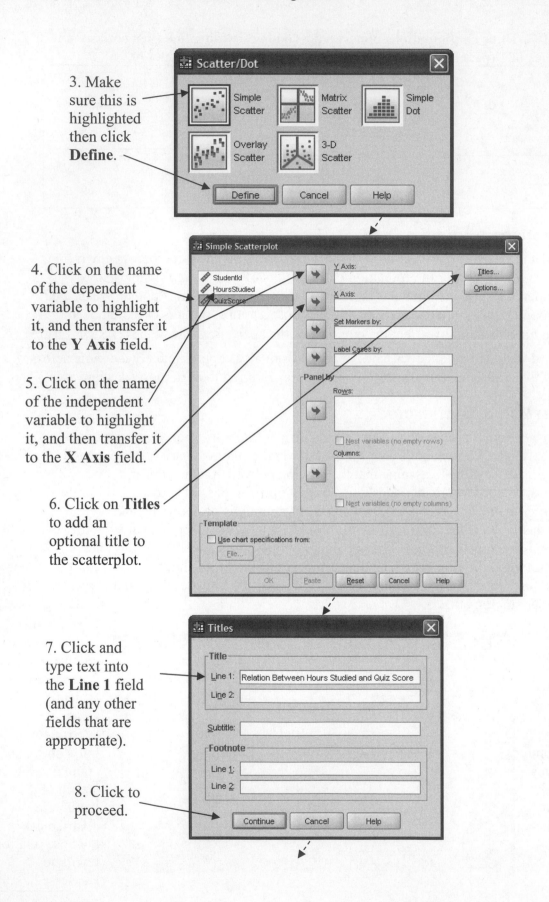

3. Make sure this is highlighted then click **Define**.

4. Click on the name of the dependent variable to highlight it, and then transfer it to the **Y Axis** field.

5. Click on the name of the independent variable to highlight it, and then transfer it to the **X Axis** field.

6. Click on **Titles** to add an optional title to the scatterplot.

7. Click and type text into the **Line 1** field (and any other fields that are appropriate).

8. Click to proceed.

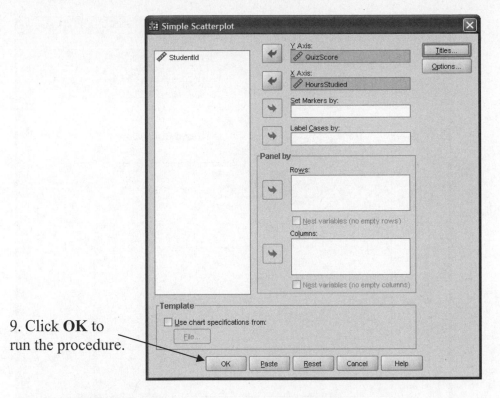

9. Click **OK** to run the procedure.

Optional Features

A Best-Fitting (Regression) Line. The steps shown above will produce a scatterplot that does not include a best-fitting straight line. The line can be added to the plot using the steps shown below:

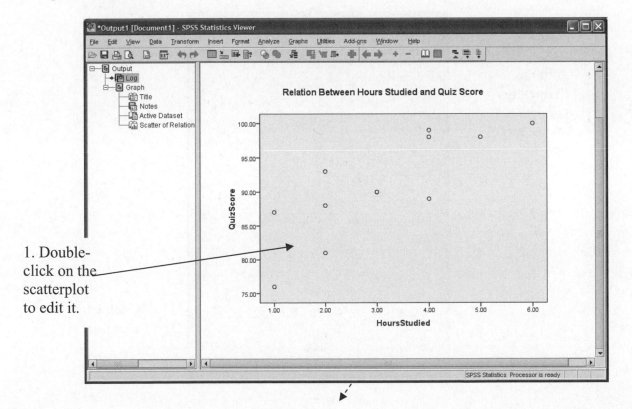

1. Double-click on the scatterplot to edit it.

2. In the **Chart Editor** that opens, select **Fit Line at Total** from the **Elements** menu.

3. In the **Properties** window that opens, select **Linear**.

4. Click **Close** to proceed.

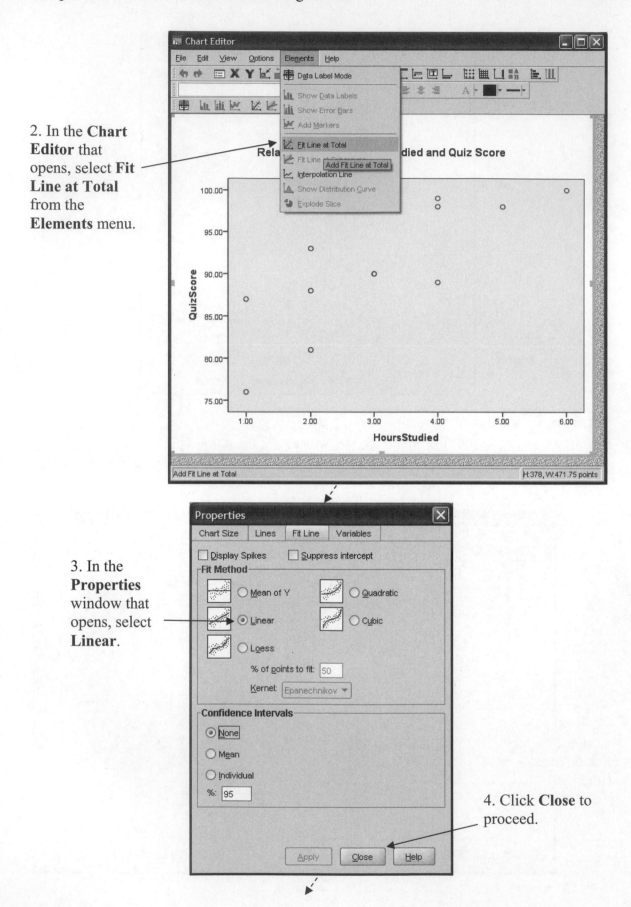

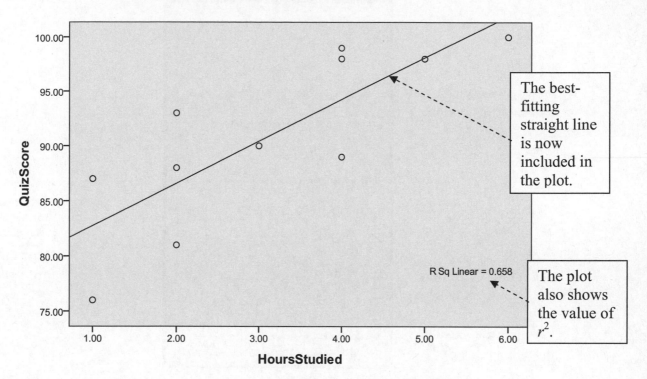

Relation Between Hours Studied and Quiz Score

The best-fitting straight line is now included in the plot.

R Sq Linear = 0.658

The plot also shows the value of r^2.

Data Labels. Another useful option for a scatterplot is a label for each data point. The label can be a case number or a value obtained from a variable in the **SPSS Statistics Data Editor**. The steps below show how to label points in a scatterplot using values of the variable **StudentId**.

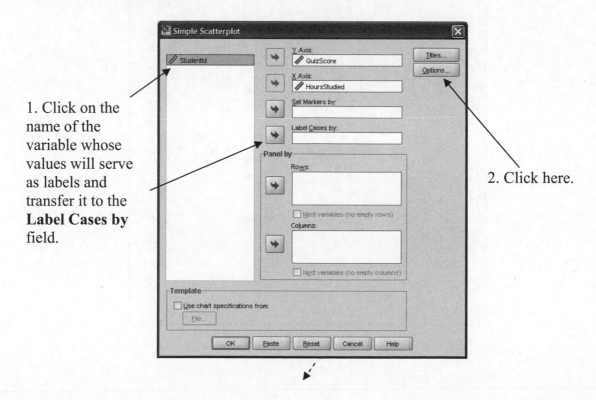

1. Click on the name of the variable whose values will serve as labels and transfer it to the **Label Cases by** field.

2. Click here.

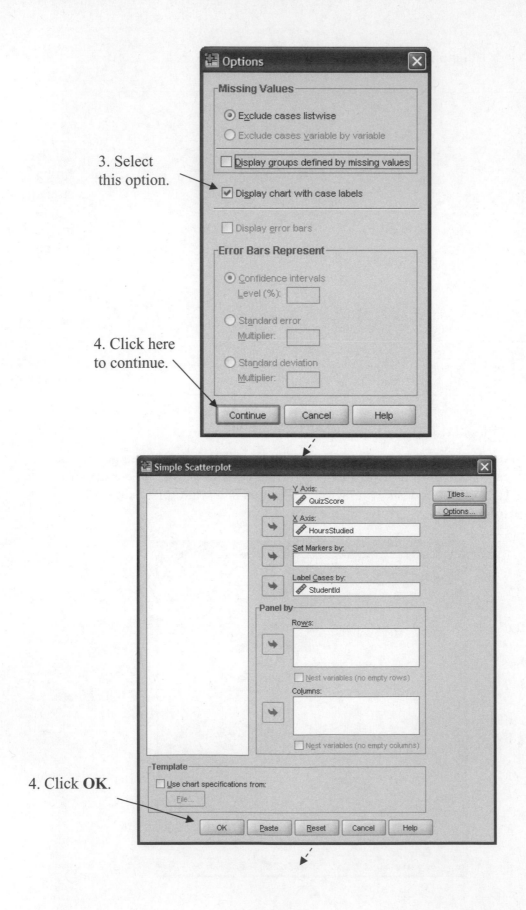

3. Select
this option.

4. Click here
to continue.

4. Click **OK**.

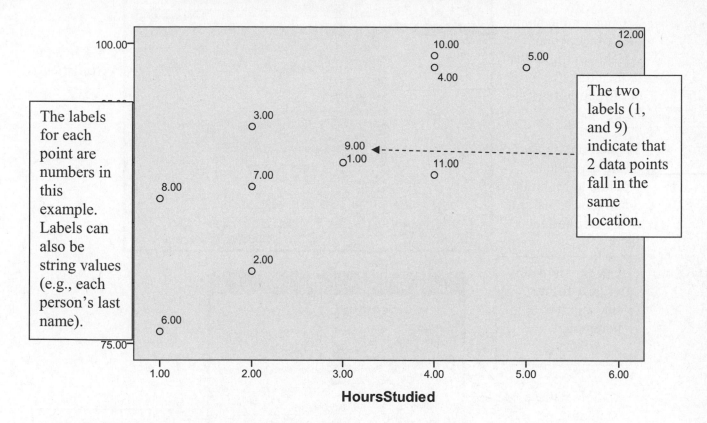

Relation Between Hours Studied and Quiz Score

Requesting a Regression Analysis

The **Regression** procedure provides parameters of the equation for a best-fitting line together with statistics that test whether the parameters differ significantly from zero. Also provided are values of r and r^2 together with tests of significance. A number of measures are available for assessing the distributional assumptions about residuals. Recommended selections for implementing the procedure are shown below:

1. From the **Analyze** menu select **Regression** then **Linear**.

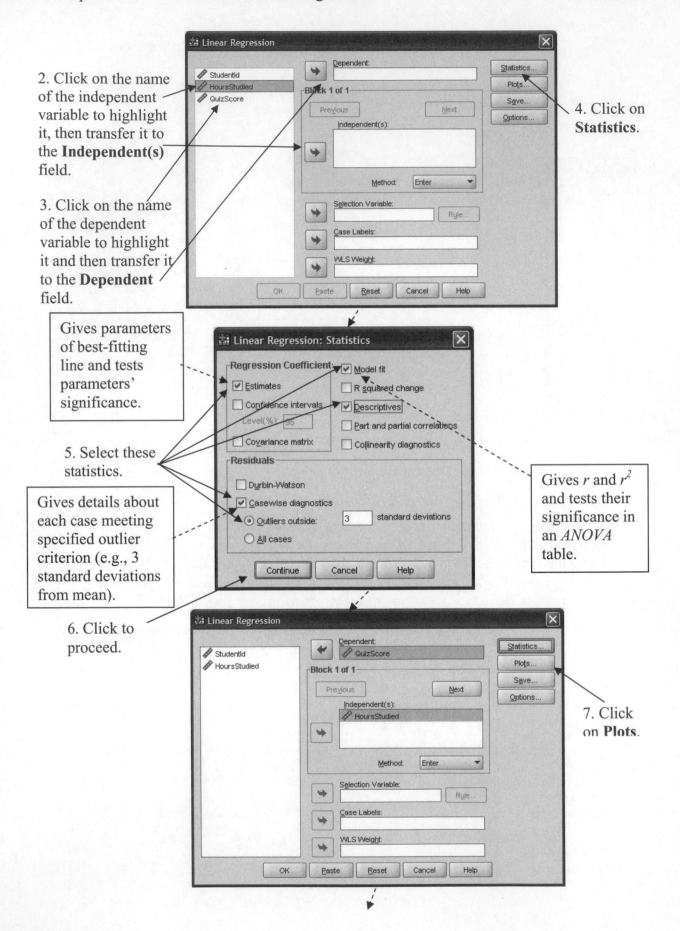

2. Click on the name of the independent variable to highlight it, then transfer it to the **Independent(s)** field.

3. Click on the name of the dependent variable to highlight it and then transfer it to the **Dependent** field.

4. Click on **Statistics**.

Gives parameters of best-fitting line and tests parameters' significance.

5. Select these statistics.

Gives details about each case meeting specified outlier criterion (e.g., 3 standard deviations from mean).

6. Click to proceed.

Gives r and r^2 and tests their significance in an *ANOVA* table.

7. Click on **Plots**.

8. Click on **ZPRED** to highlight it and then transfer it to the **X** field.

9. Click on **ZRESID** to highlight it and then transfer it to the **Y** field.

10. Select these.

11. Click to continue.

Provides a visual check if residuals are normally distributed.

This produces a plot of the predicted values of the dependent variable vs. residuals to allow a visual check of the distributional assumptions of the residuals.

This produces a histogram and superimposed normal distribution of residuals in *z*-score form.

12. Click **OK** to run the procedure.

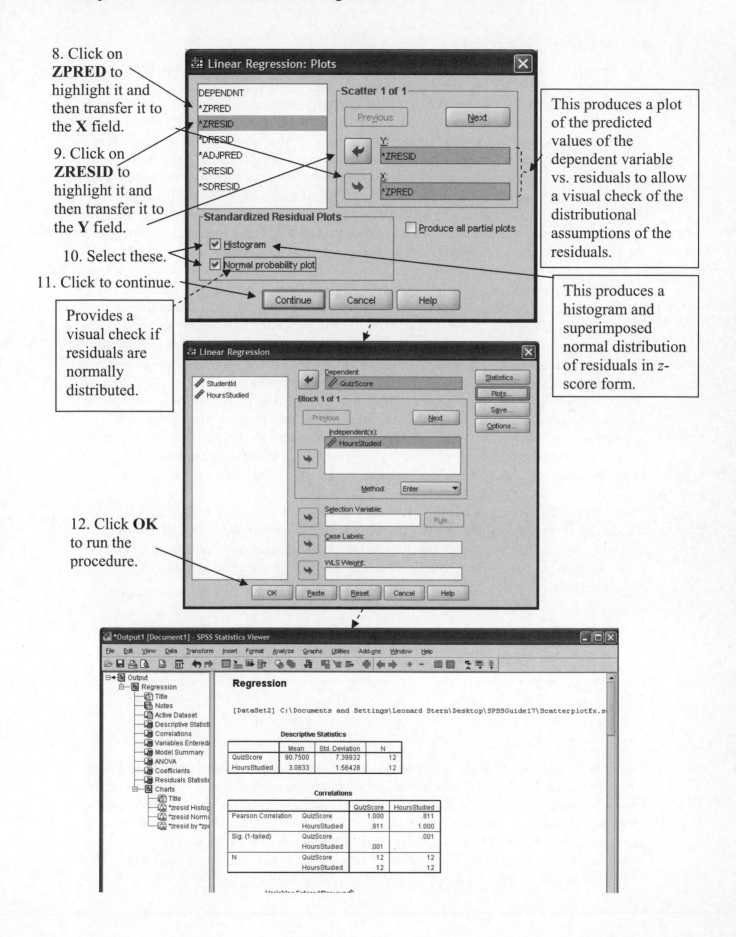

Inspecting the output

The sequence of tables and plots output by the selections just shown is reproduced below. Inspection should focus first on whether assumptions about the data have been met. If residuals are normally distributed, the histogram requested on the **Plots** window should show a distribution that generally conforms to the superimposed normal distribution. A further check is provided by inspecting the normal P-P plot which shows on the x-axis the actual proportion of residual values and on the y-axis the predicted cumulative proportion based on a normal distribution. If the distribution of residuals is normal, points in the plot will fall on the diagonal line. Points falling above the diagonal line indicate there are fewer than expected cumulative cases; points below the diagonal indicate there are more than expected cumulative cases compared to a normal distribution. Inspection of the plots shown below reveals no serious violation of the assumption of normality.

In a sense, the scatterplot showing standardized predicted values on the x-axis and standardized residual values on the y-axis provides a view of the data points from the vantage point of the best-fitting straight line. The best-fitting line may be pictured as a horizontal line going through the zero value on the y-axis. Examples of scatterplots of this kind for data that violate underlying assumptions are presented in Figure 10.4. These scatterplots each contain a straight line that goes through the zero value on the y-axis. (A line like this can be added to the scatterplot produced by *SPSS* by double-clicking on the plot in the **Viewer** to enter the edit mode and pressing the button on the toolbar that appears which has the horizontal reference line going through the y-axis—see Appendix A). Examination of the scatterplot for the variables predicting **QuizScore** from **HoursStudied** shows no suspicious patterns such as depicted in Figure 10.4.

Figure 10.4. Plots of standardized predicted values (shown on the x-axis) and standardized residual values (y-axis) that correspond to violations of an underlying assumption in a regression analysis. In panel *a* the relation between two variables is curvilinear rather than linear; panel *b* indicates a violation of the assumption of homoscedasticity; panel *c* reveals the presence of an outlier.

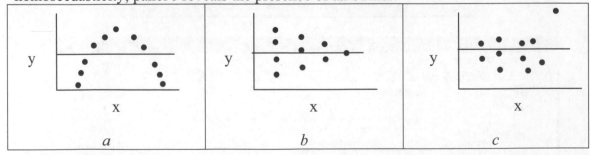

The tables output by procedure **Regression** contain some redundant information. For example, the table labeled **Correlations** presents information that also appears in other tables. Information about the strength of the relation between the variables **QuizScore** and **HoursStudied** is summarized by the coefficient *r*. The magnitudes .10, .30, and .50 correspond roughly to relations that are considered small, medium, and large, respectively (Cohen, 1988). The finding of an *r* value of .811 in the **Correlations and Model Summary** tables signals a very strong relation between the variables, one that is highly significant. The significance of the r value is reported in the **ANOVA** table as an F value and in the **Coefficients** table as a t value (having N-2 degrees of freedom) on the line reporting the value of $b_{best-fit}$. In addition to the value of $b_{best-fit}$, the table labeled **Coefficients** gives the value of $a_{best-fit}$ together with a test of the significance of each. Note that the test of the significance of the slope of the best-fitting line is equivalent to a test of the significance of r.

The steps shown below generally provide information needed for a written description of the outcome of a simple regression analysis.

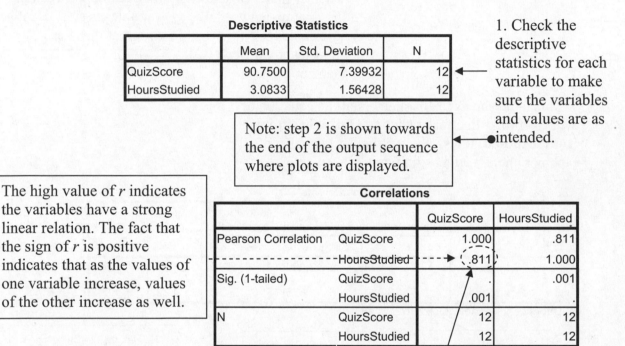

Descriptive Statistics

	Mean	Std. Deviation	N
QuizScore	90.7500	7.39932	12
HoursStudied	3.0833	1.56428	12

1. Check the descriptive statistics for each variable to make sure the variables and values are as intended.

Note: step 2 is shown towards the end of the output sequence where plots are displayed.

The high value of r indicates the variables have a strong linear relation. The fact that the sign of r is positive indicates that as the values of one variable increase, values of the other increase as well.

Correlations

		QuizScore	HoursStudied
Pearson Correlation	QuizScore	1.000	.811
	HoursStudied	.811	1.000
Sig. (1-tailed)	QuizScore		.001
	HoursStudied	.001	
N	QuizScore	12	12
	HoursStudied	12	12

3a. Look at this table to find the r value for the relation.

Variables Entered/Removed[b]

Model	Variables Entered	Variables Removed	Method
1	Hours Studied[a]	.	Enter

a. All requested variables entered.

b. Dependent Variable: QuizScore

3b. Look at this table to find the r^2 value for the relation.

Model Summary[b]

Model	R	R Square	Adjusted R Square	Std. Error of the Estimate
1	.811[a]	.658	.623	4.54084

a. Predictors: (Constant), HoursStudied

b. Dependent Variable: QuizScore

This estimates the population parameter $\sigma_{y \cdot x}^2$. Its formula is $s_{y \cdot x}^2 = \dfrac{\sum d_{y \cdot x}^2}{N-2}$

The value of r^2 assumes the data are a population; this estimates r^2 assuming the data are a random sample of a population.

ANOVA[b]

Model		Sum of Squares	df	Mean Square	F	Sig.
1	Regression	396.058	1	396.058	19.208	.001[a]
	Residual	206.192	10	20.619		
	Total	602.250	11			

a. Predictors: (Constant), HoursStudied

b. Dependent Variable: QuizScore

4. This table shows whether the r^2 value for the relation between the 2 variables is significantly different than zero.

Because this value is < .05, the relation between the 2 variables is significantly different than zero.

5. This table shows the parameters of the equation of the best-fitting line for predicting **QuizScore** from **HoursStudied**. It also shows whether the value of each parameter differs significantly from zero.

Coefficients[a]

Model		Unstandardized Coefficients		Standardized Coefficients	t	Sig.
		B	Std. Error	Beta		
1	(Constant)	78.923	3.000		26.306	.000
	HoursStudied	3.836	.875	.811	4.383	.001

a. Dependent Variable: QuizScore

This is the value of $b_{best-fit}$.

This is the value of $a_{best-fit}$.

These values test the significance of each parameter using the t statistic.

Residuals Statistics[a]

	Minimum	Maximum	Mean	Std. Deviation	N
Predicted Value	82.7585	101.9381	90.7500	6.00044	12
Residual	-6.75851	6.40557	.00000	4.32952	12
Std. Predicted Value	-1.332	1.865	.000	1.000	12
Std. Residual	-1.488	1.411	.000	.953	12

a. Dependent Variable: QuizScore

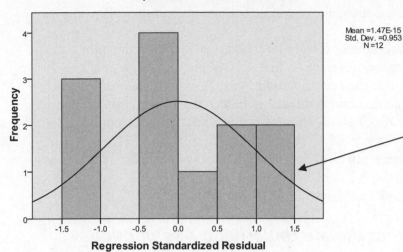

2a. Examine the distribution of the standardized residuals to detect substantial departures from normality.

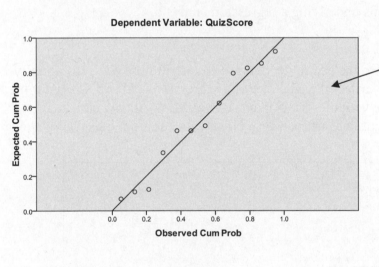

2b. Examine the normal P-P plot to detect substantial departures from normality exhibited as deviations from the diagonal line.

Given the small number of scores, the 3 plots don't signal any serious violations of the underlying assumptions.

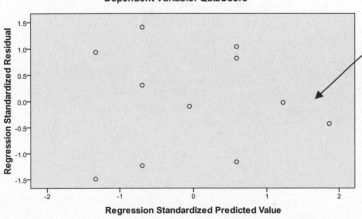

2c. Examine this plot for evidence of substantial heteroscedasticity, nonlinearity, and for outliers.

Reporting the Results

The outcome of the analysis shown above can be summarized in the following way:

> The relation between hours of study for a quiz and score on the quiz was examined with a regression analysis that used hours of study as the predictor variable. Informal examination of the data with histograms and scatterplots revealed no serious threats to underlying distributional assumptions of the residuals. A strong linear correlation was found between the variables, $r = .81$, that was highly significant, $F(1, 10) = 19.21$, $p < .01$. The equation for predicting quiz score from hours of study was
>
> Predicted quiz score $= 3.84 \times$ hours studied $+ 78.92$

Dealing with Data that Violate Underlying Assumptions

Because data are usually screened before being analyzed, problems are often detected before a scatterplot is formed. For example, if, in a preliminary data screening, a variable is clearly not normally distributed, then a scatterplot that includes the variable will likely reveal violations of assumptions underlying a regression analysis.

Removing Outliers

Data that fall extremely far from the central tendency of a distribution can substantially and sometimes inappropriately affect the outcome of a regression analysis. Consider the scatterplot shown below of the variables **MSRP** and **HiwayMPG** of new cars in 2004. Inspection reveals a relation that does not conform closely to a straight line. There appear to be outliers in both variables.

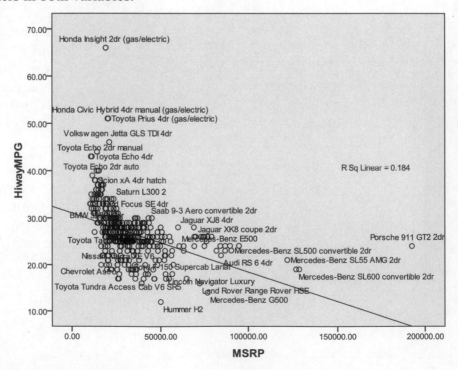

Insight into the reason for the extreme data points can be gained by inspecting the labels for the data points. The labels reveal that the extremely high values on the axis that represents highway miles per gallon result from including hybrid gas-electric vehicles in the data set. It seems reasonable to exclude these cars from the analysis and focus on the conventional vehicles. There are three hybrid cars in the data set (one is hidden behind the data point of the Toyota Prius): cases 69, 70, and 94. As shown below, the **Select Cases** window provides one way to exclude these cases from future analyses.

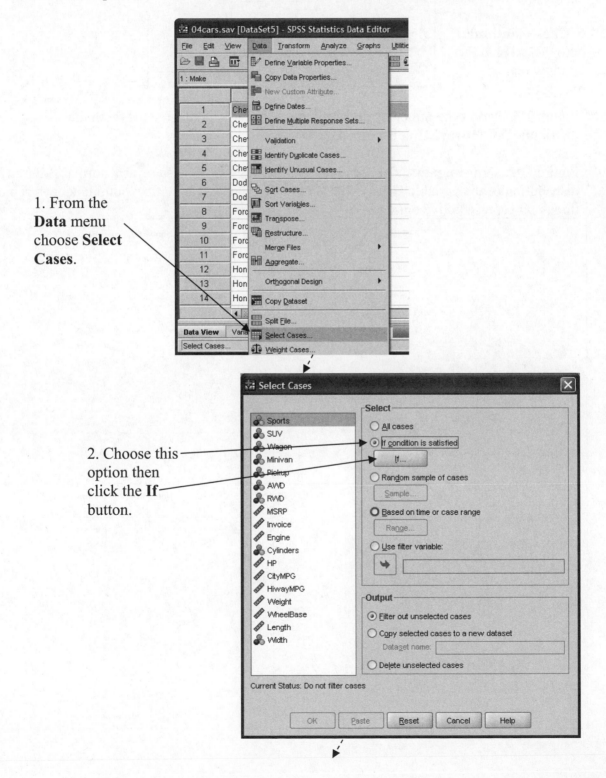

1. From the **Data** menu choose **Select Cases**.

2. Choose this option then click the **If** button.

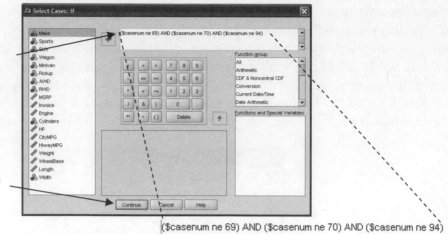

4. This statement selects all cases except 69, 70, and 94 for future analyses.

5. Click **Continue** here then **OK** in the window that reappears.

($casenum ne 69) AND ($casenum ne 70) AND ($casenum ne 94)

Figure 10.5 shows the effect of removing these cases on the degree to which the distribution of **HiwayMPG** is normal.

Figure 10.5. A histogram and a normal Q-Q plot (it's much the same as a normal P-P plot) of the distribution of the variable **HiwayMPG** before (top panels) and after (bottom panels) removing three non-representative outliers.

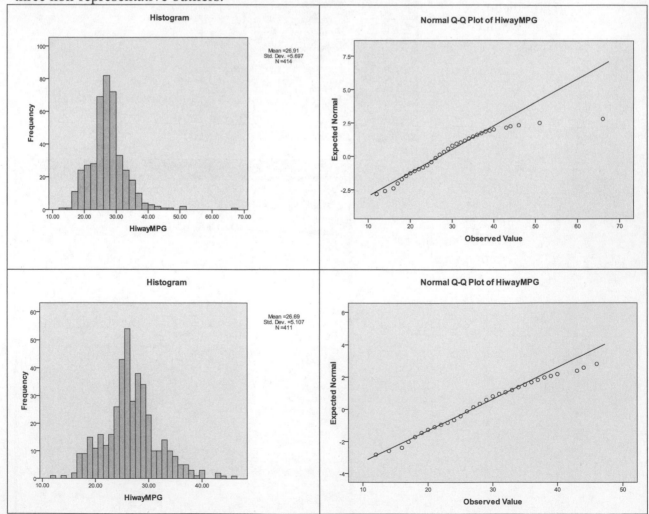

Transforming Variables

Removing data is not always a reasonable strategy for dealing with violations of underlying assumptions. Instead, transforming the variable can help correct the problems. Figure 10.6 illustrates some examples of unimodal distributions that deviate from normal to different degrees and the transformations that can help produce a normal distribution.

Figure 10.6. Transformations that can be applied to distributions that deviate from normal to help produce normal distributions.

Description of departure from normal and remedy	Plot	Equation for transforming X to X1
For moderate positive skew, take square root of each value.	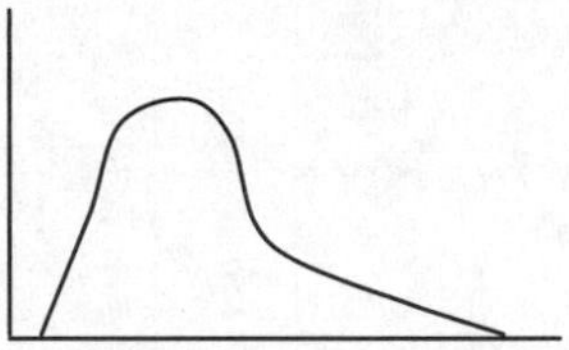	$X1=SQRT(X)$
For high positive skew, take log of each value.	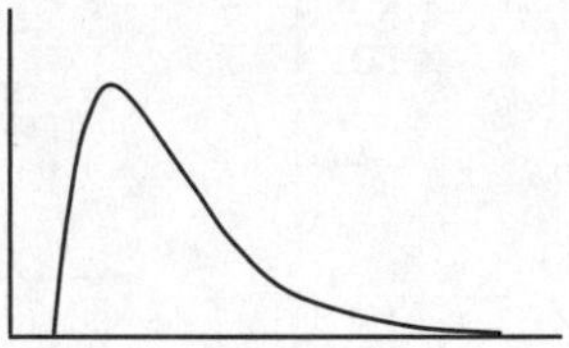	$X1=LG10(X)$
For extreme positive skew, take inverse of each value.	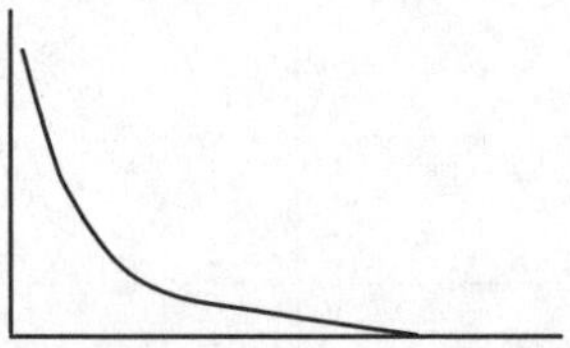	$X1=1/X$
For moderate negative skew, take square root of each reflected value.	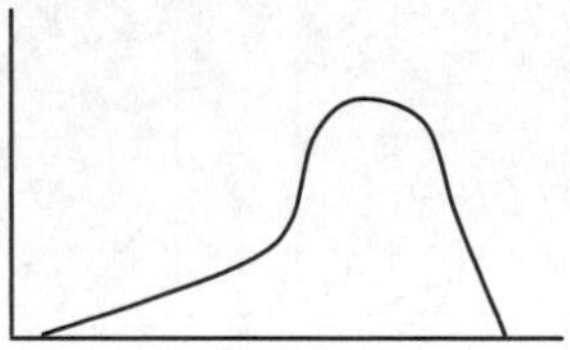	$X1=SQRT(K-X)$ where K=maximum X value + 1
For high negative skew, take log of each reflected value.	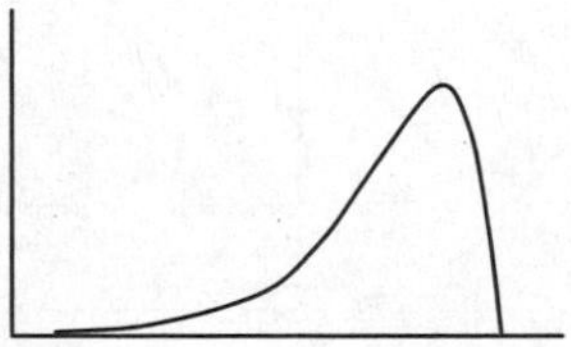	$X1=LG10(K-X)$ where K=maximum X value + 1
For extreme negative skew, take inverse of each reflected value.	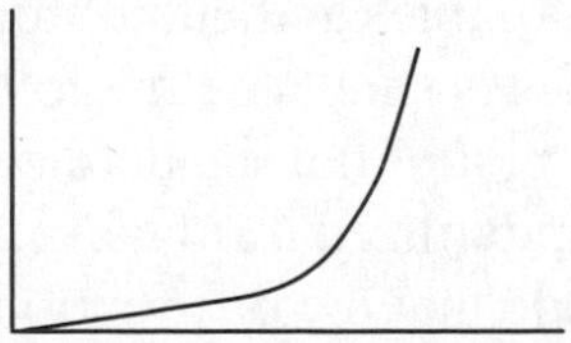	$X1=1/(K-X)$ where K=maximum X value + 1

For the variable **MSRP**, the positive skew is the result of there being a small number of very expensive cars. Because there is no good reason to exclude the expensive cars, a data transformation is appropriate. The result of applying a log transformation to produce the variable **logMSRP** is a distribution that, as shown in shown in the bottom panels of Figure 10.7, better conforms to a normal distribution.

Figure 10.7. A histogram and a normal Q-Q plot of the distribution of the variable **MSRP** before (top panels) and after (bottom panels) applying a log transformation.

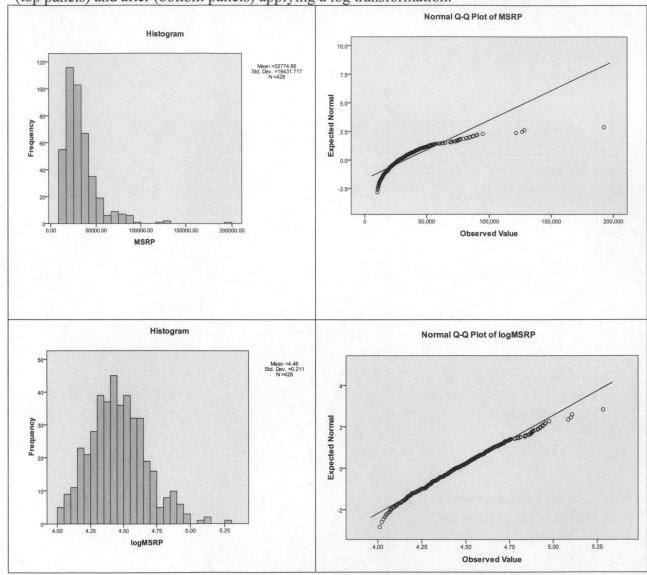

The scatterplot for the transformed variables and output for evaluating the relation between the two transformed variables is shown below followed by a histogram of the standardized residuals, a normal P-P plot of the standardized residuals, and a scatterplot of the standardized predicted and standardized residual values of **HiwayMPG**. From these plots, it is reasonable to conclude that the distributional assumptions of the residuals have been met.

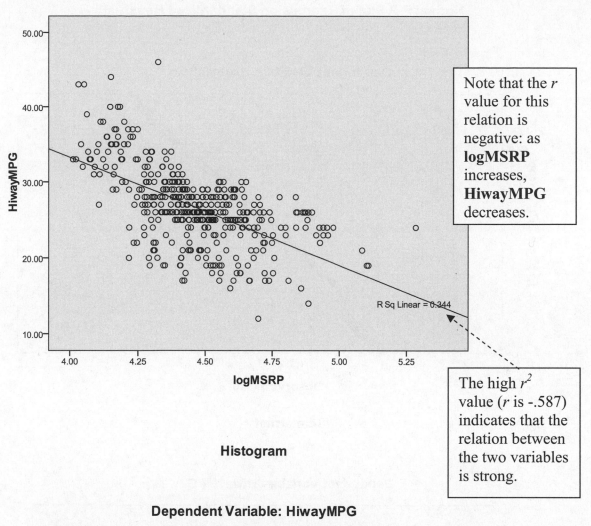

Note that the *r* value for this relation is negative: as **logMSRP** increases, **HiwayMPG** decreases.

The high r^2 value (*r* is -.587) indicates that the relation between the two variables is strong.

Histogram

Dependent Variable: HiwayMPG

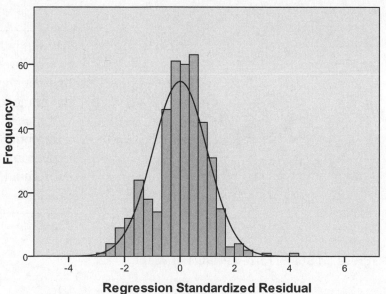

Mean =2.10E-15
Std. Dev. =0.999
N =411

The histogram and normal P-P plot (next page) show the residuals are approximately normally distributed.

Normal P-P Plot of Regression Standardized Residual

Dependent Variable: HiwayMPG

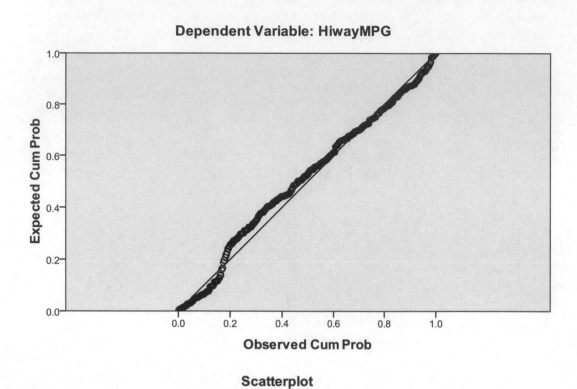

Scatterplot

Dependent Variable: HiwayMPG

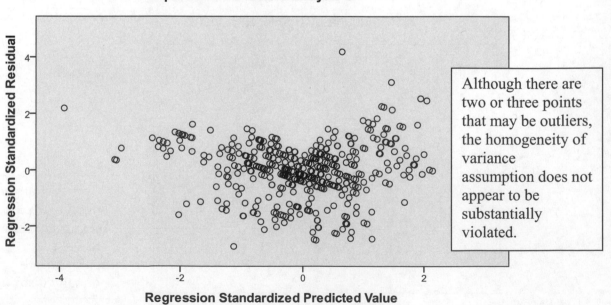

Although there are two or three points that may be outliers, the homogeneity of variance assumption does not appear to be substantially violated.

Finding all Possible r *Values for Pairs of Variables in a Data Set*

It is often of interest to determine the values of *r* for more than just one or two pairs of variables. For example, if one has data that describe the ratings given by trained judges from seven countries of 300 gymnastic performances and one wishes to determine how extensively all pairs of judges from different countries agree in their ratings, 21 *r* values would be required to make these assessments. An easy way to do this is with the **Bivariate Correlations** procedure as demonstrated below:

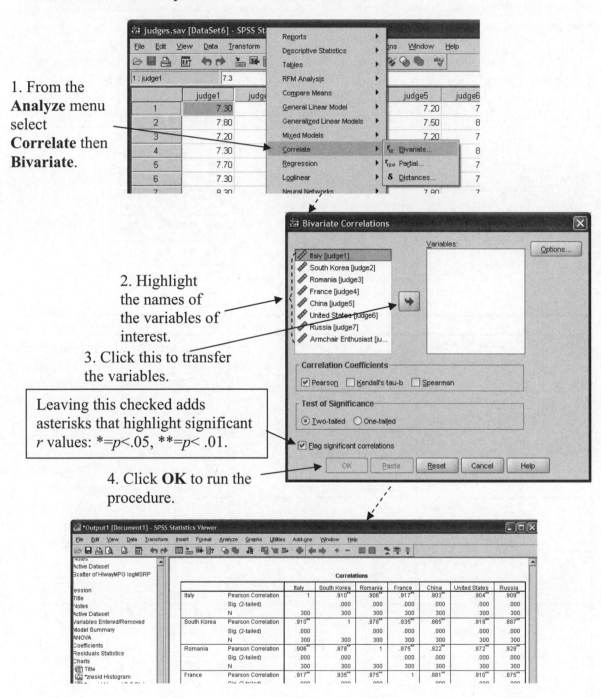

1. From the **Analyze** menu select **Correlate** then **Bivariate**.

2. Highlight the names of the variables of interest.

3. Click this to transfer the variables.

Leaving this checked adds asterisks that highlight significant *r* values: *=p<.05, **=p< .01.

4. Click **OK** to run the procedure.

Output from the procedure consists of a square matrix of r values for all possible pairs of variables included in the analysis together with the two-tailed significance level and the number of observations on which each r value is based. There is much redundant information in the table as well as information that is not informative. To interpret the data in each cell of the table, look at the variable names listed in the top row and first column of the table. Where each row and column intersects will be data that correspond to the two named variables. Note that, as illustrated in Figure 10.8, one diagonal of the table body contains the value 1 to indicate that the r value of each variable with itself is 1, and that the data on each side of the diagonal are mirror images.

Figure 10.8. Illustrates regularities found in tables of correlation values produced by the **Bivariate Correlations** procedure. Left panel shows the diagonal r values of 1 resulting when each variable is compared to itself; right panel shows mirror-image redundancies for data across the diagonal: cells connected by arrows contain the same information.

Correlations

		Italy	South Korea	Romania	France	China	Unite	
Italy	Pearson Correlation	1	.910**	.906**	.917**	.903**		
	Sig. (2-tailed)		.000	.000	.000	.000		
	N	300	300	300	300	300		
South Korea	Pearson Correlation	.910**	1	.878**	.935**	.885**		
	Sig. (2-tailed)	.000		.000	.000	.000		
	N	300	300	300	300	300		
Romania	Pearson Correlation	.906**	.878**	1	.875**	.922**	872**	.929**
	Sig. (2-tailed)	.000	.000		.000	.000		.000
	N	300	300	300	300	300		300
France	Pearson Correlation	.917**	.935**	.875**	1	.881**		.875**
	Sig. (2-tailed)	.000	.000	.000		.000		.000
	N	300	300	300	300	300		300
China	Pearson Correlation	.903**	.885**	.922**	.881**	1		.926**
	Sig. (2-tailed)	.000	.000	.000	.000			.000
	N	300	300	300	300	300	300	300
United States	Pearson Correlation	.904**	.919**	.872**	.910**	.884**	1	.885**
	Sig. (2-tailed)	.000	.000	.000	.000	.000		.000
	N	300	300	300	300	300	300	300
Russia	Pearson Correlation	.909**	.887**	.929**	.875**	.926**	.885**	1
	Sig. (2-tailed)	.000	.000	.000	.000	.000	.000	
	N	300	300	300	300	300	300	300

This cell shows the judge from France and Italy had an r value of .917

The double asterisks indicate an r value whose p <.01

**. Correlation is significant at the 0.01 level (2-tailed).

Exercises for Chapter 10

Exercise 10.1

For this exercise, use the file *04Cars.sav* available on the publisher's website for this text at the address http://www.pearsonhighered.com/stern2e. The data set is based on information obtained from Edmunds.com and is reprinted here with permission. Analyze the relation between a car's weight and the length of its wheelbase. In performing this analysis, do the following:

1. Form a scatterplot using the variable **Weight** as the y-variable and **WheelBase** as the x-variable. Include a best-fitting straight line in your scatterplot.
2. Perform a regression analysis for the two variables. From the output, answer the following questions:
   a. Does the relation between the two variables appear to be linear?
   b. What is the *r* value for the relation?
   c. Is the relation between the two variables statistically significant?
   d. What is the equation of the best-fitting straight line that predicts weight from wheelbase?
   e. Do the assumptions of normality of the distribution of residuals and homogeneity of residuals appear to be satisfied? Explain how you answered this question.

Exercise 10.2

Using the file *04Cars.sav* (see previous problem), form a new variable **Markup** calculated from the formula **Markup = MSRP – Invoice**. The variable **Markup** thus shows how much profit dealers request for each car. In this analysis the purpose is to describe the relation between profit and the price of a new car as indicated on the car's invoice. Do the following:

1. Create the variable **Markup** using the formula shown above.
2. Form a scatterplot using **Invoice** as the x-variable and **Markup** as the y-variable. Include a best-fitting straight line in your scatterplot.
3. Obtain the equation for the straight line that predicts a dealer's markup from the dealer's invoice price.
4. Based on your equation, how much does the markup change for each $1,000 increase in the invoice price of a new car?
5. Based on the equation for the best-fitting straight line, what is the predicted markup for a car with an invoice price of $27,500?
6. Obtain a list of residuals of markups that have standardized values greater than 3. Which manufacturer(s) have unusually high markups? Which have unusually low markups?
7. Is the assumption of homogeneity of variance of the residuals met? If the intent of the analysis is to describe a relation between two variables, and not to evaluate whether the relation is statistically significant, is it critical that distributional assumptions of residuals be met? Explain.

Exercise 10.3

What educational variables are related to SAT scores? Use the data if the file *SAT1994.sav* available on the publisher's website for this text at the address http://www.pearsonhighered.com/stern2e to answer these questions. This data set was made available by Professor Deborah Lynn Guber in the Department of Political Science at The University of Vermont. It also appears on the website at this address: http://www.amstat.org/publications/jse/jse_data_archive.html.

1. Was there a significant relation between the mean student/teacher ratio (the variable named **RATIO**) and mean SAT score of states in the U.S. in 1994-1995 (**TOTAL**)?
2. Did states that spent more on educating each student in elementary through secondary schools have students whose mean SAT scores changed correspondingly? For this analysis, determine if your results are more satisfactory when the variable **Cost** is transformed by taking its log to the base 10.
3. Was there a relation between the percent of students taking the SAT (the variable **PERCENT**) and mean SAT score? How does the result complicate interpretation of the results obtained for questions 1 and 2?

Exercise 10.4

Using data in the file *IQBrainsize.sav* that was prepared in **Exercise 4.3**, determine if, based on the twin data represented in the file, there is a significant linear relation between total surface area of the brain and total brain volume.

Exercise 10.5

For the data in the file *IQBrainsize.sav*, (see previous exercise) obtain *r* values to determine which of the following physiological variables are significantly correlated with IQ (variable **FIQ**): head circumference (**HC**), total brain surface area (**TOTALSA**), total brain volume (**TOTVOL**), and body weight (**WEIGHT**).

Chapter 11: Multiple Regression and Correlation

Overview

A multiple regression analysis differs from a simple (i.e., bivariate) regression analysis in that more than one independent variable (sometimes referred to as a predictor variable) is used to predict the value of a dependent variable (sometimes referred to as the criterion variable). For example, multiple regression can be used to predict a student's grade in a class (measured on a 0.0-4.0 scale) from the student's current GPA, the number of days per week the student typically skips class, and number of hours per week the student devotes to studying for the class. The result of the analysis is an equation of the general form

$$\widetilde{Y} = a + b_1 X_1 + b_2 X_2 + b_3 X_4 + ... b_k X_k \qquad \text{Equation 11.1}$$

where $\widetilde{Y}$ is the predicted value of the dependent variable, a is the $\widetilde{Y}$ value when all X_i values are zero, and each b_i is a regression coefficient that shows how the predicted value of the dependent variable changes in the context of the other independent variables for each unit change of independent variable i.

There are both similarities and differences between bivariate and multiple regression analyses. As in bivariate regression, values of the parameters a and b_i in multiple regression are selected so as to minimize the total squared deviation of predicted from actual values of the dependent variable. Figure 11.1 illustrates the distances being minimized when a dependent variable's values are predicted from values of two independent variables. Note that in the three-dimensional view depicted in the figure, the independent variables are shown at right angles to each other to represent their mutual independence (i.e., changing the value of one of these variables does not change the value of the other); however, the assumed independence among independent variables raises a complication for interpreting values of the regression coefficients, one that did not occur in the case of bivariate regression. Note also that with two independent variables, the procedure may be envisioned as producing a best-fitting plane as opposed to a best-fitting line in the bivariate case.

As in bivariate regression, success in predicting values of the dependent variable from knowledge of values of the independent variables can be summarized with a squared coefficient, symbolized now with an upper case R^2 and referred to as multiple R squared. Unlike r, R is always positive. R^2, like r^2, has a range of 0 to 1 and can be interpreted as the proportion of variance in the dependent variable that is removed (or explained) using the weighted combination of independent variables specified in the regression equation. Whether the amount of explained variance is statistically significant can be tested with an F statistic. Finding a significant F for a regression analysis indicates that, in the population being sampled, the variance of the dependent variable accounted for (i.e., removed or explained) by the weighted set of independent variables exceeds what could be expected by chance. From a significant R^2 one can also conclude that in the population represented by the data there is a nonzero linear relation between the dependent and independent variables and that the regression coefficients are not all equal to zero; all three conclusions are equivalent

Assumptions underlying proper interpretation of significance tests are similar to those for bivariate regression: Cases are randomly selected from a population of interest and independent of each other; the dependent variable is linearly related to each independent variable; and residuals of the dependent variable predicted from the combination of independent variables are normally distributed with approximately uniform variance over values of the independent variables. As for sample size, it is rare to find recommended sizes of fewer than five to ten cases per variable. It may be better, though, to select the smaller of the values obtained from two formulas considered by Greene (1991) in his assessment of techniques for determining sample size in multiple regression. The two quantities to choose between are obtained by substituting k, the number of independent variables, into the formulas $50 + 8k$ and $104 + k$. Thus for two independent variables, the recommended sample size is 66; for 10 independent variables, the recommended sample size is 114. An advantage of using suitably large sample sizes is that departures from normality of residuals become less of a threat to valid interpretations of significance tests.

Figure 11.1. The arrows show distances of data points (represented as solid circles) from predicted values (unfilled circles) located in a best-fitting plane. In a multiple regression analysis, the orientation of the plane is adjusted to locate predicted values on the plane so that their sum of the squared distances to the actual values (as determined by the joint values of X_1 and X_2) is as small as possible.

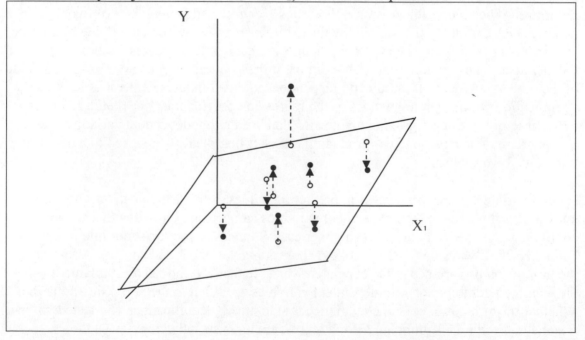

An Example

To illustrate an application of regression analysis, the data set shown in Table 11.1 will be used to examine the relation of the variable **Grade** to the set of predictors (i.e., independent variables) **GPA**, **DaysAbsnt**, and **HrsStudy**. Note that the dependent variable, **Grade**, is a scale variable as are each of the independent variables. It is possible to use nominally-scaled variables as independent variables in a regression analysis. When such variables consist of just two possible values (e.g., gender) values of the variable can be entered into a regression analysis using any two numbers (e.g., 0 and 1); when the variable consists of more than two values, data entry requires more than a single variable and will not be described here.

The equation produced by the regression analysis for the data in Table 11.1 is
$$\textbf{Estimated Grade} = 1.614 + .459 \, \textbf{GPA} - .167 \, \textbf{DaysAbsnt} + .078 \, \textbf{HrsStudy}$$
What does the equation do? It provides a way to predict the grade of a person in the class from which the data were derived, based on knowledge of values of the three independent variables. For example, the equation can be used to predict that if a person has a GPA of 3.6, does not miss any classes, and studies a mean of 6 hours per week for the class, the grade in the class will be
$$1.614 + .459 * 3.60 - .167 * 0.0 + .078 * 6.00 = 3.73.$$

Care should be taken in interpreting the magnitude of the regression coefficients (i.e., the values .459, -.167, and .078 in the above equation). The values indicate how the predicted value of grade in the class would change *over and above the changes due to all other independent variables*. That is, the value .078 for the variable **HrsStudy** means that a student's grade in the class is predicted to increase by .078 for each additional hour the student studies for the class per week beyond the independent effects on predicted grade exerted by the student's GPA and the number of days of class the student misses per week. Thus, the value .078 is relevant only in the context of the other independent variables.

Table 11.1. Fabricated data to illustrate a multiple regression analysis that predicts grade in a class from a student's GPA, mean days absent per week, and mean number of hours of study for the class.

Grade	GPA	DaysAbsnt	HrsStudy	Grade	GPA	DaysAbsnt	HrsStudy
3.50	3.60	.00	6.00	3.90	3.80	1.00	9.00
3.50	3.50	.00	4.00	3.00	3.50	.00	5.00
4.00	3.90	.00	8.00	2.00	3.30	3.00	3.00
2.90	3.20	2.00	2.00	2.20	3.40	3.00	1.00
3.70	3.50	1.00	4.00	3.90	3.70	1.00	6.00
3.60	3.30	1.00	4.00	3.50	3.50	.00	4.00
4.00	3.60	1.00	6.00	3.00	3.30	.00	4.00
3.90	4.00	.00	7.00	4.00	4.00	.00	5.00
2.70	3.00	3.00	2.00	2.90	3.30	3.00	2.00
2.80	3.20	3.00	1.00	3.30	3.20	2.00	2.00
3.00	3.10	2.00	1.00	3.20	3.10	1.00	3.00
3.00	3.30	1.00	3.00	3.30	3.40	1.00	1.00
3.70	4.00	1.00	6.00	3.00	3.30	2.00	2.00
3.50	3.50	2.00	5.00				

Caution should also be taken in interpreting the relative magnitudes of the regression coefficients: regression coefficients with bigger magnitudes do not necessarily indicate the corresponding variables are more important to predicting the value of the dependent variable. The value of a regression coefficient is affected by (in addition to the correlation of the corresponding independent variable with the all other variables in the equation) the units used to measure the corresponding variable. For example, if the variable **DaysAbsnt** were converted from mean number of classes missed per week to total number of days missed during a 10-week quarter by multiplying each value by 10, the value of the regression coefficient in the prediction equation would change (it would decrease). However, this does not mean the variable is now less important in predicting grade in the class; rather its changed magnitude is due to a change in the scale of its measurement units. Interpretation problems due to variables' different measurement units can be decreased by converting each variable's values to z-scores. When this is done, the regression coefficients are referred to as beta weights or standardized regression coefficients. The relation between a variable's standardized and unstandardized regression coefficient is shown in the following formula:

$$\beta_i = b_i \frac{s_{Xi}}{s_Y} \qquad\qquad \text{Equation 11.2}$$

where β_i is the beta weight of independent variable i,

b_i is the unstandardized regression coefficient for independent variable i,
s_{Xi} is the standard deviation of independent variable i,
s_Y is the standard deviation of the dependent variable.

The regression equation for standardized variables has the following general form:

$$\tilde{Z}_Y = \beta_1 Z_1 + \beta_1 Z_1 + \beta_1 Z_1 + ... \beta_i Z_i \qquad\qquad \text{Equation 11.3}$$

Note that when the regression equation is based on standardized scores, the constant disappears (because the mean of all z-distributions is zero). For the data shown in Table 11.1, the standardized regression equation is found to be

$$\text{Predicted } Z_{\text{grade}} = .246\ Z_{\text{GPA}} - .343 Z_{\text{DaysAbsnt}} + .322 Z_{\text{HrsStudy}}$$

The relative magnitudes of the beta weights in the standardized equation are more helpful than the regression coefficients from the unstandardized equation in indexing the relative importance of the variables in predicting the value of the dependent variable within the context of the other independent variables in the equation.

A more interpretable measure of each independent variable's influence on the dependent variable in the context of other independent variables can be obtained from a measure referred to in *SPSS* as the part (or, more commonly, semipartial) correlation. The part correlation between, for example, independent variable 1 and the dependent variable is the correlation between these variables obtained after removing from independent variable 1 all variance it has in common with all other independent variables. In a sense, part correlation is the correlation between what is unique in an independent variable (with respect to all other independent variables in an analysis) and the dependent variable. In the case of just two independent variables X_1 and X_2, the part correlation between dependent variable Y and X_1 can be found from the formula

$$r_{Y(X_1 \cdot X_2)} = \frac{r_{YX_1} - r_{YX_2} r_{X_1 X_2}}{\sqrt{\left(1 - r_{X_1 X_2}^2\right)}} \qquad\qquad \text{Equation 11.4}$$

Part correlation values for the three independent variables of our example will be pointed out when the regression output is described. It should be understood that the sum of the squared part correlations values of all independent variables does not necessarily equal R^2 because the variance that all independent variables have in common with the dependent variable is ignored. The variance that all independent variables have in common with the dependent variable may be found by subtracting the sum of the squared part correlations values of all independent variables from R^2.

The degree to which the independent variables in the regression equation help predict values of the dependent variable is summarized in the coefficient R^2. For the data shown in Table 11.1, R^2 is found to have the value .651. The value indicates that when GPA, days absent, and hours of study are used to predict a student's grade, about 65% of the variance in students' grades is removed. Whether the R^2 value is statistically significant can be assessed from an F ratio calculated from the formula

$$F = \frac{R^2 / k}{1 - R^2 / N - k - 1}$$
                                                                                          Equation 11.5

where k = the number of independent variables,
N = the number of subjects.

For our example data, F is found to be 14.33, a value that is highly significant ($p < .001$).

Another index of the effectiveness of a regression equation in predicting values of the dependent variable is the standard error of the estimate. The statistic estimates the population standard deviation of the residuals of the dependent variable (i.e., the population standard deviations of the distances represented by the arrows in Figure 11.1). The statistic is defined by the formula

$$Standard\ Error\ of\ the\ Estimate = \sqrt{\frac{\sum (Y_i - \widetilde{Y}_i)^2}{N - k - 1}}$$
                                                                                          Equation 11.6

Note that the value of the standard error or the estimate can also be obtained by taking the square root of the mean square residual shown in the *ANOVA* table that tests the significance of R. In general, small values of the standard error of the estimate indicate more accurate predictions.

Requesting a Multiple Regression Analysis

Form of the Data

To analyze data using multiple regression, each case (i.e., line of data in the spreadsheet of the **SPSS Statistics Data Editor**) should consist of a value of each independent variable and a dependent variable. If an independent variable is measured on a nominal (or ordinal) scale that consists of just two values, the values can be coded with (arbitrarily assigned) numeric values 0 and 1. The result of entering data of the 27 participants depicted in Table 11.1 into the **SPSS Statistics Data Editor** is shown below. Note that the order in which columns of variables are entered into the spreadsheet is arbitrary; furthermore, variables not essential to the analysis can be included in the spreadsheet but not subsequently selected for analysis in the multiple regression procedure.

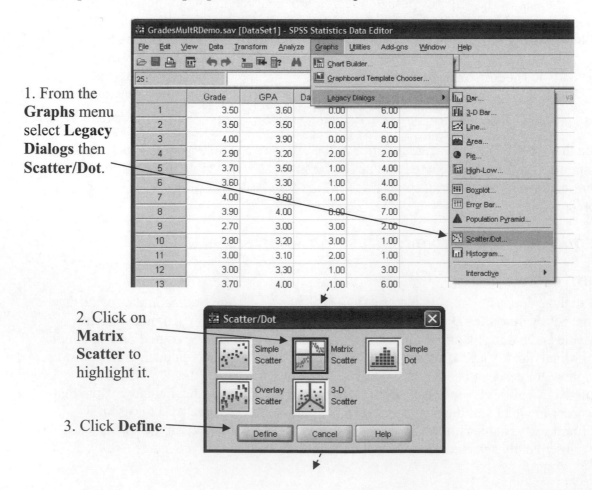

Screening the Data for Linearity

Before running a multiple regression analysis, it is advisable to check whether the dependent variable is linearly related to each of the independent variables. This can be done with the aid of scatterplots. A suitable method for requesting these multiple scatterplots and the output produced for our example are shown below.

4. Highlight the names of the dependent and independent variables and transfer them to the **Matrix Variables** pane.

5. Click **OK**.

1. Look for the name of the dependent variable.

2. Inspect the scatterplots in that row to evaluate whether the dependent variable is linearly related to each independent variable.

None of the scatterplots in this row reveal serious departures from linearity.

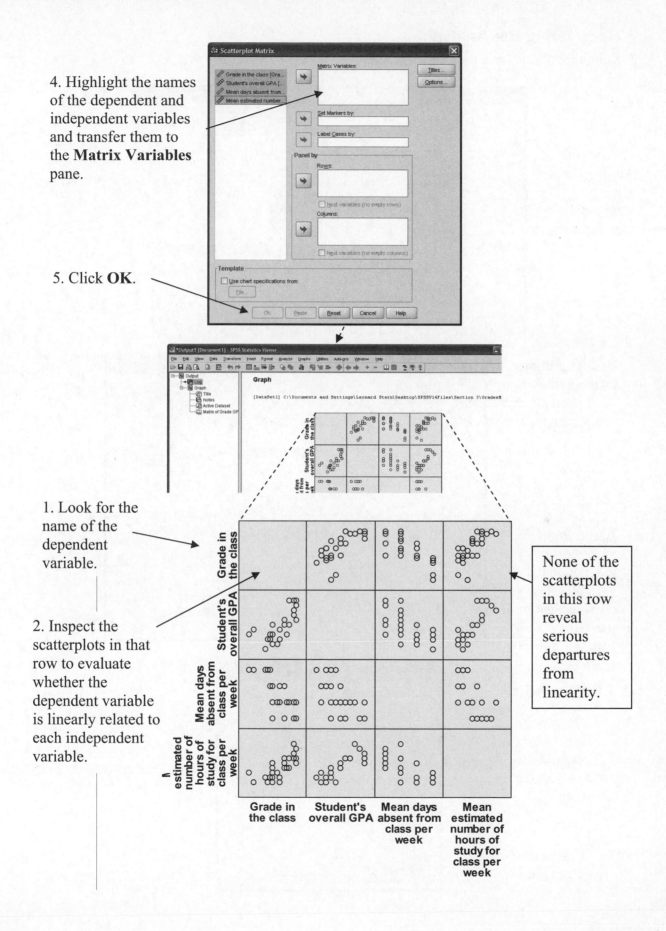

Requesting the Analysis

Suitable options for a multiple regression analysis are shown below:

1. From the **Analyze** menu select **Regression** then **Linear**.

2. Highlight the name of the dependent variable.

3. Click this arrow to transfer the variable.

4. Highlight the names of the independent variables and transfer them to the **Independent(s)** field.

5. Click **Statistics**.

6. Click in each box to select the measures shown.

7. Click **Continue**.

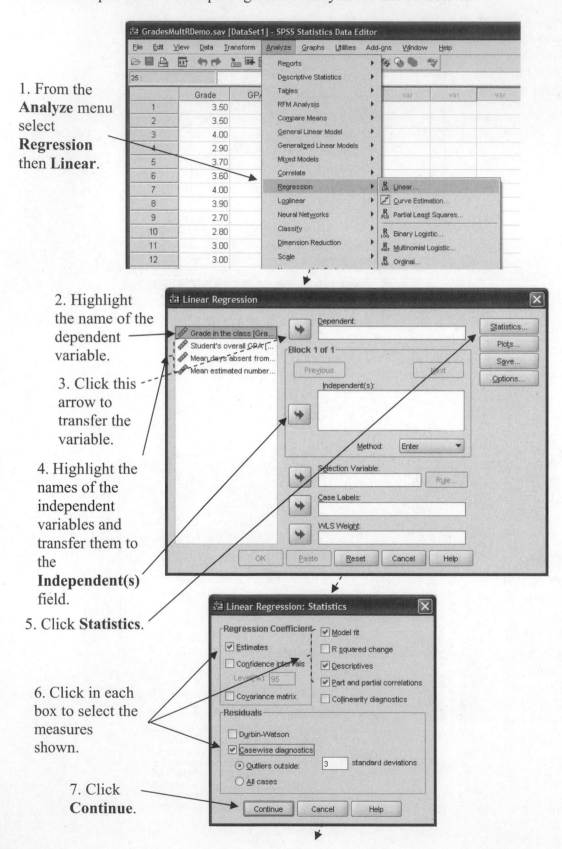

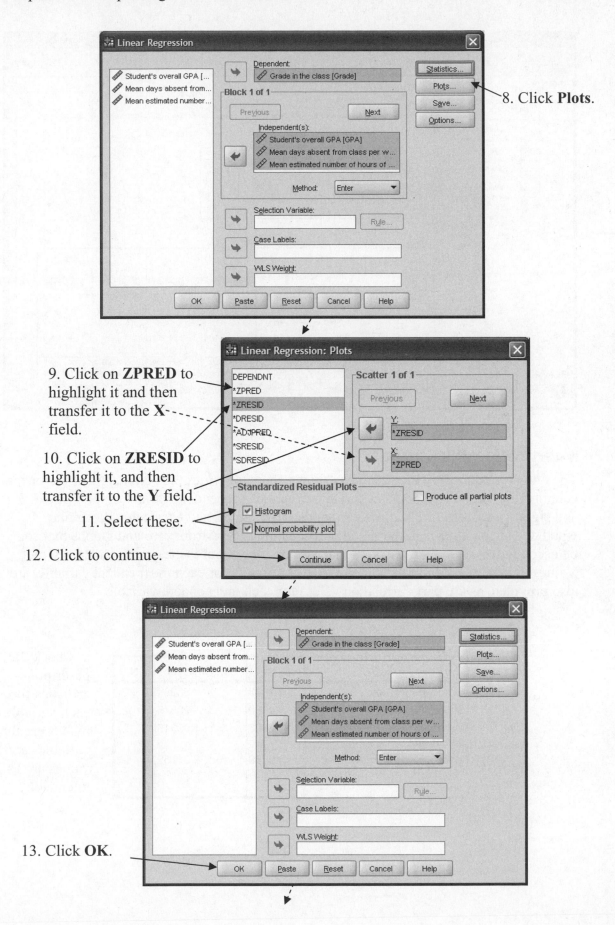

8. Click **Plots**.

9. Click on **ZPRED** to highlight it and then transfer it to the **X** field.

10. Click on **ZRESID** to highlight it, and then transfer it to the **Y** field.

11. Select these.

12. Click to continue.

13. Click **OK**.

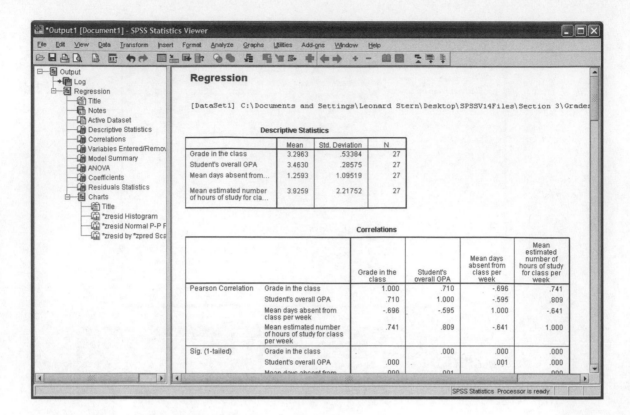

Interpreting the Output

The output produced by the selections shown above provides the parameters of the linear equation that predicts dependent variable from the independent variables, the value of R^2, and significance tests for R^2. In addition, there are significance tests that determine whether each parameter in the regression equation differs from zero and graphs that can be used to assess whether distributional assumptions about the residuals have been met. Values of beta, the standardized regression coefficient for each independent variable, are also provided, as are part correlation values for each independent variable.

Descriptive Statistics

	Mean	Std. Deviation	N
Grade in the class	3.2963	.53384	27
Student's overall GPA	3.4630	.28575	27
Mean days absent from class per week	1.2593	1.09519	27
Mean estimated number of hours of study for class per week	3.9259	2.21752	27

1. Check the descriptive statistics for each variable to make sure the variables and values are as intended.

Correlations

		Grade in the class	Student's overall GPA	Mean days absent from class per week	Mean estimated number of hours of study for class per week
Pearson Correlation	Grade in the class	1.000	.710	-.696	.741
	Student's overall GPA	.710	1.000	-.595	.809
	Mean days absent from class per week	-.696	-.595	1.000	-.641
	Mean estimated number of hours of study for class per week	.741	.809	-.641	1.000
Sig. (1-tailed)	Grade in the class		.000	.000	.000
	Student's overall GPA	.000		.001	.000
	Mean days absent from class per week	.000	.001		.000
	Mean estimated number of hours of study for class per week	.000	.000	.000	
N	Grade in the class	27	27	27	27
	Student's overall GPA	27	27	27	27
	Mean days absent from class per week	27	27	27	27
	Mean estimated number of hours of study for class per week	27	27	27	27

3. Look at this row to find the r value for each pair of variables in the analysis; this row shows the significance.

These are the r values for the dependent variable and each independent variable. Each r is highly significant.

These are the r values of pairs of independent variables. Each r is highly significant.

Variables Entered/Removed[b]

Model	Variables Entered	Variables Removed	Method
1	Mean estimated number of hours of study for class per week, Mean days absent from class per week, Student's overall GPA	.	Enter

a. All requested variables entered.

b. Dependent Variable: Grade in the class

4a. Look at this table for the R and R^2 values.

From this and the next table it can be seen that the obtained R^2 value of .651 is highly significant.

Model Summary[b]

Model	R	R Square	Adjusted R Square	Std. Error of the Estimate
1	.807[a]	.651	.606	.33509

a. Predictors: (Constant), Mean estimated number of hours of study for class per week, Mean days absent from class per week, Student's overall GPA

b. Dependent Variable: Grade in the class

This estimates the population standard deviation of the residuals (i.e., standard deviation of errors in prediction).

The obtained R^2 value of .651 is highly significant.

4b. This table shows whether the R and R^2 values are significant and gives data used in reporting the outcome of the significance test.

ANOVA[b]

Model		Sum of Squares	df	Mean Square	F	Sig.
1	Regression	4.827	3	1.609	14.329	.000[a]
	Residual	2.583	23	.112		
	Total	7.410	26			

a. Predictors: (Constant), Mean estimated number of hours of study for class per week, Mean days absent from class per week, Student's overall GPA

b. Dependent Variable: Grade in the class

Coefficients[a]

Model		Unstandardized Coefficients		Standardized Coefficients	t	Sig.	Correlations		
		B	Std. Error	Beta			Zero-order	Partial	Part
1	(Constant)	1.614	1.268		1.273	.216			
	Student's overall GPA	.459	.397	.246	1.156	.260	.710	.234	.142
	Mean days absent from class per week	-.167	.079	-.343	-2.108	.046	-.696	-.402	-.260
	Mean estimated number of hours of study for class per week	.078	.054	.322	1.447	.161	.741	.289	.178

a. Dependent Variable: Grade in the class

5a. Use this column to find the parameters of the regression equation in its unstandardized form.

5b. Use this column to find the standardized regression coefficients.

6. Details about significance tests of the regression equation's coefficients are here. They also apply to these coefficients.

Degrees of freedom for these t-tests is 23 (the same as df residual in the *ANOVA* table).

7. These are the part correlation coefficients that indicate the unique correlation of each independent variable to the dependent variable.

Residuals Statistics[a]

	Minimum	Maximum	Mean	Std. Deviation	N
Predicted Value	2.6435	4.0231	3.2963	.43088	27
Residual	-.85862	.43674	.00000	.31517	27
Std. Predicted Value	-1.515	1.687	.000	1.000	27
Std. Residual	-2.562	1.303	.000	.941	27

a. Dependent Variable: Grade in the class

For sample sizes of less than 1000, an outlier is a point whose $|std.residual| \geq 3.3$. No point in the data falls into this category.

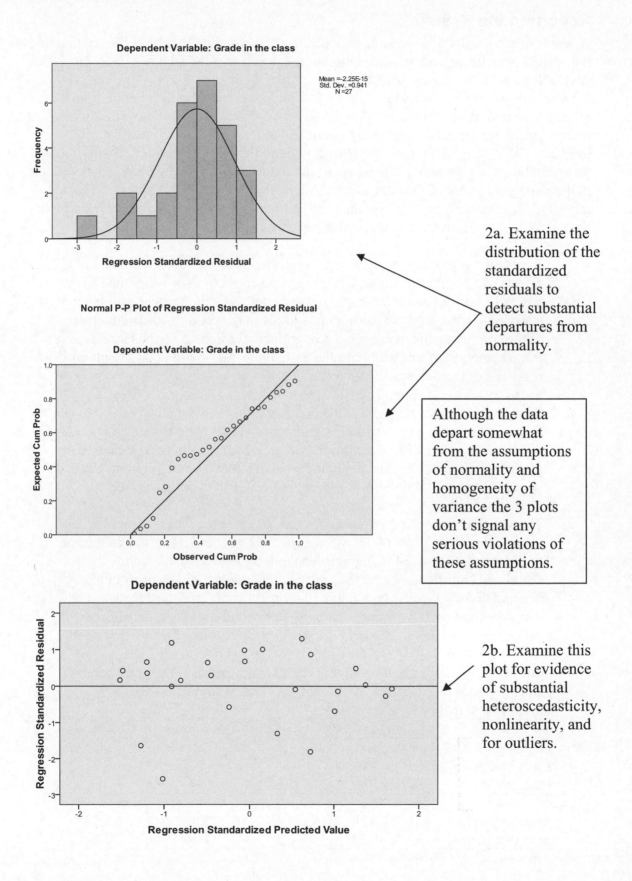

Dependent Variable: Grade in the class

Mean =-2.25E-15
Std. Dev. =0.941
N =27

Normal P-P Plot of Regression Standardized Residual

Dependent Variable: Grade in the class

Dependent Variable: Grade in the class

2a. Examine the distribution of the standardized residuals to detect substantial departures from normality.

Although the data depart somewhat from the assumptions of normality and homogeneity of variance the 3 plots don't signal any serious violations of these assumptions.

2b. Examine this plot for evidence of substantial heteroscedasticity, nonlinearity, and for outliers.

Reporting the Results

A report of the results of a multiple regression analysis should include a description of the variables involved and an explanation of the purpose of the analysis. It is also advisable to provide values (perhaps in the form of a table) of simple correlations between all pairs of variables as well as descriptive statistics for each variable. Results of the regression analysis should include values of the unstandardized and standardized regression coefficients accompanied by tests of their significance. The value of R^2 together with results of a test of its significance should also be provided. If appropriate, there can be an assessment of the independent contribution of each independent variable to predicting the value of the dependent variable. For this purpose, values of the each independent variable's part (i.e., semipartial) correlation with the dependent variable can be reported. The following summary illustrates these ideas:

> A multiple regression analysis was conducted to assess the simultaneous effects of a student's current GPA, the number of days per week the student typically skips class, and number of hours per week the student devotes to studying for the class on the student's grade in the class. Informal analysis of the data using histograms and scatterplots revealed no serious threats to the assumption of linearity or to the underlying distributional assumptions of residuals of the dependent variable.
>
> Simple correlation values of all pairs of variables in the analysis are shown in Table 11.2 together with their significance values. The table also includes the mean and standard deviation of each variable. The equation that predicts grade in the class from the three independent variables was found to be
> Grade = 1.614 + .459 GPA - .167 days absent + .078 hours studied.
>
> The value of R^2 was .65 (adjusted R^2 was .61), a value that was highly significant, $F (3, 23) = 14.33$, $MS_{residual} = .112$, $p < .001$. The standard error of the estimate was .34. Although each independent variable alone correlated significantly with the dependent variable, only days absent accounted for a significant amount of unique variance of the dependent variable. Semipartial r values and values of beta for all the independent variables are shown in Table 11.3 together with results of significance tests.

Table 11.2. Variables in the multiple regression analysis. The top panel shows r values for variables in the analysis. The bottom panel shows descriptive statistics for the variables.

	Grade (DV)	GPA	Days absent	Hours study
GPA	.71**			
Days absent	-.70**	-.60**		
Hours study	.74**	.81**	-.64**	
Mean	3.30	3.46	1.26	3.93
Standard deviation	0.53	0.29	1.10	2.22

** $p < .01$

Table 11.3. Semipartial r values and beta values together with significance tests for independent variables in the multiple regression analysis.

	Semipartial r	beta	t (23)	Significance
GPA	.14	.25	1.16	.26
Days absent	-.26	-.34	-2.11	.05
Hours study	.18	.32	1.15	.16

[handwritten annotations: Unique correlation | Relative imp. of one variable over another]

Hierarchical Multiple Regression

The example described above utilized a regression approach known as simultaneous regression because all independent variables were entered simultaneously into the equation that predicted values of the dependent variable. In an alternate procedure known as hierarchical multiple regression, independent variables are successively introduced into the prediction equation. With hierarchical multiple regression one is able to see how R^2 changes as successive independent variables (or sets of independent variables) are introduced.

Why is order of entering variables into a regression analysis important to the outcome? The reason is that in a regression analysis, the magnitude of a variable's standardized regression coefficient and its significance reflects the variable's influence on the dependent variable that is independent of influences exerted by other independent variables. It's as if an independent variable does not get credit for its overall degree of correlation with the dependent variable but for only the correlation that is independent of the correlations of all other independent variables with the dependent variable.

Consider the correlations of the individual independent variables with the dependent variable for the grade data summarized in Table 11.2. Of the three independent variables, the variable hours of study has the highest correlation with grade and the relation is highly statistically significant. However, as can be seen in Table 11.3, the beta value for hours of study and the semipartial correlation of hours of study with grade are neither the highest nor statistically significant. The different outcomes are due to the presence of other independent variables that correlate with grade and with hours of study in the multiple regression analysis. An analogy might help make this more understandable. Think of being in a class and arriving at an answer to a question posed by the instructor at the same time other students arrive at the answer. If you all call out the answer at the same time, none of you will get all the credit; however you can get some credit if you suggest a modification of the answer that improves it.

If one knows (or suspects) that a particular independent variable is causally related to a dependent variable, (and possibly to other independent variables) hierarchical regression could be appropriate. With this method, independent variables are added to the regression equation in steps according to logical or theoretical considerations. As a result, the independent variable (or set of variables) entered first gets full "credit" for the degree to which it correlates with the dependent variable. Variables entered subsequently are assessed for the degree to which each accounts for additional variance of the dependent variable. To return to our classroom analogy, this situation is comparable to a teacher calling on you to answer a question to which a number of students raise their hand in response. If your answer is correct, you get full credit; others can get credit to the extent they can "tweak" your answer to improve it.

As an illustration, assume that the number of hours a person studies and the number of class meetings the person attends are the cause of a person's grade in a class (as well as the cause of a person's GPA). We could perform a hierarchical regression analysis to look for evidence consistent with this idea (but it would not constitute proof of the idea) by first entering the variables **HrsStudy** and **DaysAbsnt** into the regression analysis and determining if they account for a significant proportion of variance in **Grade**. Then, in step 2, the variable **GPA** could be added to the equation. Of interest is how much additional variance in **Grade** is explained by the variable **GPA,** and if the additional explained variance differs significantly from chance. If the hypothesis about causal relations is correct, then in step 2 when **GPA** is added to the prediction equation, there might be little or no additional variance in grade explained (because the variables **HrsStudy** and **DaysAbsnt** also predict **GPA** and these variables have already been entered). The steps shown below illustrate the process.

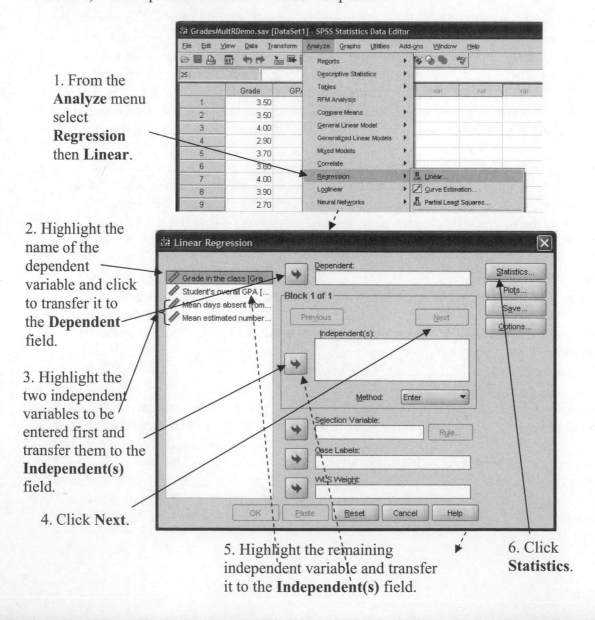

1. From the **Analyze** menu select **Regression** then **Linear**.

2. Highlight the name of the dependent variable and click to transfer it to the **Dependent** field.

3. Highlight the two independent variables to be entered first and transfer them to the **Independent(s)** field.

4. Click **Next**.

5. Highlight the remaining independent variable and transfer it to the **Independent(s)** field.

6. Click **Statistics**.

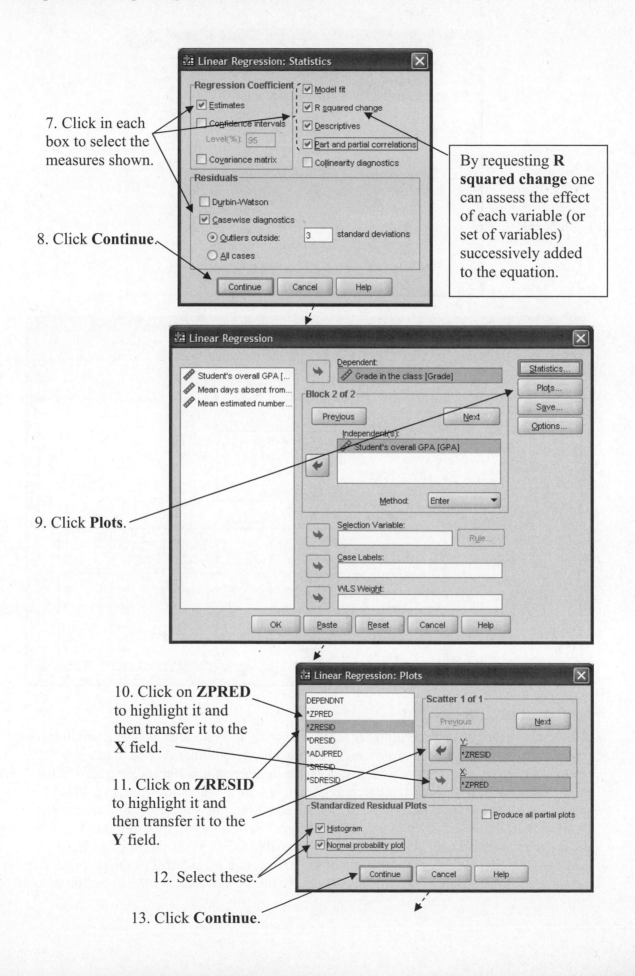

7. Click in each box to select the measures shown.

8. Click **Continue**.

By requesting **R squared change** one can assess the effect of each variable (or set of variables) successively added to the equation.

9. Click **Plots**.

10. Click on **ZPRED** to highlight it and then transfer it to the **X** field.

11. Click on **ZRESID** to highlight it and then transfer it to the **Y** field.

12. Select these.

13. Click **Continue**.

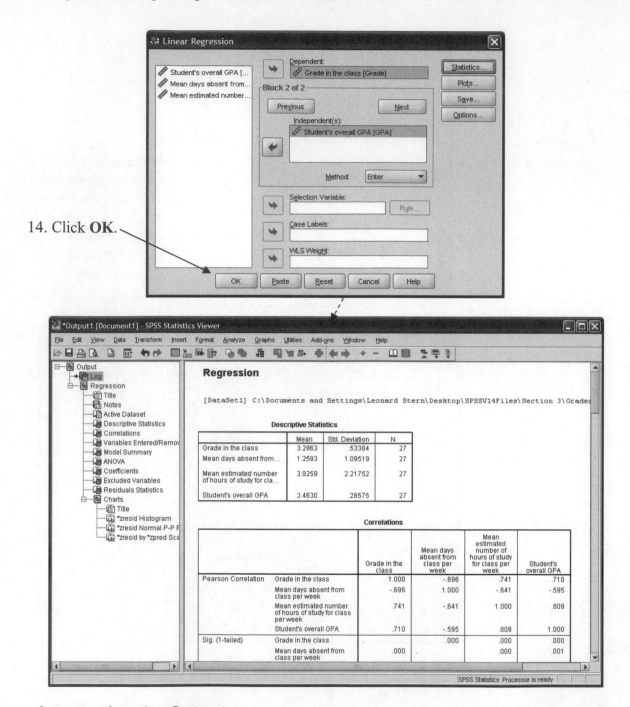

14. Click **OK**.

Interpreting the Output

Although the output of a hierarchical regression analysis resembles that of a simultaneous model in many respects, a key difference is that a model number is used to identify results of each regression analysis as successive independent variables are added to the prediction equation. In hierarchical regression there are as many models as variables (or sets of variables) entered successively into the equation. For our example, there are two models: the first predicts grade from the combination of hours studied and number of days absent per week; the second adds in the variable GPA. The success of each successive model is described in terms of R^2 change, that is, in terms of the proportion of variance of the dependent variable accounted for by the variable(s) entered for the current model over and above that accounted for by the previous model in the sequence (for step 1, R^2 change is compared to zero). These changes in R^2 and the accompanying significance tests are obtained from the table labeled **Model Summary** highlighted in step 4b below.

Descriptive Statistics

	Mean	Std. Deviation	N
Grade in the class	3.2963	.53384	27
Mean days absent from class per week	1.2593	1.09519	27
Mean estimated number of hours of study for class per week	3.9259	2.21752	27
Student's overall GPA	3.4630	.28575	27

1. Check the descriptive statistics for each variable to make sure the variables and values are as intended.

Note: the output for these two steps is identical to that for the simultaneous model and is not shown here.

2a. Examine the distribution of the standardized residuals to detect substantial departures from normality.

2b. Examine the scatterplot of **zresid** and **zpred** for evidence of substantial heteroscedasticity, nonlinearity, and for outliers.

3a. Look at this row of the table to find the r value for each pair of predictor variables in the analysis.

Correlations

		Grade in the class	Mean days absent from class per week	Mean estimated number of hours of study for class per week	Student's overall GPA
Pearson Correlation	Grade in the class	1.000	-.696	.741	.710
	Mean days absent from class per week	-.696	1.000	-.641	-.595
	Mean estimated number of hours of study for class per week	.741	-.641	1.000	.809
	Student's overall GPA	.710	-.595	.809	1.000
Sig. (1-tailed)	Grade in the class	.	.000	.000	.000
	Mean days absent from class per week	.000	.	.000	.001
	Mean estimated number of hours of study for class per week	.000	.000	.	.000
	Student's overall GPA	.000	.001	.000	.
N	Grade in the class	27	27	27	27
	Mean days absent from class per week	27	27	27	27
	Mean estimated number of hours of study for class per week	27	27	27	27
	Student's overall GPA	27	27	27	27

3b. Look at this row of the table to find the significance of each r value.

Variables Entered/Removed[b]

4a. This table shows the variables added to the equation for each model.

The first equation uses only **HrsStudy** and **DaysAbsnt**.

The second equation adds in **GPA**.

Model	Variables Entered	Variables Removed	Method
1	Mean estimated number of hours of study for class per week, Mean days absent from class per week[a]		. Enter
2	Student's overall GPA[a]		. Enter

a. All requested variables entered.

b. Dependent Variable: Grade in the class

These are the R and R^2 values for each model. Their significance is tested in the **ANOVA** table below.

4b. This table shows measures needed to evaluate the contribution of each successive model to predicting the values of the dependent variable.

Model Summary[c]

Model	R	R Square	Adjusted R Square	Std. Error of the Estimate	Change Statistics				
					R Square Change	F Change	df1	df2	Sig. F Change
1	.794[a]	.631	.600	.33743	.631	20.538	2	24	.000
2	.807[b]	.651	.606	.33509	.020	1.336	1	23	.260

a. Predictors: (Constant), Mean estimated number of hours of study for class per week, Mean days absent from class per week

b. Predictors: (Constant), Mean estimated number of hours of study for class per week, Mean days absent from class per week, Student's overall GPA

c. Dependent Variable: Grade in the class

5. Look in this table to see if each model aids significantly in predicting values of the dependent variable.

This column shows the R^2 change for each model.

Each row shows significance test data for each model's R^2 change.

Note that the F value for model 1 is identical to that shown in line 1 of the previous table.

ANOVA[c]

Model		Sum of Squares	df	Mean Square	F	Sig.
1	Regression	4.677	2	2.338	20.538	.000[a]
	Residual	2.733	24	.114		
	Total	7.410	26			
2	Regression	4.827	3	1.609	14.329	.000[b]
	Residual	2.583	23	.112		
	Total	7.410	26			

a. Predictors: (Constant), Mean estimated number of hours of study for class per week, Mean days absent from class per week

b. Predictors: (Constant), Mean estimated number of hours of study for class per week, Mean days absent from class per week, Student's overall GPA

c. Dependent Variable: Grade in the class

6. The regression coefficients for each model's equation together with their significance tests are found in this table.

Coefficients[a]

Model		Unstandardized Coefficients		Standardized Coefficients	t	Sig.	Correlations		
		B	Std. Error	Beta			Zero-order	Partial	Part
1	(Constant)	3.054	.238		12.818	.000			
	Mean days absent from class per week	-.183	.079	-.375	-2.322	.029	-.696	-.428	-.288
	Mean estimated number of hours of study for class per week	.120	.039	.500	3.096	.005	.741	.534	.384
2	(Constant)	1.614	1.268		1.273	.216			
	Mean days absent from class per week	-.167	.079	-.343	-2.108	.046	-.696	-.402	-.260
	Mean estimated number of hours of study for class per week	.078	.054	.322	1.447	.161	.741	.289	.178
	Student's overall GPA	.459	.397	.246	1.156	.260	.710	.234	.142

a. Dependent Variable: Grade in the class

These columns show details of significance tests of the regression equation's coefficients. They also apply to semipartial *r* values.

Excluded Variables[b]

Model		Beta In	t	Sig.	Partial Correlation	Collinearity Statistics Tolerance
1	Student's overall GPA	.246[a]	1.156	.260	.234	.336

a. Predictors in the Model: (Constant), Mean estimated number of hours of study for class per week, Mean days absent from class per week

b. Dependent Variable: Grade in the class

Residuals Statistics[a]

	Minimum	Maximum	Mean	Std. Deviation	N
Predicted Value	2.6435	4.0231	3.2963	.43088	27
Residual	-.85862	.43674	.00000	.31517	27
Std. Predicted Value	-1.515	1.687	.000	1.000	27
Std. Residual	-2.562	1.303	.000	.941	27

a. Dependent Variable: Grade in the class

Reporting the Results

Here's how the outcome of the regression analysis could be reported:

A hierarchical multiple regression analysis was conducted to examine the relation of the dependent variable grade in a class to the independent variables number of days per week the student is typically absent from class, number of hours per week the student devotes to studying for the class, and the student's overall GPA. Informal analysis of the data using histograms and scatterplots revealed no serious threats to the assumption of linearity or to the underlying distributional assumptions of residuals of the dependent variable. Simple correlation values of all pairs of variables in the analysis are shown in Table 11.2 together with their significance values. The table also includes the mean and standard deviation of each variable.

To evaluate the idea that a student's grade in a class (as well as a student's overall GPA) results primarily from the number of hours of study the student devotes to the class as well as the number of class sessions the student fails to attend, step 1 of a hierarchical regression procedure predicted grade in the class simultaneously from the variables hours studied and number of days per week the student typically is absent from class. In step 2, the additional contribution of overall GPA to predicting grade in the class was assessed. The R^2 change in step 1 was .63, a value that was highly significant, $F(2, 24) = 20.54$, $MS_{residual} = .114$, $p < .001$, indicating that the independent variables hours of study and number of days per week absent from class together explained a significant proportion of variance of the variable grade in the class. The inclusion of a student's GPA in the prediction equation did not significantly increase the proportion of explained variance in the variable grade in the class, R^2 change = .02, $F(1, 23) = 1.34$, $MS_{residual} = .112$, $p > .25$.

Table 11.4 shows the values of beta for independent variables included at each step of the procedure together with significance tests. As indicated in the table, in step 1 the variables number of hours of study and mean days absent from class each significantly improved prediction of grade in the class.

Table 11.4. The top panel shows semipartial r values and beta values together with significance tests for independent variables for step 1 of the hierarchical multiple regression analysis. The bottom panel shows these values for step 2.

	Semipartial r	beta	$t(24)$	Significance
Days absent	-.29	-.38	-2.32	.03
Hours study	.38	.50	3.10	.01
			$t(23)$	
GPA	.14	.25	1.16	.26
Days absent	-.26	-.34	-2.11	.05
Hours study	.18	.32	1.15	.16

Using Hierarchical Regression to Control Nuisance Variables

An important application of hierarchical regression is controlling for any role that extraneous variables may have in influencing the relation among other variables. For example, one may be interested in assessing the relation between smoking and lung cancer. If it is suggested that the relation between smoking and lung cancer are mediated by the amount of stress a person is under (i.e., stress causes both a person to smoke and compromises the immune system so that lung cancer is more likely), one can determine whether smoking and lung cancer are still related over and above the effects of stress using hierarchical regression. This could be accomplished by first entering a variable that measures stress into the equation that predicts incidence of lung cancer and then, in step 2, entering the variable that measures smoking behavior. If the R^2 change on step 2 is significant, one can conclude that smoking is related to lung cancer over and above the effect of stress on lung cancer.

The unwanted influence of more than a single independent variable can be controlled in this way. If one wishes to test whether smoking and lung cancer are related after controlling for a person's daily stress level, socioeconomic status, and size of the city in which they reside, these three variables can be included in the first step of a hierarchical regression analysis before assessing the R^2 change produced by entering a measure of smoking behavior into the equation that predicts incidence of lung cancer.

Exploring for Optimal Independent Variables

When no theory is available to help guide a researcher's selection of variables to include as predictors in a regression analysis, a variety of procedures are available to help make these selections. For example, imagine that a researcher wishes to predict the SAT score of high school students and has available 50 variables that provide information about the student's performance in high school, personality characteristics of the student obtained from standardized tests, and socioeconomic data pertaining to the student's household. Although the regression equation could include all 50 variables, it is unlikely that all will contribute significantly to predicting SAT score. Instead, pairs of variables or sets of variables may be correlated to the extent that some should not be, or even could not be, included in the prediction equation.

The possibility of strongly correlated variables not being able to be included in a regression equation is described as the problem of multicolinearity. To understand the problem, consider the data in Figure 11.2 that shows a three-dimensional scatterplot of two perfectly correlated independent variables, X_1 and X_2, and their relation to a dependent variable Y. You can see that if one attempted to locate a best-fitting plane for the data (best-fitting in that it minimized that sum of the squared differences between actual and predicted Y values), there would be nothing "supporting" the plane: the plane could be angled in many different ways. Thus, there would be no unique solution to the problem of establishing slope parameters on the Y, X_1 and Y, X_2 coordinate axes. This is the multicolinearity problem, and it occurs not just when independent variables are perfectly correlated, but when their correlation is sufficiently high.

Figure 11.2. A depiction of highly correlated independent variables X_1 and X_2. A best-fitting plane for the data would be difficult to locate because it would have no "support;" instead, it could be rotated around the axis (shown as a dotted line) formed by the perfectly correlated variables X_1 and X_2. The open circles show predicted values of Y. Actual Y values (not shown) could be directly above or below each estimated value.

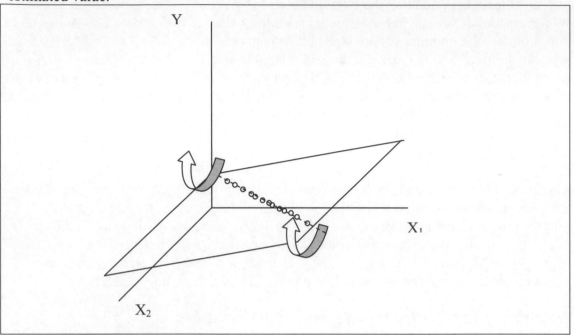

Measuring Multicolinearity

One measure of multicolinearity is tolerance. In multiple regression, tolerance is the proportion of variance that an independent variable does not have in common with other independent variables. For example, if there are three independent variables in a regression model and the tolerance value of one of the independent variables, X_3, is .34, it means that 34% of the variance of X_3 is not explained by (i.e., is independent of) the other two independent variables. Multicolinearity is said to be a problem if a variable's tolerance value is less than 0.10.

A related measure of multicolinearity is the variance inflation factor (VIF). The variance inflation factor of a variable is the reciprocal of its tolerance. Thus, if a variable has a tolerance of .34, its VIF is $1/.34 = 2.94$. Thus, multicolinearity is a problem when a variable's VIF is greater than 10.00.

Methods for Selecting Optimal Independent Variables

Table 11.5 presents some methods *SPSS* makes available for selecting variables to include in a linear regression model. The most commonly used method is the stepwise procedure.

Table 11.5. Descriptions of some procedures available in *SPSS* for selecting variables in a multiple regression analysis. The steps outlined in column three assume there are three independent variables available for inclusion in the prediction equation.

Method	Procedure	Outline of Steps in the Process
Enter	All available independent variables are entered simultaneously into the regression equation.	$Y = a + b_1 X_1 + b_2 X_2 + b_3 X_3$
Forward	In the first step, the variable is entered that has the highest correlation with the dependent variable. If the resulting r^2 is significant, another variable is selected that produces the highest R^2 change. If that R^2 change is significant, the process continues until no significant R^2 change results.	Use the X that has the highest r^2_{YX}. Is r^2 significant? y / \ n $Y = a + b_1 X_i$ Stop. Add the X that gives highest R^2 change. Is R^2 change significant? y / \ n $Y = a + b_i X_i + b_j X_j$ Stop. Repeat step 2 until have to stop.
Backward	The process begins with all variables entered into the regression equation. Then the variable is removed that changes R^2 the least, provided that R^2 change is not significant (generally, its $p > .10$). The process continues in this way until removal of a variable significantly changes R^2.	Use all X_i in equation if they give signif. R^2. $Y = a + b_i X_i + b_j X_j + b_k X_k$. Remove X that gives smallest R^2 change. Is R^2 change significant? y / \ n Stop and use previous equation $Y = a + b_i X_i + b_j X_j$ (Keep that variable out of the equation). Repeat step 2 until have to stop.
Stepwise	Combines elements of the forward and backward procedures. In step 1 the variable is selected that correlates most highly with the dependent variable. Next, the variable is added that produces the greatest R^2 change as long as that change meets a significance criterion (generally lower than .05). Variables in the equation are then examined for removal. The variable that produces the smallest R^2 change is removed if that change is sufficiently small (the convention is a significance level of greater than.10). The entry and removal sequence continues until no more variables are eligible for entry.	Use the X that has the highest r^2_{YX}. Is r^2 significant? y / \ n $Y = a + b_i X_i$ Stop. Add the X that gives highest R^2 change. Is R^2 change significant? y / \ n $Y = a + b_i X_i + b_j X_j$ Stop. Use prior equation. Remove X that gives smallest R^2 change. Is R^2 change sufficiently small? y / \ n Remove the variable Keep current equation. Repeat steps 2 and 3 until have to stop.

Implementing a stepwise procedure will be illustrated using the data in our class grade data.

1. From the **Analyze** menu select **Regression** then **Linear**.

2. Highlight the name of the dependent variable.

3. Click this arrow to transfer the variable.

4. Highlight the names of the independent variables and transfer them to the **Independent(s)** field.

5. Click in the **Method:** field to highlight it; then, in the drop-down menu, click on **Stepwise**.

6. Click **Statistics**.

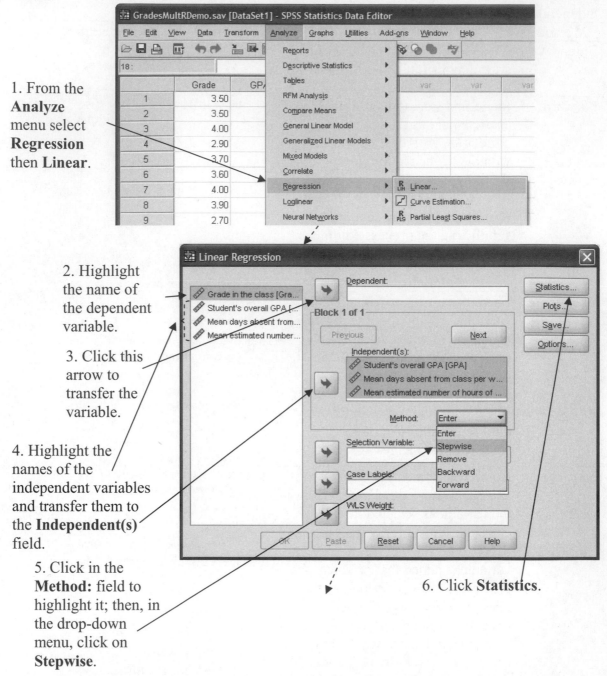

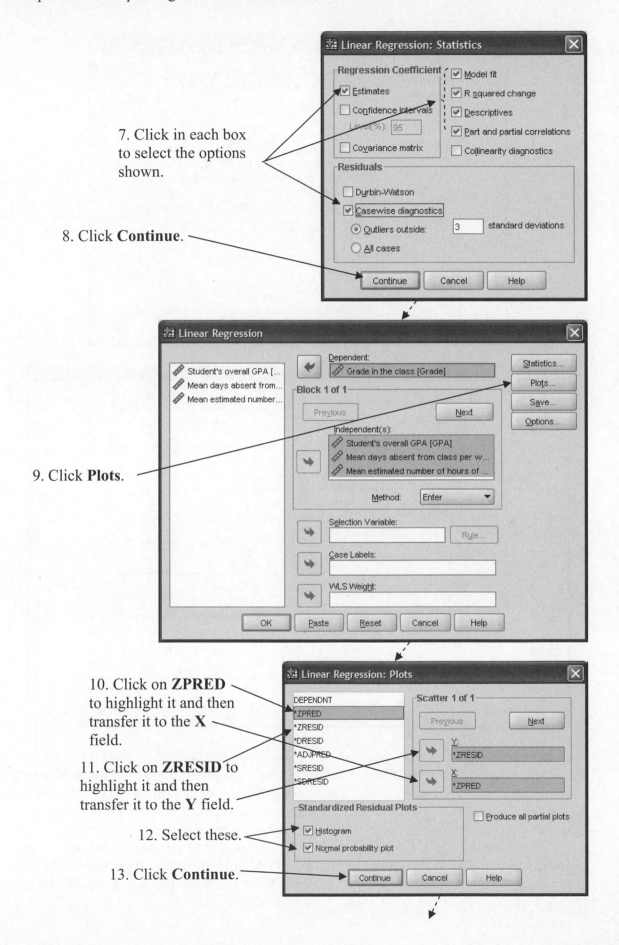

7. Click in each box to select the options shown.

8. Click **Continue**.

9. Click **Plots**.

10. Click on **ZPRED** to highlight it and then transfer it to the **X** field.

11. Click on **ZRESID** to highlight it and then transfer it to the **Y** field.

12. Select these.

13. Click **Continue**.

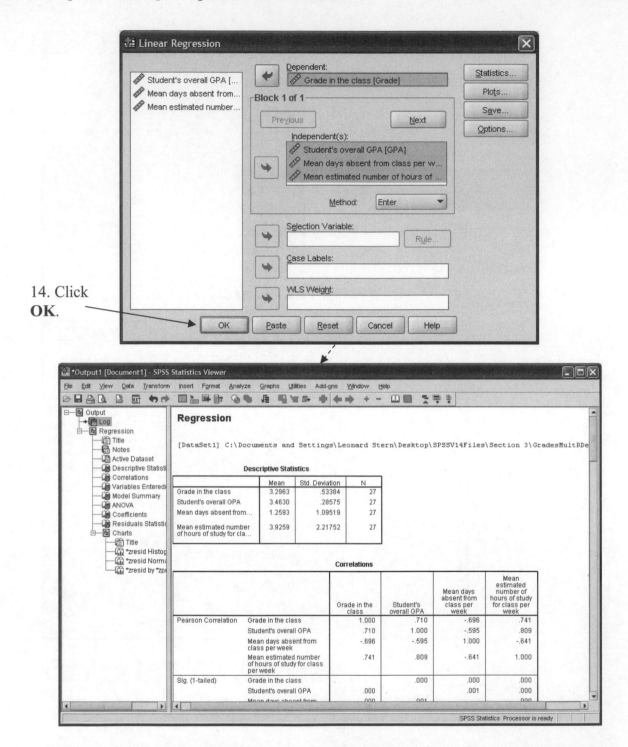

Output produced for this example is shown below. Notice in the table of correlations that the independent variable **HrsStudy** has the highest correlation (.741) with the dependent variable and that it appears in model 1 as the only independent variable. The table labeled **Excluded Variables** shows why model 2 adds the independent variable **DaysAbsnt**: the magnitude of its semipartial correlation with the dependent variable is higher than that of **GPA** and is statistically significant (it meets the criterion for entry into the model). Thus, as indicated in the **Model Change** and the **ANOVA** table, including **DaysAbsnt** in model 2 significantly improves prediction of the dependent variable to produce a model with an

R^2 of .631. Although the inclusion of **DaysAbsnt** in the model lowers the beta (and semipartial correlation) value for **HrsStudy** (due to their shared variance), the magnitude of beta for **HrsStudy** is still sufficiently high so that its significance value (.005) exceeds the level that would trigger its removal (.10). The variable **GPA** is not added in a third model because, as shown in the table of **Excluded Variables**, **GPA**'s beta value, at this point, does not reach statistical significance.

Descriptive Statistics

	Mean	Std. Deviation	N
Grade in the class	3.2963	.53384	27
Student's overall GPA	3.4630	.28575	27
Mean days absent from class per week	1.2593	1.09519	27
Mean estimated number of hours of study for class per week	3.9259	2.21752	27

1. Check the descriptive statistics for each variable to make sure the variables and values are as intended.

Correlations

		Grade in the class	Student's overall GPA	Mean days absent from class per week	Mean estimated number of hours of study for class per week
Pearson Correlation	Grade in the class	1.000	.710	-.696	.741
	Student's overall GPA	.710	1.000	-.595	.809
	Mean days absent from class per week	-.696	-.595	1.000	-.641
	Mean estimated number of hours of study for class per week	.741	.809	-.641	1.000
Sig. (1-tailed)	Grade in the class	.	.000	.000	.000
	Student's overall GPA	.000	.	.001	.000
	Mean days absent from class per week	.000	.001	.	.000
	Mean estimated number of hours of study for class per week	.000	.000	.000	.
N	Grade in the class	27	27	27	27
	Student's overall GPA	27	27	27	27
	Mean days absent from class per week	27	27	27	27
	Mean estimated number of hours of study for class per week	27	27	27	27

By looking at this column you can see which variable correlates most strongly with the dependent variable and will be selected for the first model.

Variables Entered/Removed[a]

Model	Variables Entered	Variables Removed	Method
1	Mean estimated number of hours of study for class per week	.	Stepwise (Criteria: Probability-of-F-to-enter <= .050, Probability-of-F-to-remove >= .100).
2	Mean days absent from class per week	.	Stepwise (Criteria: Probability-of-F-to-enter <= .050, Probability-of-F-to-remove >= .100).

a. Dependent Variable: Grade in the class

3. Note how many models are generated.

4. Note which variable is entered into or removed from each regression equation.

6. The R^2 change column shows how much more variance is explained as new models are generated.

Model Summary[c]

Model	R	R Square	Adjusted R Square	Std. Error of the Estimate	Change Statistics				
					R Square Change	F Change	df1	df2	Sig. F Change
1	.741[a]	.548	.530	.36586	.548	30.357	1	25	.000
2	.794[b]	.631	.600	.33743	.083	5.390	1	24	.029

a. Predictors: (Constant), Mean estimated number of hours of study for class per week

b. Predictors: (Constant), Mean estimated number of hours of study for class per week, Mean days absent from class per week

c. Dependent Variable: Grade in the class

ANOVA[c]

Model		Sum of Squares	df	Mean Square	F	Sig.
1	Regression	4.063	1	4.063	30.357	.000[a]
	Residual	3.346	25	.134		
	Total	7.410	26			
2	Regression	4.677	2	2.338	20.538	.000[b]
	Residual	2.733	24	.114		
	Total	7.410	26			

5. The bottom panel shows significance test results for the final model.

a. Predictors: (Constant), Mean estimated number of hours of study for class per week

b. Predictors: (Constant), Mean estimated number of hours of study for class per week, Mean days absent from class per week

c. Dependent Variable: Grade in the class

Coefficients[a]

Model		Unstandardized Coefficients		Standardized Coefficients	t	Sig.	Correlations		
		B	Std. Error	Beta			Zero-order	Partial	Part
1	(Constant)	2.596	.145		17.877	.000			
	Mean estimated number of hours of study for class per week	.178	.032	.741	5.510	.000	.741	.741	.741
2	(Constant)	3.054	.238		12.818	.000			
	Mean estimated number of hours of study for class per week	.120	.039	.500	3.096	.005	.741	.534	.384
	Mean days absent from class per week	-.183	.079	-.375	-2.322	.029	-.696	-.428	-.288

a. Dependent Variable: Grade in the class

7. These are the (unstandardized) regression coefficients for the final model and each one's significance

Excluded Variables[c]

Model		Beta In	t	Sig.	Partial Correlation	Collinearity Statistics
						Tolerance
1	Student's overall GPA	.321[a]	1.435	.164	.281	.346
	Mean days absent from class per week	-.375[a]	-2.322	.029	-.428	.589
2	Student's overall GPA	.246[b]	1.156	.260	.234	.336

a. Predictors in the Model: (Constant), Mean estimated number of hours of study for class per week

b. Predictors in the Model: (Constant), Mean estimated number of hours of study for class per week, Mean days absent from class per week

c. Dependent Variable: Grade in the class

By looking at this table you can see which variables are excluded at each step and the significance of each one's slope parameter.

Residuals Statistics[a]

	Minimum	Maximum	Mean	Std. Deviation	N
Predicted Value	2.6258	4.0170	3.2963	.42413	27
Residual	-.86664	.40660	.00000	.32419	27
Std. Predicted Value	-1.581	1.699	.000	1.000	27
Std. Residual	-2.568	1.205	.000	.961	27

a. Dependent Variable: Grade in the class

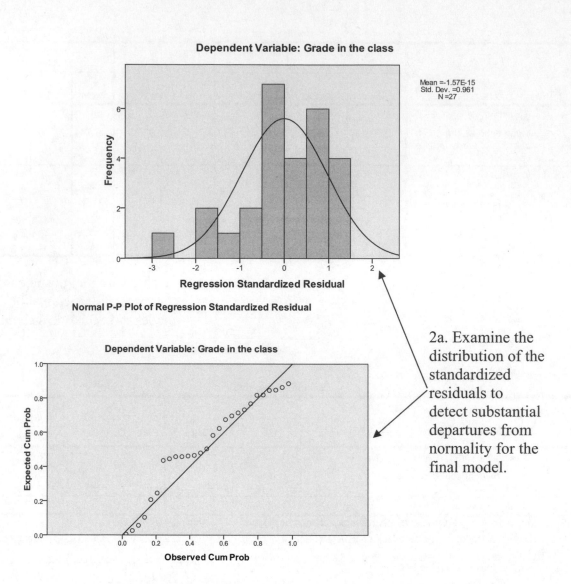

2a. Examine the distribution of the standardized residuals to detect substantial departures from normality for the final model.

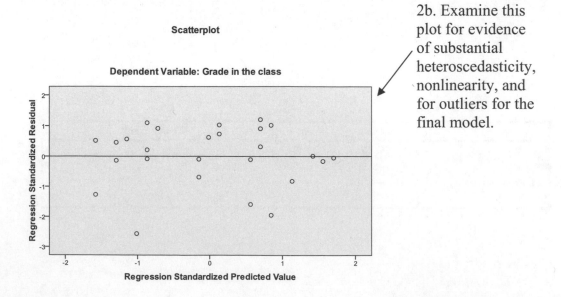

2b. Examine this plot for evidence of substantial heteroscedasticity, nonlinearity, and for outliers for the final model.

Exercises for Chapter 11

Exercise 11.1

For this exercise, use the file *04Cars.sav* available on the publisher's website for this text at the address http://www.pearsonhighered.com/stern2e. The data set is based on information obtained from Edmunds.com and is reprinted here with permission. Perform a multiple linear regression analysis to predict a car's highway gas mileage (variable **HiwayMPG**) from the following variables: **Engine**, **Cylinders**, **HP**, **Weight**, **Wheelbase**, and **Length**. Before performing the analysis, omit the data of the hybrid vehicles (case numbers 69, 70, and 94). Enter all the predictor variables simultaneously. From your printout, answer the following questions.
1.   Does it appear that the distributional assumptions of the residuals have been met?
2.   What is the numerical value of the simple correlation between the dependent variable and each predictor variable?
3.   Considering just the predictor variables, which two are most strongly related?
4.   What proportion of variance of the variable **HiwayMPG** is explained by all the predictors combined? Is that proportion statistically significant?
5.   What is the equation that predicts **HiwayMPG** from the (unstandardized) predictors?
6.   Using semipartial correlation values, list, in order of magnitude, the three variables in the equation most effective in predicting the value of **HiwayMPG**.
7.   Are there any cars in the data set that produce residuals that could be considered outliers? If so, which car(s)?

Exercise 11.2

A person investigating the relation between car weight and gas mileage reasons that because heavier cars tend to have bigger engines and because bigger engines weigh more, any relation between car weight and gas mileage may be "contaminated" by engine size. Use the data in the file *04Cars.sav* (see previous problem) to assess the relation between gas mileage (use **HiwayMPG**) and car weight (**Weight**) controlling for (i.e., over and above) the influence of engine size (**Engine**) on gas mileage. As in exercise 11.1, omit the data of the hybrid vehicles (case numbers 69, 70, and 94) before performing the analysis.

Exercise 11.3

The data in *Enroll.sav*, available on the publisher's website for this text at the address http://www.pearsonhighered.com/stern2e, show yearly fall undergraduate enrollments between 1961 and 1989 reported by the Office of Institutional Research at the University of New Mexico. The other variables show % unemployment for New Mexico (**Unemp**), number of students graduating that spring from high school (**Hgrad**), and the per capita income in Albuquerque in 1961 dollars (**Income**).
1.   Use the variables **Unemp**, **Hgrad**, and **Income** in a linear regression analysis to predict fall undergraduate enrollment. What is the equation? What is the value of R^2 for the equation?
2   What statistic could a person use to determine how much error in predicting student enrollment would have occurred if the equation specified in question 1 had been used between 1961 and 1989?

3. An administrator suggests that enrollments increase by some uniform amount each year and that it is not at all helpful to take into account any other variables included in the data file in order to optimally predict fall undergraduate enrollments. How can this idea be tested? Is there sufficient evidence to reject the administrator's idea?

Exercise 11.4

Heinz and Peterson measured the body characteristics of healthy, active adults. Ten of the measurements, including height, were of skeletal properties that could be used to define each person's body build. Twelve measurements were of girths that either were changeable (they could be affected, for example, by how much muscle or fat a person had) or constant. In addition, each person's weight was measured. Age and gender were recorded. The variables' names and each one's category are shown in the table below:

Variable Name	Description	Category
biacromial	Shoulder to shoulder (in cm)	Skeletal
biiliac	pelvic breadth (in cm)	Skeletal
bitrochanteric	Hip width (in cm)	Skeletal
chest.depth	Chest depth (in cm)	Skeletal
chest.diam	Chest diameter (in cm)	Skeletal
elbow.diam	Sum of Elbow diameters. (in cm)	Skeletal
wrist.diam	Sum of Wrist diameters. (in cm)	Skeletal
knee.diam	Sum of Knee diameters. (in cm)	Skeletal
ankle.diam	Sum of Ankle diameters (in cm)	Skeletal
shoulder.girth	Shoulder girth (in cm)	Changeable Girth
chest.girth	Chest girth (in cm)	Changeable Girth
waist.girth	Waist girth (in cm) below rib cage	Changeable Girth
navel.girth	Navel girth (in cm)	Changeable Girth
hip.girth	Hip girth at buttocks (in cm)	Changeable Girth
thigh.girth	Thigh girth, gluteal (in cm)	Changeable Girth
bicep.girth	Bicep girth, flexed (in cm)	Changeable Girth
forearm.girth	Forearm girth (in cm)	Changeable Girth
knee.girth	Knee girth (in cm)	Constant Girth
calf.girth	Calf girth, maximum (in cm)	Changeable Girth
ankle.girth	Ankle girth (in cm)	Constant Girth
wrist.girth	Wrist girth (in cm)	Constant Girth
age	Age (in years)	Other
weight	Weight (in kg)	Changeable
height	Height (in cm)	Skeletal
gender	Gender; 1 = males; 0 = females	Other

These data are available on the publisher's website for this text at the address http://www.pearsonhighered.com/stern2e in the file *BodyDimensions.sav*. This dataset is adapted from data published in the article by Heinz, Grete, Peterson, Louis J., Johnson, Roger W., and Kerk, Carter J. (2003), "Exploring relationships in body dimensions", *Journal of Statistics Education* Volume 11, Number 2, www.amstat.org/publications/jse/v11n2/

datasets.heinz.html. Full measurement descriptions are given in this article. Permission to use the data has been granted by the authors.

1. What is the equation that predicts a person's weight from the skeletal variables including the variable **height**?
2. How well does the equation derived in question 1 explain variability in weight? Is the relation statistically significant? Provide supporting data.
3. Create a prediction equation for weight from the changeable girths and height. Does it predict weight more accurately than the above equation? Which equation is a better guide for what would be a reasonable weight over the lifespan?
4. Use a stepwise procedure to determine the best equation for predicting weight from the skeletal variables, including height, and the changeable girth variables. Specify how well the equation works in predicting weight.

Exercise 11.5

In part 1 of Exercise 11.4, an equation was derived for predicting a person's weight from skeletal variables and the variable **height**. Now, the possibility will be explored that the equation derived from a stepwise model that predicts weight from these variables differs for males and females.

1. Use a stepwise method to derive an equation that predicts a male's weight from the skeletal variables and the variable **height**. The data of just the males can be selected from within the **Regression** procedure. The steps shown below illustrate the procedure:

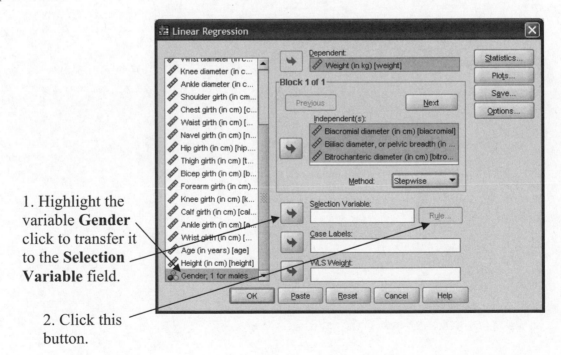

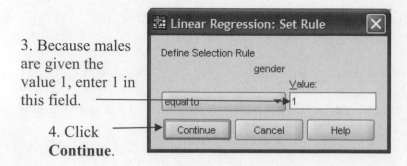

3. Because males
are given the
value 1, enter 1 in
this field. ———

4. Click
Continue.

What is the equation? How well does it explain variability in weight?

2. Repeat part 1 this time analyzing just the data of the females. What is the equation? How well does it explain variability in weight?

3. Derive an equation to predict weight from the chest girth, hip girth, and height for your gender. Use a tape measure to determine your own chest girth (above breast for females, at nipple level for males) and your hip girth (largest girth over buttocks). Insert these girths and your height in the equation to predict your current weight. Does your current weight fall within the standard error of estimate of the predicted weight?

Chapter 12: Chi-Square Tests of Independence and Goodness-of-Fit

Chi-Square Test of Independence

Overview

Many variables analyzed in the social sciences are categorical, that is, measured on a nominal scale, and so take on values that differ only qualitatively from one another. For example, gender can be thought of as a categorical variable that can take on the values male and female. Nationality (e.g., Australian, Ethiopian, Canadian), personality type (type A, type B), and hair color are other examples.

When cases are categorized simultaneously into values of two nominally-scaled variables, the outcome can be represented in the form of a contingency table. For example, if one simultaneously classifies alcoholics according to their personality type (type A, type B) and gender (male, female) the results can be depicted in a contingency table such as that shown in Figure 12.1. Note that the numbers in the body of the table represent the number of cases that fall into each joint classification. Note also that although the contingency table shown in Figure 12.1 consists of two rows and two columns (i.e., it is a 2 x 2 table), the number of rows and columns in contingency tables may assume other values (e.g., 2 x 3, 9 x 4) depending on the number of categories of each variable.

Figure 12.1. Contingency table representing the number of alcoholic patients classified as having type A or type B personalities as a function of their gender (modeled after Bottlender, Preuss, & Soyka, 2006).

		Personality Type	
		Type A	Type B
Gender	Male	128	66
	Female	33	11

A question that is sometimes appropriate to investigate for data represented in contingency tables is whether, based on the sample of scores represented in the table, the variables are independent in the population. An analysis that addresses the question is the chi-square (χ^2) test of independence.

To test the independence of two categorical variables with the chi-square test of independence, one calculates the frequency of cases in each cell of a contingency table that is expected assuming the variables are independent, and then summarizes the degree to which the obtained frequency counts in cells of the table depart from the expected values. The summary measure, called the Pearson chi-square statistic, is compared with values of an appropriate theoretical chi-square distribution. If the value of the Pearson chi-square statistic falls above a cutoff value in the distribution beyond which only a small percent of theoretical values are found, the assumption that the variables are independent is rejected.

Underlying Assumptions

Two major assumptions underlie proper use of the chi-square test of independence. One is that all observations are independent. Thus, obtaining two measurements from the same person is precluded as are other sorts of dependencies that could arise when data come from spouses or siblings of participants. A second assumption, one that is difficult to verify, is that the sampling distribution of deviations of the actual and expected frequency counts is normal in form. Satisfying this assumption generally requires that the sample size be sufficiently large. Cochran's (1954) rule addresses the requirement. The rule is that there should be no expected frequency values under 1 and that no more than 20% of the expected frequency values should be under than 5. Some have suggested that that Cochran's rule may be too conservative. Camilli and Hopkins (1978) found that in a 2 x 2 table, as long as the total sample size exceeds 20, expected values as low as one or two in up to two cells produced acceptable results in terms of type I errors. For data represented in 2 x 2 and larger tables, Wickens (1989) suggests the general rule that total sample size be at least four or five times the number of cells.

Calculations Used in the Analysis

To obtain the value of sample chi-square, expected values of the frequency counts of each cell in the summary table must first be calculated that are consistent with the assumption the two variables are independent. Because two variables are independent if values of one variable do not influence values of the other variable, expected cell frequencies that reflect independence between variables will conform to the following rule: the ratio of marginal frequency counts for one variable will be repeated at each level of the other variable. Consider the table in Figure 12.2 that includes marginal sums obtained by adding frequency counts along rows and columns of the table. Notice that, as indicated in the marginal values circled to the right of the body of the table, there are more males in the data set than females. As shown in the row marginal values, of the 238 cases, 194 are males and 44 are females. According to our rule for establishing independence, the same ratio of males and females found in the marginal values should occur among participants with type A personalities and among participants with type B personalities. Because there are 161 cases with type A personalities, independence would require that 194/238 of the 161 cases be males, and 44/238 be females. Similarly, for the 77 type B cases, independence would require that 194/238 of the 77 be males and 44/238 of the 77 be females. The outcomes of these calculations are shown in cells of the table in the middle panel of Figure 12.2.

How discrepant are the data obtained in the experiment from the data expected if the variables are independent? As shown in the bottom panel of Figure 12.2, the difference between the two is determined by subtracting from each cell frequency count that was obtained in the study (referred to as the observed frequency count) the frequency expected if the variables are independent. The results are shown in the column titled d_i in

Figure 12.2. To change the d_i values to a form appropriate for comparison to a chi-square distribution, each is squared and divided by the value expected based on the assumption of independence between the variables. When summed, the result is the Pearson chi-square value for the sample. Symbolically,

$$\chi^2_{sample} = \sum \frac{\left(f_{observed} - f_{expected}\right)^2}{f_{expected}}.$$ Equation 12.1

The value of the Pearson chi-square statistic for our example is 1.34.

Figure 12.2. Top panel shows a contingency table representing the number of alcoholic patients classified as being having type A or type B personalities as a function of their gender. Middle panel shows the calculations of expected frequencies if the variables are independent. Bottom panel shows the value of χ^2_{sample} is calculated.

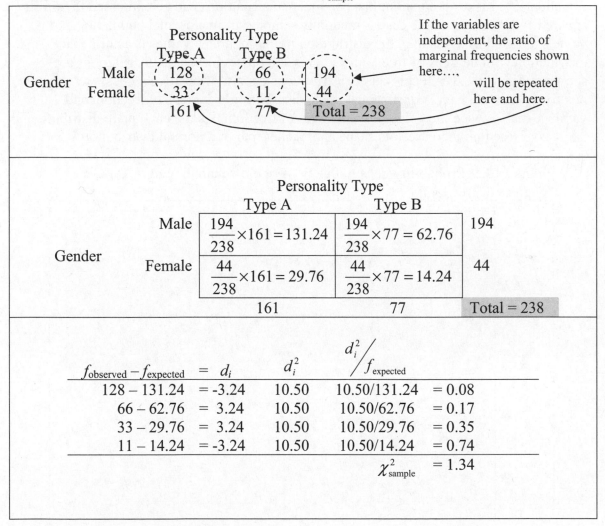

The Chi-Square Distribution

The theoretical chi-square distributions that are used as a basis for making decisions in the chi-square test of independence change shape in accord with their degrees of freedom. The distributions were derived by F.R. Helmert in 1876 (David & Edwards, 2001) to describe the population of ratios formed by dividing the variance of each randomly drawn sample of N scores weighted by its degrees of freedom to the variance of the population being sampled:

$$\chi^2 = \frac{(N-1)s^2}{\sigma^2}$$ Equation 12.2

Substituting the definition of sample variance into the formula, that is, the formula

$$s^2 = \frac{\sum(x_i - \bar{x})^2}{N-1},$$

gives

$$\chi^2 = \frac{\sum(x_i - \bar{x})^2}{\sigma^2}.$$ Equation 12.3

Equation 12.3 makes it apparent that chi-square distributions can be expressed in terms of squared z-scores. If a single case is randomly sampled from a normal population and its value expressed in terms of z, the distribution of the squared z values is a chi-square distribution with degrees of freedom = 1. This and other chi-square distributions are shown in Figure 12.3. All chi-square distributions consist of positive values, are positively skewed, have a mean equal to the distribution's degrees of freedom and a variance that is twice the value of the degrees of freedom. As the chi-square distribution's degrees of freedom increases, its shape approaches that of a normal distribution.

Figure 12.3. Probability density functions of chi-square having 1, 2, 4, or 8 degrees of freedom.

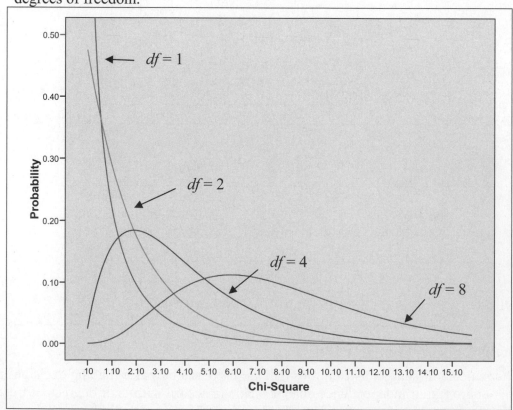

In the Pearson chi-square test of independence, degrees of freedom can be determined from the dimensions of the table used to represent the data. According to this method, degrees of freedom is given by the formula

$$df = (\# \text{ rows in the table} - 1) \times (\# \text{ columns in the table} - 1). \qquad \text{Equation 12.4}$$

Thus, for a 3 x 5 table, the degrees of freedom is 2 x 4 or 8. For the data shown in the 2 x 2 table in Figure 12.1, the degrees of freedom of the chi-square test of independence is 1. Because a table of chi-square values shows that, with one degree of freedom and an alpha of .05, the critical chi-square value is 3.84 our sample chi-square value of 1.34 is not sufficiently large to cause rejection of the assumption that the gender and personality type are unrelated.

Measuring Effect Size

Effect size for a chi-square test of independence may be summarized using the *phi* coefficient when the data conform to a 2 x 2 table and *Cramer's V* otherwise. The range of values of both coefficients is 0 to 1, values that correspond to complete independence and complete dependence of the variables, respectively. The formula for *phi* is

$$\phi = \sqrt{\frac{\chi^2}{N}} . \qquad \text{Equation 12.5}$$

In the formula for *Cramer's V* given below, L is the either the number of rows or the number of columns in the contingency table, whichever is smaller.

$$\text{Cramer's } V = \sqrt{\frac{\chi^2}{N(L-1)}} \qquad \text{Equation 12.6}$$

Cohen (1988) has suggested that *phi* values .10, .30, and .50 correspond to effects that could be described as small, medium, and large, respectively. Interpretation of the magnitude of *Cramer's V* is not as straightforward. For data represented in tables larger than 2 x 2 Cohen (1988) suggests that effect size be measured with the coefficient w (w is equivalent to *phi*). To convert *Cramer's V* to w, its *phi* equivalent, multiply its value by $\sqrt{(L-1)}$. Thus, a *Cramer's V* value of .14 obtained from a 3 x 4 table is equivalent to a *phi* or w value of .20 and so could be described as small to medium.

Preparing Data for the Analysis

A chi-square test of independence can be performed on data that represent values of two nominally-scaled variables for each case in a data file. For example, if the data of 238 participants were represented as individual cases in the **SPSS Statistics Data Editor**, and each case included a value of the variable **gender** (1 = male, 2 = female) and a value of the variable **perstype** (1 = type A, 2 = type B), a chi-square test of independence could be performed to determine if the variables are independent. A portion of such as file is shown below:

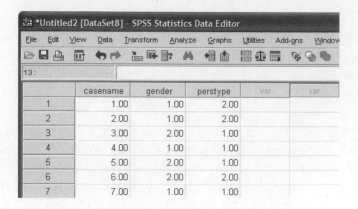

The data for each nominal scale can be represented using a variable declared as being either a string or a numeric type. Shown below are equivalent data represented with two string-type variables, **genderst** and **perstypest**:

An alternate representation of data suitable for analysis with a chi-square test of independence makes use of the **Weight Cases** function. The approach does not require coding each participant's data separately into a data file but, instead, weights the representation of each cell from a contingency table by its frequency count (i.e., the number of participants classified as falling into the joint classification represented by the cell). Three variables are required, two to represent each cell of the contingency table and one to represent the count in each cell. Data shown in the 2 x 2 table of Figure 12.1 is used to illustrate the coding scheme. Because the data are used to investigate the relation between gender and personality type, one variable in the **SPSS Statistics Data Editor** consists of the possible values of gender and a second consists of possible values of personality type. In effect, using this approach, each case is a cell in the table and there are as many cases as cells in the table. A third variable shows the frequency count of each cell identified by the other two variables.

The **SPSS Statistics Data Editor** spreadsheet shown below illustrates the coding system. The variable **gender**, using the values 1 (male) and 2 (female), and the variable **perstype,** using the values 1 (type A) and 2 (type B), identifies each cell in the contingency table. The variable **number** provides the frequency count of the cell.

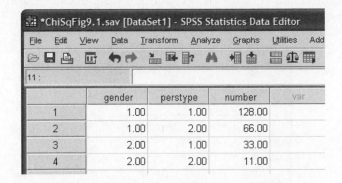

It is helpful to create variable and value labels for the variables used to identify cells. These are shown below for the data in our example:

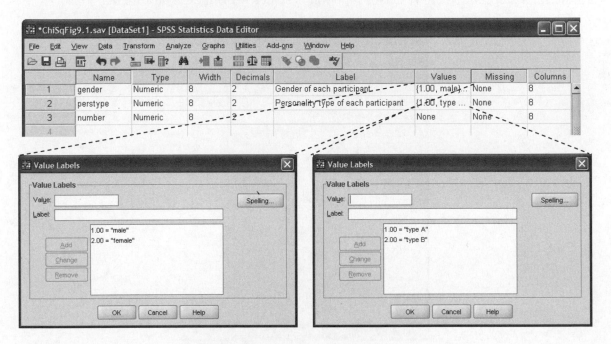

By selecting **Value Labels** in the **Data View**,

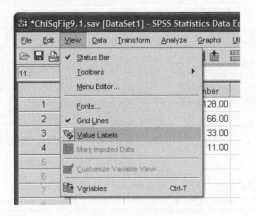

the cells become labeled and entry of the proper cell frequency count for the variable **number** is facilitated.

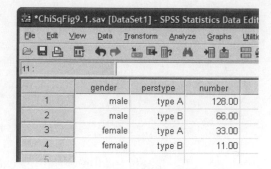

In the final step, the **Weight Cases** function is selected from the **Data** menu:

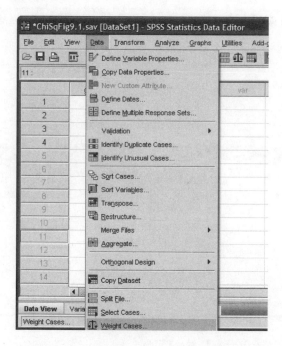

Then the selections shown below are made:

1. Click the **Weight cases by** button.

2. Click the variable name used to specify the frequency count of each cell.

3. Click to transfer the highlighted variable.

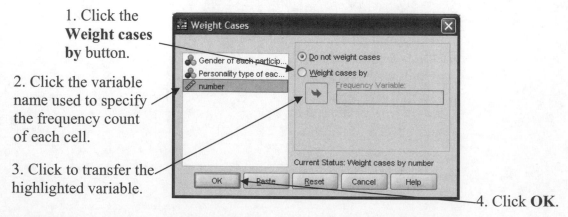

4. Click **OK**.

The data can now be analyzed using a chi-square test of independence.

Requesting a Chi-Square Test of Independence

The chi-square test of independence is accessed by selecting **Crosstabs** in the **Descriptive Statistics** menu as shown below.

1. From the **Analyze** menu select **Descriptive Statistics** and then **Crosstabs**.

2. Click to highlight the variable name that identifies different rows in the contingency table then click this button to transfer it.

3. Click to highlight the variable name that identifies different columns in the contingency table then click this button to transfer it.

4. Click **Cells**.

5. Click to select these options.

6. Click **Continue.**

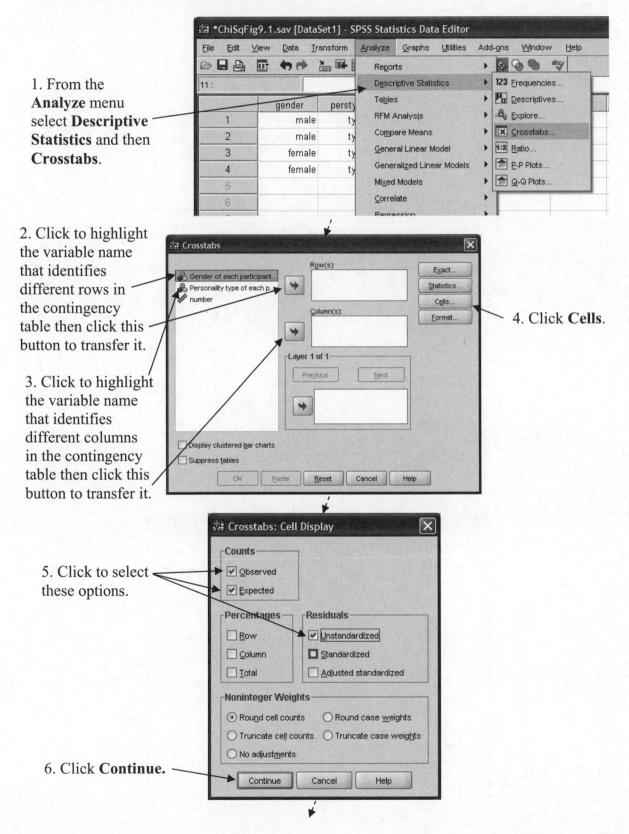

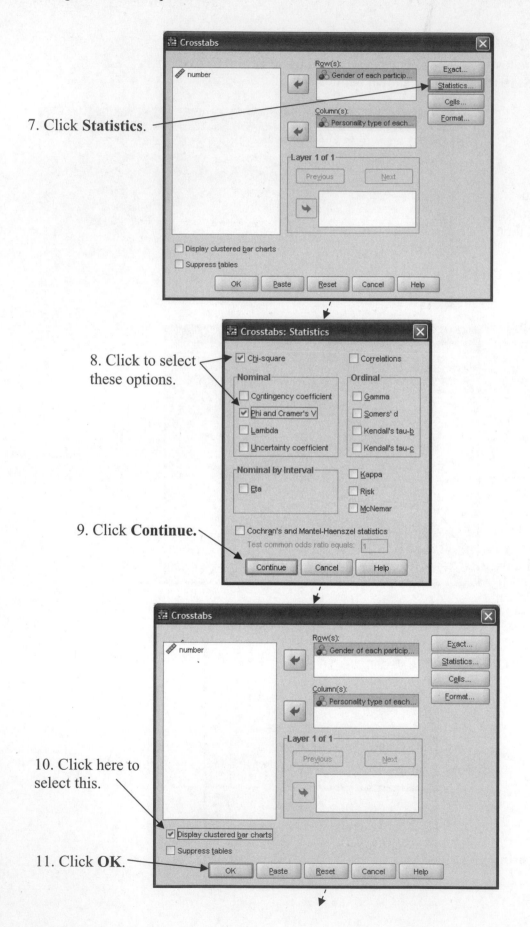

7. Click **Statistics**.

8. Click to select these options.

9. Click **Continue.**

10. Click here to select this.

11. Click **OK**.

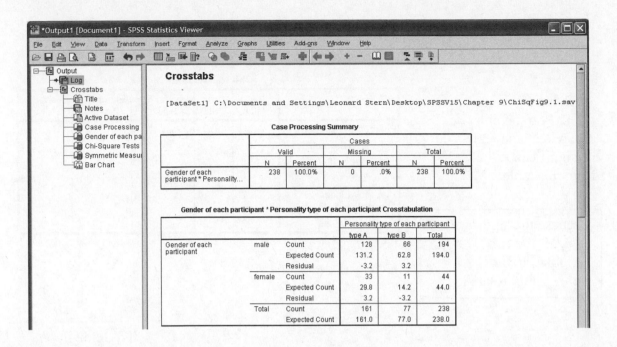

Interpreting the Output

The output includes a contingency table with the obtained and expected number of cases in each cell, a table that includes the value and significance level of the sample Pearson chi-square, a table that provides the value of *phi*, and a bar chart that shows the number of cases as a function of the category values used to identify each cell in the contingency table.

Case Processing Summary

	Cases					
	Valid		Missing		Total	
	N	Percent	N	Percent	N	Percent
Gender of each participant * Personality type of each participant	238	100.0%	0	.0%	238	100.0%

1. Inspect the contingency table to verify the data are entered correctly.

Gender of each participant * Personality type of each participant Crosstabulation

			Personality type of each participant		Total
			type A	type B	
Gender of each participant	male	Count	128	66	194
		Expected Count	131.2	62.8	194.0
		Residual	-3.2	3.2	
	female	Count	33	11	44
		Expected Count	29.8	14.2	44.0
		Residual	3.2	-3.2	
	Total	Count	161	77	238
		Expected Count	161.0	77.0	238.0

These are the observed frequency counts.

3. Obtain the value of the Pearson chi-square statistic and its significance from this table.

Chi-Square Tests

	Value	df	Asymp. Sig. (2-sided)	Exact Sig. (2-sided)	Exact Sig. (1-sided)
Pearson Chi-Square	1.333ᵃ	1	.248		
Continuity Correctionᵇ	.953	1	.329		
Likelihood Ratio	1.382	1	.240		
Fisher's Exact Test				.287	.165
Linear-by-Linear Association	1.328	1	.249		
N of Valid Cases	238				

a. 0 cells (.0%) have expected count less than 5. The minimum expected count is 14.24.

b. Computed only for a 2x2 table

Because the significance is > .05, the two variables are not significantly related.

Although *phi* can assume a negative value, it is generally reported as the positive value.

4. Obtain the value of the *phi* from this table.

Symmetric Measures

		Value	Approx. Sig.
Nominal by Nominal	Phi	-.075	.248
	Cramer's V	.075	.248
	N of Valid Cases	238	

The significance of *phi* will be identical to that of the Pearson chi-square.

Bar Chart

2. Inspect the bar chart to determine if the pattern of frequency counts among the bars within each cluster is similar over all the clusters. If it is, the variables are probably independent.

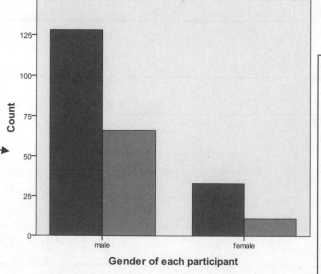

Because the patterns between the bars are so similar for the males and females, then, unless the power of the test is very high, the variables will be found not to be significantly related.

Reporting the Results

The outcome of the test could be described as follows:

> To determine whether there was a relation between personality type (type A, type B) and gender (male, female) among detoxified inpatients at an alcohol dependence treatment ward, 238 patients (194 males, 44 females) were categorized as having personality types A or B. Of the 194 males, the personalities of 128 were categorized as type A and 66 as type B; of the 44 females, the number of patients classified as type A and type B were 33 and 11, respectively. A chi-square test of independence indicated the relation between gender and personality type was not significant, χ^2 (1, $N = 238$) = 1.33, $p > .20$.

Notice that when the Pearson chi-square is not significant, there is no need to mention the value of *phi* because any difference from zero is attributed to chance. Analysis of data shown in Figure 12.4, however, produces a Pearson chi-square value sufficiently high to reject the assumption the variables are unrelated. The description of the outcome includes a report of the effect size.

Figure 12.4. Contingency table representing the number of undergraduate students reporting whether or not they ever cheated in a class as a function of their attitude towards the instructor.

		Attitude Towards Instructor	
		Liked	Disliked
Cheated?	Yes	240	41
	No	425	36

Tables that contain output that should be included in a description of the outcome are shown below:

Have you cheated? * Did you like the instructor? Crosstabulation

			Did you like the instructor?		
			yes	no	Total
Have you cheated?	yes	Count	240	41	281
		Expected Count	251.8	29.2	281.0
		Residual	-11.8	11.8	
	no	Count	425	36	461
		Expected Count	413.2	47.8	461.0
		Residual	11.8	-11.8	
	Total	Count	665	77	742
		Expected Count	665.0	77.0	742.0

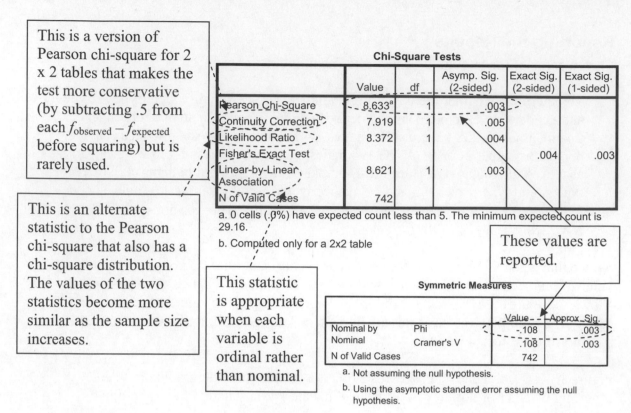

This is a version of Pearson chi-square for 2 x 2 tables that makes the test more conservative (by subtracting .5 from each $f_{observed} - f_{expected}$ before squaring) but is rarely used.

This is an alternate statistic to the Pearson chi-square that also has a chi-square distribution. The values of the two statistics become more similar as the sample size increases.

This statistic is appropriate when each variable is ordinal rather than nominal.

These values are reported.

Chi-Square Tests

	Value	df	Asymp. Sig. (2-sided)	Exact Sig. (2-sided)	Exact Sig. (1-sided)
Pearson Chi-Square	8.633[a]	1	.003		
Continuity Correction[b]	7.919	1	.005		
Likelihood Ratio	8.372	1	.004		
Fisher's Exact Test				.004	.003
Linear-by-Linear Association	8.621	1	.003		
N of Valid Cases	742				

a. 0 cells (.0%) have expected count less than 5. The minimum expected count is 29.16.

b. Computed only for a 2x2 table

Symmetric Measures

		Value	Approx. Sig.
Nominal by Nominal	Phi	-.108	.003
	Cramer's V	.108	.003
N of Valid Cases		742	

a. Not assuming the null hypothesis.

b. Using the asymptotic standard error assuming the null hypothesis.

A summary of the outcome is shown next.

> To determine if student cheating in a class is related to student attitude towards an instructor, students in a large introductory undergraduate class were asked to think of the class they took the previous year at the same or a similar time of day and to indicate both whether or not they cheated in any test or assignment for the class and whether they liked or disliked the instructor. Of the 665 students who indicated they liked the instructor, 240 (36%) reported cheating; of the 77 students who indicated they disliked the instructor 41 (53%) reported cheating. The outcome of a chi-square test of independence indicated that cheating was significantly related to attitude towards an instructor, $\chi^2 (1, N = 742) = 8.63, p < .01, \phi = .11$.

Chi-Square Goodness-of-Fit Test

Overview

A chi-square goodness-of-fit test is used to determine if the distribution of frequency counts among categories of a nominally-scaled variable (or a variable treated as though it were nominally-scaled) matches a theoretical or reference distribution. Although the test can be applied to nominally-scaled variables that have just two possible values, the preferred test for such dichotomous variables is the binomial test because it can provide exact probabilities for small sample sizes. However, for variables with more than two categories, the chi-square goodness-of-fit test may be appropriate. Consider, for example, the outcome of a survey intended to determine the attitude of a random sample of college students towards inviting a controversial speaker to campus. Of 78 students polled, 53 indicate they favor making the invitation, 20 are against making the invitation, and 5 are undecided. Consider, further, that among the entire faculty of the university, 80% had previously indicated they favored making the invitation, 10% were against making the invitation, and 10% were undecided. A chi-square goodness-of-fit test can be used to determine if student attitudes are compatible with those of the faculty.

The procedure is similar to that for the chi-square test of independence. In this case, however, the expected value of each cell is determined by the percent of cases in the corresponding cell of the reference distribution. For example, because 80% of the faculty members favored inviting the controversial speaker to campus, the expected frequency among the 78 students is .80 x 78 = 62.40. Calculation of expected frequencies for the two other attitude categories and calculations needed to obtain the value of chi-square are shown in Figure 12.5. The value of chi-square obtained for the sample is compared to a critical value from a distribution with degrees of freedom that equals the number of categories of the nominally-scaled variable − 1. Thus, in our example, because there are three possible attitudes, degrees of freedom is 2.

Figure 12.5. Top panel shows the number of students who favor, oppose, or are undecided about offering an invitation to visit the campus to a controversial speaker and the percent of faculty who hold each of these opinions. Bottom panel shows calculations for a chi-square goodness-of-fit test to assess whether student and faculty attitudes are identical.

	Attitude about Invitation			
	Favor	Oppose	Undecided	
Students	53	20	5	N = 78
Faculty	80%	10%	10%	
$f_{expected}$	.80 x 78 = 62.40	.10 x 78 = 7.80	.10 x 78 = 7.80	

$f_{observed} - f_{expected}$	$= d_i$	d_i^2	$d_i^2 / f_{expected}$
53 − 62.40	= -9.40	88.36	88.36/62.40 = 1.42
20 − 7.80	= 12.20	148.84	148.84/7.80 = 19.08
5 − 7.80	= -2.80	7.84	7.84/7.80 = 1.01
			χ_{sample}^2 = 21.51

Measuring Effect Size

Effect size for a chi-square goodness-of-fit test can be measured using the statistic w suggested by Cohen (1988) and given by the formula

$$w = \sqrt{\sum_{i=1}^{m} \frac{\left(p_{observed_i} - p_{expected_i}\right)}{p_{expected_i}}}$$ Equation 12.7

where m = the number of cells

$p_{observed\ i}$ = the proportion of cases found for cell i

$p_{expected\ i}$ = the proportion of cases expected for cell i.

The value of w can be most easily obtained from the chi-square statistic:

$$w = \sqrt{\frac{\chi^2}{N}}$$ Equation 12.8

where N = the total sample size.

Interpretation of the magnitude of w is identical to that of *phi*: the values .10, .30, and .50 correspond to small, medium, and large effects, respectively.

Preparing Data for the Analysis

The most efficient way of coding data for our example into the **SPSS Statistics Data Editor** spreadsheet utilizes a table format as shown below:

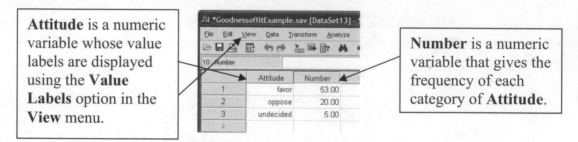

Attitude is a numeric variable whose value labels are displayed using the **Value Labels** option in the **View** menu.

Number is a numeric variable that gives the frequency of each category of **Attitude**.

The cells must then be weighted using the value specified in the variable **Number**:

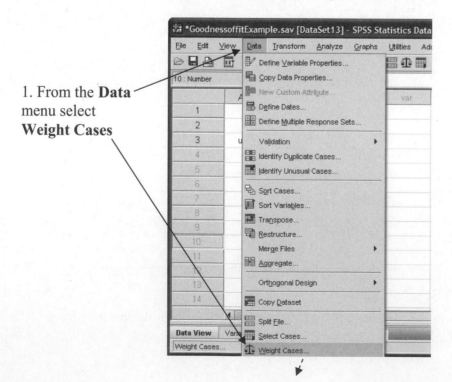

1. From the **Data** menu select **Weight Cases**

2. Click the **Weight cases by** button.

3. Click the variable name used to specify the frequency count of each cell.

4. Click to transfer the highlighted variable.

5. Click **OK**.

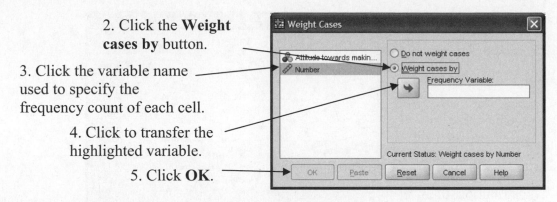

Requesting a Chi-Square Goodness-of-Fit Test

The procedure for requesting a chi-square goodness-of-fit test is shown below:

1. From the **Analyze** menu select **Nonparametric Tests** and then **Chi-Square**.

2. Click to highlight the variable name that identifies different rows in the contingency table then click this button to transfer it.

3. Click here to select **Values**.

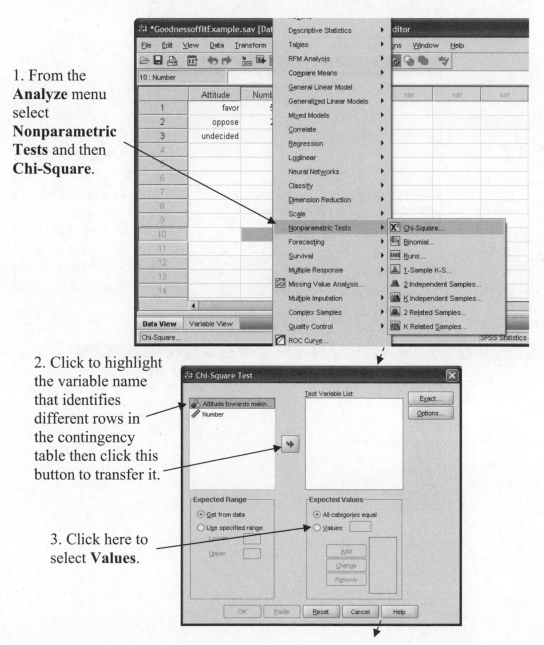

4. Click here and type in the percent value for the first cell in the reference distribution, then click **Add**.

5. Repeat step 4 to enter the % for each cell of the reference distribution.

Note: Other values proportional to these could be used (e.g., 8, 1, 1).

6. Click **OK**.

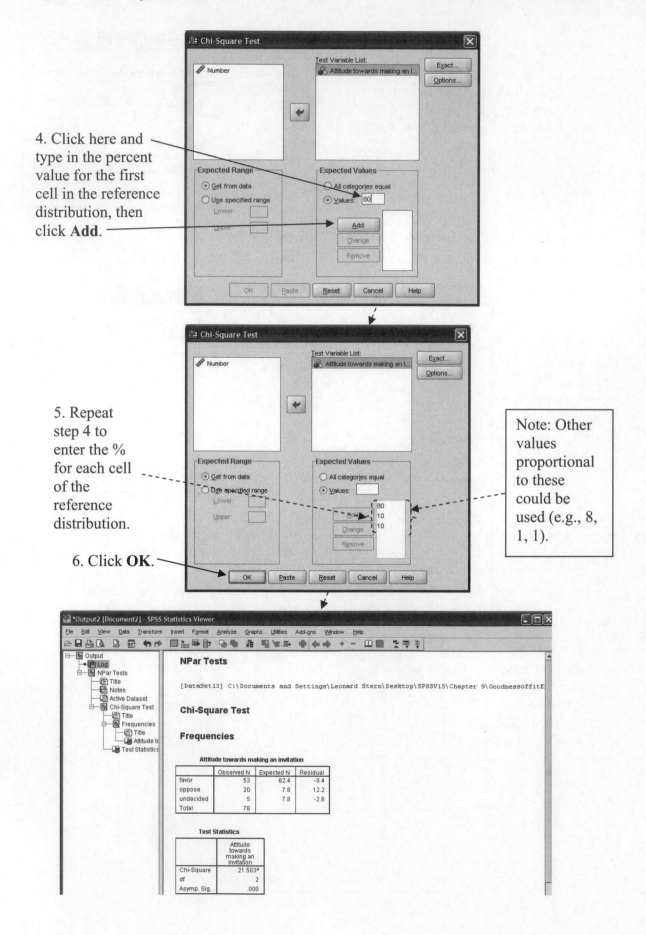

Interpreting the Output

The output includes a table with the obtained number of cases, the expected number of cases, and the difference between the two for each cell of the variable, and a table that gives the value and significance level of the sample chi-square for the goodness-of-fit test.

1. Inspect the observed N values in this table to verify the data are entered correctly.

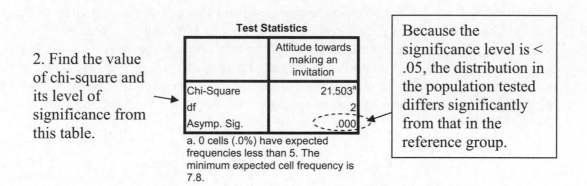

Attitude towards making an invitation

	Observed N	Expected N	Residual
favor	53	62.4	-9.4
oppose	20	7.8	12.2
undecided	5	7.8	-2.8
Total	78		

2. Find the value of chi-square and its level of significance from this table.

Test Statistics

	Attitude towards making an invitation
Chi-Square	21.503[a]
df	2
Asymp. Sig.	.000

a. 0 cells (.0%) have expected frequencies less than 5. The minimum expected cell frequency is 7.8.

Because the significance level is < .05, the distribution in the population tested differs significantly from that in the reference group.

Reporting the Results

The outcome of the goodness-of-fit test can be described as follows:

Data reported by the faculty senate indicated that among the faculty in the university, 80% favored extending an invitation to a controversial speaker to visit campus, 10% opposed extending an invitation, and 10% were undecided. To determine whether student attitudes differed significantly from those of the faculty, a randomly selected sample of 78 students was asked whether they favored, opposed, or were undecided about extending an invitation to visit campus to the controversial speaker. Of the 78 students, 53 (68%) indicated they favored extending the invitation, 20 (26%) were opposed, and 5 (6%) were undecided. A chi-square goodness-of-fit test showed the attitudes of students differed significantly from those of the faculty, χ^2 (2, $N = 78$) = 21.51, $p < .001$, $w = .53$.

Exercises for Chapter 12

Exercise 12.1

Richard B. Slatcher and James W. Pennebaker at the University of Texas at Austin (2006) randomly assigned one of two members of 86 couples who were dating to either an emotional writing condition or to a control writing condition. Participants in the emotional writing condition ($N = 44$) were instructed to write during 20 minutes for three days about their deepest emotions regarding their relationship; participants in the control condition ($N = 42$) were to write about their activities during the day. Three months later, of the 44 people who had written about their emotions, 34 were still dating; of the 42 people in the control condition, 22 were still dating. Use these data to determine if emotional writing is significantly related to relationship stability.

Exercise 12.2

To test whether people who assume a role that gives them power differ in their tendency to adopt another person's visual perspective, Galinsky, Magee, Inesi, and Gruenfeld (2006) induced 57 undergraduate participants to adopt a high or low power perspective by recalling an incident from their lives in which they either had power over another person or another person had power over them. Later in the experiment, participants were asked to draw a capital E on their forehead with a marker. The E could be drawn in a self-oriented or other-oriented way as shown below:

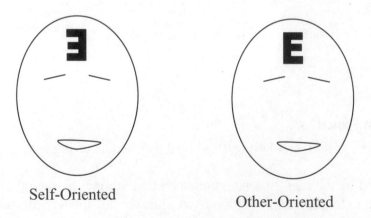

Self-Oriented   Other-Oriented

Of the 24 participants in the high power condition, 8 drew the E in the self-oriented way and 16 drew the E in an other-oriented way; of the 33 participants in the low power condition, 4 drew the E in the self-oriented way and 29 drew the E in an other-oriented way. Based on these data, is power related to visual perspective?

Exercise 12.3

The National Highway Transportation Safety Agency (NIITSA) reported that in the U.S. during 2004, the percent of speeding-related traffic fatalities as a function of speed limit on non-interstate highways was as follows:

Speed Limit	< 35 mph	35 mph	40 mph	45 mph	50 mph	55 mph
Percent	15	15	9	18	5	38

The NHTSA reported that in the state of California during 2004, the numbers of speeding-related traffic fatalities as a function of speed limit on non-interstate highways was as follows:

Speed Limit	< 35 mph	35 mph	40 mph	45 mph	50 mph	55 mph
Number	134	158	94	127	56	330

Determine whether the distribution of speeding-related traffic fatalities as a function of speed limit on non-interstate highways in California differed significantly from that in the U.S. as a whole.

Exercise 12.4

The data below show the number of crime victims as a function of the variables type of crime (rape/sexual assault, robbery) and relation between assailant and victim (stranger, non-stranger). Use the data to determine if the variables are related.

		Type of Crime	
		Rape/Sexual Assault	Robbery
Relation	Stranger	66	455
	Non-stranger	123	114

Exercise 12.5

The data file *HappyMarried.sav* contains responses of 1200 randomly selected adults to two questions asked in the General Social Survey given in 2004: "Are you currently--married, widowed, divorced, separated, or have you never been married?" and "Taken all together, how would you say things are these days--would you say that you are very happy, pretty happy, or not too happy?" Responses to the questions are coded in the data file as shown in the table below:

Marital		**Happy**	
Married =	1	Very happy =	1
Widowed =	2	Pretty happy =	2
Divorced =	3	Not too happy =	3
Separated =	4		
Never Married =	5		

Determine whether the variables **Marital** and **Happy** are significantly related.

Chapter 13: One and Two Sample *T*-tests

Overview

Consider these questions:

In 2004, students in public colleges in the U.S. who received financial aid graduated with a mean debt of $17,125. Analysis of a random sample of 20 seniors graduating in 2009 who had received financial aid at a public college in the Pacific Northwest shows they have a mean debt of $17, 735 with a standard deviation of $1,385. Based on this outcome, is it proper to conclude that the mean debt load at this college in 2009 is significantly higher than the 2004 value of $17,125?

The Beck Depression Inventory (BDI) is a 21-item multiple choice questionnaire designed to assess depression. For the revised version of the test, scores above 19 signal moderate to severe depression. If a random sample of 12 persons diagnosed with post-traumatic stress disorder (PTSD) has a mean BDI score of 20.31 with a standard deviation of 3.87, can it be concluded that the population of people with PTSD from which the sample was derived has a BDI score significantly greater than 19?

Both questions can be addressed using a single sample *t*-test. The test is used to decide whether the mean of a population represented by a sample drawn randomly from it differs significantly from a specified value. The value specified is chosen by the researcher. For variables with known means (tests can be scaled to have a mean of 100 or 50 or any other value) the known mean may be a useful benchmark against which to test samples drawn from specific populations. When testing uses multiple-choice questions having a fixed number of alternatives (e.g., 4), the chance level of correct responding (e.g., .25) can sometimes serve as an appropriate reference value.

The ideas underlying the single-sample *t*-test are extensions of those underlying the single sample z-test. Thus, the core ideas of the single sample z-test will first be reviewed.

Starting Point: The Single Sample Z-Test

If a very large population of values of the variable X that has a known mean μ_x and standard deviation σ_x is randomly sampled a great many times using samples of the same size (N), the distribution of these sample means (termed the sampling distribution of the sample mean) will have these properties:

1) Its mean, $\mu_{\bar{x}}$, will be the same as the mean of the large population of scores, μ_x.

2) Its standard deviation, $\sigma_{\bar{x}}$, will be given by the formula

$$\sigma_{\bar{x}} = \sigma_x \Big/ \sqrt{N} .$$ Equation 13.1

3) Its shape will be normal if the population being sampled is normal; if the
    population being sampled is not normal, the shape of the sampling distribution of
    the sample mean approaches that of a normal distribution as *N* increases.
This last statement is known as the central limit theorem.

When samples are drawn from normally distributed populations, or when large samples
($N \geq 30$) are drawn from populations that are not normally distributed, knowledge of the
mean and standard deviation of the population allows one to calculate the *z* value for any
sample mean and use areas under the standard normal curve to associate a probability
with the sample mean. The formula for *z* is

$$z = \frac{\bar{x} - \mu_{\bar{x}}}{\sigma_{\bar{x}}}$$ Equation 13.2

As an example, if one assumes the distribution of SAT scores in the population in general
is normal with a mean of 500 and a standard deviation of 100, then the probability of
drawing a random sample of 25 scores whose mean is 540 or higher can be obtained by
first calculating the *z*-value of the sample

$$z = \frac{540 - 500}{\frac{100}{\sqrt{25}}} = 2.00 \, .$$

Then, from a *z*-table, one finds that the probability of obtaining a *z*-score at or above 2.00
is .0228.

How does this information help us? Consider the following question: Is the SAT score of
high school students who apply to Ivy League colleges different than usual? If we assume
that in the general population of high school students, SAT scores are normally
distributed with a mean of 500 and a standard deviation of 100, we can test the question
by obtaining a random sample of SAT scores of high school students who apply to Ivy
League colleges. Assume our random sample of 25 such students has a mean SAT score
of 540. The low probability (.0228) of getting a result by chance that is this or more
extreme (it would be appropriate to double the .0228 because the test is non-directional)
would lead us to reject the assumption (i.e., the null hypothesis) that we are sampling
from the population of SAT scores in general and instead accept the idea (with the
understanding that our probability of mistakenly rejecting the null hypothesis, called a
Type I error, is .0456) that the population of SAT scores of high school students who
apply to Ivy League colleges differs from what is usual (the alternate hypothesis).

The Single Sample T-*Test*

The *T*-Distribution

If a researcher does not know the standard deviation of the single population being
examined, but, instead, estimates it from the standard deviation of a sample drawn
randomly from the population, hypothesis testing based on the mean of the single sample
should utilize the *t*-distribution. A *t*-distribution is formed when a normally distributed
population with a known mean is sampled a great many times using equal sized random
samples, and, for each sample, in the denominator of the equation for *z* (see Equation

13.2) the sample standard deviation is used to estimate the population standard deviation in the formula for calculating $\sigma_{\bar{x}}$ (see Equation 13.1). Thus, whereas z is based on this formula:

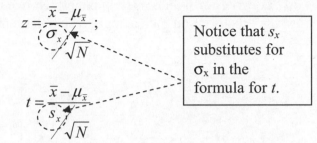

t is based on this formula:

Notice that s_x substitutes for σ_x in the formula for t.

The substitution of s_x for σ_x shown in the denominator of the formula for t produces the statistic $s_{\bar{x}}$, known as the standard error of the mean, given by the formula

$$s_{\bar{x}} = {s_x}\big/{\sqrt{N}} .$$ Equation 13.3

Thus, in a formula analogous to that of z (see Equation 13.2), t can be given by the formula

$$t = \frac{\bar{x} - \mu_{\bar{x}}}{s_{\bar{x}}} .$$ Equation 13.4

The distribution of t produced from a great many samples will not necessarily be normal, particularly when the sample size is small (<30). Instead, the distribution of t changes with sample size. For small sample sizes, compared to a normal z distribution, the t distribution, although unimodal and symmetric, has more cases in the tails and fewer in the middle. Thus the t distribution is often described as flatter than the normal distribution. However, as sample size increases, the shape of a t distribution increasingly approaches that of a normal distribution. Tables that give values of t together with associated probabilities discriminate among different t distributions using degrees of freedom (*df*) calculated, in this application, from the formula $df = N - 1$. Figure 13.1 compares the shape of a t-distribution corresponding to 4 degrees of freedom and one corresponding to 15 degrees of freedom with a normal z distribution.

Effect Size

Effect size is a measure of the extent to which a treatment (i.e., the independent variable) influences values of the dependent variable. A commonly used measure of effect size that was proposed by Cohen (1988) is d. In the case of a single sample t-test, d compares the absolute value of the difference between the test variable's mean and the reference value chosen by the experimenter to the standard deviation of the variable's scores. The formula is

$$d = \frac{|\bar{x}_i - \text{test value}|}{s_x} .$$ Equation 13.5

Figure 13.1. Pairs of plots that allow a standard normal *z* distribution (circles) to be compared to a *t* distribution (plus signs). The *t*-distribution has 4 degrees of freedom (left panel) or 15 degrees of freedom (right panel). Notice that as degrees of freedom increases, the *t* distribution increasingly resembles a normal *z* distribution.

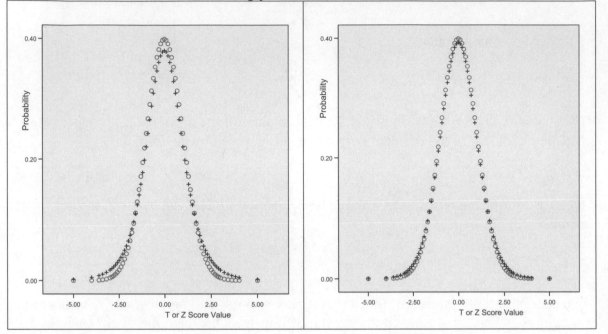

An alternate formula is

$$d = \frac{|t|}{\sqrt{N}}.$$

Equation 13.6

Guidelines for interpreting values of *d* have the values .2, .5, and .8 correspond roughly to a small, medium, and large effect size, respectively.

Underlying Assumptions

There are two assumptions underlying use of the single sample *t* test: the population being sampled is normal and scores are randomly and independently selected from the population. When the size of the sample is large (30 or higher) violation of the assumption of normality does not seriously jeopardize interpretation of the probabilities associated with the sample *t* values.

Coding the Data

To perform a single sample *t*-test with *SPSS*, each participant's score should be represented as a case of a variable in the **SPSS Statistics Data Editor** spreadsheet. The variable must be numeric and is generally assumed to be measured on an interval or ratio scale. The example below illustrates how values of the variable **debt** are coded in the **SPSS Statistics Data Editor** and analyzed with a single sample *t*-test. The variable **debt** represents the debt of college seniors graduating in 2009 described at the beginning of the chapter. The single sample *t*-test determines whether the mean debt of the sample of 20 students graduating in 2009 is significantly higher than the 2004 mean value of $17,125.

Requesting the Analysis

1. From the **Analyze** menu select **Compare Means** then **One-Sample T Test**.

2. Click to highlight the name of a variable to be analyzed and click this arrow to transfer it.

3. Type the value of the mean of the reference population.

4. Click **OK**.

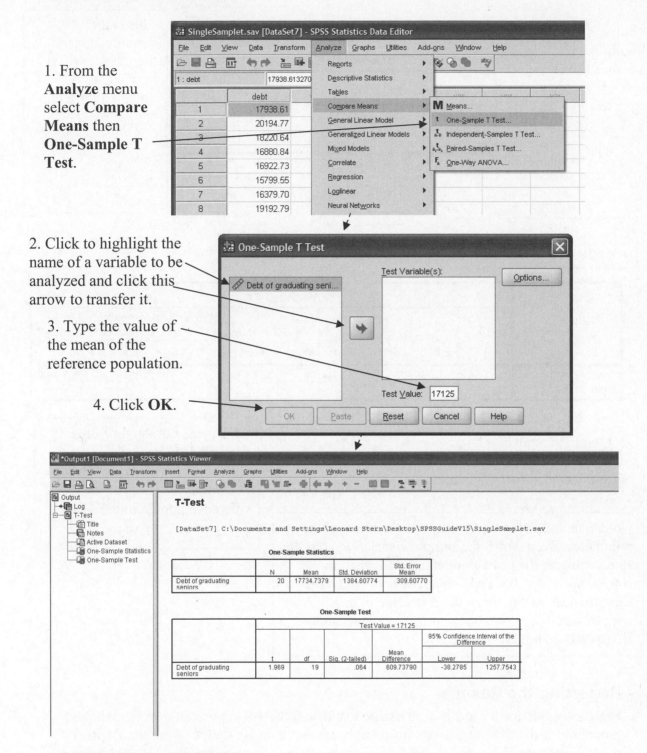

Interpreting the Output

The tables produced for the analysis just described are shown below together with guidelines for interpreting the output.

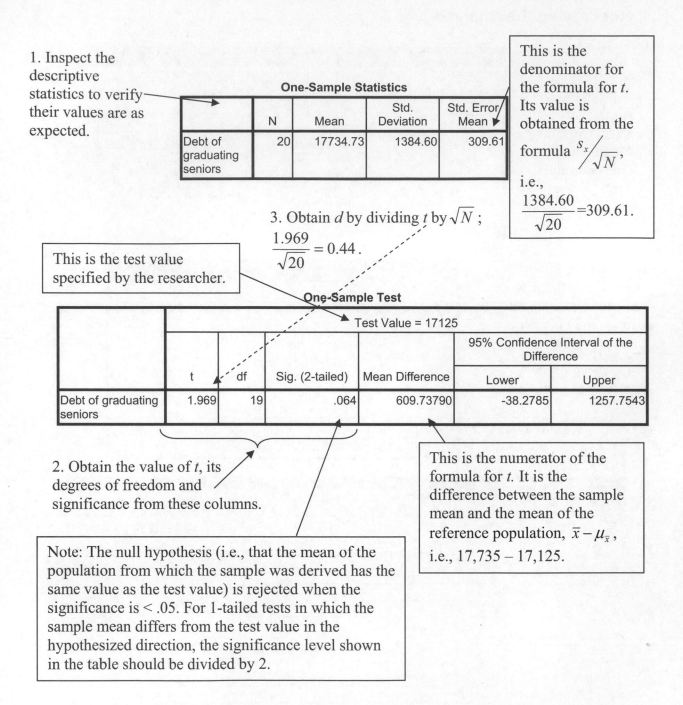

1. Inspect the descriptive statistics to verify their values are as expected.

One-Sample Statistics

	N	Mean	Std. Deviation	Std. Error Mean
Debt of graduating seniors	20	17734.73	1384.60	309.61

This is the denominator for the formula for *t*. Its value is obtained from the formula $s_x / \sqrt{N}$, i.e.,

$$\frac{1384.60}{\sqrt{20}} = 309.61.$$

3. Obtain *d* by dividing *t* by $\sqrt{N}$;

$$\frac{1.969}{\sqrt{20}} = 0.44 .$$

This is the test value specified by the researcher.

One-Sample Test

					Test Value = 17125	95% Confidence Interval of the Difference	
	t	df	Sig. (2-tailed)	Mean Difference		Lower	Upper
Debt of graduating seniors	1.969	19	.064	609.73790		-38.2785	1257.7543

2. Obtain the value of *t*, its degrees of freedom and significance from these columns.

Note: The null hypothesis (i.e., that the mean of the population from which the sample was derived has the same value as the test value) is rejected when the significance is < .05. For 1-tailed tests in which the sample mean differs from the test value in the hypothesized direction, the significance level shown in the table should be divided by 2.

This is the numerator of the formula for *t*. It is the difference between the sample mean and the mean of the reference population, $\bar{x} - \mu_{\bar{x}}$, i.e., 17,735 – 17,125.

Reporting the Results

Before conducting a *t*-test it is advisable to check if the assumption of normality holds, especially if the sample size is considerably smaller than 30. Output from the **Explore** procedure that can be used to detect serious departures from normality is shown below for the variable **debt**. As can be seen, there is no evidence in the histogram and normal Q-Q plot of any serious of violation of the underlying assumption that the variable is normally distributed.

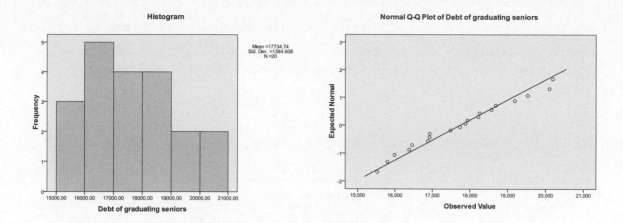

Results of the single sample t-test can be reported as follows:

> A random sample of 20 seniors graduating in 2009 from a public college in the Pacific Northwest had a mean debt of $17,735 (*SD* = $1,385). To determine if the mean debt load at this college represents a significant increase from the mean of $17,125 that occurred in 2004 among students in public colleges in the U.S., a single sample t-test was used. From an informal analysis of the 20 debt scores using a histogram and normal Q-Q plot no serious threats to the assumption of normality were apparent. The single-sample *t*-test revealed that the current mean debt load was significantly higher than the 2004 value, *t* (19) = 1.97, *p* < .05 (one-tailed). The effect size as measured by *d* was 0.44, a value that can be considered small to medium.

T-Test for Two Independent Samples

The *t*-test for independent samples allows one to compare the means of two normally distributed populations using samples drawn randomly and independently from each population. Consider, for example, how one might determine whether, between the ages of seven and eight, males differ from females in their percent of body fat. To investigate the question, a researcher could randomly sample a population of males between the ages of seven and eight, and measure the body fat of each; the process could be repeated with females. Based on the mean, standard deviation, and number of cases in each sample, a value of *t* could be derived and a decision made from the probability associated with the *t* value about whether the two populations have identical means.

The formula for *t* that allows the means of two populations to be compared based on values of the mean, standard deviation, and size of a sample drawn randomly from each population is

$$t = \frac{\bar{x}_1 - \bar{x}_2}{s_{\bar{x}_1 - \bar{x}_2}},$$
Equation 13.7

where $\bar{x}_1$ and $\bar{x}_2$ are the means of samples 1 and 2, respectively,

$s_{\bar{x}_1 - \bar{x}_2}$ is the standard error of the difference.

The statistic $s_{\bar{x}_1-\bar{x}_2}$ estimates the value of the parameter $\sigma_{\bar{x}_1-\bar{x}_2}$. Figure 13.2 illustrates that $\sigma_{\bar{x}_1-\bar{x}_2}$ is the standard deviation of the population of the differences between the pairs of means drawn randomly and independently from two identical normally distributed populations. Its numerical value is estimated from sample data using the formula

$$s_{\bar{x}_1-\bar{x}_2} = \sqrt{\frac{(N_1-1)s_1^2 + (N_2-1)s_2^2}{N_1+N_2-2}\left(\frac{1}{N_1}+\frac{1}{N_2}\right)}$$ Equation 13.8

Substituting the formula for $s_{\bar{x}_1-\bar{x}_2}$ into the formula for *t* given above, yields

$$t = \frac{\bar{x}_1 - \bar{x}_2}{\sqrt{\frac{(N_1-1)s_1^2 + (N_2-1)s_2^2}{N_1+N_2-2}\left(\frac{1}{N_1}+\frac{1}{N_2}\right)}}$$

The degrees of freedom for this test is given by the formula N_1+N_2-2.

Figure 13.2. An illustration of the quantities that $\sigma_{\bar{x}_1-\bar{x}_2}$ summarizes. Here, two identical normal distributions (each with the mean 50) are randomly sampled a great many times using equal-sized samples. For each pair of samples, the difference between their mean is calculated. The standard deviation of these difference values is given by the term $\sigma_{\bar{x}_1-\bar{x}_2}$.

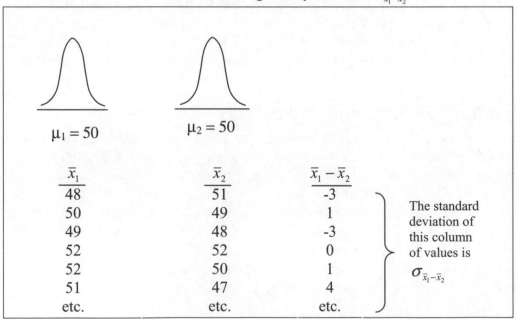

Effect Size

Effect size can be measured using *d*. The formula is

$$d = \frac{|\bar{x}_1 - \bar{x}_2|}{s_{pooled}}$$ Equation 13.9

where s_{pooled} is $\sqrt{\dfrac{(N_1-1)s_1^2 + (N_2-1)s_2^2}{N_1+N_2-2}}$.

An alternate formula is

$$d = |t| \sqrt{\frac{N_1 + N_2}{N_1 N_2}}.$$ Equation 13.10

When the sizes of the two samples are equal (each has *N* scores), one can use the formula

$$d = \frac{|2t|}{\sqrt{2N}}.$$ Equation 13.11

Assumptions Underlying the Independent Samples *T*-Test

Three assumptions underlie use of the independent samples *t*-test. 1) As with the *t*-test for a single sample, the populations being sampled are assumed to be normally distributed. Violations of the assumption become less problematic for interpretation of probabilities associated with *t* values when the size of each sample is large (i.e., 15 or greater). 2) Another assumption, known as homogeneity of variance, is that the variances of the two populations being sampled are equal. As with the assumption of normality, when the size of each sample is large, violating the homogeneity of variance assumption is less serious. Furthermore, for samples that are not very large, even moderate violations of the assumption of homogeneity of variance are not considered serious when the size of the two samples is equal. When the two samples being compared have different sizes, however, substantial differences between their variances can seriously affect conclusions drawn from the test. As shown in the example below, *SPSS* provides a test of the assumption of homogeneity of variance. If the test indicates a significant violation, a correction can be applied to the degrees of freedom of the test; results based on these adjusted degrees of freedom then should be used. 3) Cases are assumed to be drawn randomly and independently of each other, both within each population as well as between each population being sampled; thus, the selection of a case from one population has no influence on which other case is selected from the same population or from another population.

For an independent sample *t*-test, each case entered in the **SPSS Statistics Data Editor** must consist of values of two variables: a dependent variable measured on an interval or ratio scale that corresponds to the concept being assessed (e.g., percent of body fat for a test that involves comparing percent of body fat of male and female children) and an independent variable measured on (or treated as though is was measured on) a nominal scale (e.g., gender for the example of percent of body fat of male and female children) that allows the two samples to be distinguished. As illustrated below, values of the independent variable allow the two samples to be distinguished through the use of two unique whole numbers (e.g., 1 for males, 2 for females) or from cut points applied to a interval- or ratio-scaled variable (e.g., persons having IQs at or below 99 considered as falling into the low IQ group, persons having IQs of 100 or above as falling into the high IQ group).

Requesting the Analysis

The data analyzed in this demonstration are modeled after those reported by Ruxton, Reilly, and Kirk (1999) who measured physical characteristics of healthy Scottish children between the ages of 7-8. In the *SPSS* data file shown below, the variable **pctbodyfat** is the percent of body fat of each child and the variable **gender** codes males using the value 1 and females using the value 2. The intent of the analysis is to determine if the mean percent of body fat of males and females differs at the age of seven to eight.

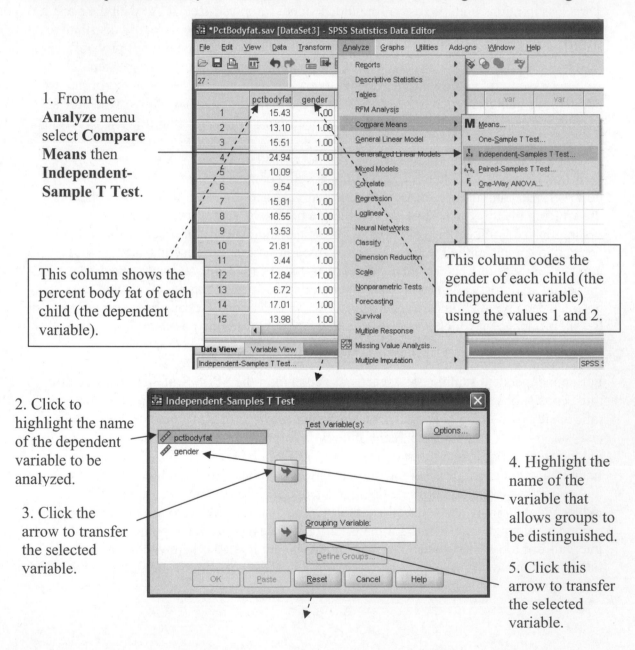

1. From the **Analyze** menu select **Compare Means** then **Independent-Sample T Test**.

This column shows the percent body fat of each child (the dependent variable).

This column codes the gender of each child (the independent variable) using the values 1 and 2.

2. Click to highlight the name of the dependent variable to be analyzed.

3. Click the arrow to transfer the selected variable.

4. Highlight the name of the variable that allows groups to be distinguished.

5. Click this arrow to transfer the selected variable.

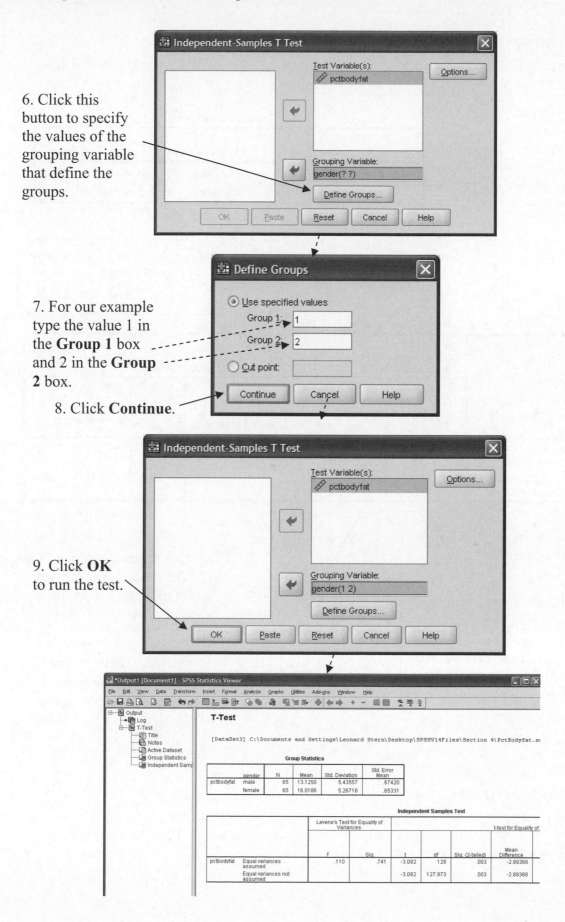

6. Click this button to specify the values of the grouping variable that define the groups.

7. For our example type the value 1 in the **Group 1** box and 2 in the **Group 2** box.

8. Click **Continue**.

9. Click **OK** to run the test.

Interpreting the Output

The two tables that comprise the output of the *t*-test for independent samples are shown below:

1. Inspect the values of the descriptive statistics to verify their values are as expected.

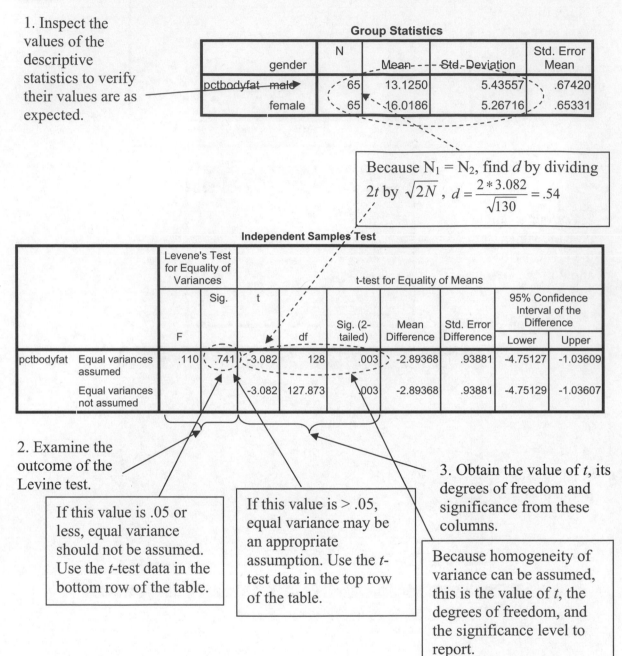

Group Statistics

	gender	N	Mean	Std. Deviation	Std. Error Mean
pctbodyfat	male	65	13.1250	5.43557	.67420
	female	65	16.0186	5.26716	.65331

Because $N_1 = N_2$, find *d* by dividing $2t$ by $\sqrt{2N}$, $d = \dfrac{2*3.082}{\sqrt{130}} = .54$

Independent Samples Test

		Levene's Test for Equality of Variances		t-test for Equality of Means					95% Confidence Interval of the Difference	
		F	Sig.	t	df	Sig. (2-tailed)	Mean Difference	Std. Error Difference	Lower	Upper
pctbodyfat	Equal variances assumed	.110	.741	-3.082	128	.003	-2.89368	.93881	-4.75127	-1.03609
	Equal variances not assumed			-3.082	127.873	.003	-2.89368	.93881	-4.75129	-1.03607

2. Examine the outcome of the Levine test.

If this value is .05 or less, equal variance should not be assumed. Use the *t*-test data in the bottom row of the table.

If this value is > .05, equal variance may be an appropriate assumption. Use the *t*-test data in the top row of the table.

3. Obtain the value of *t*, its degrees of freedom and significance from these columns.

Because homogeneity of variance can be assumed, this is the value of *t*, the degrees of freedom, and the significance level to report.

Graphing the Data

A suitable graph of the distributions of the dependent variable for the two groups being compared with an independent samples *t*-test is an error bar chart. The procedure for forming the chart is shown below:

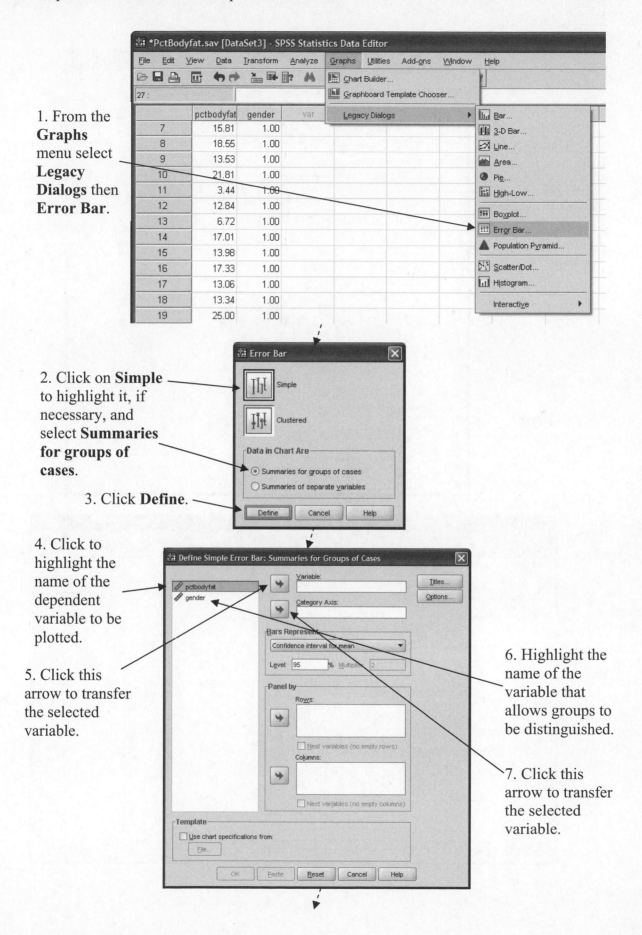

1. From the **Graphs** menu select **Legacy Dialogs** then **Error Bar**.

2. Click on **Simple** to highlight it, if necessary, and select **Summaries for groups of cases**.

3. Click **Define**.

4. Click to highlight the name of the dependent variable to be plotted.

5. Click this arrow to transfer the selected variable.

6. Highlight the name of the variable that allows groups to be distinguished.

7. Click this arrow to transfer the selected variable.

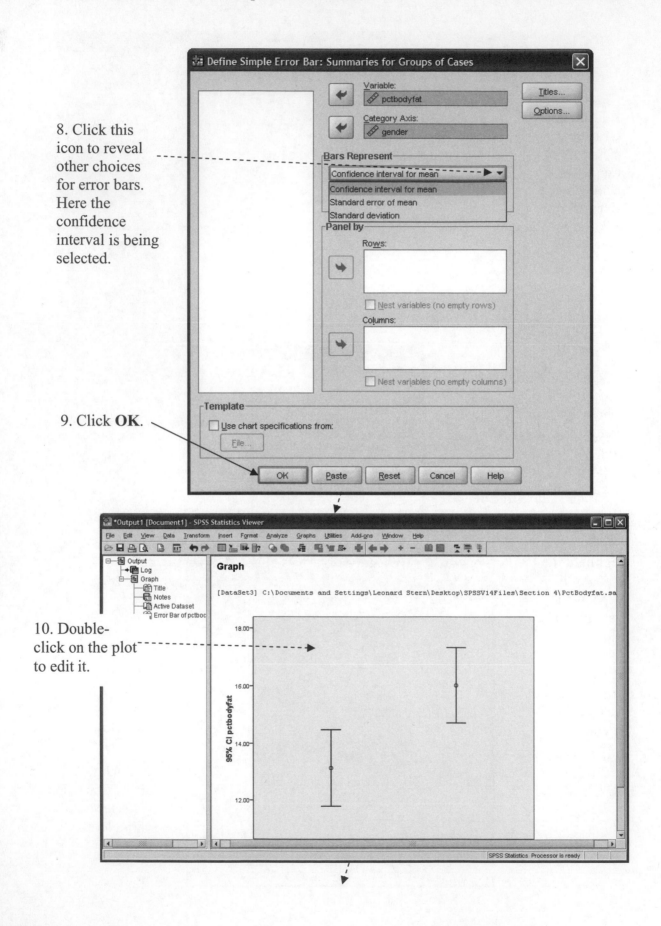

8. Click this icon to reveal other choices for error bars. Here the confidence interval is being selected.

9. Click **OK**.

10. Double-click on the plot to edit it.

11. In the **Chart Editor**, double-click on the y-axis title to edit it and type desired text.

12. Edit the title of the x-axis as above, if desired.

13. Click here to close the **Chart Editor**.

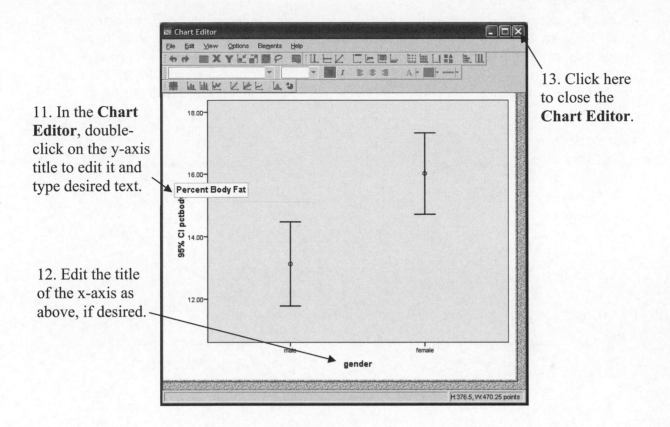

Figure 13.3. The percent of body fat of male and female seven year old children. The error bars show the 95% confidence interval of the mean.

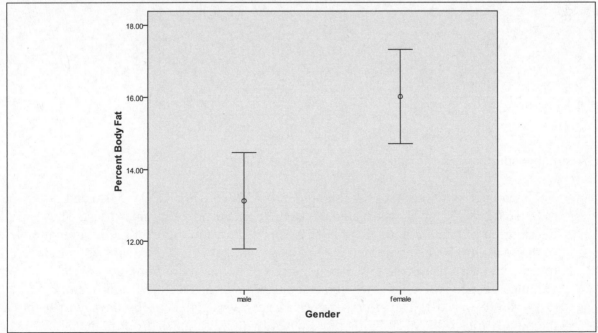

Reporting the Results

As in the case of the single sample *t*-test, it is advisable to screen the data before running the *t*-test for independent samples to assure that underlying distributional assumptions have been met. Output from the **Explore** procedure that can be used for this purpose is shown below for the variable **pctbodyfat**. The normal Q-Q plots and boxplot for the body fat data of each gender show no serious violation of underlying distributional assumptions.

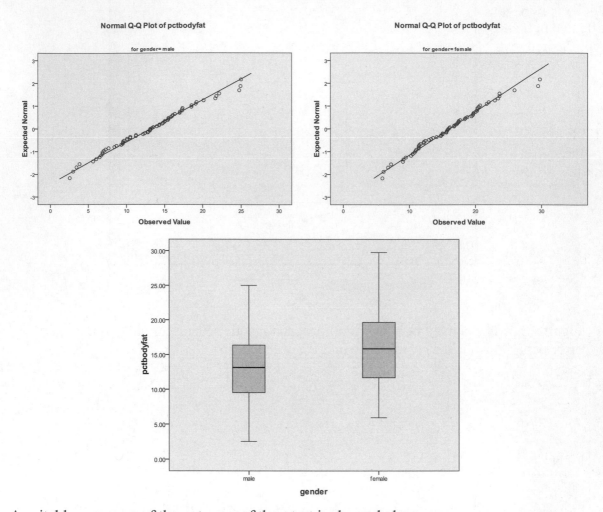

A suitable summary of the outcome of the *t*-test is shown below:

The mean percent body fat of the sample of boys (*M* = 13.13, *SD* = 5.44) and girls (*M* = 16.02, *SD* = 5.27) was examined using an independent samples *t*-test. The distribution of percent body fat of each group is shown in Figure 13.3. Examination of the two samples using normal Q-Q plots and a Levine test of equality of variance revealed no serious threats to the assumptions of normality or homogeneity of variance, respectively. The *t*-test indicated that the means differed significantly, *t* (128) = 3.08, *p* < .01. The effect size was large; *d* was .54. Thus, by the age of seven, the populations of boys and girls represented by these samples differ in their percentage of body fat.

Using a Cut Point to Define Groups

A researcher wishing to define groups based on a variable measured on an interval, ratio, or ordinal scale, may be able to do so using a **cut point** specified on the **Define Groups** window of the **Independent Samples T Test** procedure. For example, if a teacher was interested in knowing whether students who finish a test earlier score differently than those who finish later, the teacher could use the order in which tests were handed in to define the two groups. In the data set shown below, the quiz score of each of 26 students is represented in the variable **quiz**, and the order in which the quizzes are handed in is represented in the variable **order**. By specifying a cut point based on a value of the variable **order**, the mean quiz score of students handing in papers at or after that order value could be compared to the mean quiz score of students handing in papers before that order value. The sequence shown below illustrates how a cut point can be specified.

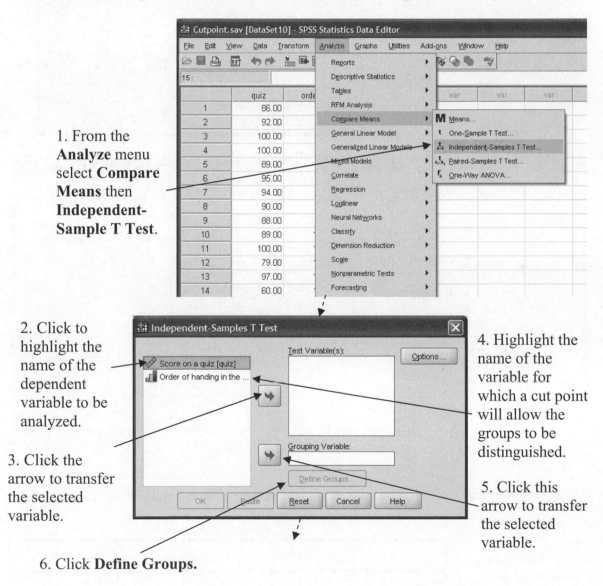

1. From the **Analyze** menu select **Compare Means** then **Independent-Sample T Test**.

2. Click to highlight the name of the dependent variable to be analyzed.

3. Click the arrow to transfer the selected variable.

4. Highlight the name of the variable for which a cut point will allow the groups to be distinguished.

5. Click this arrow to transfer the selected variable.

6. Click **Define Groups.**

7. Click on the **Cut point** button to select it then type the value of the cut point into the window.

8. Click **Continue**.

9. Click **OK**.

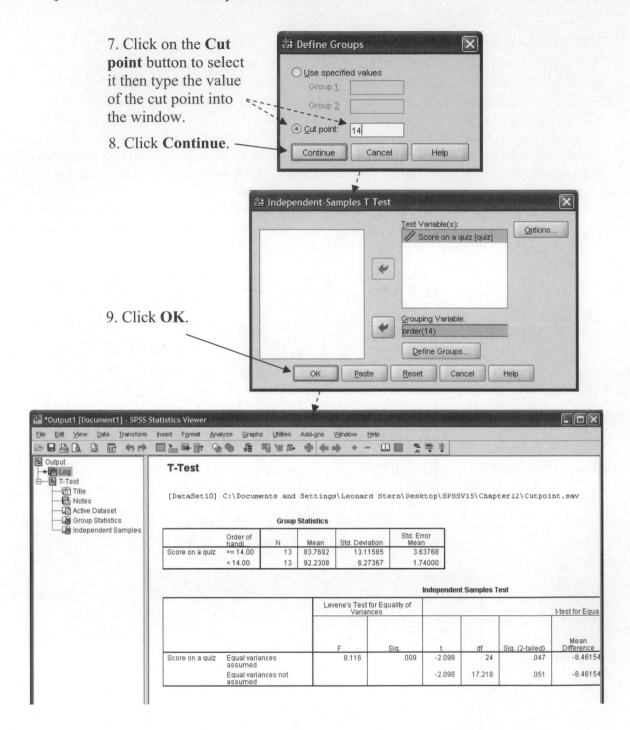

Inspecting the Output. The output produced by these selections is shown below:

Notice that two groups have been formed: one having values of **order** *less than* the cut point's value, and the other *greater than or equal to* this value.

Group Statistics

	Order of handing in the quiz	N	Mean	Std. Deviation	Std. Error Mean
Score on a quiz	>= 14.00	13	83.7692	13.11585	3.63768
	< 14.00	13	92.2308	6.27367	1.74000

Because $N_1 = N_2$, find *d* by dividing $2t$ by $\sqrt{2N}$, $d = \dfrac{2 * 2.098}{\sqrt{2 * 13}} = .82$

Independent Samples Test

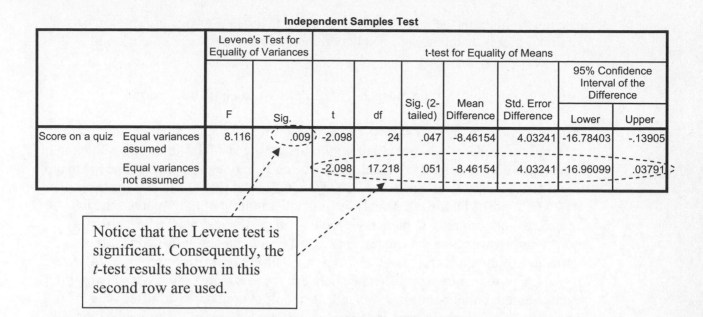

		Levene's Test for Equality of Variances		t-test for Equality of Means						
		F	Sig.	t	df	Sig. (2-tailed)	Mean Difference	Std. Error Difference	95% Confidence Interval of the Difference	
									Lower	Upper
Score on a quiz	Equal variances assumed	8.116	.009	-2.098	24	.047	-8.46154	4.03241	-16.78403	-.13905
	Equal variances not assumed			-2.098	17.218	.051	-8.46154	4.03241	-16.96099	.03791

Notice that the Levene test is significant. Consequently, the *t*-test results shown in this second row are used.

Understanding the Levene Test for Equality of Variances

The Levene test for equality of variances is an analysis of variance performed on the mean absolute deviation from its group mean of each group's scores. Derivation of the scores involved is illustrated in Table 13.1 using the quiz data of the early and late finishers analyzed above.

Table 13.1. Illustration of a Levene test of equality of variances. The *F* value in the Levene test is obtained from an *ANOVA* performed on the absolute deviation scores shown in the last two column of the table shown below.

Quiz Scores for Early and Late Finishers		Mean Absolute Deviation from the Mean Scores for Early and Late Finishers	
Early	Late	|Early-92.23|	|Late-83.77|
86.00	60.00	86.00 - 92.23 = 6.23	60.00 - 83.77 = 23.77
92.00	100.00	92.00 - 92.23 = 0.23	100.00 - 83.77 = 16.23
100.00	98.00	100.00 - 92.23 = 7.77	98.00 - 83.77 = 14.23
100.00	85.00	100.00 - 92.23 = 7.77	85.00 - 83.77 = 0.23
89.00	87.00	89.00 - 92.23 = 3.23	87.00 - 83.77 = 0.23
95.00	92.00	95.00 - 92.23 = 2.77	92.00 - 83.77 = 8.23
94.00	94.00	94.00 - 92.23 = 1.77	94.00 - 83.77 = 10.23
90.00	94.00	90.00 - 92.23 = 2.23	94.00 - 83.77 = 10.23
88.00	82.00	88.00 - 92.23 = 4.23	82.00 - 83.77 = 1.77
89.00	67.00	89.00 - 92.23 = 3.23	67.00 - 83.77 = 16.77
100.00	69.00	100.00 - 92.23 = 7.77	69.00 - 83.77 = 14.77
79.00	69.00	79.00 - 92.23 = 13.23	69.00 - 83.77 = 7.23
97.00	70.00	97.00 - 92.23 = 4.77	70.00 - 83.77 = 13.77
Mean = 92.23	Mean = 83.77	Mean Abs. Dev. = 5.02	Mean Abs. Dev. = 10.90

Because the *F* value for the Levene test is based on the means of two groups comprised of N_1 and N_2 scores, its numerator and denominator degrees of freedom are 1 and $N_1 + N_2 - 2$, respectively.

Here's how the outcome of the independent samples *t*-test could be reported:

> An independent samples *t*-test was used to determine whether the mean quiz score differed for students who were among the first or the last 50% in the class to hand in a statistics quiz (referred to henceforth as the early and late finishers). The mean quiz score for the early finishers was 92.23 (*SD* = 6.27) and that of the late finishers was 83.77 (*SD* = 13.11). Informal analysis of the distribution of quiz scores for each sample using normal Q-Q plots revealed no serious threats to the assumption of normality. However, a Levene test for equality of variances indicated that the variances of the quiz scores of the two groups differed significantly, $F(1, 24) = 8.12$, $p < .01$. Consequently, the difference between the mean quiz score of the two groups was assessed with a *t*-test for independent samples based on an adjusted degrees of freedom. The difference between the means of the two groups approached, but did not achieve significance at the .05 level, $t(17) = 2.10$, $p = .051$. These results give some support to the possibility that early and late finishers perform differently. The effect size as measured by *d* was .82, indicating an effect that can be considered large. Figure 13.4 shows the distribution of quiz scores of the early and late finishers.

Figure 13.4. The distribution of quiz scores of early and late finishers. The error bars show the 95% confidence interval of the mean.

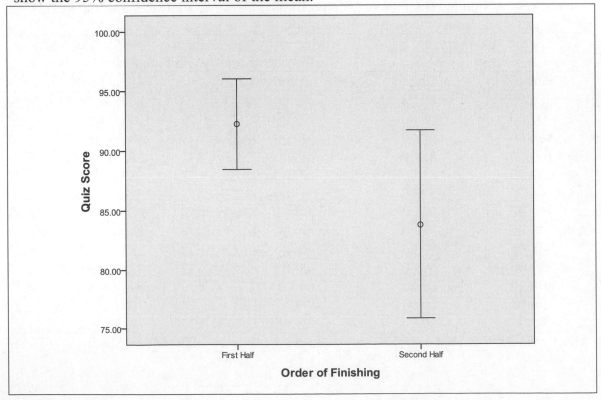

Note that in reporting the outcome of the t-test based on unequal variances, the degrees of freedom is often reported as a whole number. A reasonable, conservative procedure for arriving at the whole number is to round a fractional value down to the closest lower whole number (without ever going below 1) unless a table of *t* values gives a corresponding probability that changes the outcome of the test, in which case the fractional degrees of freedom should be rounded up to the next higher whole number.

Making Error Bar Charts when Cup Points are Used. To make the error bar chart shown in Figure 13.4, a new variable called **group** was created that served as a basis for distinguishing between the two finishing orders. To create the variable **group** the **Compute variable** procedure was used twice as shown below. First, all values of the newly created variable **group** were set to 0; then values of **group** were set to 1 just for cases having a value of **order** of 14 or above.

1. From the **Transform** menu select **Compute variable**.

2. Type the name of the new variable that will distinguish between early and late finishers and set all its values to 0 by typing 0 in this field.

3. Click **OK** to create the variable and its values.

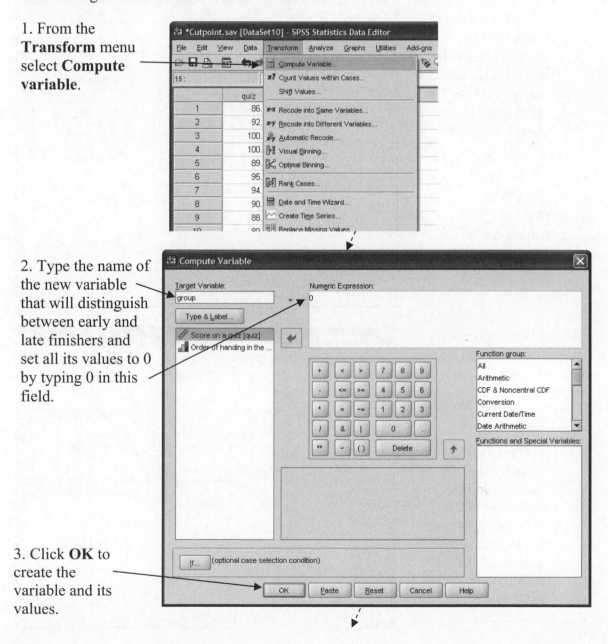

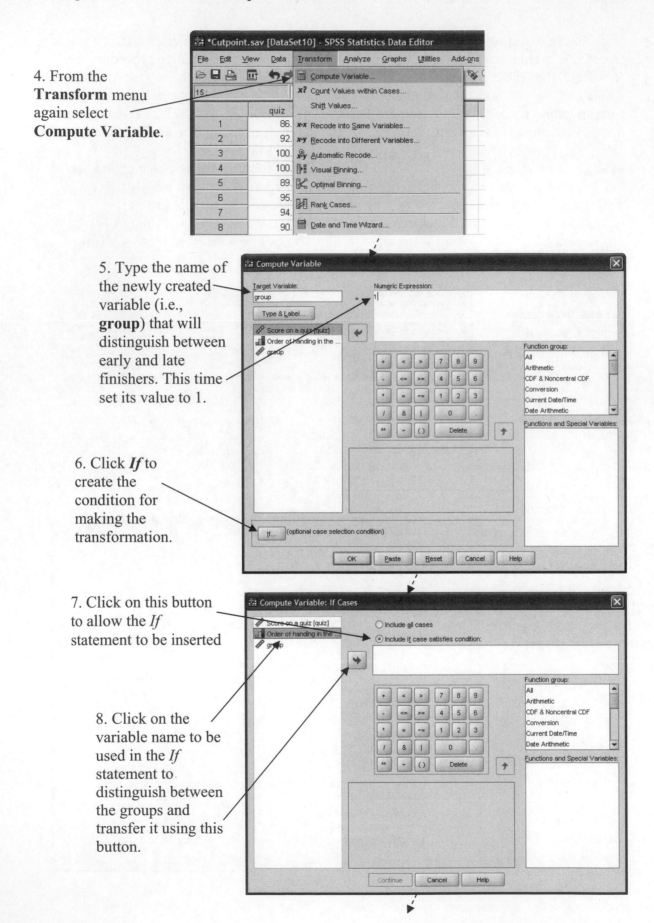

4. From the **Transform** menu again select **Compute Variable**.

5. Type the name of the newly created variable (i.e., **group**) that will distinguish between early and late finishers. This time set its value to 1.

6. Click *If* to create the condition for making the transformation.

7. Click on this button to allow the *If* statement to be inserted

8. Click on the variable name to be used in the *If* statement to distinguish between the groups and transfer it using this button.

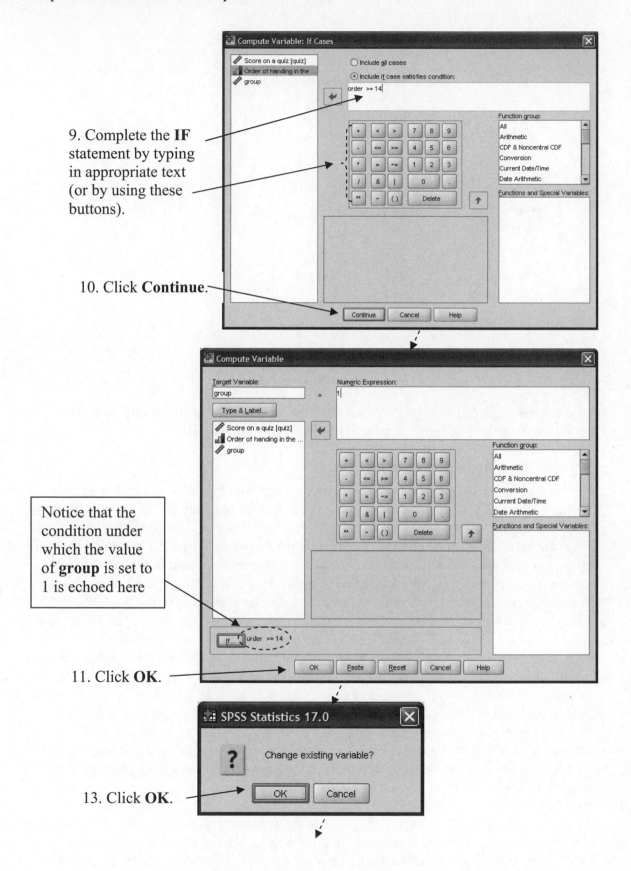

9. Complete the **IF** statement by typing in appropriate text (or by using these buttons).

10. Click **Continue**.

Notice that the condition under which the value of **group** is set to 1 is echoed here

11. Click **OK**.

13. Click **OK**.

The variable **group** now consists of the values 0 and 1.

An error bar chart can now be prepared from the variables **quiz** and **group** using the procedure described earlier in the section titled **Graphing the Data**.

T-Test for Paired Samples

A *t*-test for paired samples (also referred to as a *t*-test for correlated groups) is used to compare the means of two samples of scores when there is a logical basis for connecting each score in one sample with a particular score in the other sample. On what basis may scores be logically connected? One situation is when every participant in a study is tested twice--once in each of two conditions of a study. Because the same person (or object) contributes a score to each condition there a sensible reason for connecting a score in one condition with a particular score in the other condition. A logical connection between scores is not always based on repeated testing of the same participant. For example, if a study compares a physical characteristic (e.g., height) of a parent to the same characteristic of the parent's grown child, and each parent and child comes from the same family, then, even though the same person is not measured twice, there still is a basis for connecting scores across the two groups (i.e., Smith senior can be connected with Smith junior). As another example, consider a study that compares the mean of variable **X** obtained by testing randomly selected participants in condition 1, with the mean of variable **X** obtained by testing different randomly selected participants in condition 2. If each participant in condition 1 is first matched to a particular participant in condition 2 on variable **Y**, there is, again, a basis for pairing scores across the two groups. Here is a specific example: a researcher tests whether children taught to read using a whole language strategy subsequently differ in their mean reading speed from children taught to read using a phonics strategy; however, before conducting the study, the researcher matches the IQ of each child randomly selected to receive the whole language procedure with the IQ of a child randomly selected to receive the phonics procedure. Here, the logical basis for connecting scores across groups involves the matching IQ score so that use of a *t*-test for paired samples could be appropriate.

Formula for a Paired Samples *T*-Test

As in an independent samples *t*-test, the formula for a paired samples *t*-test compares the difference between two sample means to the standard deviation of these differences:

$$t = \frac{\overline{x}_1 - \overline{x}_2}{s_{\overline{x}_1 - \overline{x}_2}} .$$ Equation 13.12

When scores are paired, however, the population standard error of the difference (i.e., $\sigma_{\overline{x}_1 - \overline{x}_2}$) can be estimated from the standard deviation of the differences between each pair of scores, s_{d_i}. The formula for a paired samples *t*-test thus becomes

$$t = \frac{\overline{d}_i}{\frac{s_{d_i}}{\sqrt{N}}},$$ Equation 13.13

where $\overline{d}_i$ is the mean difference between all pairs of scores,

d_i is the difference between the paired scores of case *i*.

The degrees of freedom for a paired samples t-test is $N - 1$ where N is the number of paired scores. Figure 13.5 illustrates the quantities contributing to the terms that make up the formula for *t* using fabricated data of 5 pairs of cases.

Figure 13.5. Data illustrating the quantities used to calculate a *t*-test for paired samples. Five pairs of scores in two conditions are represented. The test determines whether the mean score in the two conditions differs significantly.

Pair #	Condition1	Condition 2	d_i
1	3	6	-3
2	4	7	-3
3	8	8	0
4	5	6	-1
5	4	8	-4
Means:	4.80	7.00	-2.20

s_{d_i} is the standard deviation of these values. $s_{d_i}=1.64$

$\overline{d}_i$ is the difference between the two means

$\overline{d}_i = -2.20$

$$t = \frac{-2.20}{\frac{1.64}{\sqrt{5}}} = -2.99$$

Effect Size

The effect size can be measured using *d*. The formula is

$$d = \frac{\overline{x}_1 - \overline{x}_2}{s_{d_i}}$$ Equation 13.14

where s_{d_i} is the standard deviation of the d_i values.

An alternate formula is

$$d = \frac{t}{\sqrt{N}} \qquad \text{Equation 13.15}$$

where N is the number of paired scores.

Underlying Assumptions

A t-test for paired samples is equivalent to a single-sample t-test that compares the mean difference between paired scores and zero. Thus, similar assumptions underlie both tests. Specifically, it is assumed that differences between paired scores (i.e., d_i values) are normally distributed in the population and the pairs of scores have been randomly and independently sampled. As mention previously, when sample sizes are large (30 or higher) violation of the assumption of normality does not seriously jeopardize interpretation of the probabilities associated with the sample t values.

Requesting the Analysis

To perform a paired samples t-test, each case in the **SPSS Statistics Data Editor** spreadsheet must consist of a value of the dependent variable for each pair of conditions being compared. Thus, to determine whether a diet affects weight based on the weight of each of 20 people assessed before and after the exercise program, the spreadsheet could look as follows:

	id	before	after	var
1	1.00	141.35	136.69	
2	2.00	154.44	152.65	
3	3.00	150.87	149.28	
4	4.00	149.59	149.11	
5	5.00	127.16	121.21	
6	6.00	128.49	121.93	
7	7.00	150.24	146.70	
8	8.00	179.51	175.20	
9	9.00	152.20	149.05	
10	10.00	150.25	149.24	
11	11.00	149.89	149.15	
12	12.00	137.59	135.97	
13	13.00	176.41	170.16	
14	14.00	141.92	136.80	
15	15.00	148.29	146.98	
16	16.00	128.22	127.83	
17	17.00	132.14	132.17	
18	18.00	170.20	169.22	
19	19.00	166.03	158.50	
20	20.00	163.76	152.70	

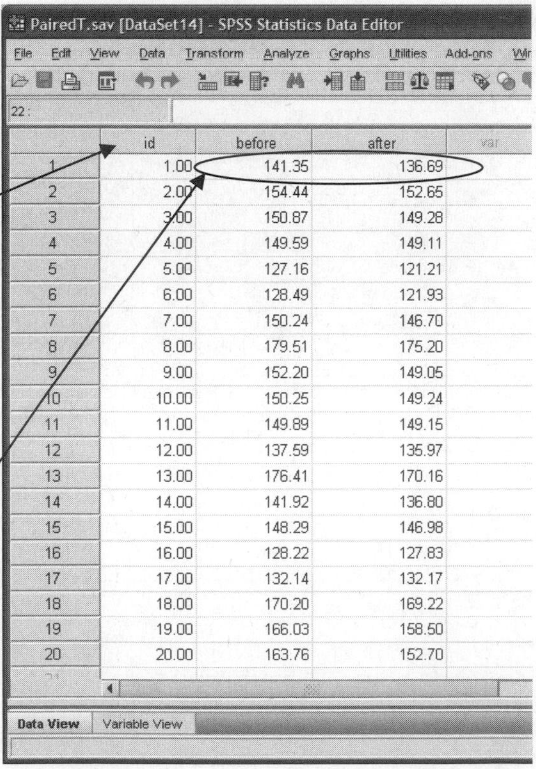

The variable **id** is used to identify each participant and is not analyzed.

The first line shows that the person 1 weighed 141.35 pounds before the diet and 136.69 pounds after the diet.

The procedure for determining whether mean weight before the diet differs from mean weight after the diet is shown below:

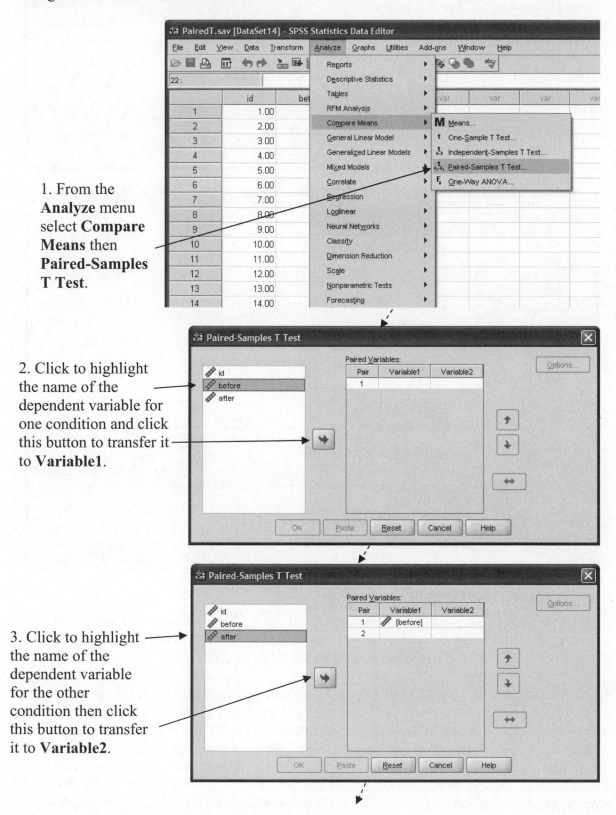

1. From the **Analyze** menu select **Compare Means** then **Paired-Samples T Test**.

2. Click to highlight the name of the dependent variable for one condition and click this button to transfer it to **Variable1**.

3. Click to highlight the name of the dependent variable for the other condition then click this button to transfer it to **Variable2**.

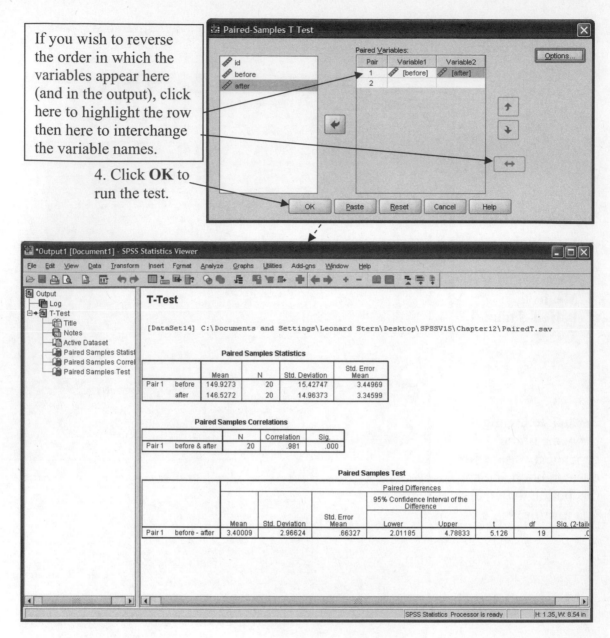

If you wish to reverse the order in which the variables appear here (and in the output), click here to highlight the row then here to interchange the variable names.

4. Click **OK** to run the test.

Interpreting the Output

The output for a paired samples *t*-test consists of three tables. Summary statistics for the dependent variable for each condition of the study are presented in the first table. The outcome of the paired samples *t*-test is summarized in the third table.

The second table, the one labeled **Paired Samples Correlations**, allows the relation between the paired scores to be assessed using Pearson's *r* together with its two-tailed significance level. Knowledge of the relation between paired scores can be helpful in assessing whether there is an advantage of using the paired samples *t*-test rather than the independent samples *t*-test. The paired samples procedure provides a more powerful test than the independent samples procedure when there is a positive correlation between paired scores; if the correlation is zero, the same value of *t* results from both procedures. However, when the correlation between the paired scores is negative, the paired procedure is less powerful. Knowledge of the correlation between the paired scores is especially helpful when a matching procedure is used. The matching process is only beneficial when the paired scores are positively correlated.

The output of a paired samples *t*-test for the diet data is shown below:

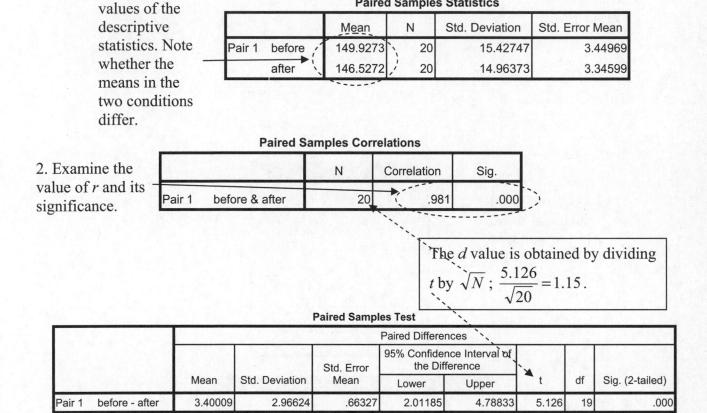

1. Inspect the values of the descriptive statistics. Note whether the means in the two conditions differ.

Paired Samples Statistics

		Mean	N	Std. Deviation	Std. Error Mean
Pair 1	before	149.9273	20	15.42747	3.44969
	after	146.5272	20	14.96373	3.34599

2. Examine the value of *r* and its significance.

Paired Samples Correlations

		N	Correlation	Sig.
Pair 1	before & after	20	.981	.000

The *d* value is obtained by dividing *t* by $\sqrt{N}$; $\frac{5.126}{\sqrt{20}}=1.15$.

Paired Samples Test

		Paired Differences							
					95% Confidence Interval of the Difference				
		Mean	Std. Deviation	Std. Error Mean	Lower	Upper	t	df	Sig. (2-tailed)
Pair 1	before - after	3.40009	2.96624	.66327	2.01185	4.78833	5.126	19	.000

This is the value of $\bar{d}_i$, the difference between the two means.

This is s_{d_i}, the standard deviation of the d_i values.

This is $\frac{s_{d_i}}{\sqrt{N}}$

3. Obtain the value of *t*, its degrees of freedom and significance from these columns.

Graphing the Data

To prepare a bar chart for data analyzed with a paired samples *t*-test, follow the procedure shown below:

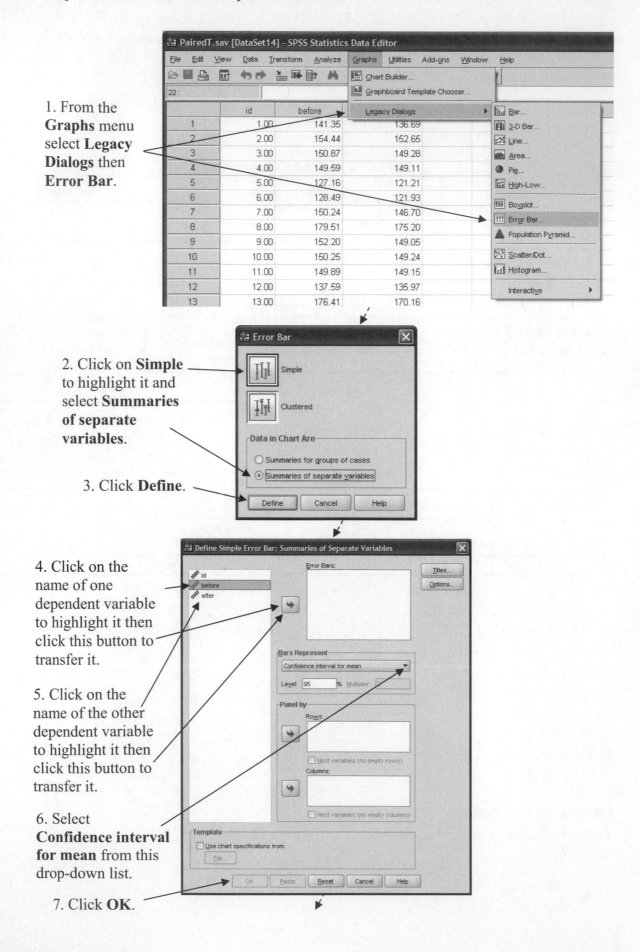

1. From the **Graphs** menu select **Legacy Dialogs** then **Error Bar**.

2. Click on **Simple** to highlight it and select **Summaries of separate variables**.

3. Click **Define**.

4. Click on the name of one dependent variable to highlight it then click this button to transfer it.

5. Click on the name of the other dependent variable to highlight it then click this button to transfer it.

6. Select **Confidence interval for mean** from this drop-down list.

7. Click **OK**.

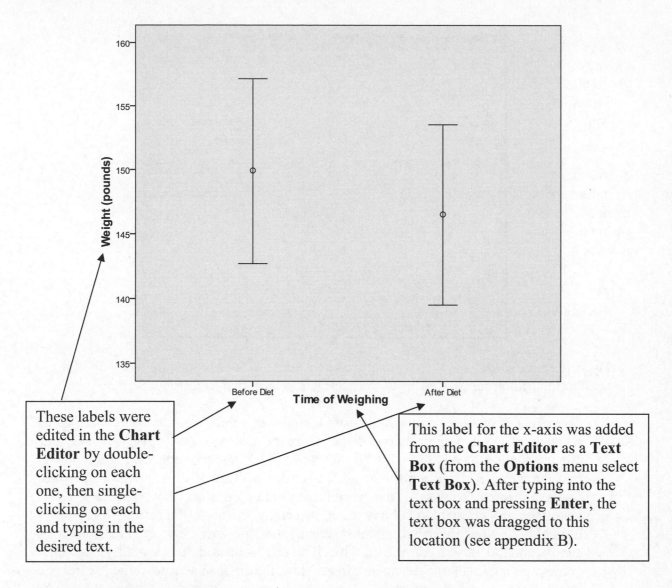

These labels were edited in the **Chart Editor** by double-clicking on each one, then single-clicking on each and typing in the desired text.

This label for the x-axis was added from the **Chart Editor** as a **Text Box** (from the **Options** menu select **Text Box**). After typing into the text box and pressing **Enter**, the text box was dragged to this location (see appendix B).

Reporting the Results

To check the assumptions underlying a paired-samples *t*-test, the d_i values should be obtained using the **Compute variable** procedure as shown below:

1. From the **Transform** menu choose **Compute variable**.

2. Type the name of the variable representing d_i values.

3. Use the existing variable names to form a formula for the d_i values.

4. Click **OK**.

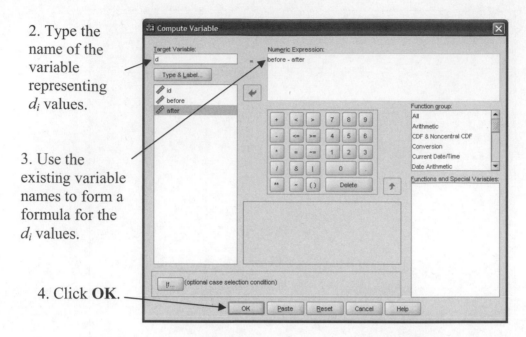

The difference scores can then be analyzed using the **Explore** procedure to check of the assumption of normality. Results of the *t*-test can be reported as follows:

> The effect of the diet on weight loss of 20 randomly selected adults was examined by weighing each participant one week before the diet ($M = 149.93$, $SD = 15.43$) and one week after the diet ($M = 146.53$, $SD = 14.96$). Difference scores were computed by subtracting each participant's weight after the diet from his/her weight before the diet. An informal analysis of the distribution of these difference scores using a histogram and normal Q-Q plot revealed no serious threats to the assumption of normality. A *t*-test for paired samples showed the difference between the means was significant, $t(19) = 5.13$, $p < .001$. The effect size as measure by *d* was 1.15, a value corresponding to a large treatment effect. Thus, the diet had a large, reliable effect on weight loss.

Exercises for Chapter 13

Exercise 13.1

The Barber Suggestibility Scale (Barber, 1969) is used to assess a person's level of hypnotic suggestibility. The scale is comprised of experimenter-evaluated responses by participants to eight scenarios such as "Imagine your arm is getting lighter." Participants whose responses exceed some minimum value (e.g., moving his/her arm up 4 inches in response to the suggestion) are given one point. The scale based on these objective measures has a minimum and maximum value of 0 and 8, respectively, with high values indicating higher suggestibility. Use the data in the file *Hypnotizablity.sav* to determine whether there is a difference in mean recognition memory ability (the variable **mem1** or a variable derived from it—see question 3 below) for participants classified as highly hypnotizable (**object** at or above 5.50) vs. low hypnotizable (**object** score at or below 2.50). Do the following:

1. Use the variable **object** to create a new variable called **group** that has the value 1 if **object** is between 0.00-2.50, 2 if **object** is between 5.50-8.00, and 0 otherwise (you can accomplish this easily using **Recode into Different Variables**).
2. Check underlying assumptions using **Explore**.
3. Create a new memory measure **mem2** that is the square of **mem1**. Run **Explore** again to determine whether distribution of the transformed variable **mem2** better meets the assumption of normality for each sample being evaluated.
4. Perform an appropriate *t*-test on a suitable dependent variable.
5. Report the results of the analysis following the format described in the text.

Exercise 13.2

The file *VoteTV.sav* includes the variable **vote** that indicates who the participant voted for in the 1992 U.S. presidential election and the variable **tv** that indicates the number of hours of TV per day that the person estimates he/she watches. The data come from randomly selected adults aged 18-65 contacted by the National Opinion Research Center from 1993-1998. Determine whether the mean number of hours of TV watched by people who voted for Clinton (**vote** = 1) differed from the mean number of hours of TV watched by people who voted for Bush (**vote** = 2). In performing this test, determine whether underlying distributional assumptions for the variable **tv** are better met by applying a $\log_{10}$ transformation. Summarize results of the analysis following the format described in the text.

Exercise 13.3

The data in file *PriusMPG.sav* consists of mileage estimates provided by 74 2006 Toyota Prius owners as reported on the website http://www.fueleconomy.gov/. Assume the data in the file represent a random sample of 2006 Toyota Prius drivers.

1. Use the variable **MPG** to determine if the mean gas mileage of the drivers differs from the EPA combined city/highway mpg estimate of 55.
2. The EPA derives their combined mpg estimate by assuming that the percent of city vs. highway driving is 55/45. Use the data in variable **hiway** to determine if the percent of highway driving reported by Prius drivers differs significantly from the EPA estimate of 45

Exercise 13.4

The data for this problem are adapted from the article by Card, David and Krueger, Alan, "Minimum Wages and Employment: A Case Study of the Fast-Food Industry in New Jersey and Pennsylvania" published in *The American Economic Review 84.4* (Sept. 1994), 772-793. The data are available at the UCLA Statistics Data Sets website, http://www.stat.ucla.edu/data/, and appear here by permission of the authors.

In April, 1992, the minimum wage in New Jersey went from $4.25 to $5.05 an hour. The data in file *MinWage.sav* was obtained from randomly selected fast food restaurants about one month before and eight months after the minimum wage increase took effect. The variable names and identifying information about the variables is shown in the table below:

Variable Name	Variable Label
StoreID	Identification number for the store
State	State in which the store was located: 1=NJ; 2=PA
Fulltime1	Number of full-time employees before wage raise
Parttime1	Number of part-time employees before wage raise
Manage1	Number of managers/assistant managers before wage raise
Fulltime2	Number of full-time employees after wage raise
Parttime2	Number of part-time employees after wage raise
Manage2	Number of managers/assistant managers after wage raise
HrsOpen1	Number of hours store was open before the wage raise
Psoda1	Price of a medium soda before the wage raise
Pfry1	Price of a small fry before the wage raise
HrsOpen2	Number of hours store was open after the wage raise
Psoda2	Price of a medium soda after the wage raise
Pfry2	Price of a small fry after the wage raise

1. Select just the stores in New Jersey. Do an appropriate statistical test to determine whether the change in minimum wage is associated with a significant effect on the number of full-time employees.
2. Repeat the analysis performed in question 1 separately for the part-time employees and managers/assistant managers. What are the outcomes of the analyses?
3. For just the stores in New Jersey, determine if the wage raise was significantly associated to the price of a medium soda or the price of a small fry.
4. Calculate the effect size for any difference that was significant for questions 1-3, and characterize the magnitude of the effect.

Exercise 13.5

Use the data in file *MinWage.sav* for this exercise.
1. Compute a new variable called **Dfry** by subtracting the price of a small fry before the wage increase (**Pfry1**) from the price of a small fry after the wage increase (**Pfry2**).
2. Select just the restaurants in Pennsylvania. Determine whether the variable **Dfry** differs significantly from zero.
3. Repeat the analysis performed in problem 2 for the restaurants in New Jersey. What is the outcome?
4. Perform a suitable test to determine whether the mean value of **Dfry** differs in New Jersey and Pennsylvania. How do the results of the test affect interpretation of the effect of the minimum wage increase in New Jersey on the price of fries in fast food restaurants?

Chapter 14: One-way Analysis of Variance

Introduction

Purpose of the analysis

A one-way analysis of variance (often abbreviated *ANOVA*) can be used to determine if two or more independent random samples come from populations with different means. The procedure is termed a one-way analysis because the distinction among samples is conceived of in terms of a single categorical variable, often termed a factor. For example, if one wishes to determine whether weight loss differs when a person engages in aerobic exercise, strength training, or does neither, the distinction among these three conditions (often referred to as levels of a factor) may be thought of as values of the categorical variable **exercise condition**. A variable such as **exercise condition** serves as the independent variable in the analysis. The dependent variable in this example could be pounds lost after 6 weeks. Generally dependent variables are scale variables (in *SPSS* parlance), that is, quantitative variables measured on an interval or ratio scale.

The null hypothesis in a one-way *ANOVA* is that the populations represented by the samples all have the same means. Rejecting the null hypothesis does not necessarily imply that the populations all have different means; rather, it is reason to conclude that the populations do not all have the same mean. Symbolically, the null and alternate hypotheses may be represented as follows:

$$H_0: \mu_1 = \mu_2 = \mu_3$$

$$H_1: \mu_1, \mu_2, \mu_3, \text{not all} =$$

Possible scenarios consistent with H_1 are shown in Figure 14.1. Testing for specific patterns among population means can be done using planned comparisons or trend analyses (see below).

Figure 14.1. Possible patterns among population means that would lead to rejecting the null hypothesis in an analysis of variance. In scenario 1, the mean of population 3 differs from that of population 1 and 2 which have the same mean. In scenario 2, populations 1 and 3 have the same mean which differs from that of population 2. Scenario 3 shows three populations having different means.

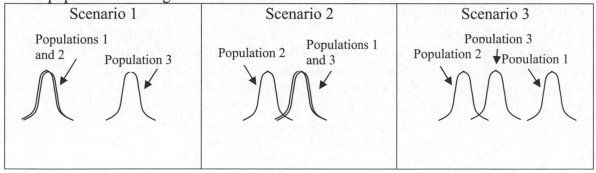

Calculations Involved in the Analysis

The decision to reject or not reject the null hypothesis in a one-way *ANOVA* is based on an *F* statistic, which, in general, is the ratio of two independent estimates of the same population variance:

$$F = \frac{s_1^2}{s_2^2}$$ Equation 14.1

In the analysis of variance one estimate of population variance, the term represented in the numerator, is based on the variance of the sample means (i.e., $s_{\bar{x}}^2$) and the other, represented in the denominator, is based on the variance of scores in each sample (i.e. s_x^2). When the null hypothesis is true, the ratio of these estimates of population variance will have an *F* distribution. When the null hypothesis is false, the numerator estimate of population variance in the *F* ratio will tend to be greater than that in the denominator because the inequality among population means will be reflected in an increased variance among sample means. As a result, *F* will have a higher value than expected. A formula for obtaining *F* when sample sizes are equal (sample size is referred to in the formula as N_x; $N_{\bar{x}}$ refers to the number of samples) is shown below. In the formula *j* indexes the sample number and *i* indexes the subject number in the jth sample:

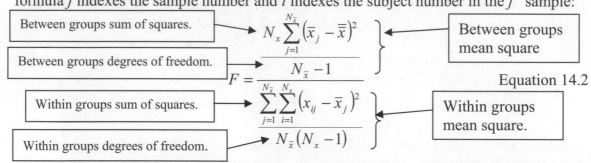

Between groups sum of squares.

Between groups degrees of freedom.

Between groups mean square

Within groups sum of squares.

Within groups mean square.

Within groups degrees of freedom.

$$F = \frac{\dfrac{N_x \sum_{j=1}^{N_{\bar{x}}} (\bar{x}_j - \bar{\bar{x}})^2}{N_{\bar{x}} - 1}}{\dfrac{\sum_{j=1}^{N_{\bar{x}}} \sum_{i=1}^{N_x} (x_{ij} - \bar{x}_j)^2}{N_{\bar{x}}(N_x - 1)}}$$

Equation 14.2

In the *ANOVA* table that summarizes the outcome of the calculations described above, the estimate of population variance obtained in the numerator of the *F* ratio is termed the Between Groups estimate and that in the denominator, the Within Groups estimate. The probability associated with the *F* value is used to decide whether or not to reject the null hypothesis. Conventionally, if the probability value is .05 or lower, the null hypothesis is rejected.

Underlying Assumptions

Several assumptions underlie a one-way *ANOVA*. One is that cases are randomly assigned to conditions. Another is that the dependent variable is normally distributed in each population that is sampled. When equal numbers of cases are assigned to each condition in a study, moderate violations of this assumption do not seriously undermine the test's validity. A third assumption is that in the populations being sampled the variance of values of the dependent variable is equal. To get a sense of whether this assumption may be violated, the standard deviations of the scores in the different conditions may be examined in the table of descriptive statistics. Validity of the assumption can be more rigorously evaluated by requesting the Levene test of homogeneity of variance (see previous chapter, page 269). If the significance value of the

Levene test is .05 or less, then the underlying assumption of homogeneity of variance may be invalid. Violating this assumption can raise the probability of Type I errors, particularly when samples have unequal sizes and smaller samples have the higher variability. When the Levene test is significant, an alternative to the one-way ANOVA is the Brown-Forsyth test (available as an option listed just below the **Homogeneity of variance test**). As with the assumption of normality, when sample sizes are equal, moderate violations of the assumption do not seriously undermine validity of the test. If the ratio of the highest to lowest cell variance is less than 3, violation of the homogeneity of variance assumption can be considered moderate; when the ratio is between 3-9, lowering alpha to .025 may be appropriate (Keppel, 1991).

Preparing Data for the Analysis

To perform a one-way analysis of variance, each case on the **SPSS Statistics Data Editor** must include values of two variables, one corresponding to the independent variable, and the other to the dependent variable. The value of the independent variable for a case should consist of an integer value that stands for one of its categories. Thus, if there are three levels of the independent variable, one could choose from among the integer values 1, 2, and 3, though any three arbitrarily chosen numbers such as 0, 4, and 15 could be used. The dependent variable should be the value measured for the participant on the variable of interest. For example, to determine if type of exercise affects mean number of pounds lost after 6 weeks, the independent variable is type of exercise; if this variable consists of three conditions, aerobic exercise, strength training, and no treatment, these conditions may be represented by the numbers 1, 2, and 3, respectively. The data set shown below indicates the first case (i.e., person) participated in exercise condition 1 and lost 8 pounds, and the second case participated in exercise condition 1 and lost 6 pounds. Although the data set shown below depicts cases grouped by levels of the independent variable, that is, the first four cases are from exercise condition 1, the next four from exercise condition 2, etc., cases can be entered in any order.

*OneWayAnova.sav [DataSet1] - SPSS Statistics D

File   Edit   View   Data   Transform   Analyze   Graphs

14:

	cond	lbslost	var
1	1.00	8.00	
2	1.00	6.00	
3	1.00	9.00	
4	1.00	11.00	
5	2.00	6.00	
6	2.00	5.00	
7	2.00	3.00	
8	2.00	3.00	
9	3.00	0.00	
10	3.00	-1.00	
11	3.00	2.00	
12	3.00	-2.00	
13			

It is helpful in interpreting the output of a one-way *ANOVA* if the independent and dependent variables have suitable labels and if values of the independent variable have been assigned suitable labels as shown below:

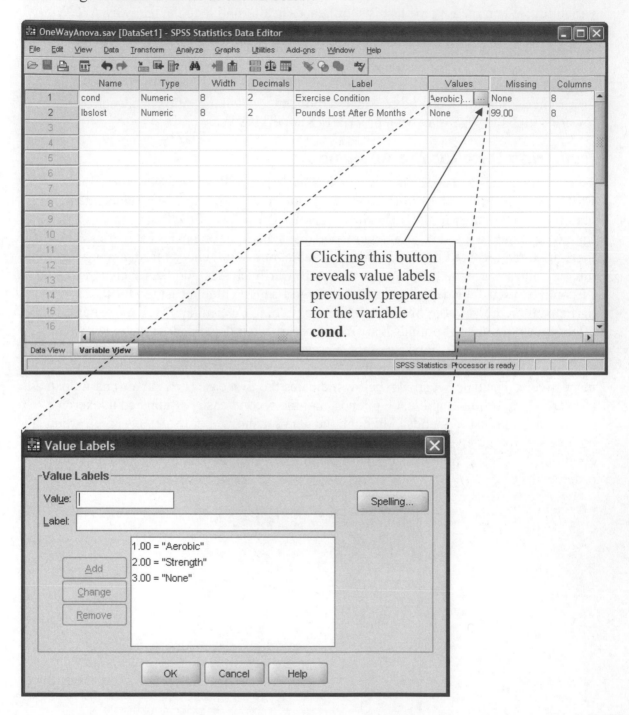

Requesting a One-Way ANOVA

After a data set has been entered in the **SPSS Statistics Data Editor** spreadsheet, a one-way *ANOVA* can be requested.

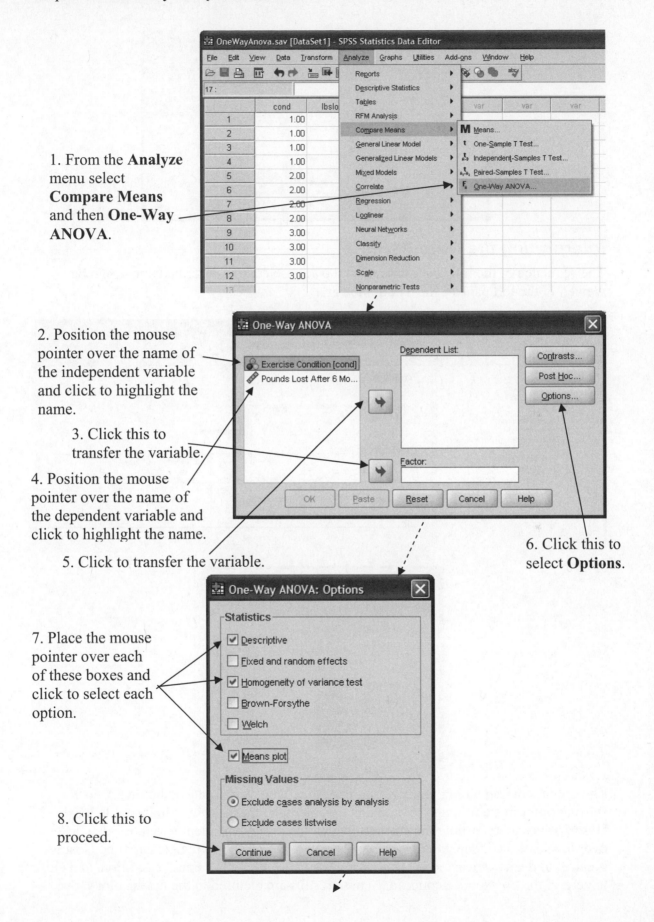

1. From the **Analyze** menu select **Compare Means** and then **One-Way ANOVA**.

2. Position the mouse pointer over the name of the independent variable and click to highlight the name.

3. Click this to transfer the variable.

4. Position the mouse pointer over the name of the dependent variable and click to highlight the name.

5. Click to transfer the variable.

6. Click this to select **Options**.

7. Place the mouse pointer over each of these boxes and click to select each option.

8. Click this to proceed.

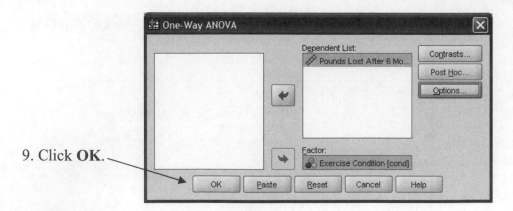

9. Click **OK**.

Interpreting the Output

The sequence of the information produced by the selections described above can be viewed in the left pane of the **SPSS Viewer**.

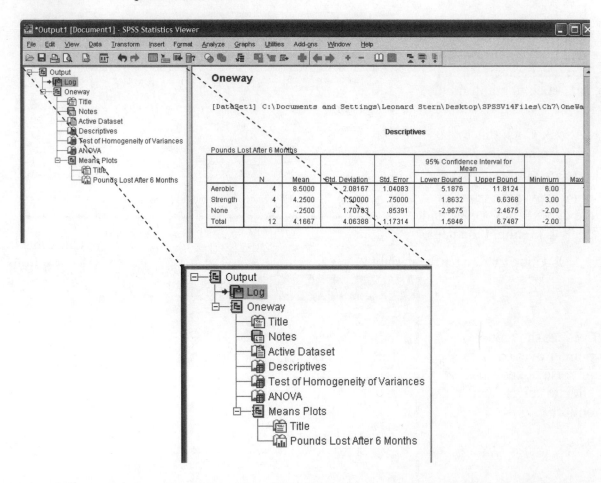

The output corresponding to the listing in outline view is reproduced below. A good starting point in examining the output is to look at the means shown in the table labeled **Descriptives** to determine the extent to which the mean dependent variable value differs over levels of the independent variable. The table below shows the mean pounds lost is greatest in the aerobic exercise condition, less in the strength training condition, and close to zero in the no exercise condition. These results are pictured in the means plot shown last in the output sequence. The *F* ratio and its significance level used to make a decision about rejecting/not rejecting the null hypothesis are displayed in the **ANOVA** table.

An index of effect size suitable for a one-way *ANOVA* is eta squared (η^2), a coefficient that is interpreted in much the same way as r^2. Like r^2 eta squared has a range of 0-1 with high values indicating a higher proportion of variance among values of the dependent variable that can be accounted for or explained by variation among values of the independent variable. Eta squared is given by the following formulas:

$$\eta^2 = \frac{SS_{Between}}{SS_{Total}} \text{ or } \frac{df_{Between} \times F}{df_{Between} \times F + df_{Within}} \qquad \text{Equation 14.3}$$

The values .01, .06, and .14 roughly correspond to a small, medium, and large effect size, respectively.

Guidelines for inspecting the output of a one-way *ANOVA* are listed below:

Descriptives

Pounds Lost After 6 Months

	N	Mean	Std. Deviation	Std. Error	95% Confidence Interval for Mean		Minimum	Maximum
					Lower Bound	Upper Bound		
Aerobic	4	8.5000	2.08167	1.04083	5.1876	11.8124	6.00	11.00
Strength	4	4.2500	1.50000	.75000	1.8632	6.6368	3.00	6.00
None	4	-.2500	1.70783	.85391	-2.9675	2.4675	-2.00	2.00
Total	12	4.1667	4.06388	1.17314	1.5846	6.7487	-2.00	11.00

1a. Inspect means of the samples. Determine if their values differ in accord with the hypothesis being tested. Examine the means plot (shown below) to see the pattern among the group means.

2a. Inspect the standard deviations of the samples to determine if the values differ substantially. Examine the Levene test to determine if the variance heterogeneity is significant.

Test of Homogeneity of Variances

Pounds Lost After 6 Months

Levene Statistic	df1	df2	Sig.
.107	2	9	.900

2b. A significance value of .05 or less indicates a significant violation of the assumption of homogeneity of variance. Here, the assumption is not violated.

Use these values to calculate the effect size, η^2.

ANOVA

Pounds Lost After 6 Months

	Sum of Squares	df	Mean Square	F	Sig.
Between Groups	153.167	2	76.583	24.184	.000
Within Groups	28.500	9	3.167		
Total	181.667	11			

3. Inspect the significance of the *F* value. A value of .05 or less indicates the independent variable has a significant effect on the dependent variable. Here, the effect is highly significant.

Means Plots

1b. Examine plot to determine how the groups means differ.

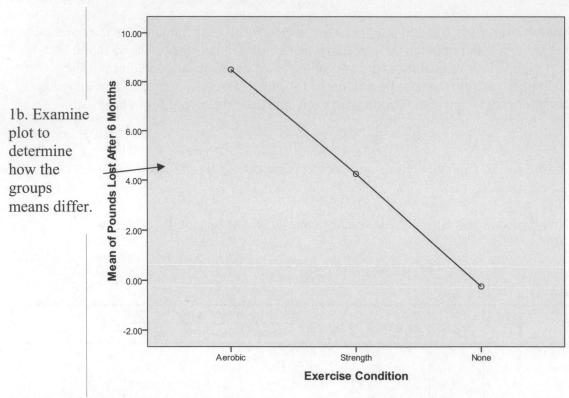

Exercise Condition

For the data in our example of the effect of exercise condition on weight loss, the results could be reported as follows:

> Twelve adults were randomly assigned in equal numbers to receive one of three forms of exercise: aerobic, strength, or none. Participants were responsible for reporting the number of pounds they had lost after six weeks of engaging in the assigned activities of their exercise condition. Means and standard deviations of the dependent variable, number of pounds lost, are shown in Table 14.1. Differences among the mean number of pounds lost by participants in the exercise conditions were assessed with a one-way *ANOVA*. A Levene test of homogeneity of variance conducted prior to the *ANOVA* did not indicate the assumption of homogeneity of variance was significantly violated ($p > .50$). The *ANOVA* was significant, $F(2, 9) = 24.18$, $p < .001$, $\eta^2 = .84$. Thus exercise condition had a significant and sizeable effect on mean number of pounds lost.

Table 14.1. Descriptive statistics for *ANOVA* example.

Exercise Condition	N	Mean	Standard Deviation
Aerobic	4	8.50	2.08
Strength	4	4.25	1.50
None	4	-0.25	1.71

Requesting Planned Comparisons

A significant *F* value for a one-way *ANOVA* indicates that the means of all populations under consideration are not equal. However, a researcher often has more specific hypotheses in mind. In our example of the effect of exercise on weight loss, the researcher may have wished to examine these more specific questions: 1) Is there a differential effect on weight loss of engaging in any form of exercise--strength or aerobic --vs. doing nothing? 2) Is there a different effect on weight loss of aerobic vs. strength training? These more specific questions call for planned comparisons.

To perform a planned comparison, one first has to propose a suitable set of comparison coefficients to test each hypothesis. Although the procedure for proposing comparison coefficients is beyond the scope of this text (see, for example, Keppel & Wickens, 2004), one can think of comparison coefficients as a set of numbers that reflect the hypothesized pattern among population means. Thus, to determine whether the combined mean weight loss of the aerobic and strength exercise conditions differs from the mean weight loss of the no exercise condition, the coefficients -1, -1, and 2 would be suitable. Note that the comparison coefficients sum to zero, there is a comparison coefficient for each level of the independent variable, and the order of the comparison coefficients corresponds to the magnitude of the values used to code levels of the independent variable (in our example, the values 1, 2, and 3 represent the aerobic, strength, and no exercise conditions, respectively). Note also that the signs of the comparison coefficients could be switched without affecting the outcome of the test (i.e., the coefficient set -1, -1, 2 is equivalent to the set 1, 1, -2). To test whether the mean weight loss in the aerobic condition differs from that in the strength condition, the coefficients -1, 1, and 0 would be suitable [note that the 0 value for condition 3 (the no exercise condition) reflects that the no exercise condition does not participate in the test]. The sequence shown below implements these planned comparisons after the data have been entered and the variables transferred to the **Dependent List** and **Factor** fields in the **One-Way** *ANOVA* window (see steps 1-5 in the section *Requesting a One-Way* **ANOVA**).

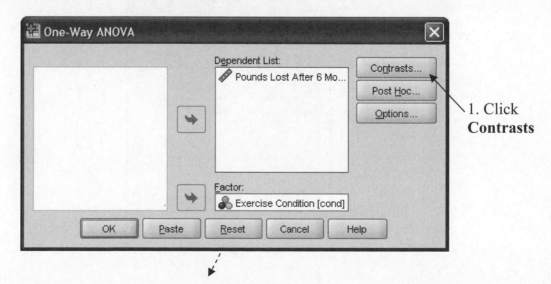

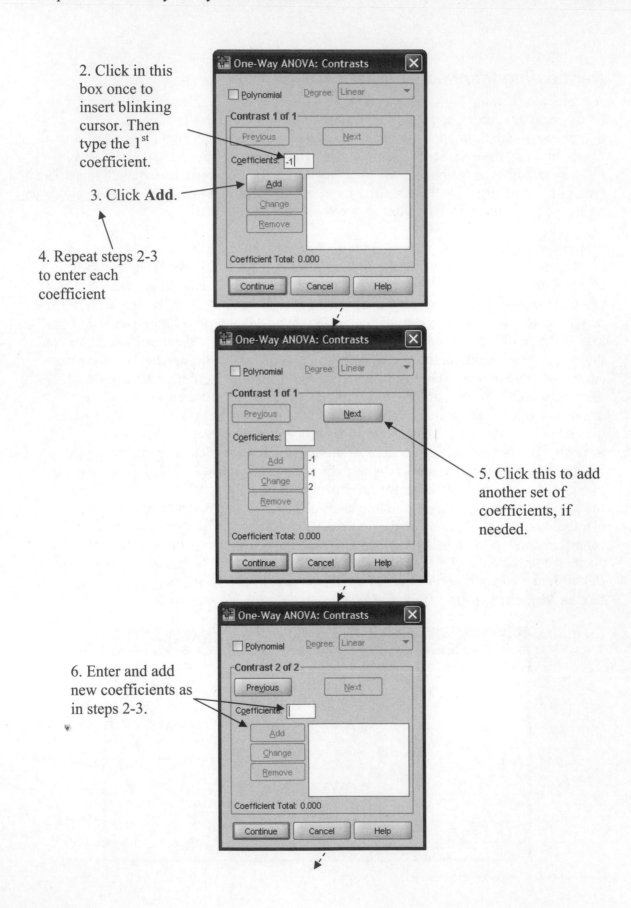

2. Click in this box once to insert blinking cursor. Then type the 1st coefficient.

3. Click **Add**.

4. Repeat steps 2-3 to enter each coefficient

5. Click this to add another set of coefficients, if needed.

6. Enter and add new coefficients as in steps 2-3.

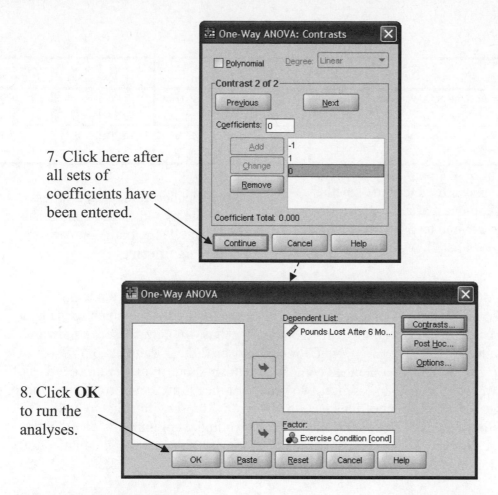

7. Click here after all sets of coefficients have been entered.

8. Click **OK** to run the analyses.

Interpreting the Output

The output for a planned comparison will present first a table showing the sets of comparison coefficients requested. You should verify that the coefficients listed in the table are those you intended to enter. Next will be significance tests for each planned comparison. Because a planned comparison basically contrasts the values of two means (those corresponding to the negative coefficients vs. the positive coefficients) the test statistic reported is t rather than F (but one can convert the t value to its corresponding F value by squaring it). Two sets of t values are reported in the table labeled **Contrast Tests**. One is based on the assumption that there is no significant difference among the variances of the populations tested, and the other assumes the variances differ. For the tests that do not assume equal variances, an adjustment is made in the degrees of freedom and the result reflected in the significance value listed in the last column of the table.

The output produced by the two sets of comparison coefficients used in our example is shown below:

Contrast Coefficients

Contrast	Exercise Condition		
	Aerobic	Strength	None
1	-1	-1	2
2	-1	1	0

1. Inspect the coefficients listed for each planned comparison. Verify that their values conform to the hypothesis being tested.

Contrast Tests

		Contrast	Value of Contrast	Std. Error	t	df	Sig. (2-tailed)
Pounds Lost After 6 Months	Assume equal variances	1	-13.2500	2.17945	-6.080	9	.000
		2	-4.2500	1.25831	-3.378	9	.008
	Does not assume equal variances	1	-13.2500	2.13600	-6.203	6.247	.001
		2	-4.2500	1.28290	-3.313	5.454	.019

2. Use the Levene test to determine whether you should or should not assume equal variances. If the Levene test's p value is < .05, use the t values listed in the lower rows of the table.

3. A significance value of .05 or less indicates the hypothesized comparison is significant. Here, both comparisons are highly significant.

Either a value of t or a value of F can be used to describe the outcome of a planned comparison. To report the outcome using an F value, square the t value given in the table labeled **Contrast Tests** to obtain the corresponding F. Thus, for comparison 1 shown above, the F value is -6.080^2 or 36.97, and for comparison 2 the F value is -3.378^2 or 11.41. When F is reported for a planned comparison, the number of numerator degrees of freedom is always 1, because, in essence, two groups of means are being compared, those corresponding to comparison coefficients with positive vs. those with negative values. The denominator degrees of freedom is the value shown in the column labeled df in the table showing **Contrast Tests**. Thus, for both comparisons shown above, the numerator and denominator degrees of freedom are 1 and 9, respectively.

The effect size for a planned comparison can be reported as a value of partial eta squared given by the formula

$$\eta^2_{partial} = \frac{F_{comparison}}{F_{comparison} + df_{denominator}}. \qquad \text{Equation 14.4}$$

Thus, for comparison 1, the following calculations provide the value of partial eta squared:

$$\eta^2_{partial} = \frac{36.97}{36.79 + 9} = .80. \qquad \text{Equation 14.5}$$

Reporting the Results

A report of the outcome of the planned comparisons for our example is shown below:

> The hypothesized difference between the mean pounds lost in the combined aerobic and strength exercise condition vs. the no exercise condition was tested with a planned comparison and found to be significantly different than chance, $F(1, 9) = 36.97, p < .001, \eta^2_{partial} = .80$.
>
> Also significant was the contrast between the mean pounds lost in the aerobic and strength exercise conditions, $F(1, 9) = 11.41, p < .001, \eta^2_{partial} = .56$.

Corrections for Multiple Tests of Data and Post-Hoc Tests

If multiple tests are made using the same set of data, and α is set at .05 for each test, the probability of making one or more Type I errors (i.e., rejecting the null hypothesis when the null hypothesis is true) in the set of multiple tests is greater than .05. To control for the increase in Type I errors with multiple testing and for tests devised after the data have been obtained (*post hoc* tests), correction procedures are often applied. There are many procedures for making corrections that are tailored to specific testing circumstances. The test selection scheme shown below is modeled after recommendations made by Keppel (1991).

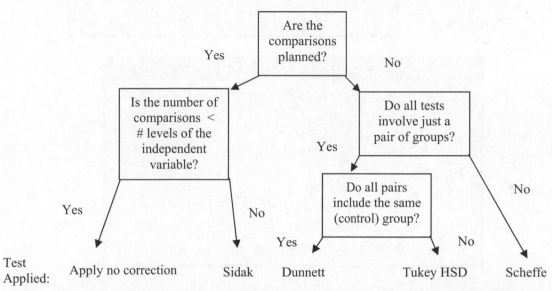

As an illustration, if a researcher testing the effect of an aerobic, strength, and no exercise condition on weight lost after 6 months has no specific hypotheses about the outcome, but decides after inspecting the data to compare all pairs of means, a reasonable choice of *post hoc* test would be the Tukey HSD test.

Implementing the procedure

After the data have been entered and the variables transferred to the **Dependent List** and **Factor** fields in the **One-Way ANOVA** window (see steps 1-5 in the *Requesting a One-Way* **ANOVA** section) the following procedure will run a Tukey HSD test:

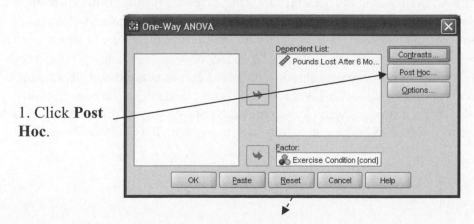

1. Click **Post Hoc**.

2. Click **Tukey** to select a Tukey HSD test.

This is the default significance level. It is usually left at .05.

3. Click **Continue**.

4. Click **OK**.

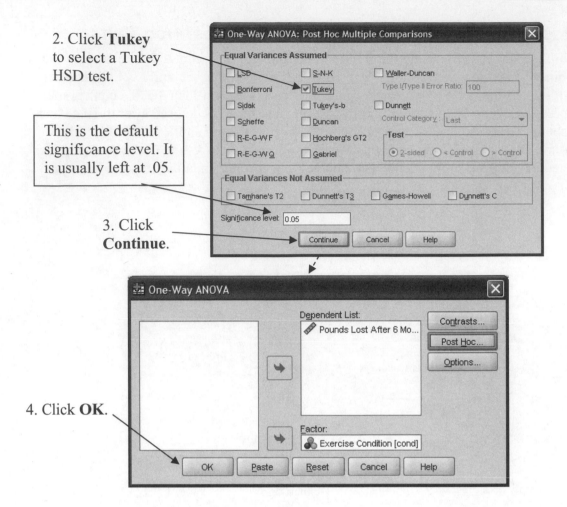

Interpreting the Output

The significance tests that compare mean dependent variable values for all possible pairings of factor levels are shown in the **Multiple Comparisons** table. There is considerable redundancy in the table. Each row compares the mean dependent variable value of one factor level separately to every other factor level. Pairs of means that differ significantly are starred in the **Mean Difference** column of the table and the exact significance level is shown in the column labeled **Sig**.

Within the columns of the table in the section of output labeled **Homogenous Subsets** are names of factor levels whose means do not differ significantly; the probability level shown at the bottom of each column is the probability of finding means as or more different by chance (this probability will always be ≥ .05 or whatever α level is selected--see comment preceding step 3 above). Listed in different columns are mean dependent variable values corresponding to factor level names whose means do differ significantly. In our example, the mean pounds lost in each exercise condition differs significantly from that in every other individual exercise condition, so each column lists only one exercise condition name.

Post Hoc Tests

> The difference in the mean pounds lost in the aerobic and strength exercise conditions is 4.25

Multiple Comparisons

Pounds Lost After 6 Months
Tukey HSD

> This row compares the aerobic exercise condition separately to every other condition.

(I) Exercise Condition	(J) Exercise Condition	Mean Difference (I-J)	Std. Error	Sig.	95% Confidence Interval	
					Lower Bound	Upper Bound
Aerobic	Strength	4.25000*	1.25831	.020	.7368	7.7632
	None	8.75000*	1.25831	.000	5.2368	12.2632
Strength	Aerobic	-4.25000*	1.25831	.020	-7.7632	-.7368
	None	4.50000*	1.25831	.015	.9868	8.0132
None	Aerobic	-8.75000*	1.25831	.000	-12.2632	-5.2368
	Strength	-4.50000*	1.25831	.015	-8.0132	-.9868

*. The mean difference is significant at the 0.05 level.

> The difference in the mean pounds lost in the aerobic and strength exercise conditions is significant

Homogeneous Subsets

Pounds Lost After 6 Months

Tukey HSD[a]

Exercise Condition	N	Subset for alpha = 0.05		
		1	2	3
None	4	-.2500		
Strength	4		4.2500	
Aerobic	4			8.5000
Sig.		1.000	1.000	1.000

Means for groups in homogeneous subsets are displayed.

a. Uses Harmonic Mean Sample Size = 4.000.

> Because the means of all conditions differ significantly from each other, each is placed in a separate column.

For our data set, the outcome of the Tukey HSD test could be reported as follows:

> A Tukey HSD test was used to examine differences in mean pounds lost between all pairs of exercise conditions. The differences in pounds lost for the no exercise and acrobic exercise conditions (M = 8.75), for the no exercise and strength exercise condition (M = 4.50) and for the aerobic and strength exercise condition (M = 4.25) were found to all be significant, $p < .025$.

The next set of tables shown is based on an alternate data set in which the mean pounds lost in the aerobic, strength, and no exercise condition are 6.75, 5.75, and -.25, respectively. For this data set, the table of **Homogenous Subsets** lists the mean pounds lost of the no exercise condition in column 1 and mean pounds lost of the strength and aerobic exercise conditions in column 2, which indicates that the mean pounds lost in the strength and aerobic exercise conditions do not differ significantly according to a Tukey HSD test but that the combined means of these two exercise conditions do differ significantly from that of the no exercise condition.

Post Hoc Tests

The difference in the mean pounds lost in the aerobic and strength exercise conditions is 1.00

Multiple Comparisons

Pounds Lost After 6 Months
Tukey HSD

(I) Exercise Condition	(J) Exercise Condition	Mean Difference (I-J)	Std. Error	Sig.	95% Confidence Interval	
					Lower Bound	Upper Bound
Aerobic	Strength	1.00000	.88976	.524	-1.4842	3.4842
	None	7.00000*	.88976	.000	4.5158	9.4842
Strength	Aerobic	-1.00000	.88976	.524	-3.4842	1.4842
	None	6.00000*	.88976	.000	3.5158	8.4842
None	Aerobic	-7.00000*	.88976	.000	-9.4842	-4.5158
	Strength	-6.00000*	.88976	.000	-8.4842	-3.5158

*. The mean difference is significant at the 0.05 level.

The difference in the mean pounds lost in the aerobic and strength exercise conditions is not significant.

Homogeneous Subsets

Pounds Lost After 6 Months

Tukey HSD[a]

Exercise Condition	N	Subset for alpha = 0.05	
		1	2
None	4	-.2500	
Strength	4		5.7500
Aerobic	4		6.7500
Sig.		1.000	.524

Means for groups in homogeneous subsets are displayed.

a. Uses Harmonic Mean Sample Size = 4.000.

Because the mean pounds lost in the aerobic and strength exercise conditions do not differ significantly, they are listed in the same column.

Because the mean pounds lost in the no exercise condition differs from that in the combined aerobic and strength exercise conditions, they are listed in different columns.

Exercises for Chapter 14

Exercise 14.1

For this problem, use the *CourseEval.sav* file provided on the publisher's website for this text, http://www.pearsonhighered.com/stern2e. The data in the file was gathered from students in various majors who were taking an introductory statistics course. Students were asked to identify their major and the grade they expected in the class. They were then given a 15-item multiple-choice test on statistical concepts.

The table shown below lists the name of each variable, an explanation of the concept assessed by each variable, and identification of the values for category variables.

Variable #	Variable Name	Concept Measured	Value Identification
1	Major	Major in College	1 = criminal justice
			2 = exercise science
			3 = nursing
			4 = psychology
			5 = other
2	Grade	Expected grade in class	9 = missing value
3	Number	Number of correct answers in statistical concepts test	

1. From the information shown in the table, provide suitable labels in the **SPSS Statistics Data Editor** for each variable. For the variable **Major**, create value labels. For the variable **Grade**, specify that the value 9 indicates a missing value.
2. Select cases that have the values 1-4 as values of the variable **Major**.
3. Do a 1-way *ANOVA* on the variable **Grade** as a function of **Majors** 1-4. Request a test of homogeneity of variance, descriptive statistics, and a means plot.
4. Describe the results of the analysis specified in question 3.
5. A person inspecting the results of the *ANOVA* described in question 3 decides to test which individual majors, criminal justice students differ from in terms of their mean expected grade. Perform a suitable analysis to address this question and describe the outcome of the test.
6. Perform the tasks specified in questions 3 using **Number** as the dependent variable. How do the results differ?

Exercise 14.2

The data in the file *voteTV.sav* provided on the publisher's website for this text at http://www.pearsonhighered.com/stern2e, show how randomly selected adults aged 18-65 who were contacted by the National Opinion Research Center between 1993-1998 report they voted in the 1992 presidential election. The candidates running for president of the U.S. were Republican George H.W. Bush, Democrat Bill Clinton, and Independent Ross Perot. The table shown below describes the variables and their values contained in the data file.

Variable #	Variable Name	Concept Measured	Value Identification
1	**year**	Year contacted	
2	**id**	Identification number of respondent	
3	**vote**	Presidential candidate voted for	1 = Clinton 2 = Bush 3 = Perot 4 = Other 6 = Didn't vote 8, 9 = Missing value
4	**tv**	Number of hours of TV watched per day	98, 99 = Missing value

1. Assume a researcher planned to investigate whether people who voted for Clinton watched a different number of hours of TV per day than those who voted for Bush and Perot, and that those who voted for Bush and Perot watched a comparable number of hours of TV per day. Conduct suitable analyses to address these questions. (Hint: use the comparison coefficients -2 1 1 to answer the first question and the coefficients 0 -1 1 to answer the second question. Be sure to select the data of only participants who voted for one of the 3 candidates.)

2. Assume a researcher planned to investigate whether the combination of people who voted for Clinton, Bush, or Perot watched a different number of hours of TV per day than the combination of those who voted for some other candidate or didn't vote. Conduct a suitable analysis to answer this question.

Exercise 14.3

The data shown in the table represent the number of words correctly spelled by different randomly selected members of four age groups.

Number of Words By Age Category			
High School	Young Adult	Middle-aged	Retired
2	3	5	6
3	6	6	7
6	5	7	5
3	3	6	7
6	4	8	9
4	2	7	10
3	3	5	8

Use the data to answer these questions:

1. Does age category significantly affect mean number of words spelled correctly? In the *ANOVA* performed to answer the question, request a test of homogeneity of variance, descriptive statistics, and a means plot.
2. After inspecting the data, a researcher decides to determine if high school students are significantly different than each of the other individual age groups on the mean number of words correctly spelled (i.e., high school vs. young adult, high school vs. middle-aged, high school vs. retired). What conclusions should be drawn?

Exercise 14.4

Based on the following tables output from by *SPSS* one-way *ANOVA*:
1. Is the mean dependent variable value in **COND 1** significantly different from that in **COND 3** and **COND 4** combined?
2. Is the mean dependent variable value in **COND 2** significantly different from that in **COND 1**?

Homogeneous Subsets

DV

Scheffe[a]

COND	N	Subset for alpha = .05	
		1	2
3.00	5	42.4000	
4.00	5	45.6000	
2.00	5	51.2000	51.2000
1.00	5		59.2000
Sig.		.287	.365

Means for groups in homogeneous subsets are displayed.

a. Uses Harmonic Mean Sample Size = 5.000.

Chapter 15: Two-Way and Higher Order Analyses of Variance

Overview

A two-way analysis of variance (*ANOVA*) extends the ideas underlying a one-way *ANOVA* to two independent variables (also called factors). When two factors are arranged in what is termed a factorial design, each level of one factor is combined with each level of the other factor. If one factor in an experiment is type of cue with three levels (none, visual, auditory), and the other is cognitive load with two levels (load present, load absent), a factorial design would produce six unique pairs of levels: no cue and load present, no cue and load absent, visual cue and load present, visual cue and load absent, auditory cue and load present, and auditory cue and load absent. These six combinations are represented as cells in the table shown in Figure 15.1. In general, the number of conditions formed by combining levels of each factor in a factorial design is found by multiplying together the number of levels of each factor. The design represented in Figure 15.1 consists of 3 x 2 or six cells.

Figure 15.1. A factorial design for the factors type of cue and cognitive load consisting of three and two levels, respectively.

		Type of Cue		
		None	Visual	Auditory
Cognitive	Load Present			
Load	Load Absent			

As in a one-way *ANOVA*, a two-way *ANOVA* is conducted on a single dependent variable that is measured on an interval or ratio scale. The purpose of the two-way *ANOVA* is to draw conclusions about the effect of the factors, either alone or in combination, on the mean of the dependent variable. In our example that combines the factors type of cue and cognitive load, if the dependent variable is number of study words recalled, our interest, if we conduct a two-way *ANOVA*, is in knowing whether type of cue and cognitive load have an effect on mean number of study words recalled.

Many specific questions can be generated about how the factors in a two-way *ANOVA* affect mean values of a dependent variable. However, the default analyses assess what are known as the main effect of each factor and the interaction of the two factors. A main effect is defined as the effect of one factor on the dependent variable, disregarding the effect of the other factor. The main effect of a factor is basically equivalent to a one-way *ANOVA*. In our example, if we ask whether there's a main effect of type of cue, we wish to know whether mean number of study words recalled differs over levels of type of cue; if we ask whether there's a main effect of cognitive load, we wish to know whether mean number of study words recalled differs when a cognitive load is present vs. absent.

Consider the values of the dependent variable shown in the cells of the table depicted in Figure 15.2. Assessing the presence of main effect of the factor type of cue involves determining whether there's a significant difference among the marginal means 5.20, 7.10, and 5.20; and assessing the presence of a main effect of the factor cognitive load involves determining whether the values 4.73 and 6.93 differ significantly.

Figure 15.2. The numbers in the cells are the mean values of the dependent variable number of words recalled. The numbers outside the cells are marginal means of the dependent variable.

		Type of Cue			
		None	Visual	Auditory	
Cognitive	Load Present	4.20	6.20	3.80	4.73
Load	Load Absent	6.20	8.20	6.60	6.93
		5.20	7.10	5.20	

An interaction is said to occur when the effect of one factor on the dependent variable differs at different levels of the other factor. The ideas underlying an interaction can be understood from inspecting a plot of the means of a dependent variable as a function of the levels of each factor. Figure 15.3 shows such a plot for the data given in Figure 15.2. When there's an interaction between two factors, the lines that represent data in the plot are not all parallel. As the output of a two-way *ANOVA* will reveal (see below), and as can be seen in Figure 15.3, while not perfectly parallel, the two lines that represent performance in the different load conditions are not sufficiently non-parallel to support the presence of a significant interaction. Thus, the effect of the factor type of cue on mean number of words recalled is not significantly different when either a cognitive load is present or when it is absent.

Figure 15.3. A line plot of data from Figure 15.2.

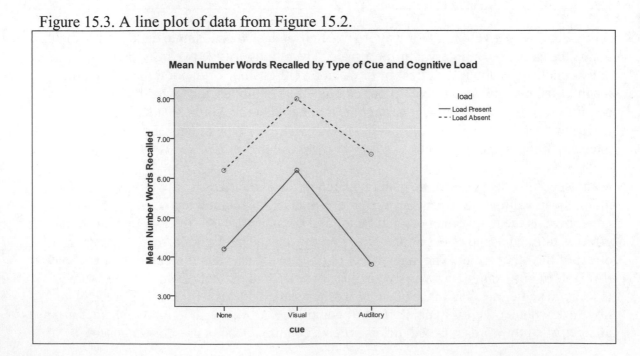

To test whether each main effect and the interaction is significant, an F value is computed. As in the one-way $ANOVA$, each F value is formed by dividing the mean square for the effect by the within-groups mean square (referred to in the $SPSS$ $ANOVA$ table as the error mean square). Each mean square is formed by dividing its sum of squares by its degrees of freedom. Table 15.1 shows formulas for the F used to assesses each effect.

Table 15.1. Formulas for calculating the F values for main and interaction effects in a two-way $ANOVA$ for independent groups assuming equal samples sizes, n, in each cell.

Effect	F	$df_{numerator}$	$df_{denominator}$
Main Effect of Factor 1	$\dfrac{SS_{factor1}/df_{factor1}}{SS_{error}/df_{error}}$	# levels of factor 1 - 1	$(n\text{-}1)$ x (# levels of factor 1) x (#levels of factor 2)
Main Effect of Factor 2	$\dfrac{SS_{factor2}/df_{factor2}}{SS_{error}/df_{error}}$	# levels of factor 2 - 1	$(n\text{-}1)$ x (# levels of factor 1) x (#levels of factor 2)
Interaction of Factor 1 and Factor 2	$\dfrac{SS_{interaction}/df_{interaction}}{SS_{error}/df_{error}}$	(# levels of factor 1 – 1) x (# levels of factor 2 – 1)	$(n\text{-}1)$ x (# levels of factor 1) x (#levels of factor 2)

Underlying Assumptions

There are three assumptions that underlie these sorts of two-way and higher order $ANOVA$s. One is that cases are randomly assigned to conditions (i.e., cells in the factorial design). Another is that, in the population sampled for each condition of the study, the dependent variable is normally distributed. When equal numbers of cases are assigned to each cell in a study, moderate violations of this assumption do not seriously undermine the test's validity. A third assumption is the assumption of homogeneity of variance; that is, the variances of the populations represented in each cell of the study are assumed to be equal. As with the assumption of normality, when sample sizes are equal, moderate violations of the assumption do not seriously undermine the validity of the test. If the ratio of the highest to lowest cell variance is less than 3, violation of the homogeneity of variance assumption can be considered moderate; when the ratio is between 3 and 9, lowering alpha to .025 may be appropriate (Keppel, 1991).

Preparing Data for the Analysis

For a two-way $ANOVA$, each case on the **SPSS Statistics Data Editor** must include values of three variables: one corresponding to the dependent variable, and the other two to each factor. To code each factor, an integer value should be chosen to represent each of its levels. Thus, if there are three levels of one factor, the integers 1, 2, and 3 could be used (though any three different arbitrarily chosen numbers could be used). If there are two levels of the other factor, the integers 1 and 2 could be used. Shown below are the data for participants in our example of the effects of type of cue (represented using the variable named **cue**) and cognitive load (**load**) on the dependent variable, number of words recalled (**nrecall**).

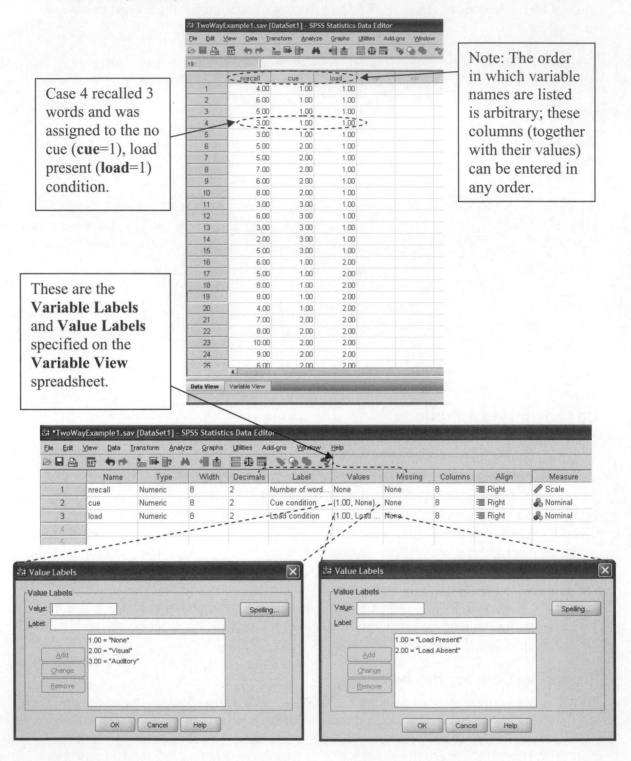

Case 4 recalled 3 words and was assigned to the no cue (**cue**=1), load present (**load**=1) condition.

Note: The order in which variable names are listed is arbitrary; these columns (together with their values) can be entered in any order.

These are the **Variable Labels** and **Value Labels** specified on the **Variable View** spreadsheet.

Requesting a Two-Way *ANOVA*

A two-way *ANOVA* can be performed using the **Univariate** procedure of the **General Linear Model**:

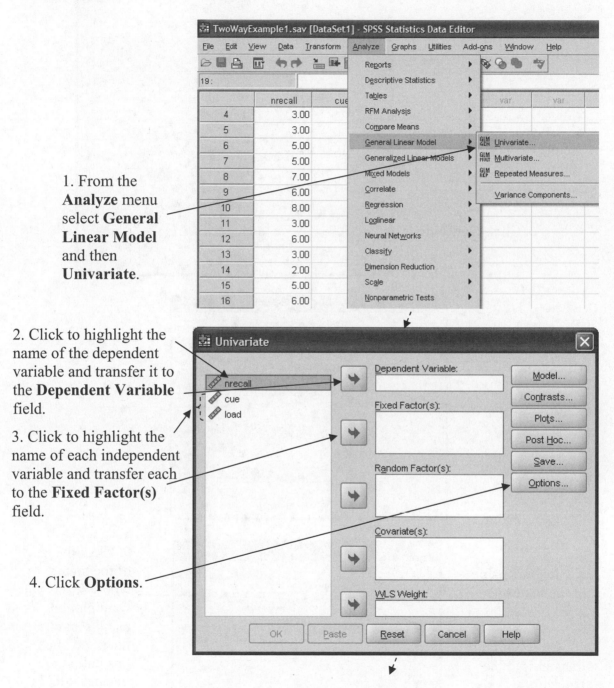

1. From the **Analyze** menu select **General Linear Model** and then **Univariate**.

2. Click to highlight the name of the dependent variable and transfer it to the **Dependent Variable** field.

3. Click to highlight the name of each independent variable and transfer each to the **Fixed Factor(s)** field.

4. Click **Options**.

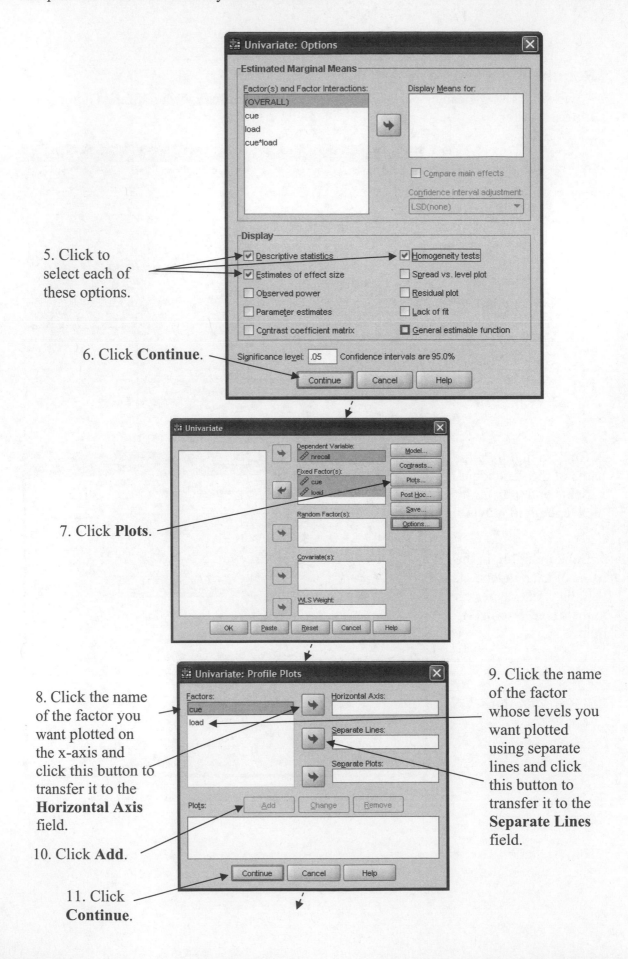

5. Click to select each of these options.

6. Click **Continue**.

7. Click **Plots**.

8. Click the name of the factor you want plotted on the x-axis and click this button to transfer it to the **Horizontal Axis** field.

9. Click the name of the factor whose levels you want plotted using separate lines and click this button to transfer it to the **Separate Lines** field.

10. Click **Add**.

11. Click **Continue**.

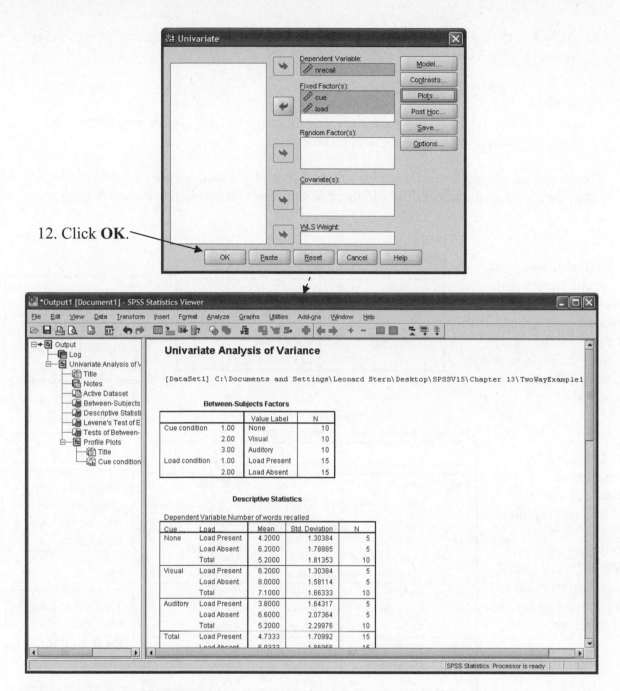

12. Click **OK**.

Interpreting the Output

The output produced by the selections shown above include descriptive statistics (mean, standard deviation and number of cases) for each cell of the factorial design, a Levene test of the equality of variances of scores within each cell of the design, an *ANOVA* table that allows determination of the significance level of tests of main and interaction effects together with a value of partial eta squared (η^2) that measures each effect size, and a line plot of the mean value of the dependent variable as a function of levels of each factor.

The measure of effect size that is often used with two-way and higher order *ANOVAs* is partial eta squared (η^2). It differs from ordinary η^2 in that, instead of using the total sum of squares in the equation's denominator, the within groups sum of squares plus the sum of squares for the effect of interest is used:

$$\text{partial } \eta^2 = \frac{SS_{effect}}{SS_{effect} + SS_{within}} \text{ or } \frac{df_{effect}F_{effect}}{df_{effect}F_{effect} + df_{within}} \qquad \text{Equation 15.1}$$

Values of partial η^2 range between 0-1; the values .01, .06, and .14 roughly correspond to a small, medium, and large effect size, respectively.

The output produced for our example of the effects of the factors type of cue and cognitive load on the dependent variable number of words recalled is shown below:

1. This table shows the names of factors and levels of each factor together with the number of cases in each level. Inspect the table to make sure are values are as expected.

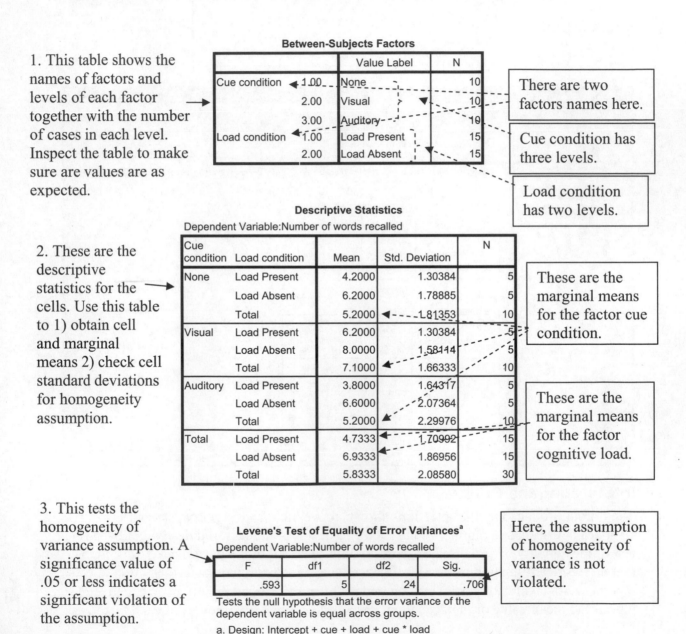

Between-Subjects Factors

		Value Label	N
Cue condition	1.00	None	10
	2.00	Visual	10
	3.00	Auditory	10
Load condition	1.00	Load Present	15
	2.00	Load Absent	15

There are two factors names here.

Cue condition has three levels.

Load condition has two levels.

2. These are the descriptive statistics for the cells. Use this table to 1) obtain cell and marginal means 2) check cell standard deviations for homogeneity assumption.

Descriptive Statistics

Dependent Variable:Number of words recalled

Cue condition	Load condition	Mean	Std. Deviation	N
None	Load Present	4.2000	1.30384	5
	Load Absent	6.2000	1.78885	5
	Total	5.2000	1.81353	10
Visual	Load Present	6.2000	1.30384	5
	Load Absent	8.0000	1.58114	5
	Total	7.1000	1.66333	10
Auditory	Load Present	3.8000	1.64317	5
	Load Absent	6.6000	2.07364	5
	Total	5.2000	2.29976	10
Total	Load Present	4.7333	1.70992	15
	Load Absent	6.9333	1.86956	15
	Total	5.8333	2.08580	30

These are the marginal means for the factor cue condition.

These are the marginal means for the factor cognitive load.

3. This tests the homogeneity of variance assumption. A significance value of .05 or less indicates a significant violation of the assumption.

Levene's Test of Equality of Error Variances[a]

Dependent Variable:Number of words recalled

F	df1	df2	Sig.
.593	5	24	.706

Tests the null hypothesis that the error variance of the dependent variable is equal across groups.

a. Design: Intercept + cue + load + cue * load

Here, the assumption of homogeneity of variance is not violated.

4. From this table, determine whether main and interaction effects are significant and determine effect sizes.

This is the *F* value and significance level for the main effect of cue condition.

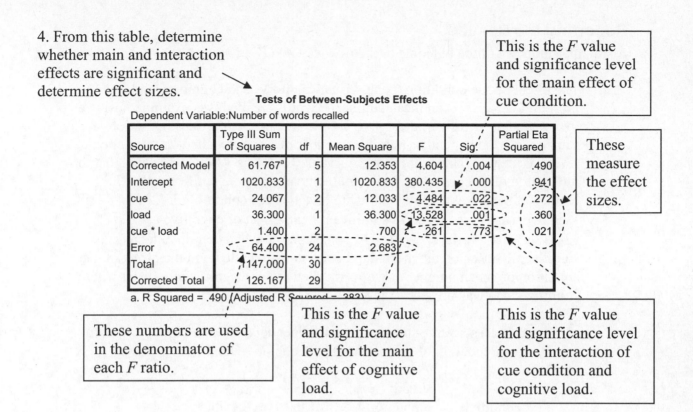

Tests of Between-Subjects Effects

Dependent Variable:Number of words recalled

Source	Type III Sum of Squares	df	Mean Square	F	Sig.	Partial Eta Squared
Corrected Model	61.767[a]	5	12.353	4.604	.004	.490
Intercept	1020.833	1	1020.833	380.435	.000	.941
cue	24.067	2	12.033	4.484	.022	.272
load	36.300	1	36.300	13.528	.001	.360
cue * load	1.400	2	.700	.261	.773	.021
Error	64.400	24	2.683			
Total	1147.000	30				
Corrected Total	126.167	29				

a. R Squared = .490 (Adjusted R Squared = .383)

These measure the effect sizes.

These numbers are used in the denominator of each *F* ratio.

This is the *F* value and significance level for the main effect of cognitive load.

This is the *F* value and significance level for the interaction of cue condition and cognitive load.

5. This is a plot of mean values of the dependent variable as a function of levels of each factor. Inspection of the plot helps reveal the source of effects that are significant.

Because the means of the three cue conditions are not all similar, the main effect of cue condition is significant.

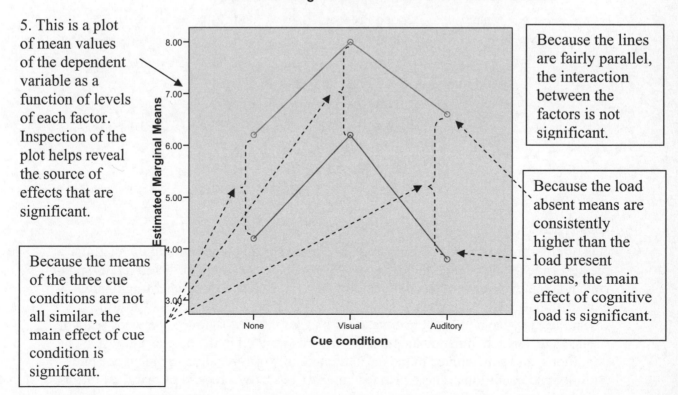

Estimated Marginal Means of Number of words recalled

Because the lines are fairly parallel, the interaction between the factors is not significant.

Because the load absent means are consistently higher than the load present means, the main effect of cognitive load is significant.

Reporting the Results

A suitable summary of the outcome of the two-way *ANOVA* is as follows:

The effect of cue condition (none, visual, auditory) and cognitive load (load present, load absent) on mean number of words recalled was examined using a two-way analysis of variance (*ANOVA*) for independent groups. Descriptive statistics for the dependent variable, number of words recalled, as a function of levels of the two factors are shown in Table 15.2. The *ANOVA* revealed that the interaction of cue condition and cognitive load was not significant, $F < 1$. However, there was a significant main effect of cue condition, $F (2, 24) = 4.48$, $p < .025$, partial $\eta^2 = .27$, and a significant main effect of cognitive load, $F (1, 24) = 13.53$, $p < .01$, partial $\eta^2 = .36$. Thus, cue condition and cognitive load each significantly affected the mean number of words recalled, but the effect of cue condition on mean number of words recalled did not significantly differ when a cognitive load was present or absent.

Table 15.2. Descriptive statistics for the dependent variable number of words recalled as a function of cue condition and cognitive load.

Cue condition	Load condition	Mean	Std. Deviation	N
None	Load Present	4.20	1.30	5
	Load Absent	6.20	1.79	5
	Total	5.20	1.81	10
Visual	Load Present	6.20	1.30	5
	Load Absent	8.00	1.58	5
	Total	7.10	1.66	10
Auditory	Load Present	3.80	1.64	5
	Load Absent	6.60	2.07	5
	Total	5.20	2.30	10
Total	Load Present	4.73	1.71	15
	Load Absent	6.93	1.87	15
	Total	5.83	2.09	30

Contrasts

It is often of interest to probe for particular patterns of outcomes among the marginal means of the levels of each factor in an *ANOVA*. In our example of the effect of type of cue and cognitive load on mean number of words recalled, a researcher might have expected that only visual cues would enhance recall, not auditory cues. Thus, the researcher may have planned in advance to check for two differences between pairs of means: a difference in the mean number of words recalled in the no cue and visual cue conditions, and a difference in the mean number of words recalled in the no cue and auditory cue conditions. These planned comparisons between pairs of marginal means can be request from the **Contrasts** window from within the **Univariate** procedure:

1. From the **Analyze** menu select **General Linear Model** and then **Univariate**.

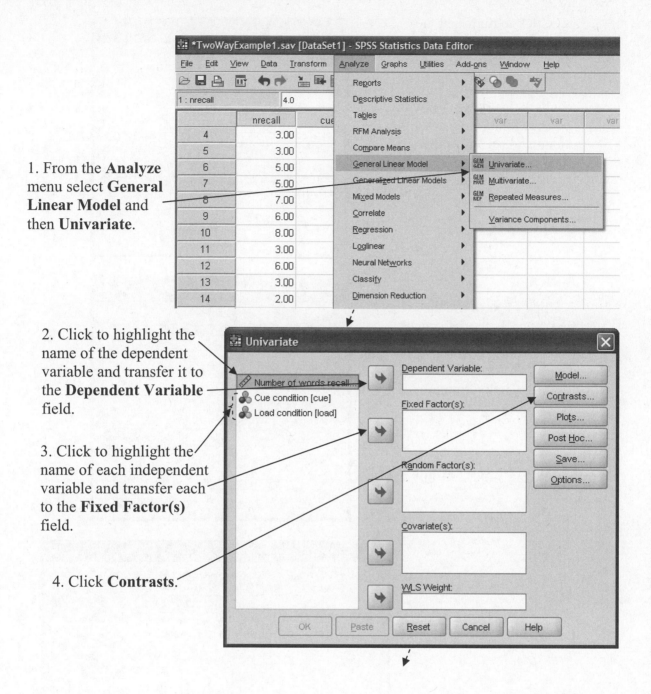

2. Click to highlight the name of the dependent variable and transfer it to the **Dependent Variable** field.

3. Click to highlight the name of each independent variable and transfer each to the **Fixed Factor(s)** field.

4. Click **Contrasts**.

5. Click to highlight the name of the variable whose levels are to be examined.

6. Click this down-arrow to activate the drop-down menu and select **Simple**.

7. Click **First** to use the first mean as the reference group to compare in each pair of means.

8. Click **Change**.

9. Click **Continue**.

10. Click **OK**.

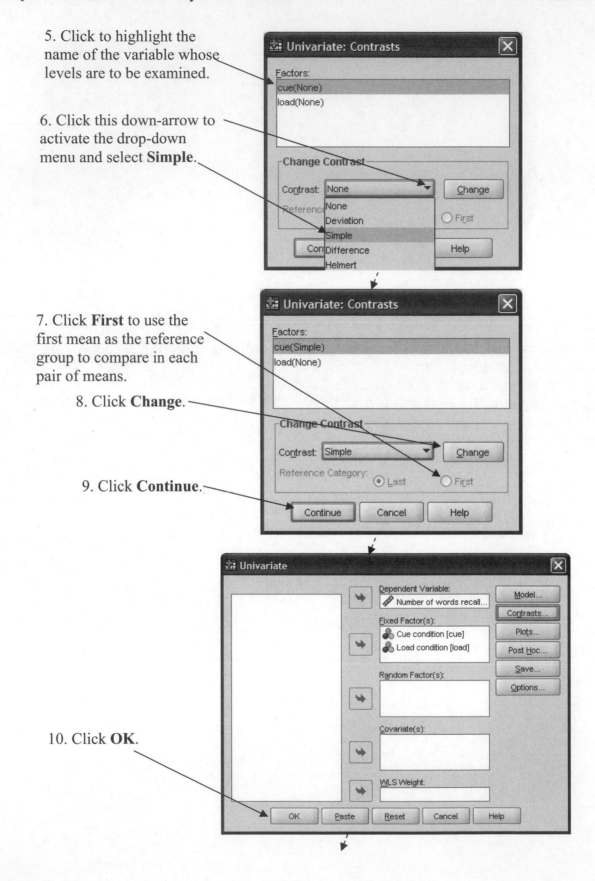

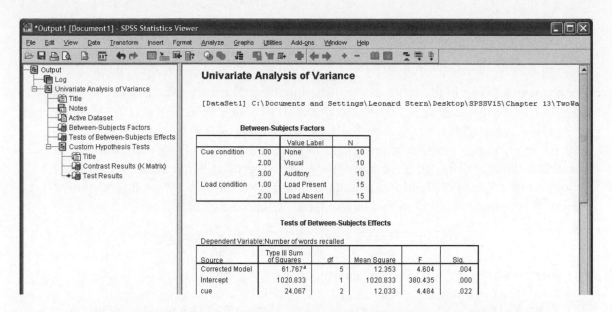

Because a planned comparison compares a pair of means, one can assess its significance using a *t*-test. The numerator of the *t* ratio is the difference between the means of the two samples and the denominator is the standard error of the difference. These values can be obtained from the table labeled **Contrast Results** shown below:

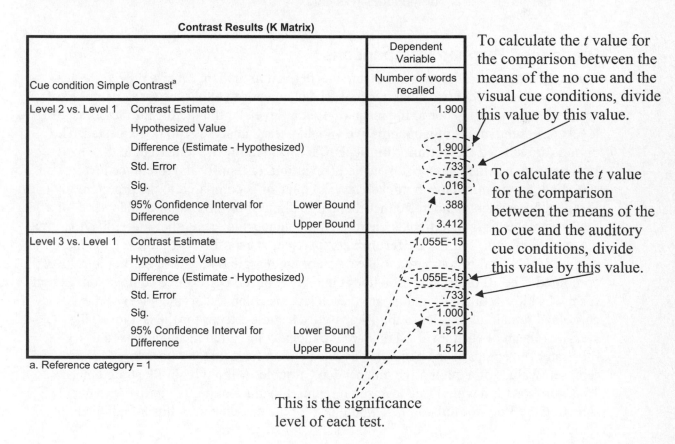

Contrast Results (K Matrix)

Cue condition Simple Contrast[a]		Dependent Variable Number of words recalled
Level 2 vs. Level 1	Contrast Estimate	1.900
	Hypothesized Value	0
	Difference (Estimate - Hypothesized)	1.900
	Std. Error	.733
	Sig.	.016
	95% Confidence Interval for Difference Lower Bound	.388
	Upper Bound	3.412
Level 3 vs. Level 1	Contrast Estimate	-1.055E-15
	Hypothesized Value	0
	Difference (Estimate - Hypothesized)	-1.055E-15
	Std. Error	.733
	Sig.	1.000
	95% Confidence Interval for Difference Lower Bound	-1.512
	Upper Bound	1.512

a. Reference category = 1

To calculate the *t* value for the comparison between the means of the no cue and the visual cue conditions, divide this value by this value.

To calculate the *t* value for the comparison between the means of the no cue and the auditory cue conditions, divide this value by this value.

This is the significance level of each test.

The calculations for these t values are $t_{comparison\ 1} = 1.90/.73 = 2.60$, and $t_{comparison\ 2} = 0.00/.73 = 0.00$. Note that the difference between the means for the second planned comparison is given in the table in scientific notation. The value -1.1E-15 is equivalent to -1.10×10^{-15} whose value is -.0000000000000011 (which rounds to 0.00). Note also that a t can be converted to an equivalent F by squaring; that is $F = t^2$. Thus, the t value of 2.60 for the first comparison is equivalent to and F value of 2.60^2 or 6.76 with 1 numerator degree of freedom (because there are two groups being compared) and 24 denominator degrees of freedom (as in the overall $ANOVA$). The second formula for partial η^2 previously provided can be used to calculate the effect size:

$$\text{Partial } \eta^2 = \frac{df_{effect}F_{effect}}{df_{effect}F_{effect} + df_{within}} = \frac{1 \times 6.76}{1 \times 6.76 + 24} = .22$$

The outcomes of these tests can be reported in the following way:

> Planned comparisons were used to test whether the mean number of words recalled differed significantly for participants in the no cue and visual cue conditions but not for participants in the no cue and auditory cue conditions. As hypothesized, the former comparison was significant, $F(1, 24) = 6.76$, $p < .025$, partial $\eta^2 = .22$, but the latter was not, $F < 1$.

Predefined Planned Comparisons

There are a number of planned comparisons defined in the **Univariate** procedure that compare an individual marginal mean of a level a factor to either the marginal mean of another individual level or to the mean of a set of levels of the factor; for factors whose levels represent values of a quantitative variable, trend analyses can be requested. The options are labeled **Deviation**, **Simple**, **Difference**, **Helmert**, **Repeated**, and **Polynomial**. For the comparison labeled **Deviation**, except for the reference level specified, the marginal mean of each level of a factor is compared to the grand mean. The **Simple** comparison compares either the marginal mean of the first or the last level of a factor (whichever is specified as the reference category) to each other individual marginal mean of the factor. For the **Difference** comparison, except for the first level, the marginal mean of each level is compared to the mean of the marginal means of all previous levels combined. The **Helmert** selection does the reverse of the **Difference** comparison: except for the last level, the marginal mean of each level is compared to the mean of the combined remaining levels. In the **Repeated** selection, except for the last level, the marginal mean of each level is compared to the next marginal mean. Table 15.3 illustrates the comparisons generated by each option for a factor whose three levels represent values of a qualitative independent variable. Although not illustrated in Table 15.3, for a factor having three levels that represent values of a quantitative variable, selecting the **Polynomial** contrast would test for the presence of a linear and quadratic trend.

Table 15.3. Illustrations of the means that would be compared by various contrasts available in the **Univariate** procedure of the **General Linear Model**. The contrasts are pictured as being applied to the marginal means of factor A with three levels that are referred to as a_1, a_2, and a_3.

Name	Reference Category	Illustration Of Means Being Compared
Deviation	first	Two grids with columns a_1 a_2 a_3, rows b_1 b_2; marginal means $\bar{x}_1$ $\bar{x}_2$ $\bar{x}_3$ compared to Grand mean
Simple	first	Two grids; $\bar{x}_1$ $\bar{x}_2$ $\bar{x}_3$ compared to Grand mean
Difference	none	Two grids; second circles $\bar{x}_1$ $\bar{x}_2$; Grand mean
Helmert	none	Two grids; first circles $\bar{x}_2$ $\bar{x}_3$; Grand mean
Repeated	none	Two grids; $\bar{x}_1$ $\bar{x}_2$ $\bar{x}_3$; Grand mean

Post Hoc and Multiple Comparison Tests

When conducting multiple planned comparisons or unplanned tests on the same data set, corrections are often applied to adjust for possible increases in Type I errors (see Chapter 14). These corrections can be conducted on factors in *ANOVA*s having independent groups of cases in each level. To access these procedures for a two-way *ANOVA*, click the **Post Hoc** button on the **Univariate** window after transferring factor names to the **Fixed Factors** field:

1. Click the **Post Hoc** button after transferring variables to the **Fixed Factor(s)** field.

2. Click to highlight the name of each independent variable to which a post hoc or multiple comparison test is to be applied and transfer the variable by clicking this button.

3. Select the name of each test to be applied by clicking a box. Here, a Tukey test has been selected.

4. Click **Continue**.

5. Click **OK**.

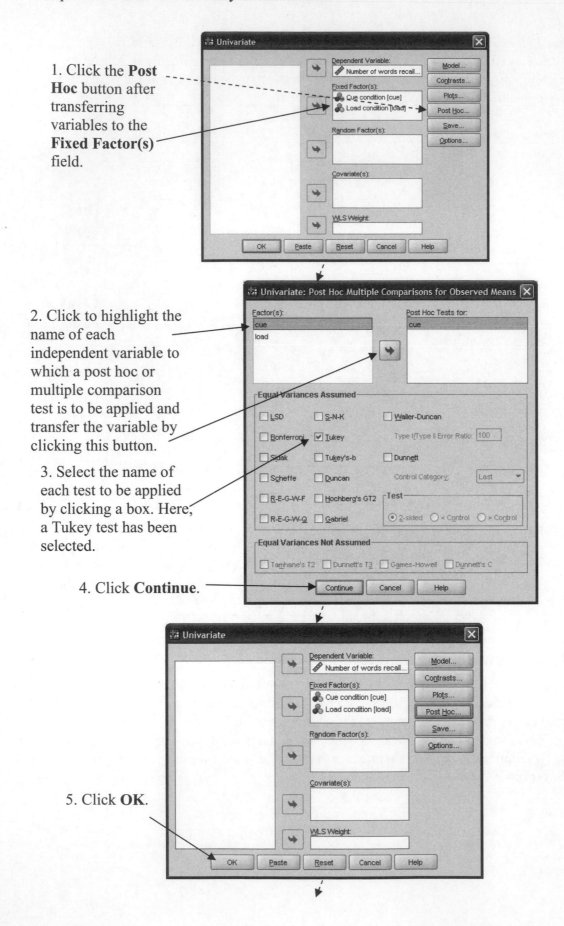

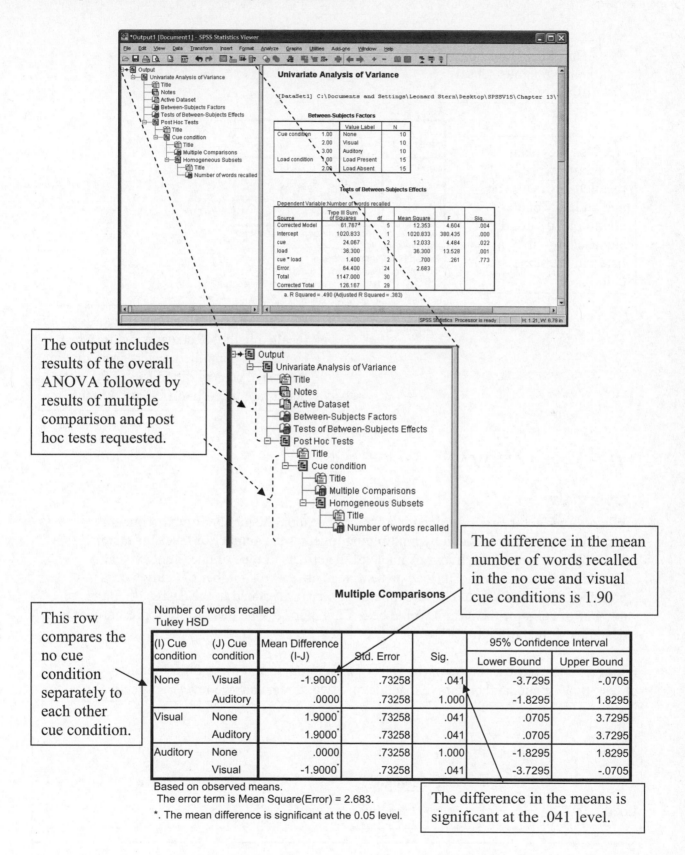

Univariate Analysis of Variance

[DataSet1] C:\Documents and Settings\Leonard Stern\Desktop\SPSSV15\Chapter 13\

Between-Subjects Factors

		Value Label	N
Cue condition	1.00	None	10
	2.00	Visual	10
	3.00	Auditory	10
Load condition	1.00	Load Present	15
	2.00	Load Absent	15

Tests of Between-Subjects Effects

Dependent Variable:Number of words recalled

Source	Type III Sum of Squares	df	Mean Square	F	Sig.
Corrected Model	61.767ᵃ	5	12.353	4.604	.004
Intercept	1020.833	1	1020.833	380.435	.000
cue	24.067	2	12.033	4.484	.022
load	36.300	1	36.300	13.528	.001
cue * load	1.400	2	.700	.261	.773
Error	64.400	24	2.683		
Total	1147.000	30			
Corrected Total	126.167	29			

a. R Squared = .490 (Adjusted R Squared = .383)

The output includes results of the overall ANOVA followed by results of multiple comparison and post hoc tests requested.

Output
  Univariate Analysis of Variance
    Title
    Notes
    Active Dataset
    Between-Subjects Factors
    Tests of Between-Subjects Effects
    Post Hoc Tests
      Title
      Cue condition
        Title
        Multiple Comparisons
        Homogeneous Subsets
          Title
          Number of words recalled

The difference in the mean number of words recalled in the no cue and visual cue conditions is 1.90

Multiple Comparisons

This row compares the no cue condition separately to each other cue condition.

Number of words recalled
Tukey HSD

(I) Cue condition	(J) Cue condition	Mean Difference (I-J)	Std. Error	Sig.	95% Confidence Interval	
					Lower Bound	Upper Bound
None	Visual	-1.9000*	.73258	.041	-3.7295	-.0705
	Auditory	.0000	.73258	1.000	-1.8295	1.8295
Visual	None	1.9000*	.73258	.041	.0705	3.7295
	Auditory	1.9000*	.73258	.041	.0705	3.7295
Auditory	None	.0000	.73258	1.000	-1.8295	1.8295
	Visual	-1.9000*	.73258	.041	-3.7295	-.0705

Based on observed means.
 The error term is Mean Square(Error) = 2.683.

*. The mean difference is significant at the 0.05 level.

The difference in the means is significant at the .041 level.

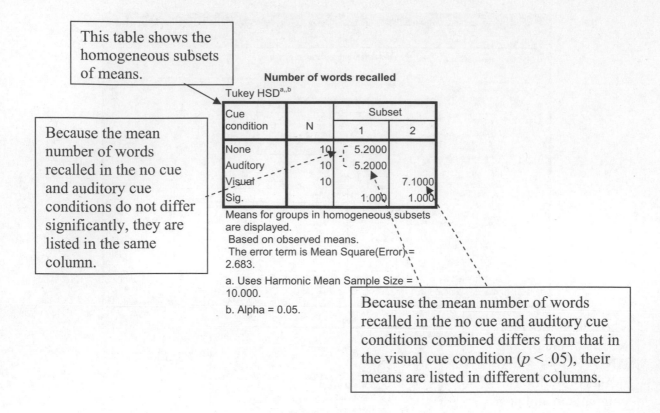

This table shows the homogeneous subsets of means.

Because the mean number of words recalled in the no cue and auditory cue conditions do not differ significantly, they are listed in the same column.

Number of words recalled

Tukey HSD[a,b]

Cue condition	N	Subset	
		1	2
None	10	5.2000	
Auditory	10	5.2000	
Visual	10		7.1000
Sig.		1.000	1.000

Means for groups in homogeneous subsets are displayed.
Based on observed means.
The error term is Mean Square(Error) = 2.683.

a. Uses Harmonic Mean Sample Size = 10.000.

b. Alpha = 0.05.

Because the mean number of words recalled in the no cue and auditory cue conditions combined differs from that in the visual cue condition ($p < .05$), their means are listed in different columns.

Three-Way ANOVAs

Overview

When three factors are combined in a factorial design, the number of experimental conditions resulting is found by multiplying together the number of levels of factor 1, factor 2, and factor 3. If, in our example of the effects of type of cue (none, visual, auditory) and cognitive load (load present, load absent) on number of study words produced, the factor type of test (explicit, implicit) was added to the design, then the number of cells for the design would be 3 x 2 x 2 or 12. One method for representing the design is shown in Figure 15.4.

Figure 15.4. A representation of the cells of a factorial design formed for the factors type of test, type of cue, and cognitive load, having two, three, and two levels, respectively.

		Type of Test									
		explicit						implicit			
		Cue						Cue			
		none	visual	auditory				none	visual	auditory	
Load	present					Load	present				
	absent						absent				

The effects tested for by the default analysis in a three factor *ANOVA* conducted on the variables represented in Figure 15.4 include the following: main effects of the factors type of test, type of cue, and cognitive load; two way interactions between the pairs of factors type of test and type of cue, type of test and cognitive load, and type of cue and cognitive load; and a three way interaction among the factors type of test, type of cue, and cognitive load. The ideas underlying the main effects and two-way interactions are the same as in a two-way design. However, the ideas underlying a three-way interaction are new.

A three way interaction occurs when the interaction between two factors changes over levels of the third factor. Again, as with a two-way interaction, the presence of a three-way interaction is most easily detected by inspecting line plots of means of the dependent variable as a function of levels of the three factors. In Figure 15.5, mean number of study words produced as a function of the factors type of cue and cognitive load are plotted separately for the explicit and implicit test conditions of the factor type of test. It can be seen that the interaction between cue condition and cognitive load that occurs for the explicit test (see right panel of Figure 15.5) appears to be absent for the implicit test (left panel of Figure 15.5). Thus, because a two-way interaction appears to change over levels of a third factor, a significant three-way interaction may be occurring.

Figure 15.5. Line plots of the mean number of words produced as a function of cue condition and cognitive load for an implicit (left panel) and explicit (right panel) test of memory.

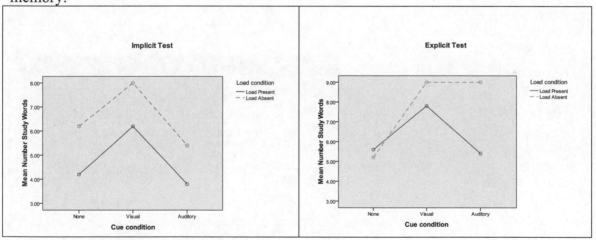

Preparing Data for the Analysis

For a three-way *ANOVA*, each case on the **SPSS Statistics Data Editor** must include values of four variables: one corresponding to the dependent variable, and the other three to each factor. As for a two-way *ANOVA*, to code each factor, a different integer value should be chosen to represent each of its levels. Shown below are data for some participants in our example of the effects of type of cue (represented using the variable named **cue**), cognitive load (**load**), and type of test (**test**) on the dependent variable number of words produced (**nwords**).

The new variable **test** is included whose values have been declared in the **Value Labels** window shown below.

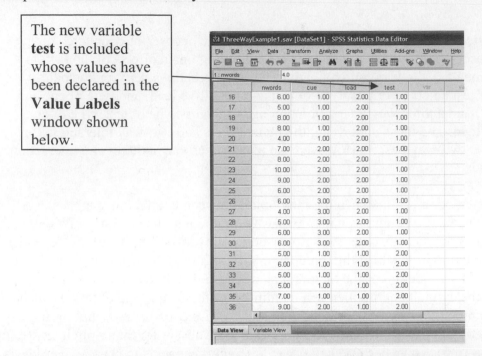

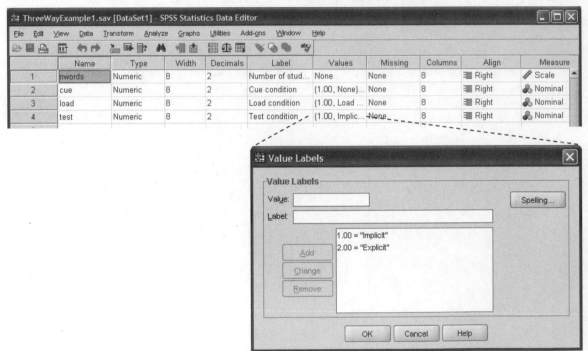

Requesting a Three-Way *ANOVA*

The procedure for requesting a three-way *ANOVA* for factorial designs with independent samples of cases in each cell (often referred to as between-subject designs) is illustrated below for our example of the effects of type of cue (none, visual, auditory), cognitive load (load present, load absent), and type of test (implicit, explicit) on number of study words produced.

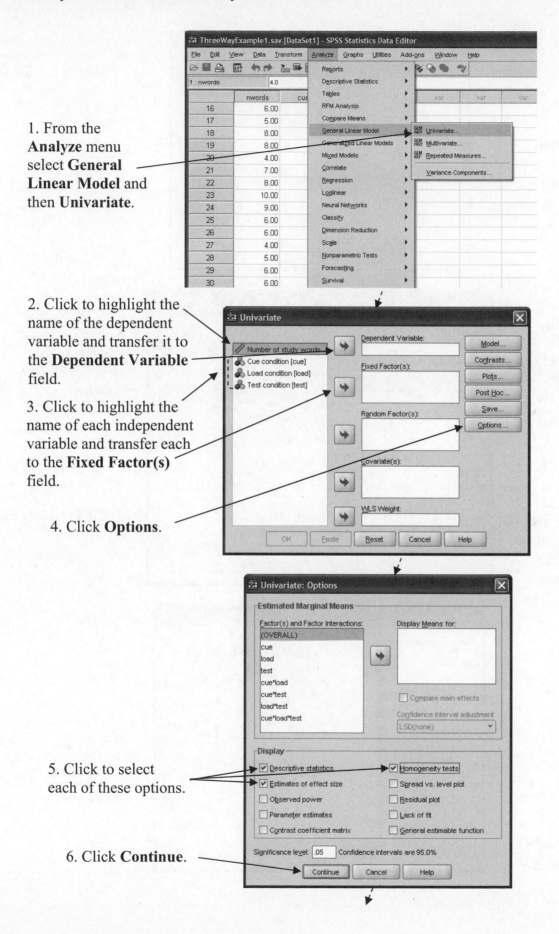

1. From the **Analyze** menu select **General Linear Model** and then **Univariate**.

2. Click to highlight the name of the dependent variable and transfer it to the **Dependent Variable** field.

3. Click to highlight the name of each independent variable and transfer each to the **Fixed Factor(s)** field.

4. Click **Options**.

5. Click to select each of these options.

6. Click **Continue**.

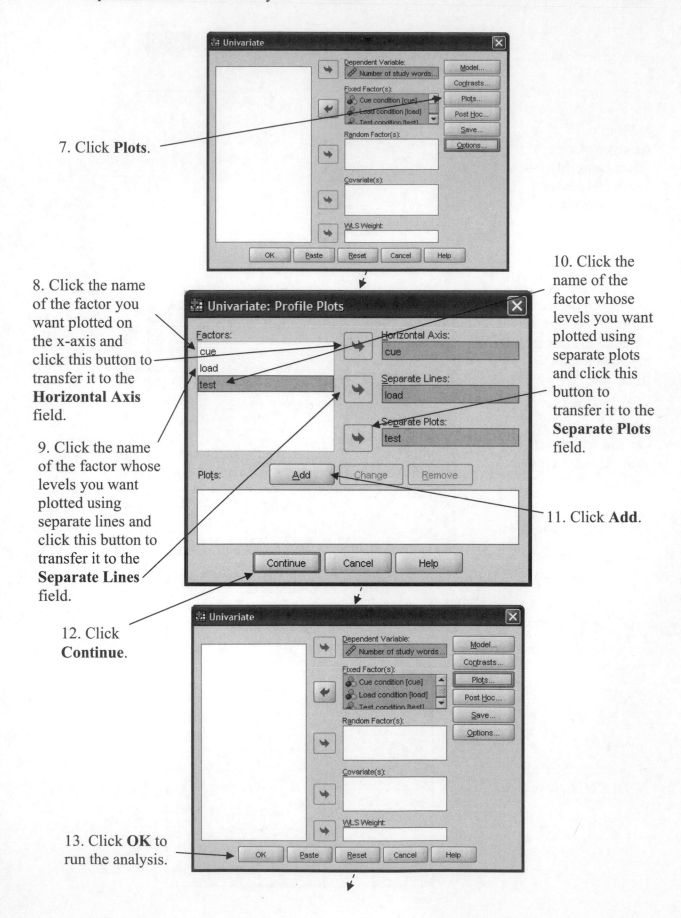

7. Click **Plots**.

8. Click the name of the factor you want plotted on the x-axis and click this button to transfer it to the **Horizontal Axis** field.

9. Click the name of the factor whose levels you want plotted using separate lines and click this button to transfer it to the **Separate Lines** field.

10. Click the name of the factor whose levels you want plotted using separate plots and click this button to transfer it to the **Separate Plots** field.

11. Click **Add**.

12. Click **Continue**.

13. Click **OK** to run the analysis.

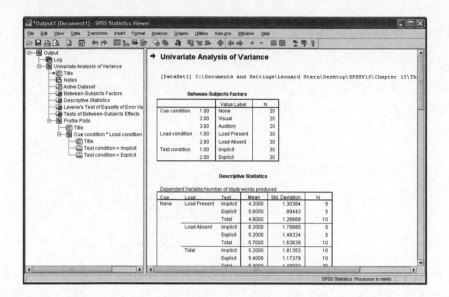

Interpreting the Output

The sequence of tables and plots produced by the selections shown above corresponds to that for the two-way *ANOVA* described earlier. The *ANOVA* table is shown below from which one can determine the main and interaction effects that are significant and the effect sizes.

Tests of Between-Subjects Effects

Dependent Variable:Number of study words produced

Source	Type III Sum of Squares	df	Mean Square	F	Sig.	Partial Eta Squared
Corrected Model	168.583[a]	11	15.326	9.383	.000	.683
Intercept	2394.017	1	2394.017	1465.724	.000	.968
cue	65.233	2	32.617	19.969	.000	.454
load	40.017	1	40.017	24.500	.000	.338
test	28.017	1	28.017	17.153	.000	.263
cue * load	8.233	2	4.117	2.520	.091	.095
cue * test	14.433	2	7.217	4.418	.017	.155
load * test	.417	1	.417	.255	.616	.005
cue * load * test	12.233	2	6.117	3.745	.031	.135
Error	78.400	48	1.633			
Total	2641.000	60				
Corrected Total	246.983	59				

a. R Squared = .683 (Adjusted R Squared = .610)

All main effects are significant.

These numbers are used in the denominator of each *F* ratio.

This is the only significant 2-way interaction.

The three-way interaction is significant.

Planned comparisons as well as post-hoc tests and corrections for multiple comparisons can be applied to marginal means of each factor of a three factor design using procedures similar to those described earlier for the two-way *ANOVA*.

Exercises for Chapter 15

Exercise 15.1

Each cell of the table below shows values of a dependent variable for different groups of five participants who were randomly assigned to a cell of the factorial design formed from factors A and B each with two levels.

A

		a_1	a_2
B	b_1	7, 6, 8 5, 5	12, 13, 13, 10, 11
	b_2	14, 15, 14, 18, 19	8, 9, 10, 11, 7

1. Enter the data into *SPSS* in a manner suitable for conducting a two-way *ANOVA* that assesses the effects of factors A and B on the mean values of the dependent variable.
2. Perform the two-way *ANOVA*. Include a line plot that shows levels of Factor A on the x-axis. Describe the outcome of the analysis.

Exercise 15.2

To determine if a new drug affects feelings of depression, a drug company tests randomly selected depressed males and females who either get the new drug or the standard drug at one of 4 dosage levels (0, 20, 40, or 60 mg). The depression scores (low values = less depressed) for the participants are shown below:

	Males 0mg	20mg	40mg	60mg		Females 0mg	20mg	40mg	60mg
Std. Drug	12, 13, 14, 15	11, 15, 16, 14	10, 12, 13, 14	10, 9, 8, 12	Std. Drug	14, 18, 15, 15	12, 13, 14, 11	11, 9, 13, 10	8, 10, 7, 6
New Drug	14, 14, 15, 16	12, 15, 12, 14	10, 12, 11, 13	9, 12, 10, 10	New Drug	14, 16, 17, 16	14, 13, 10, 9	8, 9, 10, 6	5, 6, 7, 8

1. Enter the data into *SPSS* in a manner suitable for conducting a three-way *ANOVA* that assesses the effects of gender (male, female), drug (standard, new), and dose (0, 20, 40, 60) on the mean depression score.
2. Perform the three-way *ANOVA*. Include separate line plots for males and females that show dose levels on the x-axis and use separate lines for each drug. Describe the outcome of the analysis.
3. Determine whether there is a linear effect on the marginal means of drug dose. Report the result as an *F* value and specify the value of partial eta squared.

Exercise 15.3

Table 15.3 illustrated the means that are compared by various contrasts that are available in the **Univariate** procedure of the **General Linear Model** for marginal means of a factor having three levels. Using arrows show the means that are compared for each contrast in the table below of the factor that has four levels.

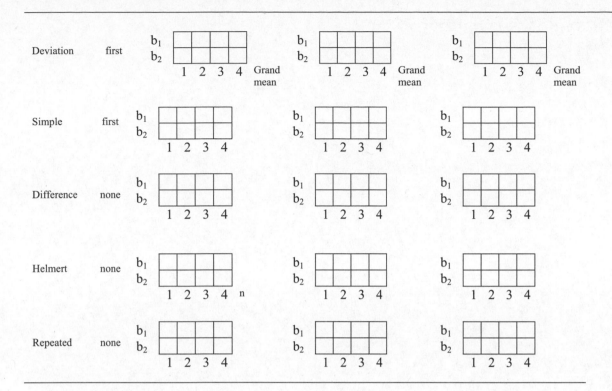

Exercise 15.4

Randomly selected participants in the U.S. were surveyed between 1988 and 1998 by the National Opinion Research Center and asked to evaluate how happy they were on a scale of 1-3 where 1=very happy, 2=pretty happy, and 3=not too happy. Another question requested participants to report how many sex partners they had during the past year. In the file *HappyPartner2.sav* provided on the publisher's website for this text, http://www.pearsonhighered.com/stern2e, the variable **Happy** contains responses to the question about happiness and the variable **Partner2** codes responses about number of sex partners using the values 0-3 where the numbers have the following meaning:

Value	Meaning
0	No partners
1	1 partner
2	2 partners
3	3 or more partners

The data file also contains the variable **gender** (1 = male and 2 = female).

Although the variable **Happy** does not measure happiness on an interval or ratio scale, treat it as though it did. Perform a two-way *ANOVA* to determine whether mean happiness as measured by the variable **Happy** is significantly related to the number of sex partners a person reports (**Partner2**) and the respondent's gender as measured by the variable **gender**. Based on your output, answer the following questions:

1. What effects are significant?
2. Is it appropriate to conclude that males are happier than females or must that conclusion be made conditional on the number of partners a person has?

Chapter 16: One-Way Within-Subjects ANOVA [*]

Overview

A factor whose means are examined with an analysis of variance (*ANOVA*) can have either independent groups of participants in each level (often referred to as a between-subjects factor) or the same group of participants in each level (referred to either as a within-subjects factor or a repeated measure). The situation is analogous to what occurs in a *t*-test. As discussed in a previous chapter, *t*-tests that examine the means of two samples are applied to either independent or paired samples.

For example, if a researcher examines the effect of number of study sessions (the factor) on memory for a list of words (the dependent variable) by testing the memory of each participant after one, two, and three study sessions, then the factor number of study sessions is a within-subjects factor. Similarly, if a researcher examines the effect of four different types of music (the factor) on mood (the dependent variable) by assessing mood score immediately after each participant is exposed to each of the four types of music, then type of music is a within-subjects factor.

In designing a study, a researcher often can choose whether a factor should be between- or within-subjects. An advantage of making a factor within- rather than between-subjects is that it provides for a more sensitive (i.e., more powerful) test of hypotheses concerning means of the factor. This occurs because, as in the calculation of *t* for paired samples, the value of *F* for a within-subjects design is generally larger than it would be had the factor been between-subjects due to the value of the denominator term being smaller.

Efficiency is another advantage of making a factor within- rather than between-subjects because, by measuring each participant a number of times, fewer are needed. Consider the situation depicted in Figure 16.1 that shows a factor with three levels each comprised of either three different participants or the same three participants. The factor shown in the left panel is between-subjects and requires a total of nine participants while that in the right panel is within-subjects are requires only three participants.

Figure 16.1. Number of participants (p_i) required to assess the effect of factor A on mean values of the dependent variable when factor A is between-subjects (left panel) vs. within-subjects (right panel).

Factor A			Factor A		
a_1	a_2	a_3	a_1	a_2	a_3
p_1	p_4	p_7	p_1	p_1	p_1
p_2	p_5	p_8	p_2	p_2	p_2
p_3	p_6	p_9	p_3	p_3	p_3
$\bar{x}_1$	$\bar{x}_2$	$\bar{x}_3$	$\bar{x}_1$	$\bar{x}_2$	$\bar{x}_3$

[*] Requires the *Advanced Statistics* module in *SPSS*

A disadvantage of a within-subjects design is the possible presence of practice effects. That is, a participant tested first at level a_1 of factor A gains experience in performing the task measured by the dependent variable so that performance improves during subsequent tests in levels a_2, a_3, and so on. Other related problems are carryover effects (i.e., the treatment administered in level a_1 does not completely dissipate when treatment a_2 is administered) and order effects (i.e., the effect on the dependent variable of presenting level a_1 first is different than presenting it last). Counterbalancing, that is, administering levels of a factor in different orders to different participants, can sometimes be used to control for these effects. For example, in the design shown in Figure 16.1, participant 1 could get the three levels of factor A in the order a_1, a_2, a_3, participant 2 in the order a_2, a_3, a_1, and participant 3 in the order a_3, a_1, a_2. The result is that each treatment is presented equally often in each order so that, although not eliminated, practice or order effects are spread out over all orders (see Keppel & Wickens, 2004, for other forms of counterbalancing). Counterbalancing cannot be used to counter all difficulties associated with within-subjects factors. Factors whose levels produce long-lasting effects on the dependent variable or differential carryover effects may not be suitable for analysis using within-subject designs. For example, if one of three possible treatments for depression produces a long-lasting alleviation, then the effects of treatments administered shortly after the successful treatment would not be detected.

Underlying Assumptions

Three of the four assumptions that underlie single factor within-subjects *ANOVA*s are similar to those that underlie between-subject *ANOVA*s. One is that cases represent a random sample of the population of interest and so are independent of each other. The second is that, in each condition of the study, the dependent variable is normally distributed in the population. The third is the assumption of homogeneity of variance; that is, the variances of the populations represented in each cell of the study are assumed to be equal.

An assumption unique to a within-subject *ANOVA*, one that can be considered an extension of the homogeneity of variance assumption, is the sphericity assumption. The assumption is that the variances of differences between all pairs of scores over all levels of the factor are identical in the population. The assumption is best understood in terms of an example. Consider the data shown in Table 16.1. The top panel of the table shows the scores of four participants who are tested in each of three levels of factor A. To assess whether the assumption of sphericity is met, all possible pairs of difference scores are calculated for each participant. Because there are three levels of factor A, three pairs of difference scores can be obtained: the difference between a_1 and a_2, the difference between a_1 and a_3, and the difference between a_2 and a_3. These difference scores are shown in the bottom panel of Table 16.1. The sphericity assumption is that the variances of difference scores for all pairs of conditions do not differ significantly in the populations. For the data shown in Table 16.1, the values of $s^2_{a_1-a_2}$, $s^2_{a_1-a3}$, and $s^2_{a_2-a_3}$ are used to test whether $\sigma^2_{a_1-a_2} = \sigma^2_{a_1-a3} = \sigma^2_{a_2-a3}$.

Table 16.1. An illustration of the ideas underlying the assumption of sphericity. The top panel shows the scores of each of four participants (labeled p_1-p_4) tested in each of three levels of factor A. The middle panel shows difference scores for each participant between pairs of levels of factor A. The bottom panel shows the sample variances of the difference scores.

	a_1	a_2	a_3
p_1	3	4	8
p_2	4	6	11
p_3	2	3	6
p_4	5	4	10

$a_1 - a_2 = d_1$	$a_1 - a_3 = d_2$	$a_2 - a_3 = d_3$
3 – 4 = -1	3 – 8 = -5	4 – 8 = -4
4 – 6 = 2	4 – 11 = -7	6 – 11 = -5
2 – 3 = -1	2 – 6 = -4	3 – 6 = -3
5 – 4 = 1	5 – 10 = -5	4 – 10 = -6

d_1	d_2	d_3
-1	-5	-4
2 $s_{a_1-a_2}^2 = 1.58$	-7 $s_{a_1-a3}^2 = 1.58$	-5 $s_{a_2-a_3}^2 = 1.67$
-1	-4	-3
1	-5	-6

In *SPSS* the assumption of sphericity is tested in the **General Linear Model** procedure using the Mauchly test of sphericity (see details below). When the sphericity assumption is violated and the *F* value for an *ANOVA* is obtained from a standard table to evaluate the null hypothesis, the table *F* value will be smaller than is appropriate, so too many Type I errors will occur (i.e., the null hypothesis will be rejected when it is correct). Three methods are available in *SPSS* for correcting this positive bias in *F*. As will be explained below, all involve evaluating the null hypothesis using a critical value of *F* based on degrees of freedom that have been adjusted to make them smaller than otherwise.

Terms Used in the Analysis

The basic ratios used to calculate the denominator terms for the *F* value of a one-way within-subjects *ANOVA* are different than for the one-way between-subjects *ANOVA*. Consider the data shown in Figure 16.2. In the body of the table are scores for a dependent variable of three participants who are administered each of three levels of factor A. In the margins of the table are means of either each participant's scores (the last column) or of each factor level (the bottom row). The grand mean shown in the shaded box is the mean of all scores in the body of the table. Formulas for calculating the sums of squares and degrees of freedom (*df*) of *F* to evaluate the significance of factor A, and mean values of the dependent variable are shown in Table 16.2. The formula for calculating F and its value is $\dfrac{SS_{factorA}/df_{factorA}}{SS_{error}/df_{error}} = \dfrac{MS_{factorA}}{MS_{error}} = \dfrac{42/2}{1.33/4} = \dfrac{21}{0.33} = 63.00$

Figure 16.2. Scores of three participants who receive treatments in levels a_1, a_2, and a_3 of factor A. Row marginal values show means of each participant's 3 scores; column marginal values show means of all participants in a level of the factor.

Participant #	Factor A			
	a_1	a_2	a_3	$\bar{P}_j$
1	2	4	7	4.33
2	3	3	8	4.67
3	4	5	9	6.00
$\bar{x}_i =$	3	4	8	$\bar{\bar{x}}$ = Grand mean = 5.00

Table 16.2. Formulas for calculating terms used in the numerator and denominator of the F ratio of a one-way within-subjects *ANOVA*. The calculations illustrate use of the formulas with data shown in Figure 16.2. In the df column, n is the number of participants.

Source of Variance Estimate	Sum of Squares	df
Factor A	$n\sum_i (\bar{x}_i - \bar{\bar{x}})^2$	# levels of factor A - 1
Calculations:	$3[(3-5)^2 + (4-5)^2 + (8-5)^2] = 42$	$3 - 1 = 2$
Error (A x P)	$\sum_i \sum_j (x_{ij} - \bar{P}_j - \bar{x}_i + \bar{\bar{x}})^2$	$(n-1)$ x (# levels of factor A $-$ 1)
Calculations:	$(2 - 4.33 - 3 + 5)^2 +$ $(3 - 4.67 - 3 + 5)^2 +$ $(4 - 6.00 - 3 + 5)^2 +$ $(4 - 4.33 - 4 + 5)^2 +$ $(3 - 4.67 - 4 + 5)^2 +$ $(5 - 6.00 - 4 + 5)^2 +$ $(7 - 4.33 - 8 + 5)^2 +$ $(8 - 4.67 - 8 + 5)^2 +$ $(9 - 6.00 - 8 + 5)^2 = 1.33$	$(3 - 1)$ x $(3 - 1) = 4$

Note that the error term that appears in the denominator of the F ratio of a one-way within-subjects ANOVA measures the *factor x participants* interaction and so, if the factor is called factor A, can be designated as $MS_{A \, x \, P}$.

Preparing Data for the Analysis

To analyze data for a one-way within-subjects ANOVA using the *SPSS* **General Linear Model**, each level of the factor that is to be analyzed should be entered into the **SPSS Statistics Data Editor** as a separate variable. For example, if the data shown in the top panel of Table 16.1 are to be analyzed, then, because the factor contains three levels, three variables must be represented in the **SPSS Statistics Data Editor**. Because there are four participants in each level of the factor, four values must be entered for each variable. The name of each variable is arbitrary. In the representation shown below, the variables are named **a1**, **a2**, and **a3**.

> Note that the data in the spreadsheet are arranged just like those in the top panel of Table 16.1.

	a1	a2	a3	var
1	3.00	4.00	8.00	
2	4.00	6.00	11.00	
3	2.00	3.00	6.00	
4	5.00	4.00	10.00	
5				
6				

OneWayWithinExample.sav [DataSet1] - SPSS Statistics Data Editor

Requesting a One-Way Within-Subjects ANOVA

The procedure for requesting a one-way within-subjects *ANOVA* using the **General Linear Model** is illustrated below:

1. From the **Analyze** menu select **General Linear Model** and then **Repeated Measures**.

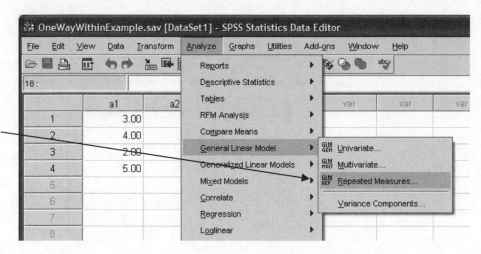

2. Type into this field the name you wish to assign to the factor. Here it is called **factorA**.

3. Type into this field the number of levels of your factor.

4. Click **Add**.

5. Click **Define**.

6. Shift-Click to highlight each level name then transfer them by clicking this button.

7. Click **Options**.

8. Click to select these options.

9. Click **Continue.**

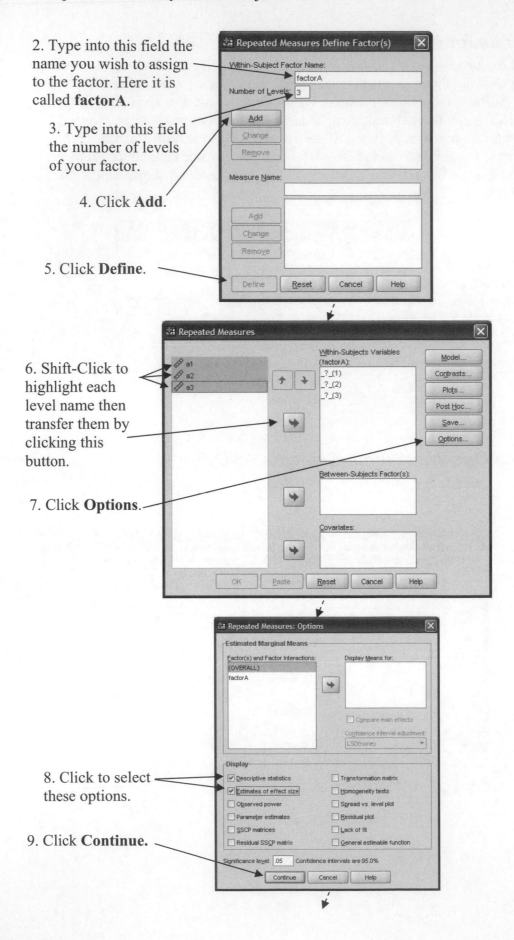

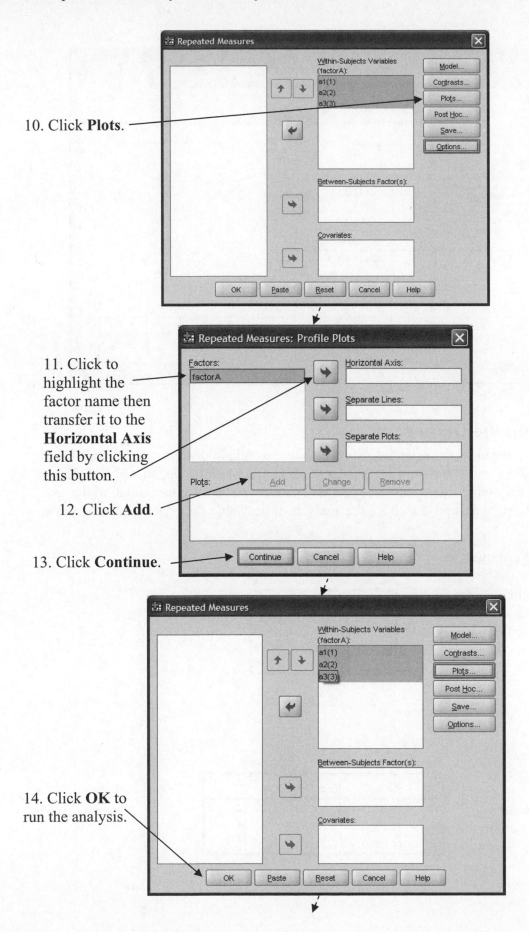

10. Click **Plots**.

11. Click to highlight the factor name then transfer it to the **Horizontal Axis** field by clicking this button.

12. Click **Add**.

13. Click **Continue**.

14. Click **OK** to run the analysis.

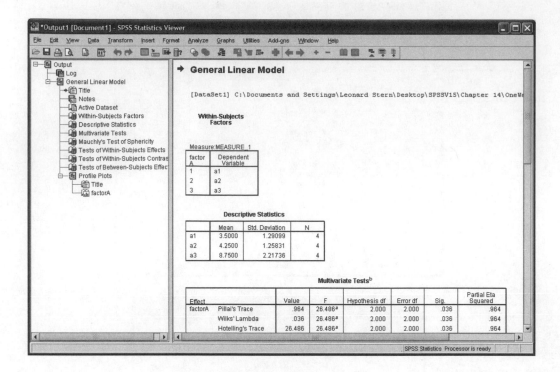

Interpreting the Output

The output produced by the selections specified above include descriptive statistics for each level of the factor, the Mauchly test of the sphericity assumption, an *ANOVA* table, and a line plot showing the mean value of the dependent variable at each level of the factor. The entire output produced for the analysis of the Table 16.1 data is shown below.

1. This table shows the name given to the factor and the number of levels of the factor together with their names. Verify that these are as expected.

Within-Subjects Factors

Measure:MEASURE_1

factorA	Dependent Variable
1	a1
2	a2
3	a3

2. Inspect the means and standard deviations of scores in each level. Verify that they are as expected.

Descriptive Statistics

	Mean	Std. Deviation	N
a1	3.5000	1.29099	4
a2	4.2500	1.25831	4
a3	8.7500	2.21736	4

Multivariate Tests[b]

Effect		Value	F	Hypothesis df	Error df	Sig.	Partial Eta Squared
factorA	Pillai's Trace	.964	26.486[a]	2.000	2.000	.036	.964
	Wilks' Lambda	.036	26.486[a]	2.000	2.000	.036	.964
	Hotelling's Trace	26.486	26.486[a]	2.000	2.000	.036	.964
	Roy's Largest Root	26.486	26.486[a]	2.000	2.000	.036	.964

a. Exact statistic

b. Design: Intercept
 Within Subjects Design: factorA

3. Examine this table to determine if the sphericity assumption has been violated. If the significance value is ≤ .05, the assumption has been violated.

Because this value is >.05 the assumption of sphericity is not violated.

Mauchly's Test of Sphericity[b]

Measure:MEASURE_1

Within Subjects Effect	Mauchly's W	Approx. Chi-Square	df	Sig.	Epsilon[a]		
					Greenhouse-Geisser	Huynh-Feldt	Lower-bound
factorA	.999	.002	2	.999	.999	1.000	.500

Tests the null hypothesis that the error covariance matrix of the orthonormalized transformed dependent variables is proportional to an identity matrix.

a. May be used to adjust the degrees of freedom for the averaged tests; tests are displayed in the Tests of Within-Subjects Effects table.

b. Design: Intercept
 Within Subjects Design: factorA

These are the multipliers used to adjust the numerator and denominator degrees of freedom of *F* when sphericity does not hold.

Tests of Within-Subjects Effects

Measure: MEASURE_1

Source		Type III Sum of Squares	df	Mean Square	F	Sig.	Partial Eta Squared
factorA	Sphericity Assumed	64.500	2	32.250	40.034	.000	.930
	Greenhouse-Geisser	64.500	1.998	32.288	40.034	.000	.930
	Huynh-Feldt	64.500	2.000	32.250	40.034	.000	.930
	Lower-bound	64.500	1.000	64.500	40.034	.008	.930
Error(factorA)	Sphericity Assumed	4.833	6	.806			
	Greenhouse-Geisser	4.833	5.993	.807			
	Huynh-Feldt	4.833	6.000	.806			
	Lower-bound	4.833	3.000	1.611			

4. This table gives the *F* value and its level of significance for testing the equality of means of the factor.

These numbers are used in the numerator and denominator of the *F* ratio.

This measures the effect size.

This is the *F* value and significance level for the effect of factor A.

Tests of Within-Subjects Contrasts

Measure: MEASURE_1

Source	factorA	Type III Sum of Squares	df	Mean Square	F	Sig.	Partial Eta Squared
factorA	Linear	55.125	1	55.125	69.632	.004	.959
	Quadratic	9.375	1	9.375	11.441	.043	.792
Error(factorA)	Linear	2.375	3	.792			
	Quadratic	2.458	3	.819			

Tests of Between-Subjects Effects

Measure: MEASURE_1

Transformed Variable: Average

Source	Type III Sum of Squares	df	Mean Square	F	Sig.	Partial Eta Squared
Intercept	363.000	1	363.000	55.373	.005	.949
Error	19.667	3	6.556			

Estimated Marginal Means of MEASURE_1

5. This plots the means of the levels of factor A. The plot can be edited to insert appropriate axis names.

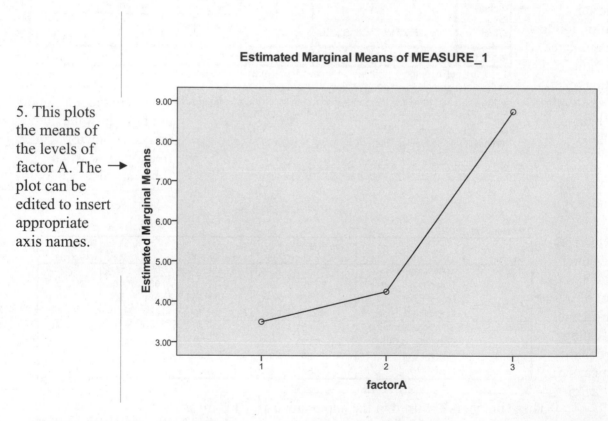

Reporting the Results

Assume that in the analysis shown above, factor A represents type of background sound and that levels a_1, a_2, and a_3 represent white noise, classical music, and rock music, respectively. Assume, further, that the dependent variable is number of errors on a test of reasoning. A suitable summary of the results of the *ANOVA* can take the following form:

The effect of type of background sound (white noise, classical music, rock music) on number of errors on a test of reasoning was examined using a one-way within-subjects *ANOVA*. Table 16.3 shows the means and standard deviations of scores on the test of reasoning as a function of type of background sound. Because the Mauchly test of sphericity was not significant, (approximate $\chi^2 < 1$), the difference among the means was examined using the uncorrected F value. The test indicated that type of background sound had a significant effect of mean number of errors on the reasoning test, $F(2, 6) = 40.03$, $p < .001$, partial $\eta^2 = .93$.

Table 16.3. Means and standard deviations of the number of errors on the reasoning task as a function of type of background sound.

Background Sound	Mean	Std. Deviation	n
White noise	3.50	1.29	4
Classical Music	4.25	1.26	4
Rock Music	8.75	2.22	4

Dealing with Violations of Sphericity

The Mauchly test assesses the sphericity assumption with the statistic W whose significance is evaluated using a chi-square test that, when significant, indicates the sphericity assumption is unlikely to be valid. Under these circumstances one can apply a correction factor (using a value of *epsilon* reported in the *SPSS* output) to adjust the degrees of freedom of the test or one can evaluate the null hypothesis with a multivariate test (because the multivariate approach is not based on the sphericity assumption). *SPSS* provides three methods for adjusting degrees of freedom (and thus, the F value used to evaluate the null hypothesis). In order of the degree to which they adjust the value of F, these methods are 1) the Huynh-Feldt 2) the Greenhouse-Geisser, and 3) the lower-bound procedure.

There are a variety of recommendations about how to proceed (see, e.g., Keppel & Wickens, 2004). One reasonable strategy is to use the F value corresponding to a multivariate test. Another is to rely exclusively on planned comparisons to test hypotheses. The latter approach takes advantage of the sphericity assumption being irrelevant when the within-subjects factor of an *ANOVA* has only two levels (because there is only one possible set of difference scores). In accord with this, the Mauchly sphericity test is not included in *SPSS* output when either the within-subjects factor has two levels or when performing a contrast (e.g., comparing the mean of condition 1 to the mean of condition 3 or comparing the mean of condition 1 with the mean of conditions 2 and 3 combined). Because planned comparisons are generally more informative than the overall (often referred as omnibus) *ANOVA*, this approach is generally advantageous. Thus, it is advisable, when including a within-subjects factor in an *ANOVA*, to couch hypotheses in terms of single *df* contrasts.

Contrasts

The same contrasts that were described in **Chapter 15** on the two-way and higher order between-subjects *ANOVA*s are available on a one-way within-subjects *ANOVA*. For convenience, the contrasts that were demonstrated in Table 15.3 of that chapter are adapted for a one-way design and shown again in Table 16.4.

Use of one of the contrasts is illustrated with data from an experiment that measured the proportion of test words participants signaled they recognized having studied in each of three conditions: in condition 1, the test words had been included in a list of words the participants had previously studied; in condition 2, the test words had not been presented, but had earlier been "primed" by presentation of associates of the word (e.g., presentation of words such as *bed* and *tired* had primed the word *sleep*); in condition 3, the test words had neither been studied nor primed. The intent of the experiment was 1) to verify that recognition performance in conditions 1 and 2 combined differed from that in condition 3, and 2) to test whether there was any significant difference between performance in conditions 1 and 2. These hypotheses were examined using the **difference** contrast.

Table 16.4. Illustrations of the means compared by various contrasts available in the **Repeated Measures** procedure of the **General Linear Model**. The contrasts are pictured as being applied to the marginal means of factor A having three levels that are referred to as a_1, a_2, and a_3.

To request one of these sets of contrasts, at some point after the within-subjects factor has been defined and the variable names transferred to the levels of the within-subjects factor listed in the **Repeated Measures** window (i.e., after step 6 shown in the section entitled **Requesting a One-Way Within-Subjects *ANOVA***) the **Contrasts** button on the **Repeated Measures** window is activated to bring up the **Repeated Measures: Contrasts** window shown below:

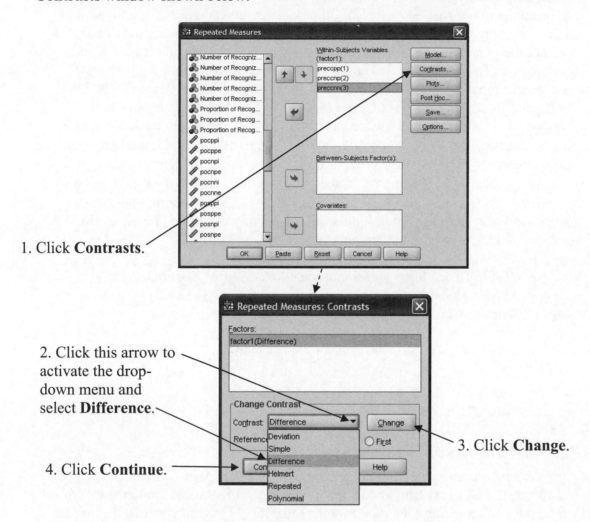

1. Click **Contrasts**.

2. Click this arrow to activate the drop-down menu and select **Difference**.

3. Click **Change**.

4. Click **Continue**.

The output will now include a table such as the one shown below:

This table gives each *F* value and its level of significance for planned comparisons.

This tests if means of conditions 1 and 2 differ.

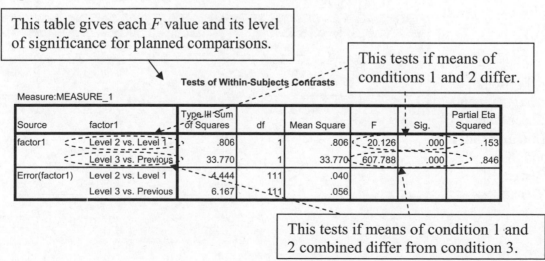

Tests of Within-Subjects Contrasts

Measure:MEASURE_1

Source	factor1	Type III Sum of Squares	df	Mean Square	F	Sig.	Partial Eta Squared
factor1	Level 2 vs. Level 1	.806	1	.806	20.126	.000	.153
	Level 3 vs. Previous	33.770	1	33.770	607.788	.000	.846
Error(factor1)	Level 2 vs. Level 1	4.444	111	.040			
	Level 3 vs. Previous	6.167	111	.056			

This tests if means of condition 1 and 2 combined differ from condition 3.

A suitable summary of the results of the *ANOVA*s are shown below:

The effect of study condition [primed and studied (P/S), primed not studied (P/NS), not primed and not studied (NP/NS)] on proportion of test words recognized was examined using two within-subjects planned comparisons. Comparison one tested whether the mean proportion of test words recognized of the combined P/S and P/NS conditions differed from that in the NP/NS condition and comparison two tested whether the mean proportion of test words recognized differed in the P/S and the P/NS condition. Table 16.5 shows the means and standard deviations of the proportion of test words recognized as a function of study condition. Comparison one was significant, $F(1, 111) = 607.79$, $p < .001$, partial $\eta^2 = .85$, indicating that for both studied and non-studied words, priming enhances the tendency to treat words on a recognition test as having previously been studied. Comparison two was also significant, $F(1, 111) = 20.13$, $p < .001$, partial $\eta^2 = .15$, indicating that, on a recognition test, studying a word in addition to having it primed, enhances the tendency to treat words as having previously been studied.

Table 16.5. Means and standard deviations of proportion words recognized in an experiment as a function of study condition.

Study Condition	Mean	Std. Deviation	n
P/S	.88	.16	112
P/NS	.80	.20	112
NP/NS	.29	.21	112

Multiple Comparison Tests

When performing a number of planned comparisons between pairs of means of a within-subjects factor, the **General Linear Model** allows application of the Bonferroni and Sidak methods for controlling the type I error probability. These are accessed using the **Repeated Measures: Options** window, as shown below:

1. From the **Analyze** menu select **General Linear Model** and then **Repeated Measures**.

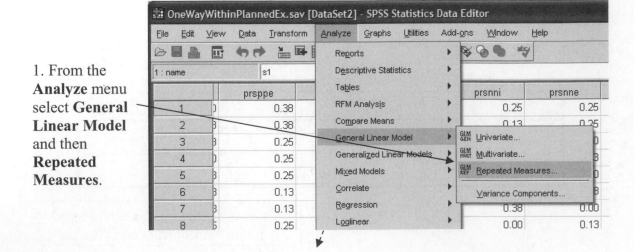

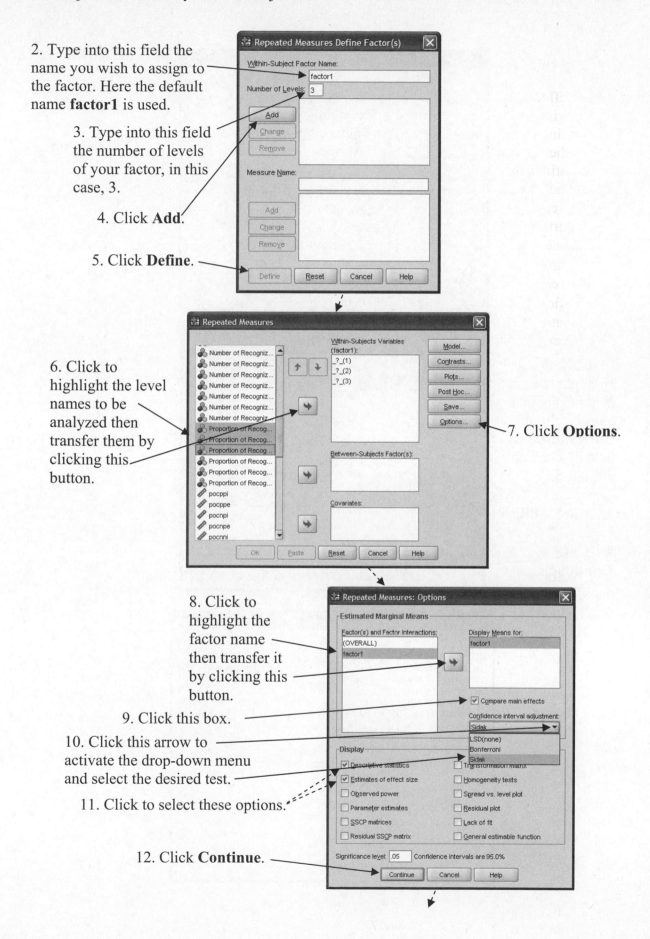

2. Type into this field the name you wish to assign to the factor. Here the default name **factor1** is used.

3. Type into this field the number of levels of your factor, in this case, 3.

4. Click **Add**.

5. Click **Define**.

6. Click to highlight the level names to be analyzed then transfer them by clicking this button.

7. Click **Options**.

8. Click to highlight the factor name then transfer it by clicking this button.

9. Click this box.

10. Click this arrow to activate the drop-down menu and select the desired test.

11. Click to select these options.

12. Click **Continue**.

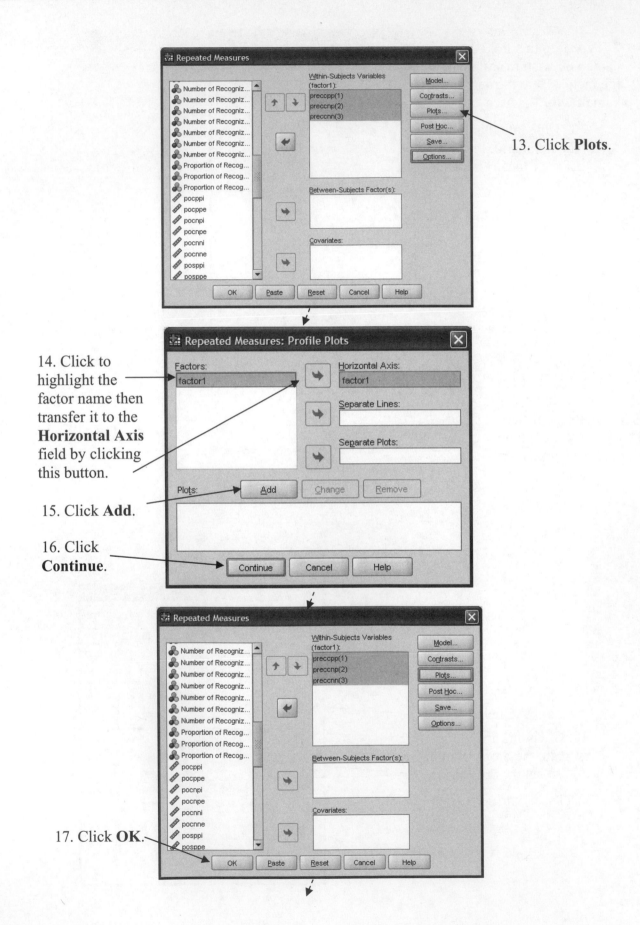

13. Click **Plots**.

14. Click to highlight the factor name then transfer it to the **Horizontal Axis** field by clicking this button.

15. Click **Add**.

16. Click **Continue**.

17. Click **OK**.

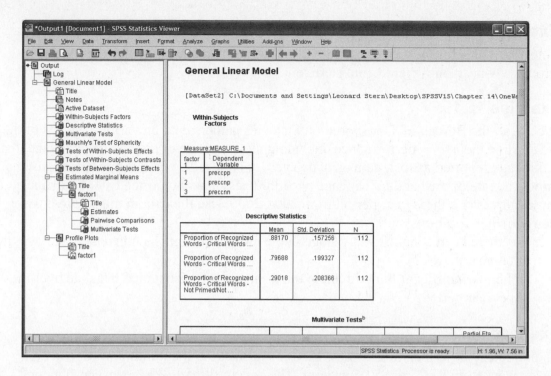

The output now includes a table showing the mean of the dependent variable at each level of the within-subjects factor together with its confidence interval adjusted using the method selected in the **Options** window and a table showing pairwise comparisons:

This table shows the mean of each level and the 95% confidence interval adjusted using the Sidak method.

Estimates

Measure:MEASURE_1

factor1	Mean	Std. Error	95% Confidence Interval	
			Lower Bound	Upper Bound
1	.882	.015	.852	.911
2	.797	.019	.760	.834
3	.290	.020	.251	.329

This shows the significance of the comparison between conditions 1 and 2.

Pairwise Comparisons

Measure:MEASURE_1

(I) factor1	(J) factor1	Mean Difference (I-J)	Std. Error	Sig.[a]	95% Confidence Interval for Difference[a]	
					Lower Bound	Upper Bound
1	2	.085*	.019	.000	.039	.131
	3	.592*	.023	.000	.537	.646
2	1	-.085*	.019	.000	-.131	-.039
	3	.507*	.026	.000	.444	.569
3	1	-.592*	.023	.000	-.646	-.537
	2	-.507*	.026	.000	-.569	-.444

Based on estimated marginal means

*. The mean difference is significant at the .05 level.

a. Adjustment for multiple comparisons: Sidak.

This shows the significance of the comparison between conditions 2 and 3.

This shows the significance of the comparison between conditions 1 and 3.

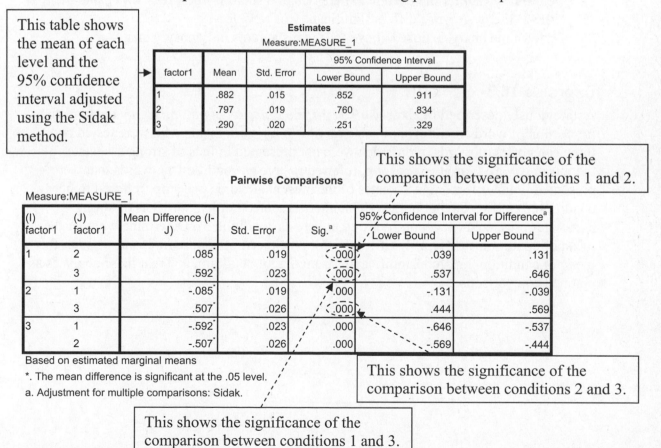

Exercises for Chapter 16

Note: Data files for these exercises are available at the publisher's website for this text, http://www.pearsonhighered.com/stern2e.

Exercise 16.1

Each year, the Bureau of Transportation Statistics gathers data on various aspects of the U.S. airline industry's performance, including the incidence of mishandled baggage, that is, luggage reported as lost, damaged, delayed, or stolen. The data in file *Airline.sav* shows the rate of mishandled baggage per 1,000 passengers reported by U.S. airline companies over a three year period from 2004-2006. Use the data in this file to answer the following questions:

1. Has there been a significant change in the mean rate of mishandled baggage over the three-year period?
2. Is there a significant linear trend in the mean rate of mishandled baggage over the three-year period?

Exercise 16.2

As previously described in **Exercise 12.4**, in April, 1992, the minimum wage in New Jersey went from \$4.25 to \$5.05 an hour. The data in file *MinWage.sav* was obtained from randomly selected fast food restaurants about one month before and eight months after the minimum wage increase took effect.

1. Determine whether the change in the price of a small fry before (**Pfry1**) and after (**Pfry2**) the wage raise differs significantly in New Jersey
2. Perform the analysis posed above for the restaurants in Pennsylvania.

Exercise 16.3

As previously described in **Exercise 9.2**, the file *FalseRecognitionExp.sav* contains the proportion of words recognized in an experiment by participants who were tested on three categories of words: words that were not presented in lists of strong associates of the missing word (variable **preccnp**, referred to here as condition 1); words that were presented in lists of strong associates of the presented word (**preccpp**, referred to here as condition 2); or words that both were neither presented nor had any lists of strong associates presented (**preccnn**, referred to here as condition 3). Determine whether the mean of condition 1 differs significantly from the mean of condition 2, and whether the mean of condition 2 differs significantly from that of condition 3. Treat these analyses as planned comparisons.

Chapter 17: Nonparametric or Distribution Free Tests

Overview

Statistical tests based on strict assumptions about a population from which each sample is obtained, for example, that the population is normally distributed or that, if several populations are sampled, they all have equal variance, can be considered parametric techniques. On the other hand, nonparametric tests, sometimes referred to as distribution-free tests, base inferences on populations about which more relaxed (or fewer) assumptions are made. Advantages of nonparametric tests include their applicability to variables measured on nominal or ordinal scales and to small samples derived from populations whose distributions may not conform to those required by a parametric test (see Siegel & Castellan, 1988).

Tests Involving Single Samples

The Binomial Test

The binomial test is used to determine whether the proportion of cases with a particular value of a dichotomous variable differs from a theoretical or reference proportion. Consider, for example, the dichotomous variable gender. We may know that the proportion of males in a college is .42 (thus the proportion of females is .58) and we may wish to know whether the proportion of males enrolled in a particular program in the college is significantly lower than this reference value. Imagine that in a random sample of 20 psychology majors there are 4 males and 16 females. The binomial test can determine whether finding a proportion of .20 males in a random sample of size 20 indicates the proportion of psychology majors at the school is significantly lower than the proportion of males in the university population (i.e., .42).

The test utilizes the binomial distribution. A binomial distribution results when there are just two possible mutually exclusive outcomes of an event, one that occurs with a probability p and the other with a probability $(1 - p) = q$. For example, in tossing a fair coin, the outcome is either a head or a tail; these outcomes are mutually exclusive because both cannot simultaneously occur. If the coin is fair the probability of obtaining a head (p) is ½ and the probability of obtaining a tail (q) is $(1 - ½)$ or ½. The binomial distribution shows the probability of obtaining a particular number of outcomes (n) from N independent trials, for example, 9 heads out of 10 coin tosses. The exact probability is given by a formula that specifies the number of ways a particular outcome can occur (the expression composed of factorials, i.e., terms followed by the symbol !) and the probability of that outcome. The formula is

$$\frac{N!}{n!(N-n)!} p^n q^{N-n} \qquad \text{Equation 17.1}$$

Thus, the probability of obtaining 9 heads ($n = 9$) out of 10 coin tosses ($N = 10$) is

$$\frac{10\times9\times8\times7\times6\times5\times4\times3\times2\times1}{9\times8\times7\times6\times5\times4\times3\times2\times1(1)}\left(\frac{1}{2}\right)^9\left(\frac{1}{2}\right)^1 = .009765$$

When testing hypotheses, our interest is in calculating the probability of outcomes that are as or more extreme than some obtained value. For the question about the proportion of male psychology majors, the calculation requires that we find the probability of obtaining 4 or fewer males (or 16 or more females) in samples of size 20 when the theoretical probability of finding a male is .42 (and, therefore, .58 for females). These calculations are shown in Table 17.1. Because the probabilities sum to less than .05, we can reject the null hypothesis that the proportion of male psychology majors matches or is higher than that of males in the university.

Table 17.1. Calculations involved in finding the probability of obtaining four or fewer males in randomly drawn samples of size 20 from a population in which males occur at a rate of .42.

Probability Being Calculated	Calculations	Exact Probability
Four males in a sample of 20	$\dfrac{20!}{4!\times16!}.42^4.58^{16} =$	.02473
Three males in a sample of 20	$\dfrac{20!}{3!\times17!}.42^3.58^{17} =$	.00803
Two males in a sample of 20	$\dfrac{20!}{2!\times18!}.42^2.58^{18} =$	.00185
One males in a sample of 20	$\dfrac{20!}{1!\times19!}.42^1.58^{19} =$	.00027
Zero males in a sample of 20[*]	$\dfrac{20!}{0!\times20!}.42^0.58^{20} =$	.00002
		Total = .03490

[*]$0! = 1$

Some properties worth knowing about binomial distributions are that the mean of a binomial distribution is Np and its standard deviation is $\sqrt{Npq}$. Thus, if a fair coin is tossed 10 times, the expected mean of the distribution of heads is 10 x .5 = 5 and the standard deviation is $\sqrt{10\times.5\times.5}$ =1.58. Another property that is useful to know is that as the sample size, N, increases, the binomial distribution increasingly resembles a normal distribution. The approximation to the normal distribution will be approached with lower sample sizes when p and q are both close to ½; the more disparate the values of p and q, the larger the sample size, N, must be for the binomial distribution to approximate a normal distribution. A general rule is that for p and q values near ½, the binomial distribution will be approximately normal for sample sizes that exceed 25; when p or q are near 0 or 1, the binomial distribution will be approximately normal if the standard deviation of the binomial distribution, $\sqrt{Npq}$, exceeds 3 (see Siegel and Castellan, 1988). Thus, if p = .10 and q = .90, a sample size of 100 will be required for the binomial distribution to be considered approximately normal.

For the example that had 20 students drawn randomly from a population consisting of .42 males and .58 females, the theoretical probability of obtaining samples with particular numbers of males is shown in Figure 17.1. It can be seen that the distribution is positively skewed. The probability of obtaining a random sample consisting of 16 or more males is not equal to that of obtaining a sample consisting of 4 or fewer males: the probability of obtaining a sample consisting of 16 males is .0022716; the probability of obtaining a sample consisting of 17 males is .0000876; the probability of finding 18 males is .0000106; the probability of finding 19 males is .0000008; and the probability of finding 20 males is essentially zero.

Figure 17.1. The probability of finding a particular number of males in samples of size 20 drawn randomly from a population consisting of .42 males and .58 females.

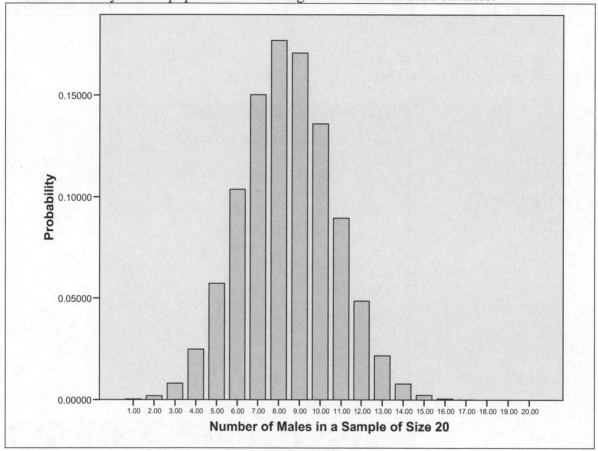

Underlying Assumptions. To use a binomial test to determine if the distribution of values of a dichotomous variable in a sample comes from a population with specified proportions of the two values, two assumptions must hold. One is that cases are randomly and independently sampled from the population. A second is that if the normal approximation to the binomial distribution is used to obtain probabilities, the sample size must be sufficiently large.

Preparing Data for the Analysis. The most efficient way of coding data into the **SPSS Statistics Data Editor** spreadsheet makes use of the **Weight Cases** function. For our example of the sample of 4 males and 16 females, data entry using this method is shown below:

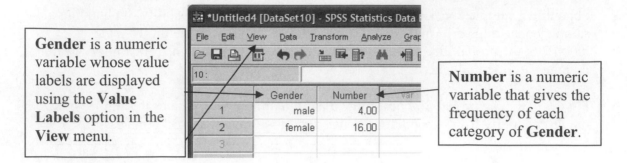

Gender is a numeric variable whose value labels are displayed using the **Value Labels** option in the **View** menu.

Number is a numeric variable that gives the frequency of each category of **Gender**.

The two categories of the variable **Gender** must then be weighted using the value specified in the variable **Number**:

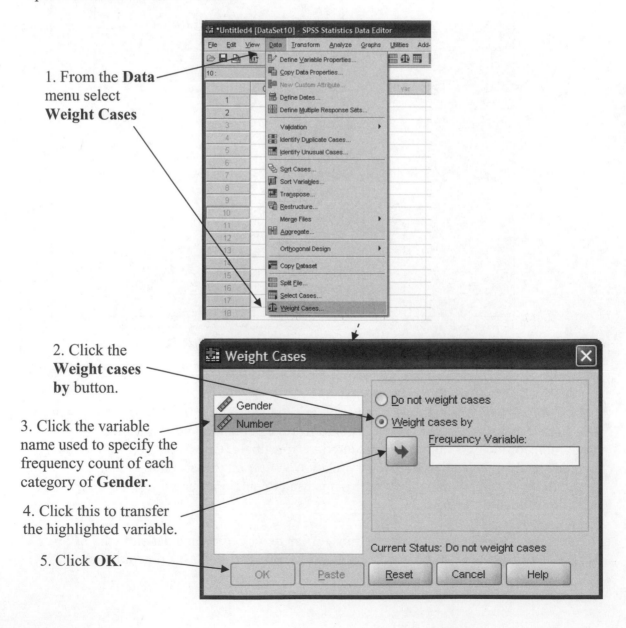

1. From the **Data** menu select **Weight Cases**

2. Click the **Weight cases by** button.

3. Click the variable name used to specify the frequency count of each category of **Gender**.

4. Click this to transfer the highlighted variable.

5. Click **OK**.

Requesting a Binomial Test. The procedure for requesting a binomial test is shown next:

1. From the **Analyze** menu select **Nonparametric Tests** and then **Binomial**.

The first category of gender entered here (male) determines which reference test value is entered in the next step (.42).

2. Click to highlight the name of the dichotomous variable whose frequencies you want to test then click this button to transfer it.

4. Click **Options**.

3. Click here and type in the test proportion you wish to use as a reference value for the first gender value entered.

5. Click to select this option.

6. Click **Continue.**

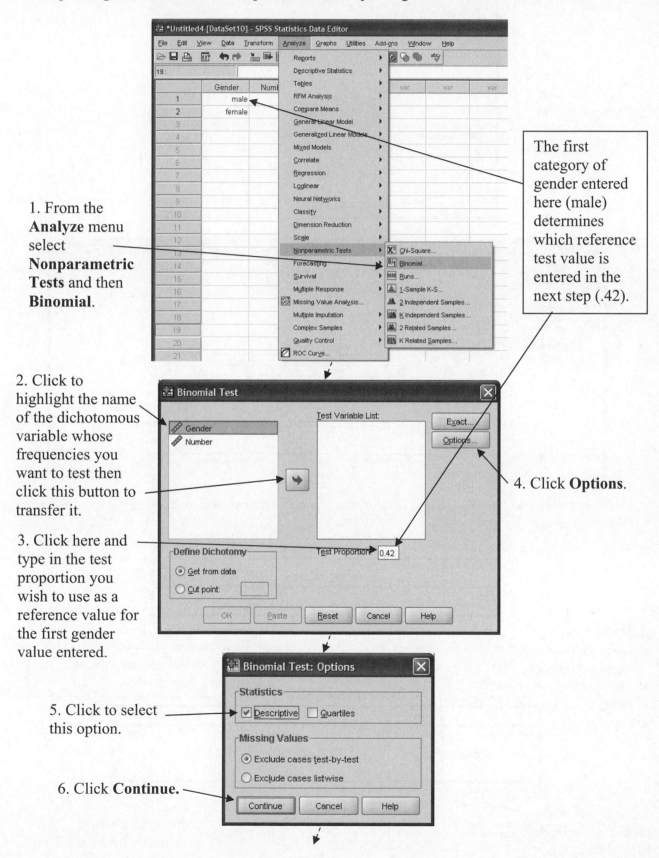

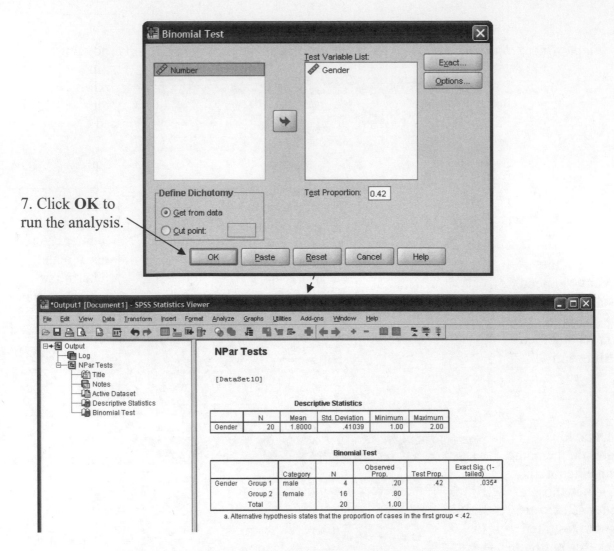

7. Click **OK** to run the analysis.

Interpreting the Output. Output for the analysis requested above consists of the two tables shown next:

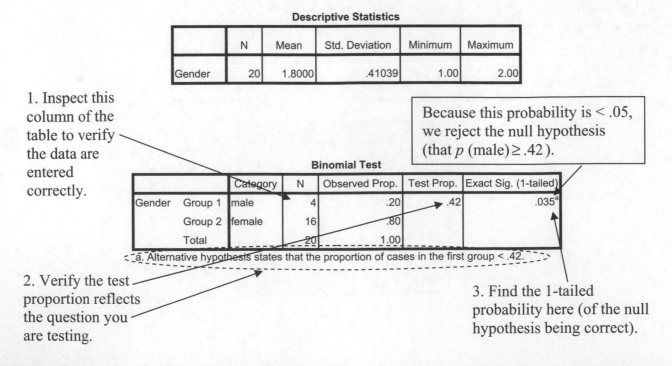

Descriptive Statistics

	N	Mean	Std. Deviation	Minimum	Maximum
Gender	20	1.8000	.41039	1.00	2.00

1. Inspect this column of the table to verify the data are entered correctly.

Because this probability is < .05, we reject the null hypothesis (that p (male) $\geq$ .42).

Binomial Test

		Category	N	Observed Prop.	Test Prop.	Exact Sig. (1-tailed)
Gender	Group 1	male	4	.20	.42	.035[a]
	Group 2	female	16	.80		
	Total		20	1.00		

a. Alternative hypothesis states that the proportion of cases in the first group < .42.

2. Verify the test proportion reflects the question you are testing.

3. Find the 1-tailed probability here (of the null hypothesis being correct).

Reporting the Results. A report of the outcome of a binomial test should include the theoretical and observed proportions, the sample size, the outcome of the test including mention of whether the probability is exact or derived from the normal approximation to the binomial distribution, and, if the outcome is significant, a measure of effect size. Although an effect size measure is not often reported, the measure h suggested by Cohen (1988) is appropriate, and is given by the formula

$$h = 2\arcsin\sqrt{p_{obtained}} - 2\arcsin\sqrt{p_{theoretical}}$$ Equation 17.2

where $p_{obtained}$ is the proportion of "successes" obtained in the sample,

$p_{theoretical}$ is the theoretical or reference proportion of successes.

Note that both proportions should be expressed in radians rather than degrees. A relatively easy way to obtain h is with a **Compute** statement in *SPSS*:

1. From the **Transform** menu select **Compute Variable**.

2. Type in a variable name here, such as **h**.

3. With the aid of the **Arithmetic** function group, insert an expression like this.

4. Click **OK**.

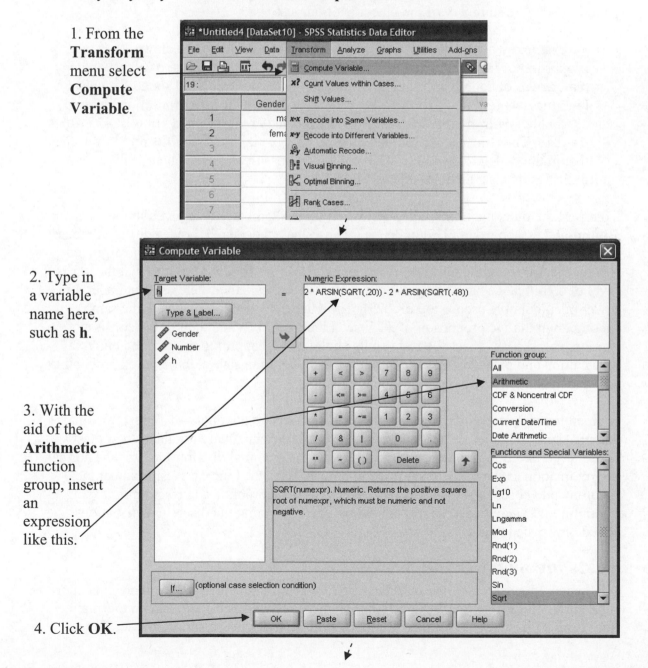

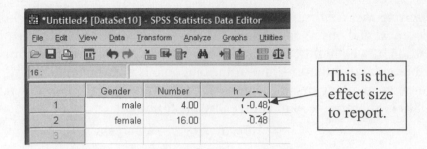

Cohen recommends providing the h value together with its sign if the test is 1-tailed (i.e., directional) and reporting the absolute value of h otherwise. Cohen categorizes values of h of .20, .50, and .80 as reflecting, respectively, small, medium, and large effect sizes. Here is a suitable summary of the outcome of our test.

> To examine whether the proportion of male psychology majors is lower than the proportion of males enrolled in the college (.42) a random sample of 20 psychology majors was obtained. The sample contained four males (.20) and sixteen females. A binomial test revealed that the exact probability of obtaining a proportion value of .20 and below from a sample of this size when the expected proportion is .42 is .035, $h = -.48$. Thus, the proportion of male psychology majors is significantly lower than that in the college as a whole. The effect size measure, h (see Cohen, 1988), indicates this is a medium effect.

To report the outcome of a 2-tailed test when 1-tailed probability is given in the **Binomial Test** table, simply double the given value. Understand, however, that if the test proportion differs from .50, the observed proportions being tested will not be arranged symmetrically about the mean. In the example just described, a 2-tailed test at the .05 level of significance based on a sample of size 20 tests whether there are just under 4-or-fewer (a cumulative proportion of .025) or just under 13-or-more males in the sample (another cumulative proportion of .025, see Figure 17.1). When the sample consists of 26 or more cases, *SPSS* bases the test results on the normal approximation to the binomial distribution and provides a 2-tailed probability value. In this case, the 1-tailed probability value is obtained by halving the value reported.

As mentioned previously in the chapter on the chi-square goodness-of-fit test, for small sample sizes, the binomial test is more precise that the chi-square goodness-of-fit test and is preferred. Even for larger sample sizes, when the binomial distribution uses the normal approximation as the basis for estimating probabilities, the binomial test is sometimes recommended because the values reported by *SPSS* incorporate a correction for continuity that may make them more appropriate for testing the discrete distributions based on frequency counts.

Tests Involving Two Samples

In Chapter 13, *t*-tests were described to assess whether the means of two independent or related samples differ significantly. Nonparametric procedures are available to examine comparable questions for data measured on ordinal scales or for small samples that use interval- or ratio-scaled dependent variables derived from populations with distributions that may violate assumptions required for a *t*-test.

The Mann-Whitney *U* Test

A nonparametric test that is analogous to the *t*-test for independent samples is the Mann-Whitney *U* test. The Mann-Whitney *U* test, applied to a dependent variable that assesses some concept using a measurement scale that is at least ordinal, tests the hypothesis that two independent population distributions are identical. If the forms of the distributions of scores in the two populations are assumed to be identical, for example, if both distributions are rectangular in shape with about the same variability, the test is equivalent to a test that their medians are the same. Scores are assumed to be randomly and independently sampled from continuous distributions (the last assumption makes ties unlikely).

The procedure for calculating the value of *U*, the test statistic used to evaluate the null hypothesis, is shown in Figure 17.2. The data consist of ease of understanding ratings (1 = extremely easy to understand, 7 = extremely difficult to understand) given by participants randomly assigned to receive one of two forms of instruction for a task. The table shows that scores of both samples are combined and ranked, ties are broken, ranks are identified as belonging to one sample or the other, ranks are summed for each sample, and the value of *U* is calculated using the sum of ranks for each sample. Note that the procedure for breaking ties is to determine what ranks would have been assigned among the tied scores if they had not been tied, then to assign to each score the mean of these ranks.

U_1 is the number of times a score in condition 1 precedes a score in condition 2 when the scores are ranked from low to high (ties that occur across conditions complicate the determination). Shown below are the ratings of the two instruction conditions taken from Figure 17.2, arranged from low to high. Scores from the first group are shown in bold grey font:

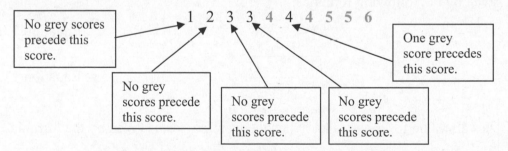

It can be seen that only once does a score from group 1 (standard instructions) precede a score from group 2, thus $U_1 = 1$. On the other hand, for the first grey 4, four scores from group 2 precede it, for the next grey 4, five scores from group 2 precede it, and for each of the remaining grey scores, five scores from group 2 precede each. Thus, $U_2 = 24$. The procedure shown in Figure 17.2 utilizes computational formulas to obtain values of U_1 and U_2. Note that the relation between the two *U* values is

$$U = n_1 n_2 - U'$$

Thus, one can obtain the value of U_2 from the value of U_1.

For a non-directional test, the smaller of the two values of U is compared to a critical U value to make a decision about the null hypothesis. Tables of critical U values can be found in many introductory statistics text books.

Figure 17.2. Procedure for obtaining U for a Mann-Whitney U test.

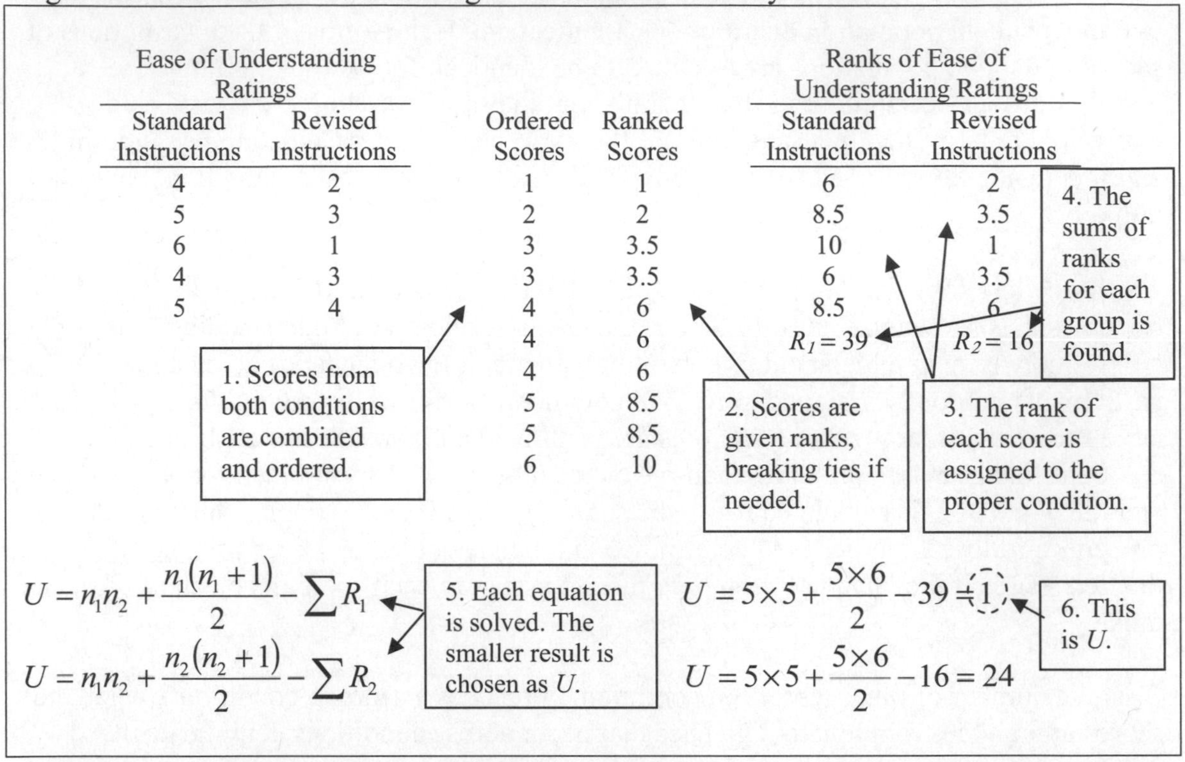

For large sample sizes, that is, when the number of scores in either condition exceeds 20, the sampling distribution if U will be approximately normal with a mean and standard deviation given by the following formulas:

$$\mu_U = \frac{n_1 n_2}{2}$$

Equation 17.8

$$\sigma_U = \sqrt{\frac{n_1 n_2 (N+1)}{12}}$$

Equation 17.9

where $N = n_1 + n_2$.

SPSS provides a z value for each U that, when there are no ties, is given by the formula

$$z = \frac{U - \frac{n_1 n_2}{2}}{\sqrt{\frac{n_1 n_2 (N+1)}{12}}}.$$

Equation 17.10

An adjustment is made to the denominator when there are ties:

$$z = \frac{U - \dfrac{n_1 n_2}{2}}{\sqrt{\dfrac{n_1 n_2 (N+1)}{12}\left[1 - \dfrac{\sum \left(t_i^3 - t_i\right)}{N^3 - N}\right]}}$$

Equation 17.11

where t_i = the number of tied scores having a particular value.
In the example shown in Figure 17.2, there are two tied scores with the value 3, three with the value 4, and two with the value 5. Thus,

$$\sum \left(t_i^3 - t_i\right) = \left(2^3 - 2\right) + \left(3^3 - 3\right) + \left(2^3 - 2\right) = 36 .$$

Preparing Data for the Analysis. Data for a Mann-Whitney U test are entered into the **SPSS Statistics Data Editor** spreadsheet in the same way as for a t-test for independent samples. One variable, declared as a numeric **type** represents values of the independent variable to allow cases to be distinguished as belonging to one condition or another, and a second variable, also declared as a numeric **type**, represents values of the dependent variable. The coding of data from Figure 17.2 is shown below:

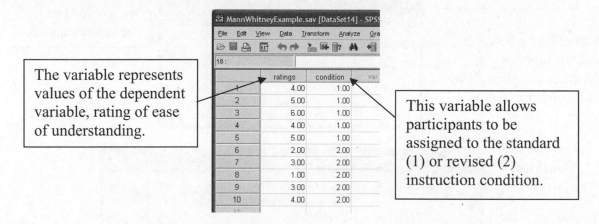

The variable represents values of the dependent variable, rating of ease of understanding.

This variable allows participants to be assigned to the standard (1) or revised (2) instruction condition.

Requesting the Analysis. The procedure for requesting a Mann-Whitney U test is shown below:

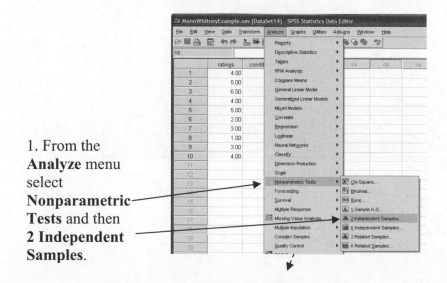

1. From the **Analyze** menu select **Nonparametric Tests** and then **2 Independent Samples**.

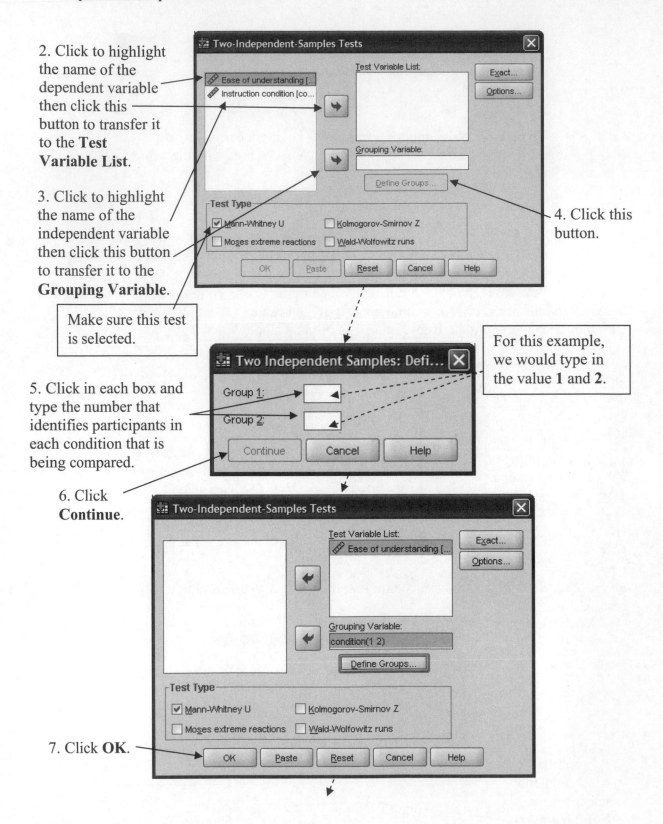

2. Click to highlight the name of the dependent variable then click this button to transfer it to the **Test Variable List**.

3. Click to highlight the name of the independent variable then click this button to transfer it to the **Grouping Variable**.

Make sure this test is selected.

4. Click this button.

For this example, we would type in the value **1** and **2**.

5. Click in each box and type the number that identifies participants in each condition that is being compared.

6. Click **Continue**.

7. Click **OK**.

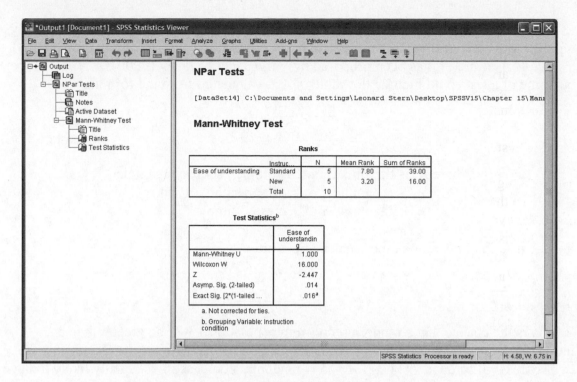

Interpreting the Output. The output consists of the tables shown below:

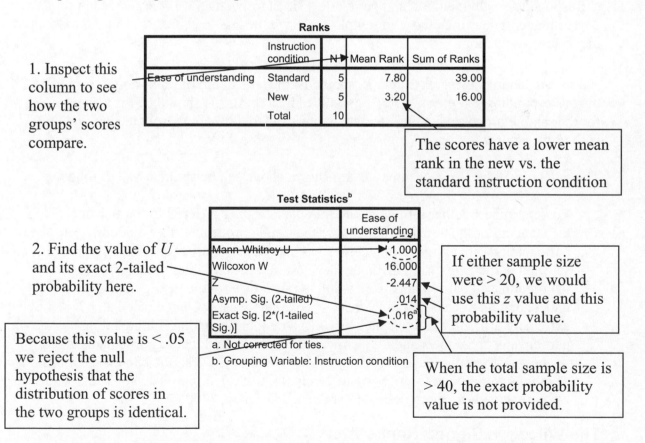

Ranks

1. Inspect this column to see how the two groups' scores compare.

The scores have a lower mean rank in the new vs. the standard instruction condition

Test Statistics

2. Find the value of *U* and its exact 2-tailed probability here.

If either sample size were > 20, we would use this *z* value and this probability value.

Because this value is < .05 we reject the null hypothesis that the distribution of scores in the two groups is identical.

When the total sample size is > 40, the exact probability value is not provided.

Reporting the Results. A report of the outcome of a test should include the number of participants in each condition of the study, the value of *U,* and, if either sample size exceeds 20, the value of z that is used to evaluate the significance of the outcome together with the significance level. Although measures of effect size are not commonly reported, a suitable measure, A, has been proposed by Vargha and Delaney (2000). A report of the outcome of a test could include the value of A as calculated from the formula

$$A_{12} = \frac{\left(\dfrac{R_1}{n_1} - \dfrac{n_1 + 1}{2}\right)}{n_2}$$ Equation 17.12

Where R_1 is the sum of ranks for the n_1 scores in sample 1,
n_1 is the number of scores in sample 1, and
n_2 is the number of scores in sample 2.

For the data in our example, these calculations are

$$A_{s\,\tan dard,new} = \frac{\left(\dfrac{39}{5} - \dfrac{6}{2}\right)}{5} = .96$$

A_{12} gives the chance that a random score from population 1 will be greater than an independently-drawn random score from population 2, plus ½ times the chance that the two scores will be equal. Thus, if $A = .5$, a randomly drawn score is equally likely to have come from either population. A has a range of 0-1. A values of .56, .64, and .71 correspond to small, medium, and large effect sizes, respectively. If the scores in sample 2 have higher values than those in sample 1, A_{12} will be less than .50. A_{12} and A_{21} have the following relation:

$$A_{12} = 1 - A_{21}.$$

If a two-tailed hypothesis is tested, R_1 should be the larger sum of ranks and n_1 should be the corresponding sample size. For a one-tailed hypothesis, R_1 should be the sum or ranks for the sample proposed (in the alternate hypothesis) to have come from the population with higher scores.

The outcome of the Mann-Whitney U test shown above can be summarized as follows:

> To determine whether ratings of ease of understanding differed for participants given the standard or the new instructions for the testing procedure, five randomly selected participants were assigned to receive the standard test instructions and five randomly selected participants were given the new test instruction. After reading the instructions, all participants were asked to rate how easy the instructions were to understand on a scale of 1 to 7 where 1 = extremely easy to understand and 7 = extremely difficult to understand. The mean rank of the understanding ratings for participants given the standard instructions was 7.80, and that of participants given the new instructions was 3.20. Using a Mann-Whitney U test, the two distributions of ratings were found to differ significantly, $U = 1.0$, $p < .025$, $A = .96$. The A value .96 corresponds to a large effect (Vargha and Delaney, 2000).

The Wilcoxon Signed-Ranks Test

The Wilcoxon signed-ranks test is a nonparametric test that is analogous to the t-test for paired samples. Because the test analyzes differences between pairs of scores, it is suitable for dependent variables measured on an interval scale. The test is nonparametric in that, unlike a *t*-test for paired samples, it does not assume that the distribution of difference scores in the population is normal. Rather, the distribution is assumed to be continuous and of any shape; if the distribution is, however, assumed to be symmetrical, the test addresses whether the population medians differ in the two conditions under examination. The test can be applied to paired or matched scores. Thus, if the number of math problems solved by each of several randomly selected participants is assessed alternately while classical music is playing and while rock music is playing, one can use the Wilcoxon signed-ranks test to determine if math ability differs significantly in the two background music conditions. As another example, if randomly selected participants are matched on a measure of working memory capacity and then assigned to a distraction or no-distraction condition in which a timed test of problem solving is administered, one can use the Wilcoxon signed-ranks test to determine if the distributions of problem solving times differ in the two distraction conditions.

The procedure for calculating a test statistic for the Wilcoxon signed-ranks test is shown in Figure 17.3. The figure shows that the difference for each pair of scores is calculated and any difference score of zero is removed from further consideration. The absolute values of the differences are then ranked with ties being broken by determining what ranks would have been assigned among the tied scores if they had not been tied, then assigning to each tied score the mean of these ranks. The signs of the differences between paired scores are then returned to the ranks, and the sum of the positive and the sum of the negative ranks is found. For sample sizes of 15 or fewer, one of these two sums is found in a table available in many introductory statistics texts and the exact probability associated with the sum is obtained.

Figure 17.3. Procedure for obtaining a test statistic for a Wilcoxon signed-ranks test.

Participant #	Classical Music	Rock Music	d	Rank of $|d|$	Return signs to d	Positive Ranks	Negative Ranks
1	13	12	1	2	2	2	-2
2	14	15	-1	2	-2	2	-5
3	8	11	-3	5	-5	$\Sigma| = 4$	-7
4	10	15	-5	7	-7		-4
5	5	7	-2	4	-4		-6
6	9	13	-4	6	-6		-8
7	9	15	-6	8	-8		$\Sigma- = 32$
8	6	6	0				
9	11	10	1	2	2		

1. The difference, d, between each pair of scores is calculated.

2. Any difference of 0 is removed.

3. The signs of the differences are ignored, and the differences are ranked, breaking ties if necessary.

4. The signs are returned to the ranks.

5. The sum of the positive and negative ranks is found.

For samples comprised of more than 15 pairs of scores, the distribution of the sum of the positive ranks (or the sum of the negative ranks) is approximately normal with a mean and standard deviation given by these formulas:

$$Mean = \frac{N(N+1)}{4}$$

Equation 17.13

$$SD = \sqrt{\frac{N(N+1)(2N+1)}{24}}$$

Equation 17.14

where N = the number of paired scores.

Thus, the z value corresponding to the sum of the positive ranks, $\Sigma Ranks_+$, is found from the formula

$$z = \frac{\Sigma Ranks_+ - N(N+1)/4}{\sqrt{N(N+1)(2N+1)/24}}.$$

Equation 17.15

SPSS uses a formula for the standard deviation of the distribution that adjusts for ties.

$$SD = \sqrt{\frac{N(N+1)(2N+1)}{24} - \frac{1}{48}\sum_{j=1}^{g} t_j(t_j - 1)(t_j + 1)}$$

Equation 17.16

where g = the number of groups of different tied ranks,
t_j = the number of ties within grouping j.

Preparing Data for the Analysis. Data for a Wilcoxon signed ranks test are entered into the **SPSS Statistics Data Editor** spreadsheet in the same way as for a *t*-test for paired samples. Each case consists of a value of the dependent variable for each of the two conditions being compared. For the data shown in Figure 17.3 that compares the number of math problems solved in a classical music and a rock music condition, two numeric variables must be represented, one for the number of problems solved in the classical music condition, and the other for the number of problems solved in the rock music condition. As shown below, data are entered pair-wise, that is, each case consists of a particular participant's (or the matched participants') dependent variable values in the two conditions.

The order in which the two variables appear in the spreadsheet is arbitrary.

	classical	rock
1	13.00	12.00
2	14.00	15.00
3	8.00	11.00
4	10.00	15.00
5	5.00	7.00
6	9.00	13.00
7	9.00	15.00
8	6.00	6.00
9	11.00	10.00
10		

Requesting the Analysis. The procedure for requesting a Wilcoxon signed ranks test is shown below:

1. From the Analyze menu select Nonparametric Tests and then 2 Related Samples.

2. Click to highlight the name of one dependent variable and click this to transfer it.

3. Click to highlight the name of the other dependent variable and click this to transfer it.

5. Click OK.

SPSS will obtain difference scores by subtracting **Variable1** from **Variable2**. To interchange the dependent variables assigned to **Variable1** and **Variable2**, click anywhere here, then press this.*

*This was done here to make the output conform to the data shown in Figure 17.3.

4. Select this test if it's not already selected.

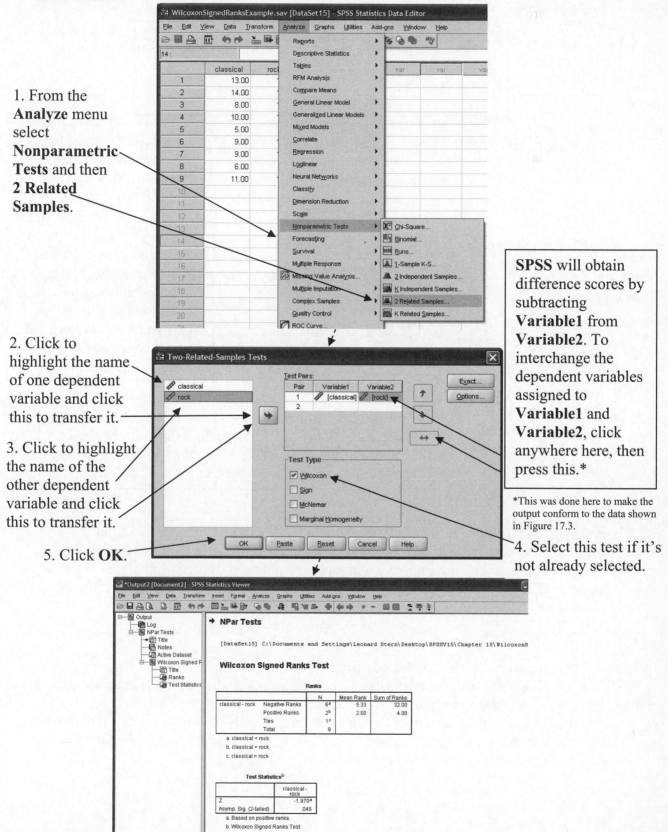

Interpreting the Output. The output consists of the tables shown below:

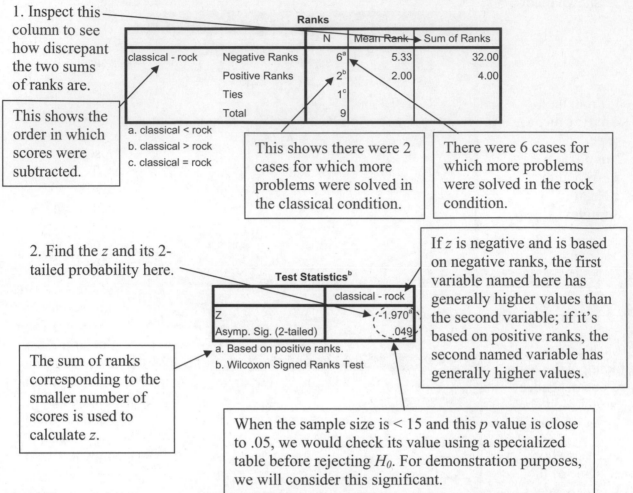

1. Inspect this column to see how discrepant the two sums of ranks are.

Ranks

		N	Mean Rank	Sum of Ranks
classical - rock	Negative Ranks	6[a]	5.33	32.00
	Positive Ranks	2[b]	2.00	4.00
	Ties	1[c]		
	Total	9		

a. classical < rock
b. classical > rock
c. classical = rock

This shows the order in which scores were subtracted.

This shows there were 2 cases for which more problems were solved in the classical condition.

There were 6 cases for which more problems were solved in the rock condition.

2. Find the z and its 2-tailed probability here.

If z is negative and is based on negative ranks, the first variable named here has generally higher values than the second variable; if it's based on positive ranks, the second named variable has generally higher values.

Test Statistics[b]

	classical - rock
Z	-1.970[a]
Asymp. Sig. (2-tailed)	.049

a. Based on positive ranks.
b. Wilcoxon Signed Ranks Test

The sum of ranks corresponding to the smaller number of scores is used to calculate z.

When the sample size is < 15 and this p value is close to .05, we would check its value using a specialized table before rejecting H_0. For demonstration purposes, we will consider this significant.

Reporting the Results. A report of the outcome of a test should include the number of negative and positive ranks, the smaller sum of ranks, and, when the test of the null hypothesis is based on the z approximation, the z value and its probability level. As a measure of effect size one can report the value of A described by Vargha and Delaney (2000) calculated by the formula

$$A_{xy} = \frac{[n(x > y) + .5n(x = y)]}{N}$$ Equation 17.17

where $n(x>y)$ is the number of paired scores in which the value of x exceeds y,
$n(x=y)$ is the number of paired scores in which the value of x equals y, and
N = the number of pairs of scores.
A is interpreted as the probability that in a pair of randomly drawn scores (x, y), the value of x will exceed that of y plus .5. For the data shown in Figure 17.3, the calculations for finding the value of A are shown below:

$$A_{rock,classical} = \frac{[6 + .5(1)]}{9} = .72$$

Because the *A* values 56, .64, and .71 correspond to small, medium, and large effect sizes, respectively, the effect size obtained for our example can be described as large. Note that because $A_{12} = 1 - A_{21}$, the value $A_{classical,rock}$ is .28.

The outcome of the Wilcoxon signed-ranks test illustrated above can be summarized as follows:

> To determine whether math performance differs when students solve problems with classical vs. rock music in the background, the number of problems solved in 20 minutes was recorded for nine randomly selected students who were exposed to four alternating 5-minute periods in which classical or rock music was played. The median number of problems solved with the classical music background was 9.00 and that with the rock music background was 12.00. This difference, tested with a Wilcoxon signed ranks test was significant, $z = 1.98$, $p < .05$. For this test, the smaller sum of ranks, based on two pairs of scores, had the value of 4.00. Of the nine paired scores one pair of ranks was tied. The *A* value for the effect was .72, which corresponds to a large effect (Vargha and Delaney, 2000).

Exercises for Chapter 17

Note: The data files named in these exercises are available at the publisher's website for this text, http://www.pearsonhighered.com/stern2e.

Exercise 17.1

Between 1944 and 2004 the proportion of Atlantic storms that were classified as hurricanes during the hurricane season (June 1-November 30) was .248. During 2005, which was an exceptional year for hurricanes, 7 storms reached hurricane strength and 20 did not. Determine if the proportion of storms that were hurricanes during 2005 differed significantly from the historical rate of .248.

Exercise 17.2

The data file *HappyMarried.sav* contains data gathered by the General Social Survey given in 2004. It includes ratings of happiness measured on a scale of 1-3 where 1 = very happy, 2 = pretty happy, and 3 = not too happy. The file also identifies the marital status of each participant. Determine if the distribution of happiness ratings of married people (**marital** = 1) differs from that of the never married people (**marital** = 5).

Exercise 17.3

Reaction time data tend to be positively skewed. The data file *ReadingTimes.sav* contains the reading times of participants shown one of two versions of an instruction for a laboratory task, a standard form of the instructions (labeled **control**) and a new form of the instructions (labeled **new**). The reading time in tenths of a second is recorded in the variable **time**. Conduct a test to determine whether the distributions of reading times in the two instruction conditions differ. What is the effect size, *A*?

Exercise 17.4

During 2002, .34 (i.e., 34%) of the births to teenage mothers in the U.S. were to unmarried women. To determine if this proportion differs for Americans of Japanese descent, a random sample is obtained of 112 American teenage women of Japanese descent who give birth. The number of these women who are unmarried is found to be 10. Determine if the proportion of births to unmarried teenagers of Japanese descent differs from that of the U.S. population in general in 2002.

Exercise 17.5

An experimenter asks participants to read two pages of instructions for a task. Each participant's reading times are recorded in tenths of a second for each page. The file *ReadtimesTwoPage.sav* contains the reading time of each participant for page one in the variable **time1** and for page two in the variable **time2**. Determine whether the median time to read pages one and two differs significantly.

Exercise 17.6

Olson, Banaji, Dweck, and Spelke (2006) read male and female children between 5-7 years old are scenarios that included positive uncontrollable outcomes for a target child (e.g., the child found $10.00 on the street) or negative uncontrollable outcomes (e.g., the child's soccer game was cancelled due to bad weather). Each child heard and number of such scenarios and rated how much he/she liked the target child on a 6-point scale where 1 = really don't like the target child and 6 = really like the target child. The mean liking rating for each set of positive and negative scenarios produced by each child was compared. Use the data shown in the table below to determine whether there was a significant difference in the median ratings given to positive vs. negative outcomes. (Note: the data shown below were created to resemble some of the data described by Olson et al.).

	Outcome	
Child #	Positive	Negative
1	6.8	4.6
2	6.7	3.5
3	4.7	5.2
4	5.2	3.2
5	6.1	5.8
6	6.2	5.5
7	4.4	4.3
8	4.5	3.1
9	5.8	3.0
10	5.0	1.9

Chapter 18: Exploratory Factor Analysis

Introduction

Many concepts in the social sciences are difficult to define and measure precisely. What, for example, do we mean when we use the term intelligence? How should intelligence be measured? Other concepts examined in social science research such as shyness, curiosity, and altruism also resist precise definition and measurement. But even though we may not be able to provide a good definition of a concept, we often feel we understand the concept; that is, we know an intelligent or a shy or a curious person when we encounter one. How do we do this?

One view of concepts is that they represent the commonalities embodied in a set of specific instances. For example, cars generally share basic physical and functional properties such as the presence of wheels, an engine, and a use in transporting people and objects. Perhaps we come to know what shyness or intelligence or curiosity is, in part, by detecting similarities in the behaviors of people under various circumstances.

Exploratory factor analysis may be thought of as a quantitative method for aiding concept formation; it is a set of data analytic procedures that allow similarities among a set of measures to be detected, distinguished, and labeled.

Varieties of Approaches and Procedures

There are two major forms of factor analysis that differ in their fundamental objectives: exploratory factor analysis is intended to discover commonalities that may exist among subsets of variables while confirmatory factory analysis is used to test the appropriateness of a theory involving latent processes. Exploratory factor analysis tends to be used at early stages of a research program when discovering underlying processes is valuable whereas confirmatory factor analysis is more appropriate at later stages of research to confirm hypotheses generated about underlying processes. The two types of factor analysis utilize different procedures. Confirmatory factor analysis is often based on a set of statistical techniques known as structural equation modeling whereas exploratory factor analysis often utilizes principal components analysis. In the discussions that follow, exploratory factor analysis will be described. Although there are a number of possible methods to extract factors from a set of variables, most produce similar results. In discussions that follow, principal components analysis, the most popular method of factor extraction, will be described. In the discussions the terms principal components and factors are used interchangeably even though, strictly speaking, principal component analysis produces principal components, not factors.

An Example

To understand some ideas underlying exploratory factor analysis, imagine that a number of randomly selected adults are asked to assess, on a scale of 1 to 10, the importance of several life goals (10 = most important). The goals are earning a lot of money, being independent, having a family, and residing in a prestigious neighborhood. Ratings given by five hypothetical people to these questions are shown in Table 18.1.

Table 18.1. Ratings of the importance of four life goals of five hypothetical participants. The ratings are on a scale of 1 to 10 where 1 = least important and 10 = most important.

| | Importance Ratings | | | |
	Income	Independence	Family	Neighborhood
Participant 1	8	3	8	9
Participant 2	7	6	5	9
Participant 3	2	4	6	3
Participant 4	3	7	3	5
Participant 5	5	5	4	4

How could we discover the similarities among ratings of these variables? One way is to examine correlations among ratings of all pairs of goals. A table of Pearson r values for the data in Table 18.1 is shown in Table 18.2. From the correlations, it can be seen that the variables **Income** and **Neighborhood** are highly positively correlated, that the variables **Independence** and **Family** are highly negatively correlated, and that other correlations among different pairs of variables exhibit lower correlations that range from -.31 to .51.

Table 18.2. Correlations between ratings for all pairs of variables shown in Table 18.1.

	Income	Independence	Family	Neighborhood
Income	1	-.31	.51	.90
Independence	-.31	1	-.90	-.11
Family	.51	-.90	1	.46
Neighborhood	.90	-.11	.46	1

Steps in Performing an Exploratory Factor Analysis

The correlation matrix shown in Table 18.2 indicates that the variables **Income** and **Neighborhood** are rated in a similar way, and that **Independence** and **Family** are rated in generally opposite ways. Thus we might expect a factor analysis to reveal that these pairs of variables correspond to two underlying factors that may be substantially independent of each other. Of course, if more variables were involved, detecting the possible presence of underlying, independent factors from a table of pair-wise correlations would be more difficult. As described below, an exploratory factor analysis generally goes through two stages: deriving the factors, then rotating them to enhance their interpretability.

Deriving Principal Components

To understand how the principal component analysis approach to exploratory factor analysis works, it is helpful to think of values of each variable in the form of z-scores. When a variable has been converted to z-scores, the variable is standardized so that its mean is zero and its standard deviation (and variance) is one. The conversion to z-scores does not alter correlations between pairs of variables. There are, however, benefits to converting all variables to z-scores. One is that, because the variance of each variable in standardized form is one, the total variance of all the variables is equal to the number of variables. A second is that, for two or three dimensional situations, lines known as principal components can readily be located. In two dimensional space (i.e., if two variables are plotted on x, y coordinate axes) one principal component will go through the origin at a 45 degree angle in relation to the x-axis; the other principal component will also go through the origin but will be oriented at 90 degrees to the first principal component. In three dimensions, (i.e., if three variables are plotted) there will be a third principal component oriented at 90 degrees to the other two.

Of what use are principal components? They help us determine the extent to which there are similarities among variations in values of subsets of variables. As shown in the left panel of Figure 18.1, for perfectly correlated variables ($r = 1$), a scatterplot reveals a set of points that define a straight line passing through the origin at a 45 degree angle with respect to the x-axis. That straight line is the first principal component. The second principal component is independent of the first; its independence corresponds to its being oriented at an angle of 90 degrees to the first principal component. As shown in the table in the left panel of Figure 18.1, the variance of the points on the first principal component is 2, the total variance of the combined two variables in standardized form; the variance of the points on the second principal component is zero. If three variables are represented, their total variance in standardized form is three. If they are perfectly correlated, their representation in an x, y, z, coordinate axis system would again conform to a straight line possibly in the orientation shown in the right panel of Figure 18.1; the variance of points along this first principal component is three. The two other principal components, all oriented at 90 degrees to one another, capture no additional variance. In general, the total combined variance of a set of standardized variables and the total number of principal components needed to account for their combined variance will equal the number of variables.

Figure 18.1. The left panel shows two perfectly correlated variables and two principal components. The right panel shows three perfectly correlated variables and three principal components. The tables below each figure give the coordinates of the four data points, their z values, and their coordinates on the principal components. The means and variances of the z and principal component scores are given below the tables.

x	y	z_x	z_y	C_1	C_2	x	y	z	z_x	z_y	z_z	C_1	C_2	C_3
1	2	-1.34	-1.34	-1.90	0	1	2	3	-1.34	-1.34	-1.34	-2.32	0	0
2	3	-0.45	-0.45	-0.63	0	2	4	6	-0.45	-0.45	-0.45	-0.78	0	0
3	4	0.45	0.45	0.63	0	3	6	9	0.45	0.45	0.45	0.78	0	0
4	5	1.34	1.34	1.90	0	4	8	12	1.34	1.34	1.34	2.32	0	0
μ:		0.00	0.00	0.00	0				0	0	0	0.00	0	0
σ^2		1.00	1.00	2.00	0				1.00	1.00	1.00	3.00	0	0

The success of a principal component in accounting for combined variance of a set of variables is measured in units called eigenvalues. An eigenvalue is the variance of a single standardized variable, that is, it is the value 1. If a principal component accounts fully for the variance of two variables, its eigenvalue is 2; if there are four variables in an analysis and the eigenvalue of a principal component is 2, the principal component accounts for the variance of two variables, that is, for 50% of the total variance of all the variables.

It is rare to find variables that are perfectly correlated. If principal component analysis is applied to two imperfectly correlated standardized variables, the principal components will still be oriented at 45 and 135 degrees to the x-axis. The first principal component will be the one that accounts for the majority of the combined variance of the two variables; the second principal component will then account for the remaining variance. In general, successive principal components will each account for successively less remaining variance of the combined variables.

Interpreting Principal Components

Consider the data depicted in Figure 18.2 which shows the distribution of two unrelated variables (i.e., $r = 0$). Principal component analysis would reveal two principal components that each had an eigenvalue of one. How should we interpret these principal components? One way of making sense of a principal component is to determine the extent to which it correlates with values of each variable in the data set. For example, in Figure 18.1, if we correlate the x, y, and z values of the data points shown in the right panel, with the values of the points' representation on the first principal component, we would find that each correlated perfectly (i.e., $r_{x,C1} = 1$, $r_{y,C1} = 1$, $r_{z,C1} = 1$). These correlation values, called loadings, indicate that our first principal component corresponds perfectly to the three variables. If variables x, y, and z were ratings of the extent to which a person avoids social situations, fears speaking in public, and prefers to spend time alone, we might choose to think of this component as representing the concept shyness.

For the data shown in Figure 18.2, the variable loadings on each principal component, that is, r values of each variable and each principal component, are shown in table on the bottom right. It can be seen that each principal component accounts for 50% ($r^2 = .707^2 = .50$) of the variance of each variable. Thus, in a sense, each principal component represents both variables equally.

At this point the second step in an exploratory factor analysis occurs. To enhance the interpretability of each component, the principal components can be rotated to make each correspond more uniquely to one or more variables. The process is illustrated graphically in Figure 18.3 where, in the left panel, the loadings (i.e., r values) of each variable on each principal component are plotted. The right panel shows how rotating the principal components brings component 1 into perfect correspondence with variable x and component 2 into perfect correspondence with variable y. Thus, component 1 can be viewed as equivalent to x, and component 2 as equivalent to y. Of course, this result is trivial in the sense that the components do not help us go beyond the separate variables that were entered into the analysis; that is, we end up identifying one principal component with variable x and the other with an unrelated variable y, the two variables we started with. Although we have not found useful, underlying similarities in the data, the point of the example is to illustrate how rotating principal components that are independent of each other can aid in simplifying how we interpret them.

Figure 18.2. A plot of two unrelated standardized variables. Open circles show the location of the data points on the principal components. These locations correspond to where a line from each data point perpindicular to the principal component would intersect with the principal component. The left table shows the coordinates of the points on the unstandardized, standardized, and component axes. The right table shows loadings of the x and y values on the components.

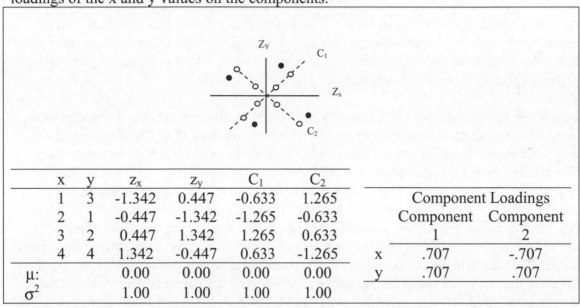

x	y	z_x	z_y	C_1	C_2			Component Loadings	
1	3	-1.342	0.447	-0.633	1.265			Component 1	Component 2
2	1	-0.447	-1.342	-1.265	-0.633				
3	2	0.447	1.342	1.265	0.633				
4	4	1.342	-0.447	0.633	-1.265		x	.707	-.707
μ:		0.00	0.00	0.00	0.00		y	.707	.707
σ^2		1.00	1.00	1.00	1.00				

Figure 18.3. Correlations of variables x and y with components 1 and 2 before rotation of the components (left panel) and after rotation (right panel).

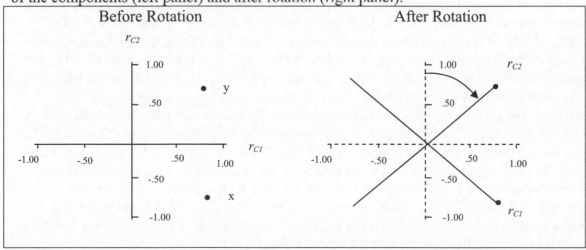

Underlying Assumptions

Because a factor analysis based on a principal components approach does not utilize significance tests, strict assumptions of normality of individual variables and multivariate normality can be relaxed. However, variables are assumed to be linearly related to each other, an assumption that can be verified by examining pairwise scatterplots of the variables. In addition, variables that are dichotomous (e.g., those having only pairs of possible values such as yes/no or true/false) should not be included in a factor analysis because their binary nature introduces problems with assumptions of linearity.

Practical Considerations Concerning the Data

Number of Variables and Sample size. The number of variables and sample size are important considerations that influence interpretation of a factor analysis. A general recommendation about number of variables is to include at least three or more for each factor that may result. If three variables have high loadings with each factor, the results of the factor rotation are most interpretable (MacIntyre, 1990).

Guidelines for sample size are numerous and varied. A suitable set of recommendations come from Guadagnoli and Velicer (1988) who demonstrated that sample size and the degree to which variables are correlated with factors are both important in determining the extent to which a factor analysis performed on a sample reflects the component structure of the population. These authors give the following recommendations for sample size: If all variables have low loadings (.40) on each factor, and there are fewer than four variables per factor, a sample size in excess of 300 is appropriate; if all variables have low loadings and there are 10-12 variables per factor, a sample size greater than 150 is recommended; and if all variables have high loadings (.60 and above) and there are four or more variables per factor, the outcome is interpretable "whatever the sample size" (p. 274)—note that the minimum sample size used by these authors was 50.

Factorability of the Correlation Matrix. Although one can perform a factor analysis on a suitable set of variables and see what happens, that is, see if the analysis detects a small number of principal components (relative to the number of variables) that account for a substantial amount of the variance of the variables, it is often recommended that the factorability of the matrix of pairwise correlations first be examined. The Kaiser-Meyer-Olkin (KMO) measure provides and index of factorability that ranges from 0-1. The measure is the ratio of the sum of squared r values for all pairs of different variables to the sum of squared r values for all pairs of different variables plus the sum of squared partial r values for all pairs of different variables. When the value of this statistic is less than .5, the matrix is considered not to be suited to factor analysis; values from .5 to .7 are considered marginal; and values greater than .7 are considered adequate. Recall that partial correlation assesses the correlation between two variables with the influence of other variables removed. Thus, if three variables are all correlated with a single component, that is, if they all measure the same concept, all partial correlations will be close to zero because removing the influence of, say, variable 1 from variables 2 and 3 will leave very little correspondence between them.

Number of Principal Components. Another important decision that affects the outcome of a factor analysis is the number of principal components retained. Changing the number of principal components kept in the analysis affects the total amount of variance captured by the retained components as well as the interpretation of the rotated components. One common guideline utilizes a cutoff value specified in eigenvalues by which components with eigenvalues greater than one are retained; another, which is more highly recommended (Zwick & Velicer, 1982), utilizes visual inspection of a scree plot. A scree plot has each successive factor or principal component plotted on the x-axis and its eigenvalue plotted on the y-axis. An example is shown in Figure 18.4. One draws a straight line through the smaller eigenvalues and looks for a definite break in the remaining eigenvalues. Factors with eigenvalues above the straight line are retained.

Figure 18.4. A scree plot. A straight line has been drawn through the smallest values to detect the components having eigenvalues falling above the straight line. According to the scree test, these principal components are retained.

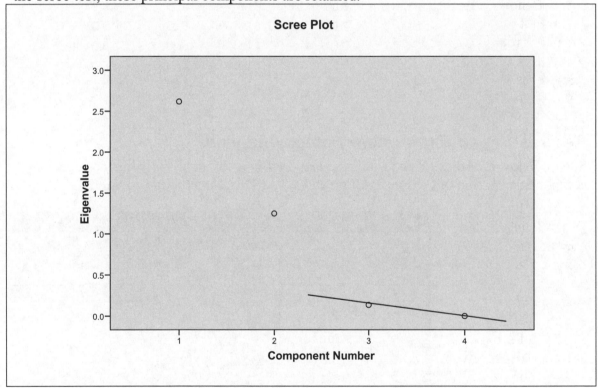

Method of Factor Rotation. Two types of factor rotation are available, orthogonal and oblique rotation. For orthogonal rotation, the more commonly-used approach, the factors or components are kept uncorrelated with one another. In Figure 18.3, the rotation is pictured as orthogonal because the components maintain their 90 degree relation to each other and so are independent. A number or orthogonal rotation methods are available, the most popular being the VARIMAX method that seeks to maximize variance of the factor loadings by making high loadings higher and low loadings lower on each factor. Oblique rotation produces factors that may be correlated with each other. As a result, interpretation of the factors will not be as straightforward as with orthogonal rotation (but see Fabrigar, Wegener, MacCallum, and Strahan, 1999).

Preparing Data for the Analysis

To conduct an exploratory factor analysis, the values of each variable must be entered into the **SPSS Statistics Data Editor** for each randomly selected case (i.e., participant). Even though the data shown in Table 18.1 are inadequate for an exploratory factor analysis in both numbers of variables and cases, the data will be used to illustrate the basics steps in requesting and interpreting such an analysis. Note in data set shown below, each case is identified with a unique number using the variable **ID**.

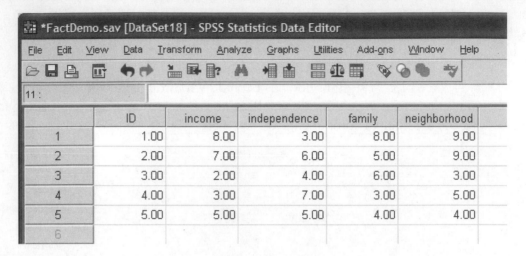

Requesting an Exploratory Factor Analysis

Shown below are steps for requesting an exploratory factor analysis using a principal components method of factor extraction and a VARIMAX method of rotation.

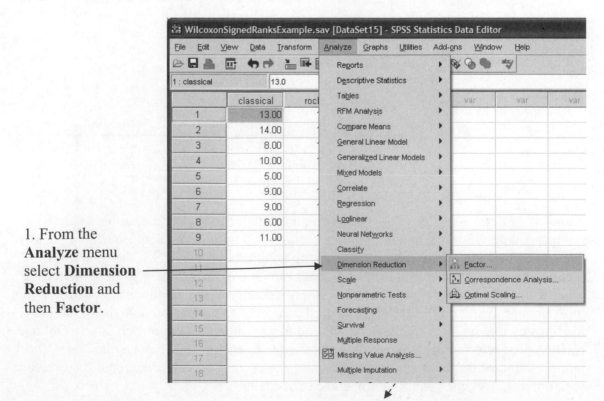

1. From the **Analyze** menu select **Dimension Reduction** and then **Factor**.

2. Select all the variables to be included in the analysis then click this button to transfer them to the **Variables** pane.

3. Click **Descriptives.**

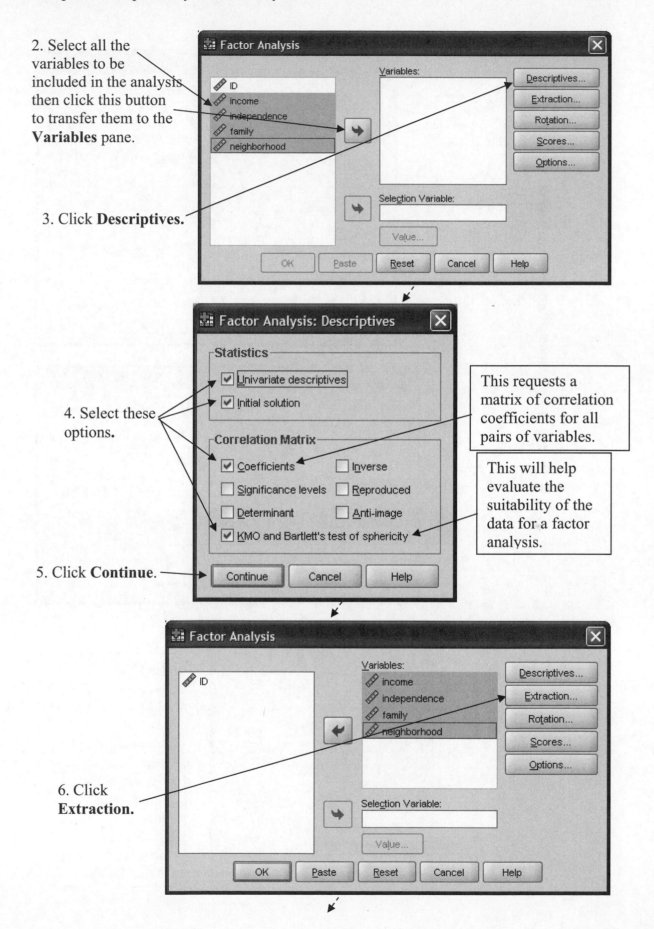

This requests a matrix of correlation coefficients for all pairs of variables.

This will help evaluate the suitability of the data for a factor analysis.

4. Select these options.

5. Click **Continue**.

6. Click **Extraction.**

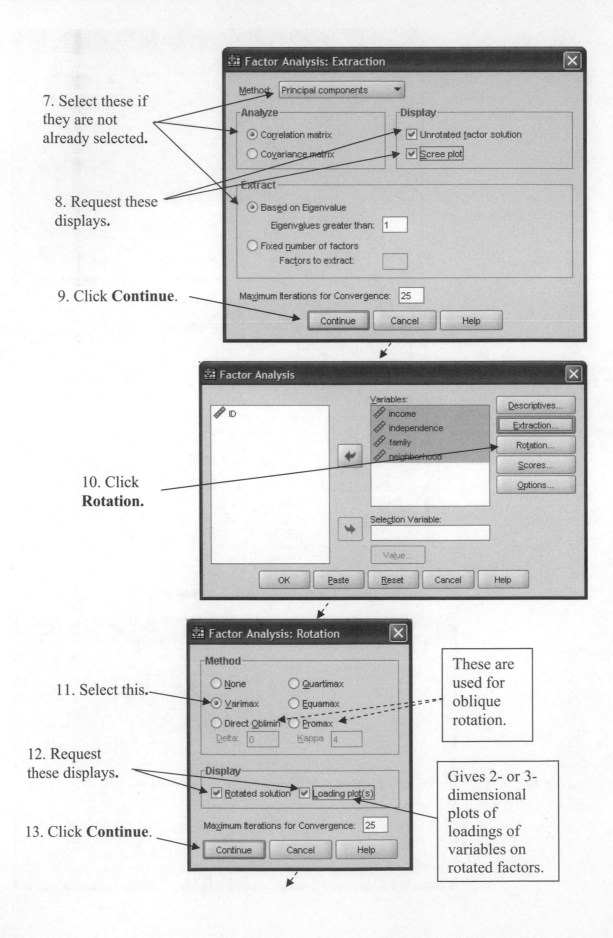

7. Select these if they are not already selected.

8. Request these displays.

9. Click **Continue**.

10. Click **Rotation.**

11. Select this.

12. Request these displays.

13. Click **Continue**.

These are used for oblique rotation.

Gives 2- or 3-dimensional plots of loadings of variables on rotated factors.

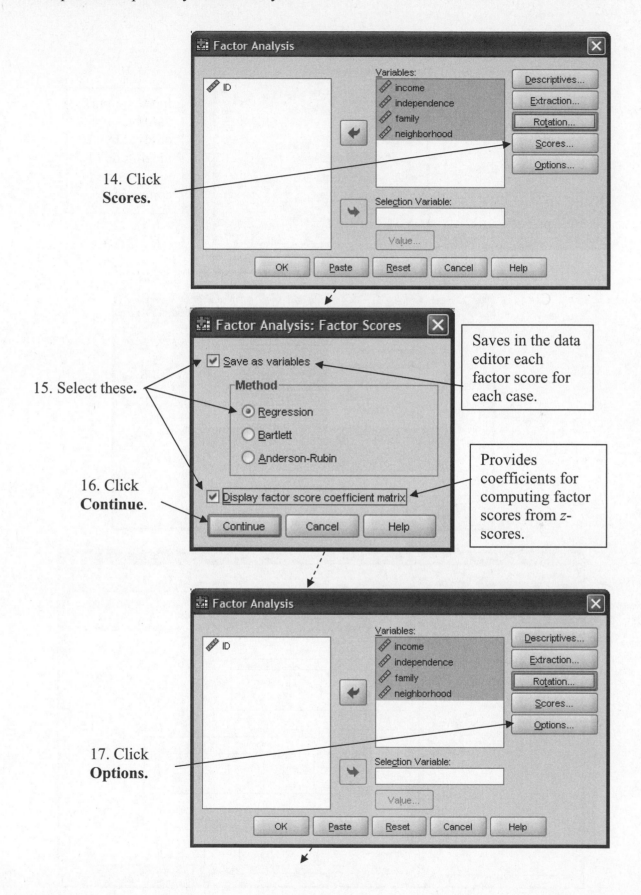

14. Click **Scores.**

15. Select these.

16. Click **Continue**.

17. Click **Options.**

Saves in the data editor each factor score for each case.

Provides coefficients for computing factor scores from z-scores.

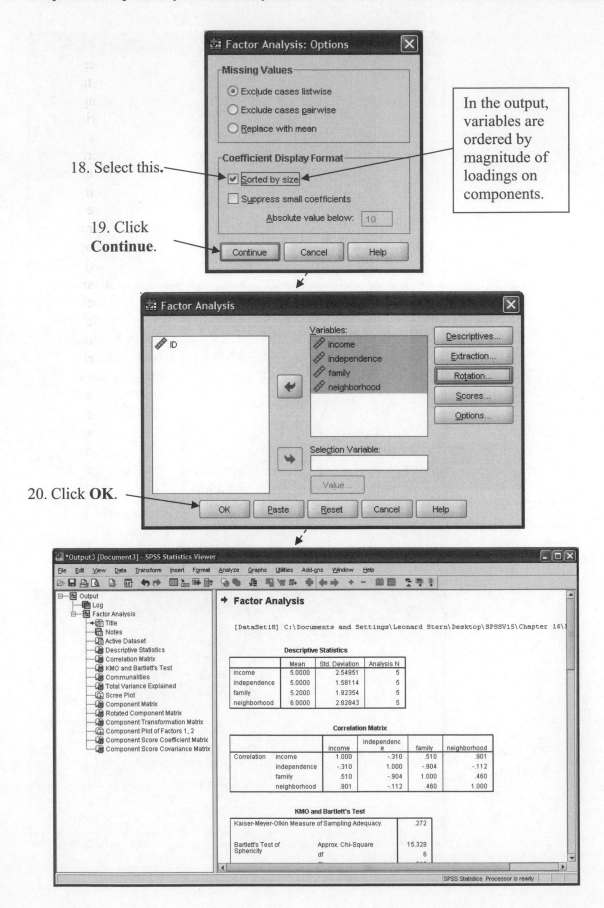

18. Select this.

19. Click **Continue**.

In the output, variables are ordered by magnitude of loadings on components.

20. Click **OK**.

Interpreting the Output

Output produced by the selections specified above is shown next. The output begins with a table of descriptive statistics for the variables included in the study. From the table one can determine the number of variables and the number of cases with non-missing data used in the analysis. The correlation matrix shows *r* values between pairs of variables requested to be analyzed. The table labeled **KMO and Bartlett's Test** provides data to assess the suitability of the variables for a factor analysis. Bartlett's test of sphericity tests the null hypothesis that in the correlation matrix the correlations between pairs of different variables (i.e., the off-diagonal *r* values) are zero. A significant result indicates the data may be suitable for factor analysis, but because the test is very sensitive to sample size, it is not recommended for samples containing more than about four cases per variable (Tabachnick & Fidell, 2007). The table of communalities shows the proportion of variance of each variable accounted for either initially (before factor analysis) or by the combined factors retained in the analysis. For a principal components analysis, the initial communality values are always 1.00. The values listed in the column labeled **Extraction** can be calculated by squaring and summing the loadings of the variable on the unrotated or rotated principal components retained in the analysis; these values can be found in the tables labeled **Component Matrix** and **Rotated Component Matrix**, respectively. A variable with a low communality (e.g., .40 or lower) is not well represented by the combined factors. As noted below, the table labeled **Total Variance Explained** and the **Scree Plot** are helpful in deciding the number of factors to retain in the analysis. The factor loadings on the rotated component matrix and the corresponding plot of the loadings are used to interpret the components. In interpreting components, loadings of magnitude lower than .30 or .40 are considered low and variables with these loadings are "typically ignored" (Zwick & Verlicer, 1982, p. 258) while loadings in the .50 to .80 range are considered substantial.

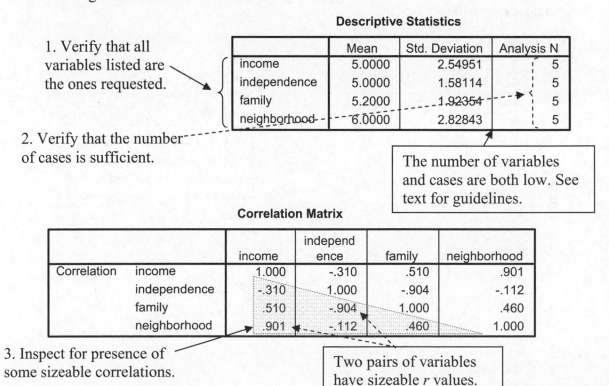

Descriptive Statistics

1. Verify that all variables listed are the ones requested.

	Mean	Std. Deviation	Analysis N
income	5.0000	2.54951	5
independence	5.0000	1.58114	5
family	5.2000	1.92354	5
neighborhood	6.0000	2.82843	5

2. Verify that the number of cases is sufficient.

The number of variables and cases are both low. See text for guidelines.

Correlation Matrix

		income	independence	family	neighborhood
Correlation	income	1.000	-.310	.510	.901
	independence	-.310	1.000	-.904	-.112
	family	.510	-.904	1.000	.460
	neighborhood	.901	-.112	.460	1.000

3. Inspect for presence of some sizeable correlations.

Two pairs of variables have sizeable *r* values.

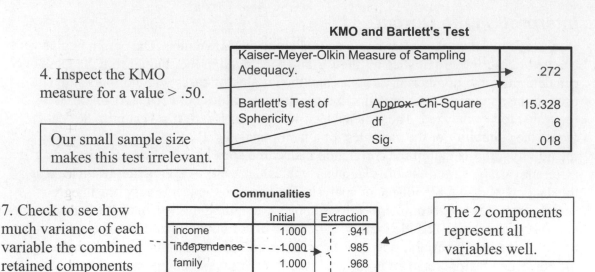

KMO and Bartlett's Test

Kaiser-Meyer-Olkin Measure of Sampling Adequacy.		.272
Bartlett's Test of Sphericity	Approx. Chi-Square	15.328
	df	6
	Sig.	.018

4. Inspect the KMO measure for a value > .50.

Our small sample size makes this test irrelevant.

7. Check to see how much variance of each variable the combined retained components explain.

Communalities

	Initial	Extraction
income	1.000	.941
independence	1.000	.985
family	1.000	.968
neighborhood	1.000	.970

Extraction Method: Principal Component Analysis.

The 2 components represent all variables well.

Rotation spreads the eigenvalues more evenly.

Total Variance Explained

Component	Initial Eigenvalues			Extraction Sums of Squared Loadings			Rotation Sums of Squared Loadings		
	Total	% of Variance	Cumulative %	Total	% of Variance	Cumulative %	Total	% of Variance	Cumulative %
1	2.616	65.400	65.400	2.616	65.400	65.400	1.965	49.129	49.129
2	1.248	31.202	96.602	1.248	31.202	96.602	1.899	47.473	96.602
3	.135	3.385	99.987						
4	.001	.013	100.000						

Extraction Method: Principal Component Analysis.

6. Check to see how much variance of the combined variables the retained components explain.

Components with eigenvalues < 1 have been removed.

Scree Plot

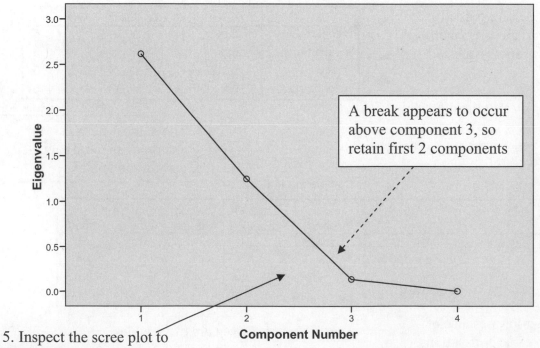

A break appears to occur above component 3, so retain first 2 components

5. Inspect the scree plot to determine number of components to retain.

Component Matrix[a]

	Component	
	1	2
family	.887	-.426
income	.849	.470
neighborhood	.775	.608
independence	-.713	.691

Extraction Method: Principal Component Analysis.

a. 2 components extracted.

The communality of income (see table of communalities) is the sum of $.849^2 + .470^2$.

Rotated Component Matrix[a]

	Component	
	1	2
neighborhood	.980	.095
income	.939	.245
independence	-.040	-.992
family	.349	.920

Extraction Method: Principal Component Analysis.
Rotation Method: Varimax with Kaiser Normalization.

a. Rotation converged in 3 iterations.

8. Base interpretations of each component on variables that load high one each.

The positive loading of family and negative loading of independence on component 2 means that as the importance of having a family increases, the importance of independence decreases.

The loadings in this table are plotted here.

Component Transformation Matrix

Component	1	2
1	.724	.690
2	.690	-.724

Extraction Method: Principal Component Analysis.
Rotation Method: Varimax with Kaiser Normalization.

Component Plot in Rotated Space

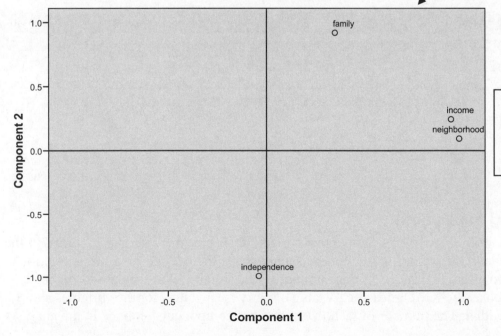

Plots can represent up to three factors.

Component Score Coefficient Matrix

	Component	
	1	2
income	.495	-.049
independence	.184	-.589
family	.010	.481
neighborhood	.550	-.148

> This table provides coefficients for calculating factor scores for each participant. The coefficients act on z-scores (see below).

Extraction Method: Principal Component Analysis.
Rotation Method: Varimax with Kaiser Normalization.
Component Scores.

Component Score Covariance Matrix

Component	1	2
1	1.000	.000
2	.000	1.000

Extraction Method: Principal Component Analysis.
Rotation Method: Varimax with Kaiser Normalization.

Component Scores.

Because a request was made to save factor scores in the **Factor Scores** window, two new variables have been created in the **Data Editor.** Factor scores are calculated using the coefficients given in the table labeled **Component Score Coefficient Matrix**. The coefficients act on standardized variables. The formula for obtaining a factor 1 score is shown below:

$$Factor\ 1 = .495 \times z_{income} + .184 \times z_{independence} + .010 \times z_{family} + .550 \times z_{meighborhood}$$

*FactDemo.sav [DataSet18] - SPSS Statistics Data Editor

File   Edit   View   Data   Transform   Analyze   Graphs   Utilities   Add-ons   Window   Help

11 :

	ID	income	independence	family	neighborhood	FAC1_1	FAC2_1
1	1.00	8.00	3.00	8.00	9.00	0.94739	1.22985
2	2.00	7.00	6.00	5.00	9.00	1.08726	-0.61760
3	3.00	2.00	4.00	6.00	3.00	-1.27810	0.78671
4	4.00	3.00	7.00	3.00	5.00	-0.36106	-1.20375
5	5.00	5.00	5.00	4.00	4.00	-0.39550	-0.19522

Reporting the Results

A summary of the results of a factor analysis should specify the variables included in the analysis, the number of cases with non-missing values, the method of factor extraction and factor rotation, and statistics that summarize the suitability of the data for factor analysis such as the KMO measure. A table of pairwise r values for the variables should also be provided. The number of factors or principal components retained in the analysis and the basis for deciding on this number should be described. To help account for the interpretation of the retained factors, include a table of loadings of variables on the retained factors. The summary shown below illustrates these points based on the output produced by our analysis of the life goals questions.

Five randomly selected participants were asked to rate the importance of four life goals using a scale of 1 to 10. The goals were earning a lot of money, being independent, having a family, and residing in a prestigious neighborhood. Correlations between ratings of all pairs of goals are shown in Table 18.3. To determine if there were underlying redundancies among the rated goals, the data were factor analyzed. Suitability of the data for factor analysis assessed with the Kaiser-Meyer-Olkin measure of sampling adequacy yielded the value .27, a value that ordinarily would be interpreted as indicating the data were inappropriate for factor analysis; however the small sample size used for this demonstration makes interpretation of this KMO result suspect. A principal components method was used to extract factors and orthogonal rotation of factors was performed using the VARIMAX method. Based on analysis of the scree plot (see Figure 18.5) two factors were retained. The combined factors accounted for approximately 97% of the combined variance of ratings of the four goals. Loadings of the four goals on the two rotated factors are shown in Table 18.4. Based on these loadings, factor 1 was interpreted as representing material concerns and factor 2 was interpreted as representing social interaction concerns. Communality values indicated that the two factors accounted well for the data of each individual goal (all values > .94).

Table 18.3. Correlations between all pairs of goals rated in the study.

	Income	Independence	Family	Neighborhood
Income	1.00			
Independence	-.31	1.00		
Family	.51	-.90	1.00	
Neighborhood	.90	-.11	.46	1.00

Figure 18.5. Scree plot for demonstration data.

Table 18.4. Loadings of the goals on the two rotated factors.

	Factor 1	Factor 2
Neighborhood	.98	.10
Income	.94	.25
Independence	-.04	-.99
Family	.35	.92

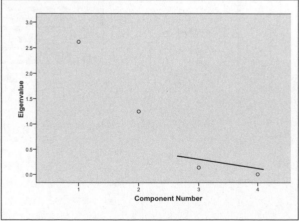

Plotting Factor Scores of Individual Cases

In the data set used to demonstrate factor analysis, factor scores for components 1 and 2 were saved in the **Data Editor** (see step 15 in the procedure shown above) in variables with the default names **FACT1_1** and **FACT2_1**. These factor scores are standardized (their means are zero and standard deviations are 1); they indicate where each case falls on the rotated components based on the case's scores on the individual variables. It can be informative to plot each case on a pair of axes that represent each factor. The steps to produce such a scatterplot are shown below.

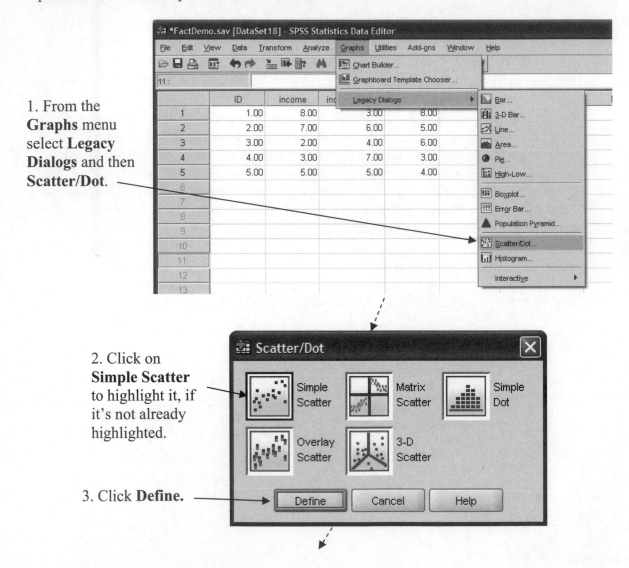

1. From the **Graphs** menu select **Legacy Dialogs** and then **Scatter/Dot**.

2. Click on **Simple Scatter** to highlight it, if it's not already highlighted.

3. Click **Define**.

4. Click on the name of factor 1 to highlight it then transfer it to the **X Axis** field.

5. Click on the name of factor 2 to highlight it then transfer it to the **Y Axis** field.

6 Click on the name of the variable containing case labels to highlight it then transfer it to the **Label Cases by** field.

7. Click **Options.**

8. Click to select this option.

9. Click **Continue**.

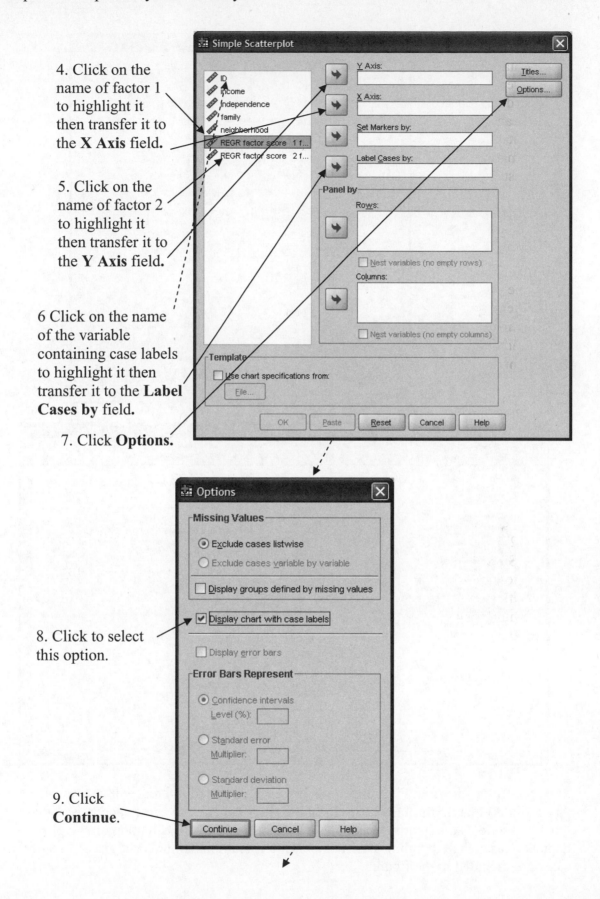

10. Click **OK**.

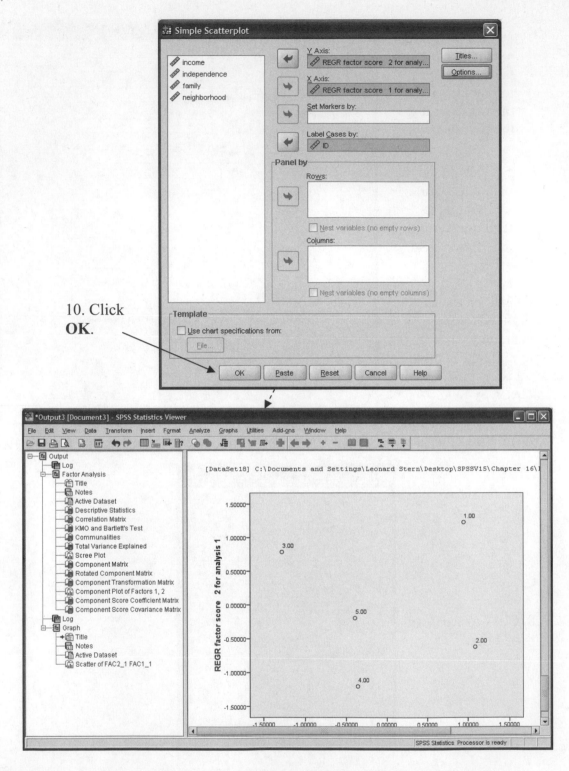

The scatterplot shown in Figure 18.6 has been edited to add reference lines (see Appendix A) that go through each axis at the zero point and to name each axis with a label that reflects the interpretation of the factor represented. Each point on the plot depicts a case labeled with its case number. Interpretations of the locations of two of the cases are included in the figure.

Figure 18.6. Scatterplot showing the location of each case on the two rotated components obtained by a factor analysis. Interpretations of the location of cases 1 and 4 are displayed.

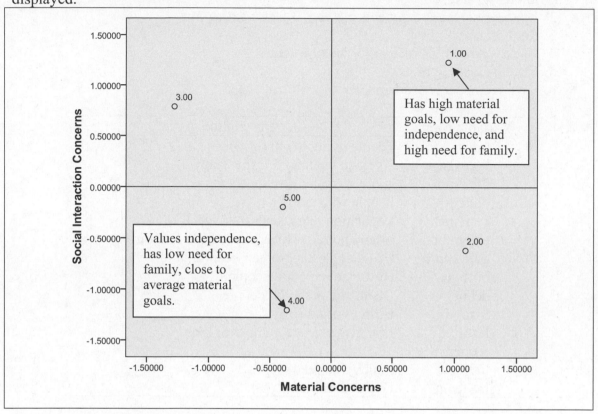

Exercises for Chapter 18

Exercise 18.1

The data file *World95.sav* is located in the SPSS subdirectory of C:\Program Files. It can be opened from the **File** menu in *SPSS* by requesting **Open** then **Data** and, if the proper location is not produced by default, locating it using the drop-down menu available from the **Look in**: window, as shown below:

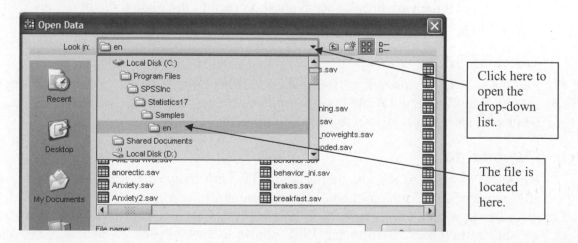

Factor analyze the variables shown in the table below. In performing the analysis
1. Show a table of descriptive statistics for each variable, a correlation matrix, and the KMO statistic.
2. Use a principal components method of factor extraction.
3. Request a scree plot.
4. Use a VARIMAX method of factor rotation.
5. Request loading plots.
6. Save factor scores as variables.

Variable Name	Description
urban	People living in cities (%)
lifeexpf	Average female life expectancy
lifeexpm	Average male life expectancy
literacy	People who read (%)
pop_incr	Population increase (% per year)
babymort	Infant mortality (deaths per 1000 live births)
gdp_cap	Gross domestic product / capita
birth_rt	Birth rate per 1000 people
death_rt	Death rate per 1000 people
b_to_d	Birth to death ratio
fertilty	Fertility: average number of kids
cropgrow	
lit_male	Males who read (%)
lit_fema	Females who read (%)

On the basis of your output for the analysis, answer the following questions.
1. How many countries were included in the analysis?
2. What does the magnitude of the KMO statistic indicate about the data?
3. What two variables had the lowest communality values?
4. How many factors were retained in the analysis?
5. What were the eigenvalues of each retained factor?
6. What proportion of the total variance of the variables in the analysis was accounted for by the combined retained factors?
7. What three variables loaded highest on each of the rotated factors?
8. How would you label (i.e., interpret) each of the rotated factors?

Exercise 18.2

Plot the factor scores saved in Exercise 18.1. Label the data points in the scatterplot using the variable **Country**. Locate the USA in the scatterplot. In terms of the factors you labeled in Exercise 18.1, where does it fit in on these dimensions?

Exercise 18.3

Patricia K. Kerig and Kurt K. Stellwagen at the University of North Carolina at Chapel Hill gathered data from children diagnosed primarily with externalizing behavior disorders at a large psychiatric institution in North Carolina. The data included a 15-item questionnaire (Crick & Grotpeter, 1995) shown in the table below. Each was answered on a scale of 1 to 5 with 1 = Never and 5 = All the Time. Factor analyze the data shown in the file *Ex18.3.sav*. The file is available at the website for this text at the address http://www.pearsonhighered.com/stern2e. The data appear here by permission of Professors Kerig (now at Miami University) and Stellwagen (now at Eastern Washington University). The questions have the variable names **q1** to **q15** in the data file. Arrive at an interpretation of each factor retained in the analysis based on loadings of questions on the rotated factors.

Questions 1-15

1. Some boys/girls tell lies (fibs/make up stories) about a kid so that others won't like that kid anymore. How often do you do this?
2. Some boys/girls try to keep certain people from being in their group when it is time to play or do an activity. How often do you do this?
3. Some boys/girls try to cheer up other kids who feel upset or sad.
4. When they are mad at someone, some boys/girls get back at the kid by not letting the kid be in their group anymore. How often do you do this?
5. Some boys/girls hit other kids. How often do you do this? How often do you do this?
6. Some boys/girls let other know that they care about them. How often do you do this?
7. Some boys/girls help out other kids when they need it .How often do you do this?
8. Some boys/girls yell at other and call them mean names. How often do you do this?
9. Some boys/girls push and shove other kids. How often do you do this?
10. Some boys/girls tell their friends that they will stop liking them unless the friends do what they say. How often do you tell friends this?
11. Some boys/girls have a lot of friends. How often do you have a lot of friends?
12. Some boys/girls try to keep other from liking a kid by saying mean things about the kid. How often do you do this?
13. Some boys/girls wish that they had more friends. How often do you feel this way?
14. Some boys/girls say or do nice things for other kids. How often do you do this?
15. Some boys/girls have a lot of kids who like to play with them. How often do the other kids like to play with you?

Chapter 19: Discriminant Analysis

Introduction

Discriminant analysis can be used to determine whether the classification of cases known to fall into particular groups can be successfully based on each case's score on one or more quantitative variables. For example, assume that a company that sells automobile insurance knows on the basis of records of its customers, which drivers do and do not get into accidents over a 6-year period. Assume, further, that the insurance company has much information about each customer, such as income, age, years of education, number of miles driven per year, and years lived at the current address. Discriminant analysis can be used to determine how successfully the customer information variables (income, age, etc.) can be used to correctly classify these customers into those who have or have not had an accident over the 6-year period. In general, a discriminant analysis can generate one or more rules for classifying cases based on linear combinations of the quantitative variables. Inspecting the composition of the functions can provide an insight into the variables that are most influential in allowing groups to be discriminated from one another.

Huberty (1984) distinguishes between two applications of discriminant analysis. One, predictive discriminant analysis, is intended to discover whether and how effectively groups can be distinguished using a set of predictors. The other, descriptive discriminant analysis, is used to determine an optimal set of predictors that distinguish groups and then to interpret the underlying dimensions that separate the groups. Huberty and Hussein (2003) suggest that when a research question clearly has one of these two intents, different aspects of the outcomes should be emphasized in a report.

An Example

A Single Predictor and Two Groups

Consider the data depicted in Figure 19.1 that lists the IQ scores of two groups of hypothetical people who either don't own (**own** = 1) or own (**own** = 2) a home computer. How could we determine if knowledge of the IQ score of each case can be used to discriminate between those who own or don't own a computer? Notice that in the plot of the IQ data on the number line shown at the top of the right panel of Figure 19.1, the IQ scores of the people who own computers are generally higher than those of the people who don't own computers. Specifically, the mean IQ of all cases is 100, and computer owners generally have IQs above the mean and non-owners generally have IQs below the mean. The analysis begins with the derivation of a discriminant function having a mean of zero (obtained by subtracting the mean of 100 from each IQ score to form the equation $D_i = IQ_i - 100$) and a pooled standard deviation for the groups of one (obtained here by dividing the equation for D_i by the mean standard deviation of the IQ scores in each group--the value 4.082) to form the discriminant function

$$D_i = .245 \times IQ_i - 24.498 .$$

Equation 19.1

The value of D for each case obtained from this formula is shown in the last column in the table in the left panel of Figure 19.1.

How does the function help us? Notice that by having the function centered at zero, we can make the rule that all cases with a positive D value (i.e., cases at or above the mean IQ) belong in one group and all cases with a negative D value belong in the other group. The rule allows us to correctly classify all cases but one.

In a sense, what we have done is locate a discriminating point on the number line that represents IQ by setting our equation for D equal to zero and solving for the value of IQ:

$$IQ = \frac{24.498}{.245} = 100.$$

The dashed line at the bottom of the right panel of Figure 19.1 goes through this point. The dimension used to classify cases is shown as a line (labeled D) that extends at a right angle from the discriminating (dashed) line.

Figure 19.1. Left panel shows data of hypothetical owners and non-owners of computers, their IQ scores, and values of a discriminant function. The top part of the right panel displays the IQs of the owners and non-owners on a number line; at the bottom of the right panel are shown values of a discriminant function D corresponding to the IQ values.

Own	IQ		D	
1	95	s_1=4.082	-1.22	s_1=1.00
1	90		-2.45	
1	100		.00	
1	95		-1.22	
2	100	s_2=4.082	.00	s_1=1.00
2	105		1.22	
2	110		2.45	
2	105		1.22	
	μ=100		μ=0	

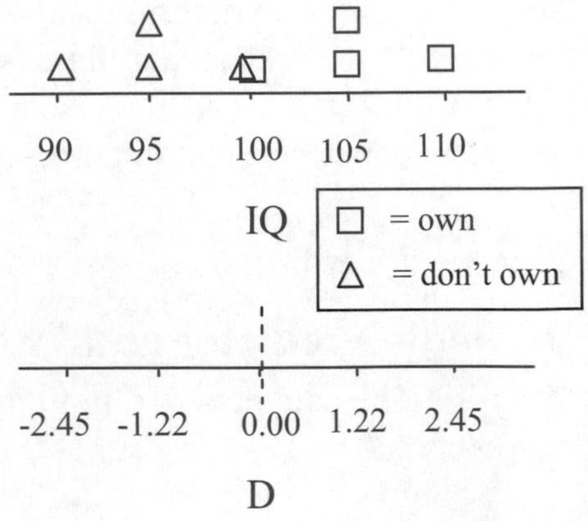

Two Predictors and Two Groups

Consider now an extension of this example that includes a second quantitative variable—years of education—that may contribute to distinguishing cases into a group of computer owners vs. non-owners. Data for the new predictor variable, **YrsEd**, are shown in the table in the left panel of Figure 19.2. A scatterplot of the data appears in the right panel of Figure 19.2. The equation for discriminating owners and non-owners based on each case's values of **IQ** and **YrsEd** produced by the *SPSS* procedure **Discriminant** is

$$D_i = .159 \times IQ_i + .211 \times YrsEd - 18.947. \qquad \text{Equation 19.2}$$

Setting D in this equation to zero and transforming the resulting equation into slope-intercept form ($Y = bX + a$) with **IQ** serving as the x variable and **YrsEd** as the y variable produces the equation

$$YrsEd = -.754 \times IQ + 89.80 \qquad \text{Equation 19.3}$$

The line is plotted as the dotted line in the graph in the right panel of Figure 19.2. The dotted line illustrates the rule for separating cases into groups: cases on opposite sides of the dotted line are classified into different groups. The solid line drawn approximately perpendicular to the dotted line helps illustrate the values of D for each point in the scatterplot. Each point's approximate D value is located on the solid line where a projection from the data point parallel to the dotted line intersects with the solid line.

Figure 19.2. The left panel shows values of two predictors, **IQ** and **YrsEd**, one grouping variable, **Own**, and values of a discriminant function, D, for each of 8 hypothetical cases. The right panel shows a scatterplot of the variables **IQ** and **YrsEd** for owners (squares) and non-owners (triangles). The dotted line in the scatterplot shows the straight line that separates predicted owners and non-owners in the scatterplot; the solid line illustrates the dimension composed of the combined predictors obtained from the discriminant analysis.

Own	IQ	YrsEd	D
1	95	9	-1.93
1	90	12	-2.09
1	100	14	-.08
1	95	12	-1.30
2	100	16	.34
2	105	18	1.56
2	110	20	2.78
2	105	14	.72
	$\mu=100$	$\mu=14.4$	$\mu=0$

Outcome of an Analysis

Number of Discriminant Function

The number of discriminant functions produced by a discriminant analysis is the smaller of the following values: the number of groups minus 1 or the number of predictor variables. Thus, if there are three groups that are to be distinguished, but only a single predictor, then just a single discriminant function can be produced. If there are three groups to be distinguished and 17 predictors, then just two discriminant functions can be produced. The first discriminant function will likely best separate one of the groups from two others combined, perhaps groups 2 from groups 1 and 3 combined, and the second discriminant function—successive discriminant functions are independent of one another--may separate the remaining two, in this example, groups 1 and 3.

Effectiveness of a Discriminant Function

A measure of the degree to which a discriminant function succeeds in discriminating among groups can be based on the correlation of the D values and group membership. The measure is known as a canonical correlation. A canonical correlation is one involving a variable that is derived from a combination of other variables; the discriminant function is such a variable. For the data in Figures 19.1 and 19.2, canonical correlations calculated between the variables **own** and D are .816 and .841, respectively.

When more than one discriminant function is produced, it can be helpful to determine the relative amount of discrimination provided by each function. Eigenvalues (λ) are useful for this purpose. In the context of a discriminant analysis an eigenvalue is the ratio of two sums of squares involving the D values:

$$\lambda = \frac{SS_{Between}}{SS_{Within}}$$
Equation 19.4

These quantities are usually associated with output of an *ANOVA*. If the mean D values for groups shown in Figure 19.1 are compared using an *ANOVA*, the data in Table 19.1 is obtained:

Table 19.1. *ANOVA* table for analyzing mean D values for the two groups shown in Figure 19.1.

	Sum of Squares	df	Mean Square	F	Sig.
Between Groups	12.000	1	12.000	12.000	.013
Within Groups	6.000	6	1.000		
Total	18.000	7			

A single eigenvalue is the quantity 6.00 shown in Table 19.1 as the Within Groups Sum of Squares. In general, because the pooled standard deviation of D values is 1.00, an eigenvalue will equal $N - g$ where N is the total number of cases and g is the number of groups. The eigenvalue of the discriminant function for our example is 2.00 because the between groups sum of squares is 12, a value twice as great as the within groups sum of squares.

An eigenvalue of 0 indicates the D values do not help distinguish among groups at all. However, even small eigenvalues can correspond to sizeable canonical correlations. For example, an eigenvalue of .01 corresponds to a canonical correlation of .10. In general eigenvalues may be converted to canonical correlation values (R^*) with the formula

$$R^* = \sqrt{\frac{\lambda}{1+\lambda}}\,.$$
Equation 19.5

Significance of a Discriminant Function

A question that can be asked when discriminant analysis has been applied to distinguish cases from a sample into groups is whether the analysis discriminates significantly among groups, that is, whether the separation among groups for the sample being analyzed is beyond what could be produced by chance. The question is addressed using Wilks' lambda (Λ) which is the proportion of the total variance in D scores that *is not* explained or accounted for by differences among the groups. Wilks' lambda is measured here with D values as the ratio of the within-groups sum of squares to the total sum of squares (i.e., the sum of the between- and within-group sum of squares):

$$\Lambda = \frac{SS_{Within}}{SS_{Between} + SS_{Within}}.$$ Equation 19.6

When there is no separation among group means, the between groups term will be zero and Wilks' lambda will have its maximum value, 1; when there is a high degree of separation among group means relative to the variation of D within groups, Wilks' lambda will approach its minimum value, 0. Thus small values of Wilks' lambda correspond to a high degree of discrimination among groups. For the data analyzed in Table 19.1, the value of Wilks' lambda is .33. To interpret the value of Wilks' lambda, it may help to note that Wilks' lambda is related to the squared canonical correlation value, $R*^2$, which measures the proportion of variance in D values that *is* accounted for by the variability among groups. Thus, if the squared canonical correlation value is .67, Wilks' lambda will be .33 because the two terms sum to 1.00.

An alternate formula for Wilks' lambda is based on the eigenvalue of a discriminant function:

$$\Lambda = \frac{1}{1+\lambda}.$$ Equation 19.7

If there are several discriminant functions, Wilks' lambda for measuring the combined proportion of residual variance is given by the formula:

$$\Lambda = \frac{1}{1+\lambda_1} \times \frac{1}{1+\lambda_2} \times \frac{1}{1+\lambda_3} \ldots$$ Equation 19.8

The method of testing significance begins with an assessment of the effectiveness of all the discriminant functions combined in distinguishing among the groups; after testing whether all the discriminant functions together explain an amount of variance among the group means that differs significantly from chance, the first (and most effective) discriminant function is removed and the ability of the combined remaining discriminant functions is tested to determine if together they explain an amount of residual variance among the groups that differs significantly from chance. The process repeats until the last discriminant function has been examined.

The significance of Wilks' lambda in this process can be assessed with a χ^2 or F statistic. The formula for χ^2 is a function of the total number of cases (N), the number of predictors (p), the number of groups (g) and Wilks' lambda:

$$\chi^2 = -\left[N - \left(\frac{p+g}{2}\right) - 1\right]\ln\Lambda$$ Equation 19.9

For the kth discriminant function that is removed ($k = 0$ in the first step when no discriminant function is removed), degrees of freedom of the test is $(p-k)(g-k-1)$. For the data shown in Figure 19.1 which had two groups, one predictor, and a single discriminant function that produced a Wilks' lambda of .33, the value of chi-square is

$$\chi^2 = -\left[8 - \left(\frac{1+2}{2}\right) - 1\right]\ln.33 = 6.04.$$

Degrees of freedom of the test is $(1 - 0) \times (2 - 0 - 1) = 1$.

Interpreting Discriminant Functions

Unstandardized Discriminant Function Coefficients. Each discriminant function coefficient specifies how each case's location on a dimension that best separates cases into groups is affected by unit changes in each predictor variable. For example, the discriminant function derived to distinguish computer owners and non-owners based on IQ (Equation 19.1) was found to be $D_i = .245 \times IQ_i - 24.498$. The value .245 is the unstandardized discriminant function coefficient for the predictor **IQ**. The coefficient indicates that for each unit increment in IQ, a person's location on the discriminant function increases by .245 units. In the more complex situation shown in Table 19.2 in which computer ownership status is determined by both IQ and years of education, the function (Equation 19.2) was found to be $D_i = .159 \times IQ_i + .211 \times YrsEd - 18.947$. This equation indicates that both IQ and years of education affect a score's position on the dimension that best separates the two groups: from the unstandardized discriminant function coefficients we can see that a unit change in IQ increases D by .159 units (if **YrsEd** doesn't change), and a unit change in years of education increases D by .211 units (if **IQ** doesn't change).

Standardized Discriminant Function Coefficients. To interpret the relative magnitudes of coefficients in a discriminant function, the variables should first be standardized because the magnitude of a variable's unstandardized coefficient is affected by the units used to measure the variable. The result of applying a discriminant analysis to standardizinged variables (i.e., z-scores) will be a discriminant function with standardized coefficients. If one already has an equation in an unstandardized form, such as Equation 19.2, the conversion from unstandardized to standardized coefficients can be made by multiplying each unstandardized coefficient by the square root of the variable's within-groups sum of squares divided by $N - g$ as shown below:

$$\begin{array}{ccc} Standardized \\ coefficient \end{array} = \begin{array}{c} Unstandardized \\ coefficient \end{array} \times \sqrt{\frac{\sum_{j=1}^{g}\sum_{i=1}^{n}\left(X_{ij} - \overline{X}_g\right)^2}{N-g}} \qquad \text{Equation 19.10}$$

where g is the number of groups,
n is the number of cases in a group,
N is the total number of cases, and
X is the score of case i in group g.

Applying this formula to the unstandardized coefficients in Equation 19.2 gives an equation for D in standardized form:

$$D_i = .650 \times IQ_i + .492 \times YrsEd$$

By examining the magnitude (ignoring the sign) of each standardized coefficient in equations like this, one can determine the relative magnitude of each variable's contribution to the value of D. Thus, in the equation shown above, the net effect of IQ is greater than that of years of education in influencing a case's location on the discriminating dimension.

Structure Coefficients. It should be understood that standardized and unstandardized coefficients in discriminant functions, like the b coefficients in a regression equation, measure the independent effect of each variable on the value of D over and above contributions of all other variables. Thus, the value of a variable's standardized and unstandardized coefficients can change depending on which other variables are used as predictors and the degree of correlation of that variable with the other predictors.

Structure coefficients, unlike the standardized and unstandardized coefficients, are not influenced by a predictor's relation to other predictors. A structure coefficient is the bivariate correlation of a predictor and the D value for each group that is then pooled over all groups. For example, the structure coefficient for **IQ** for the data in Table 19.2 is found by obtaining the r value for **IQ** and D among the computer owners ($r = .90$) and among the non-owners ($r = .92$) and averaging the values ($.91$). A similar process gives a structure coefficient value of approximately $.83$ for **YrsEd**. Thus, the discriminant function shown in Equation 19.2 is strongly correlated with both predictors, but somewhat more strongly with **IQ** than with **YrsEd**. Klecka (1980) suggests that the complex inter-relations among predictors can make structure coefficients better guides to the meaning of a discriminant function that standardized coefficients, though both measures should be considered (Huberty, 1975)

Classifying Cases

An important application of discriminant analysis is to predict group membership based on knowledge of values of predictor variables. In the automobile insurance company example described at the beginning of this chapter, the goal was to use information about a driver to determine whether or not the driver will be involved in an automobile accident. Such predictions can be based on discriminant functions produced by the analysis. For example, the data shown in Figure 19.2 that used IQ and years of education to discriminate between computer owners and non-owners yielded the function $D_i = .159 \times IQ_i + .211 \times YrsEd - 18.947$. Substituting a case's values for **IQ** and **YrsEd** will produce a value of D that, if positive, will suggest the case is an owner and if negative, a non-owner.

When more than one discriminant function is derived and prediction is based on the multiple discriminant functions, classifications are more effectively made by using what are known as Fisher classification functions. There is a separate classification function for each group. The functions provided by *SPSS* for the data given in Figure 19.2 are

$$G_1 = 6.96.9IQ - 4.232YrsEd - 306.883$$
$$G_2 = 7.399IQ - 3.663YrsEd - 358.001.$$

Although derivation and interpretation of these functions is complex, using them is not. One substitutes each case's values of the predictors into each function to yield a value of

G_i. The case is categorized as being a member of the group (as designated by the value of i) that has the highest G value. For example, substituting the IQ value 100 and years of education value 16 into each of these equations (see case 5 in Figure 19.2) yields the value $G_1 = 322.31$ and $G_2 = 323.29$. Because the value of G_2 is higher than the value of G_1, the case is categorized as being a member of group 2, which in this example is a non-owner.

A summary of classification success is provided by *SPSS* in the form of a table that gives the actual and predicted number of cases falling in each grouping category (e.g., owners, non-owners) as well as the actual and predicted percent of cases falling into each group. Figure 19.3, adapted from *SPSS* output, provides this information for the data of Figure 19.2.

Figure 19.3. Actual and predicted number (top 2 x 2 grid) and percent (lower 2 x 2 grid) of cases classified as owners or non-owners of computers based on a discriminant analysis using IQ and years of education as predictors (see Figure 19.2).

	Measure		Predicted Group Membership		Total
			Owner	Non-owner	
	Count	Owner	4	0	4
		Non-owner	0	4	4
Actual Group Membership					
	%	Owner	100.0	0.00	100.0
		Non-owner	0.00	100.0	100.0

100.0% of original grouped cases correctly classified.

How effective will the classification process be when another sample is used? The question is important because the classifications based on a sample of cases whose group membership is already known may overestimate classification accuracy by capitalizing on idiosyncratic errors in the sample that may not be representative of a population. One method of validating the sample result is to split the sample into two subsets. One of the subsets—sometimes advised to consist of relatively more cases—is used to derive classification functions and the other is used to test classification accuracy. This split sample validation approach requires there be sufficient numbers of cases (see below).

Another technique used for this same purpose is called a leave-one-out procedure. With this technique, each case is classified from an equation derived with the case omitted from the data set. This option will be illustrated in the *SPSS* analysis shown below.

Underlying Assumptions

A number of assumptions underlie proper use and interpretation of a discriminant analysis. Some assumptions apply to the number and types of variables utilized. The analysis requires that there be at least two groups each comprised of two or more cases; however, the number of cases in the smallest group should be greater than the number of predictors. Although it is possible to conduct a discriminant analysis with few cases per group, outcomes based on small sample sizes will be highly variable and the variability will be reflected in significance tests of the effectiveness of discriminant functions such as chi-square based on Wilks' lambda. A sensible recommendation is that the number of cases should be about five times the number of predictors. Predictors should be variables measured on interval or ratio scales. For analyses that include dichotomous predictors logistic regression may be appropriate.

There are a number of distributional assumptions for the analysis. If the predictors are related to one another, their relation is assumed to be linear. The assumption can be verified from scatterplots of all pairs of predictors. In addition, the predictors are assumed to have a multivariate normal distribution; that is, at every combination of values of all other predictors, each predictor variable will be normally distributed. This assumption is, in practice, not easily verified, but because individual variables that are not normally distributed will produce violations of the multivariate normal assumption, the distribution of each the individual predictor is examined to verify it is approximately normal. Of particular concern is the presence of outliers; outliers can seriously compromise the ability of an analysis to significantly discriminate among groups.

In addition to assumptions involving predictors as a whole, a discriminant analysis rests on assumptions about the distributions of the predictors and their inter-relations within each set of cases defined by the grouping variable. Specifically, it is assumed that the population variances and covariances among the predictors are the same in each group of cases. The assumption can be examined using the Box's M statistic (see below). If the F value associated with the test is not significant, the assumption is not violated. However, because the test is very sensitive to sample size (the bigger the sample size, the more likely small violations of the equal variance/covariance assumption will be significant), a significant result does not always invalidate interpretation of the results of a discriminant analysis.

A better understanding of the equal within-group variance/covariance assumption can be obtained by referring to the data in Figure 19.2. The equal variance/covariance assumption means that for the computer owners and non-owners 1) the variance of IQ scores is the same; 2) the variance in years of education is the same; and 3) the correlation between IQ and years of education is the same. To check these assumptions, 1) the variance of IQ scores for computer owners and non-owners is obtained (the values are 16.67 and 16.67, respectively); 2) the variance of years of education for computer owners and non-owners is obtained (4.25 and 6.67, respectively); and the r values (a formula for r is the covariance of two variables divided by the square root of the product of the variance of the variables) between IQ and years of education for computer owners and non-owners is obtained (.396 and .632, respectively). Although the variance of IQ scores is identical for the two groups of computer owners, the variance of years of education and the correlation between IQ and years of education differ. Thus, we might expect that the assumption of equal population variances and covariances may not hold, a possibility that can be examined with the Box M statistic.

Requesting a Discriminant Analysis

Form of the Data

For each case in a discriminant analysis there must be a value of the grouping variable and a value for each predictor variable. The grouping variable should consist of integer values that code group membership, usually the values 1, 2, 3, etc., though any arbitrary value can be used. Value labels assigned to each number used to code group membership can be helpful reminders of the coding choices. Each predictor must be represented as a variable. The data of Figure 19.2 coded for analysis by *SPSS* procedure **discriminant** is shown below.

	own	iq	yrsed	va
1	1.00	95.00	9.00	
2	1.00	90.00	12.00	
3	1.00	100.00	14.00	
4	1.00	95.00	12.00	
5	2.00	100.00	16.00	
6	2.00	105.00	18.00	
7	2.00	110.00	20.00	
8	2.00	105.00	14.00	

Requesting the Analysis

Suitable options used in requesting a discriminant analysis are shown below:

1. From the **Analyze** menu select **Classify** then **Discriminant**.

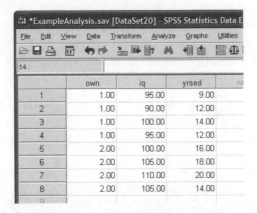

2. Highlight the names of the predictor variables and transfer them to the **Independent(s)** field.

3. Highlight the name of the grouping variable and transfer it to the **Grouping Variable** field.

4. Click **Define Range.**

5. Type in the lowest and highest values used to code the groups you want included in the analysis, here 1 and 2.

6. Click **Continue**.

7. Click **Statistics**.

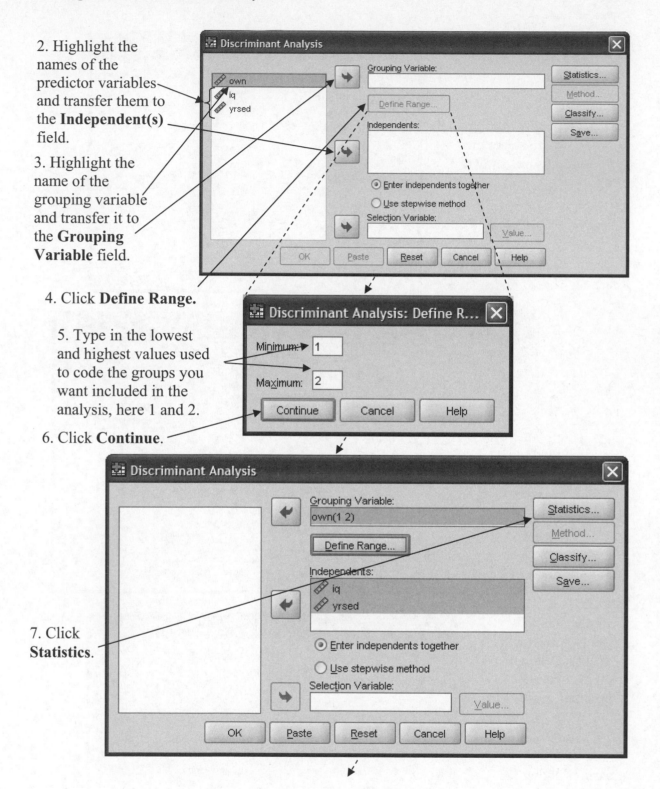

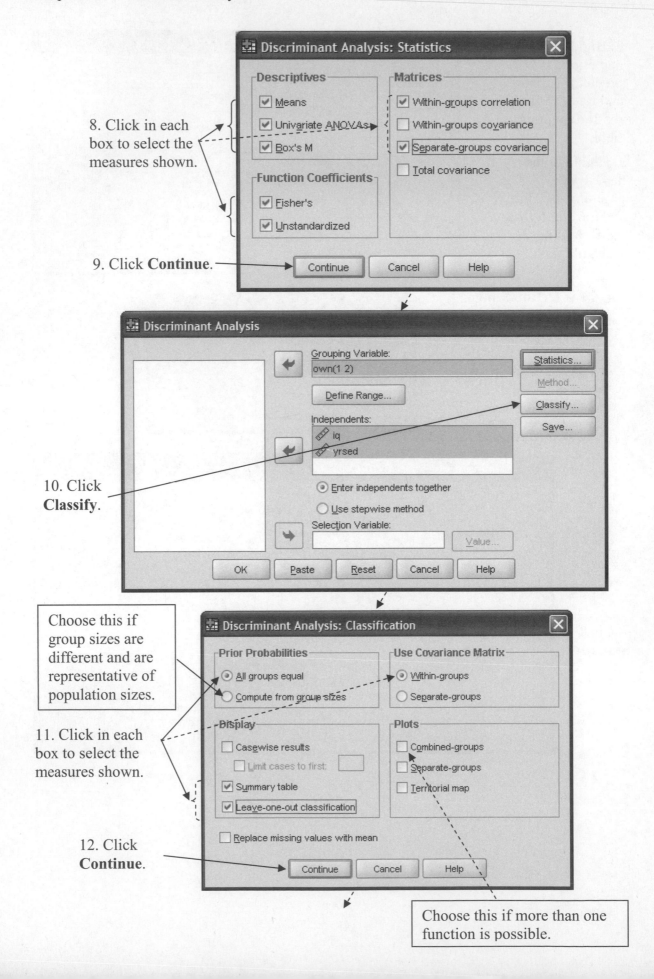

8. Click in each box to select the measures shown.

9. Click **Continue**.

10. Click **Classify**.

Choose this if group sizes are different and are representative of population sizes.

11. Click in each box to select the measures shown.

12. Click **Continue**.

Choose this if more than one function is possible.

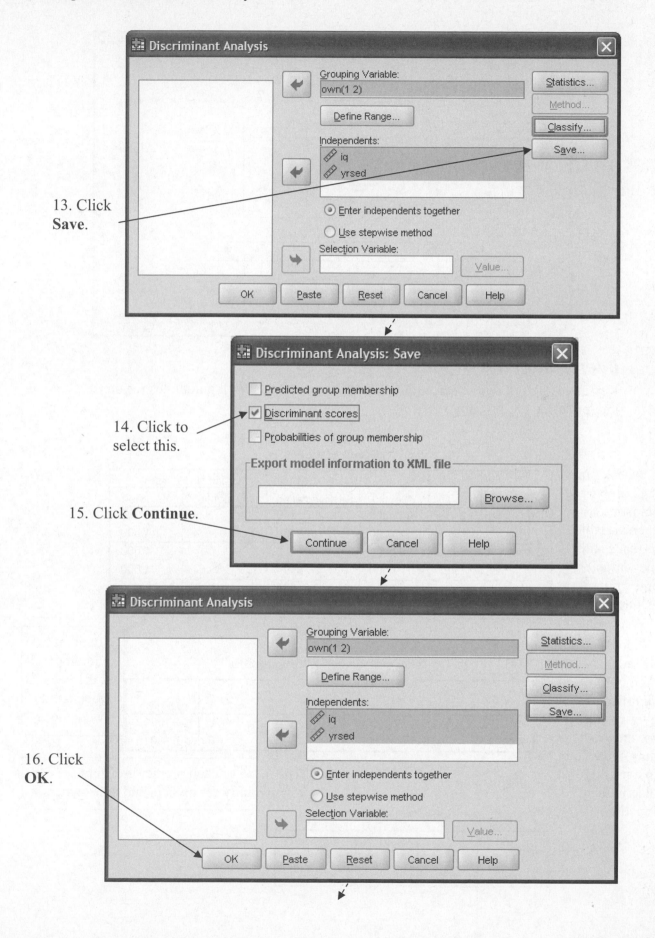

13. Click **Save**.

14. Click to select this.

15. Click **Continue**.

16. Click **OK**.

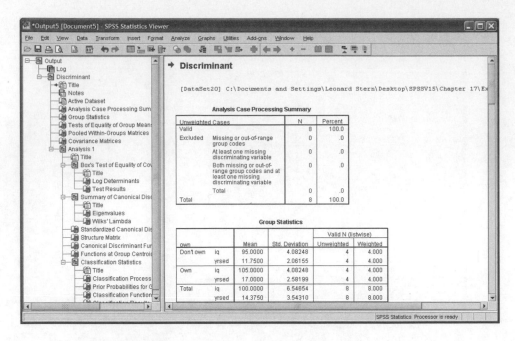

Interpreting the Output

Key tables output by the selections shown above together with guidelines for their interpretation are given next:

Group Statistics

1. Check the descriptive statistics for each variable to make sure the variables and values are as intended.

own		Mean	Std. Deviation	Valid N (listwise) Unweighted	Weighted
Don't own	iq	95.0000	4.08248	4	4.000
	yrsed	11.7500	2.06155	4	4.000
Own	iq	105.0000	4.08248	4	4.000
	yrsed	17.0000	2.58199	4	4.000
Total	iq	100.0000	6.54654	8	8.000
	yrsed	14.3750	3.54310	8	8.000

Note that s_{iq} is identical in the two groups, but s_{yrsed} is not.

2. See if mean of each predictor differs significantly over groups. If so, the predictor may contribute to a useful discriminant function.

Tests of Equality of Group Means

	Wilks' Lambda	F	df1	df2	Sig.
iq	.333	12.000	1	6	.013
yrsed	.373	10.099	1	6	.019

The mean of each predictor differs significantly for owners and non-owners.

Pooled Within-Groups Matrices

		iq	yrsed
Correlation	iq	1.000	.524
	yrsed	.524	1.000

3. Use this table to
help assess validity
of equal within group
variance/covariance
matrices.

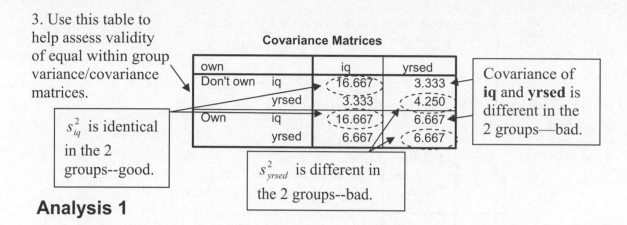

Covariance Matrices

own		iq	yrsed
Don't own	iq	16.667	3.333
	yrsed	3.333	4.250
Own	iq	16.667	6.667
	yrsed	6.667	6.667

s_{iq}^2 is identical
in the 2
groups--good.

Covariance of
iq and **yrsed** is
different in the
2 groups—bad.

s_{yrsed}^2 is different in
the 2 groups--bad.

Analysis 1

Box's Test of Equality of Covariance Matrices

Log Determinants

own	Rank	Log Determinant
Don't own	2	4.090
Own	2	4.200
Pooled within-groups	2	4.189

The ranks and natural logarithms of determinants
printed are those of the group covariance matrices.

4. Look at this table for
a significance test of
the equal within group
variance/covariance
assumption.

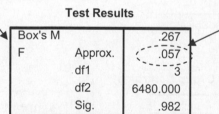

Test Results

Box's M		.267
F	Approx.	.057
	df1	3
	df2	6480.000
	Sig.	.982

Tests null hypothesis of equal population covariance matrices.

A value < .05 may signal significant
violation of the assumption of equal
group variance/covariance matrices,
but the test is overly sensitive with
larger group sizes.

Summary of Canonical Discriminant Functions

5. Look at these
tables to see
how effectively
each function
separates the
groups.

Eigenvalues

Function	Eigenvalue	% of Variance	Cumulative %	Canonical Correlation
1	2.426[a]	100.0	100.0	.842

a. First 1 canonical discriminant functions were used in the
analysis.

Function 1 correlates highly
with *D* values and is
statistically significant.

Wilks' Lambda

Test of Function(s)	Wilks' Lambda	Chi-square	df	Sig.
1	.292	6.157	2	.046

Standardized Canonical Discriminant Function Coefficients

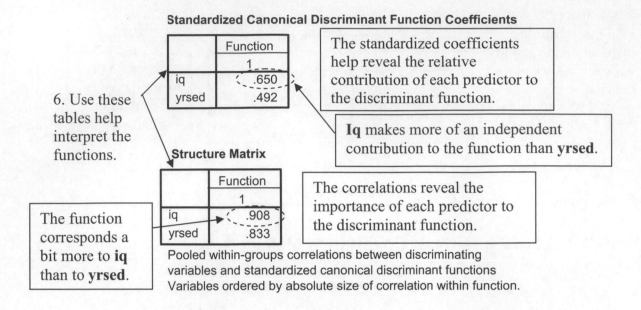

	Function
	1
iq	.650
yrsed	.492

6. Use these tables help interpret the functions.

The standardized coefficients help reveal the relative contribution of each predictor to the discriminant function.

Iq makes more of an independent contribution to the function than **yrsed**.

Structure Matrix

	Function
	1
iq	.908
yrsed	.833

The function corresponds a bit more to **iq** than to **yrsed**.

The correlations reveal the importance of each predictor to the discriminant function.

Pooled within-groups correlations between discriminating variables and standardized canonical discriminant functions
Variables ordered by absolute size of correlation within function.

Canonical Discriminant Function Coefficients

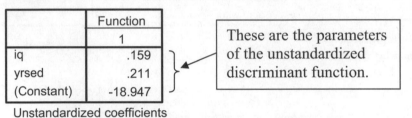

	Function
	1
iq	.159
yrsed	.211
(Constant)	-18.947

Unstandardized coefficients

These are the parameters of the unstandardized discriminant function.

Functions at Group Centroids

	Function
own	1
Don't own	-1.349
Own	1.349

These are the mean *D* values of the groups on the unstandardized function.

Unstandardized canonical discriminant functions evaluated at group means

Classification Statistics

Prior Probabilities for Groups

own	Prior	Cases Used in Analysis	
		Unweighted	Weighted
Don't own	.500	4	4.000
Own	.500	4	4.000
Total	1.000	8	8.000

Classification Function Coefficients

	own	
	Don't own	Own
iq	6.969	7.399
yrsed	-4.232	-3.663
(Constant)	-306.883	-358.001

Fisher's linear discriminant functions

These are the parameters of the Fisher functions that can be used to classify cases into groups.

Classification Results[b,c]

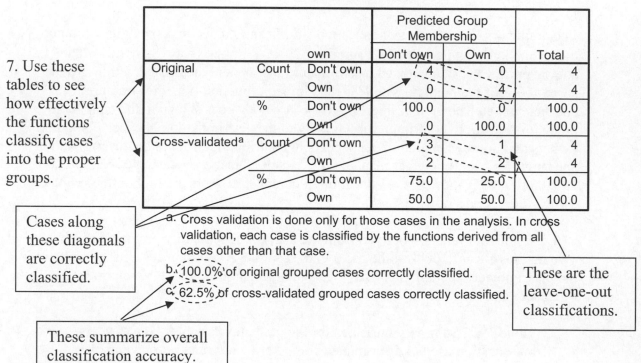

7. Use these tables to see how effectively the functions classify cases into the proper groups.

			own	Predicted Group Membership		Total
				Don't own	Own	
Original	Count	Don't own		4	0	4
		Own		0	4	4
	%	Don't own		100.0	.0	100.0
		Own		.0	100.0	100.0
Cross-validated[a]	Count	Don't own		3	1	4
		Own		2	2	4
	%	Don't own		75.0	25.0	100.0
		Own		50.0	50.0	100.0

Cases along these diagonals are correctly classified.

a. Cross validation is done only for those cases in the analysis. In cross validation, each case is classified by the functions derived from all cases other than that case.

b. 100.0% of original grouped cases correctly classified.

c. 62.5% of cross-validated grouped cases correctly classified.

These are the leave-one-out classifications.

These summarize overall classification accuracy.

Reporting the Results

A summary of the outcome of the discriminant analysis is shown next. Notice that the summary includes a description of the grouping and predictor variables together with descriptive statistics of each predictor variable as a function of group. Also provided is information about whether the underlying assumptions are met and how this is determined. The outcome of the discriminant analysis provides measures of the effectiveness of the discriminant function in distinguishing among groups and a summary of coefficients useful in interpreting the function(s).

A discriminant analysis was performed using *SPSS V17* to determine whether people who own home computers can be distinguished from people who do not own home computers based on the knowledge of each person's IQ and years of education. The analysis was conducted on a sample of four randomly selected people who owned a home computer and a sample of four randomly selected people who did not own a home computer. The two sample sizes are considered representative of the relative sizes of the populations to which the results are intended to generalize. A summary of the means and standard deviations of the predictor variables is shown in Table 19.2 as a function of the grouping variable, computer ownership. Informal analysis of the variables using histograms and scatterplots did not reveal the presence of outliers in the distribution of each predictor, nonlinearity in the relation between the two predictors, or serious violations of the assumption of bivariate normality for the predictors. The value of Box's M approached, but did not reach statistical significance ($p > .05$), an outcome interpreted as indicating no significant violation of the assumption of homogeneity of variance-covariance matrices between the two populations.

The predictors IQ and years of education significantly aided in separating computer owners and non-owners (Wilks' lambda = .29, χ^2 (2, $N = 8$) = 6.18, $p < .05$). The coefficients of the standardized discriminant function and the pooled within-group correlations of the predictors and the discriminant function (i.e., the structure coefficients) are shown in Table 19.3. Based on the values shown in the table, both predictors appear to contribute substantially to the discrimination between computer owners and non-owners, but the independent contribution of IQ to the discrimination appears to be slightly greater than that of years of education. As can be seen in Table 19.2, both the IQ and years of education of computer owners are higher for computer owners than for non-owners.

The discriminant function derived from the analysis successfully predicted computer ownership status of 100% of the cases in the sample. As an indication of the ability of the discriminant function to classify cases in other samples, the leave-one-out procedure correctly classified 62.50 % of the cases.

Table 19.2. Summary measures for the predictor variables IQ and years of education used to discriminate computer owners and non-owners.

Computer Ownership Status	Summary Measure	IQ	Years of Education
Don't own	Mean	95.00	11.75
	N	4	4
	Std. Deviation	4.08	2.06
Own	Mean	105.00	17.00
	N	4	4
	Std. Deviation	4.08	2.58
Total	Mean	100.00	14.38
	N	8	8
	Std. Deviation	6.55	3.54

Table 19.3. Standardized discriminant function coefficients and structure coefficients for the predictors IQ and Years of education.

Predictor	Standardized Function Coefficients	Structure Coefficients
IQ	.65	.91
Years of Education	.49	.83

Another Example

Consider a more complicated discriminant analysis that is applied to three groups. The data coded in the **SPSS Statistics Data Editor** shown below depicts three fictional groups of computer owners: those who have bought a home computer (**own** = 1), those who don't have a home computer (**own** = 2), and those who rent a home computer (**own** = 3). The variables **IQ** and **yrsed** serve as predictors of group membership. Because there are three groups (and two predictors) in the analysis, two discriminant functions are derived.

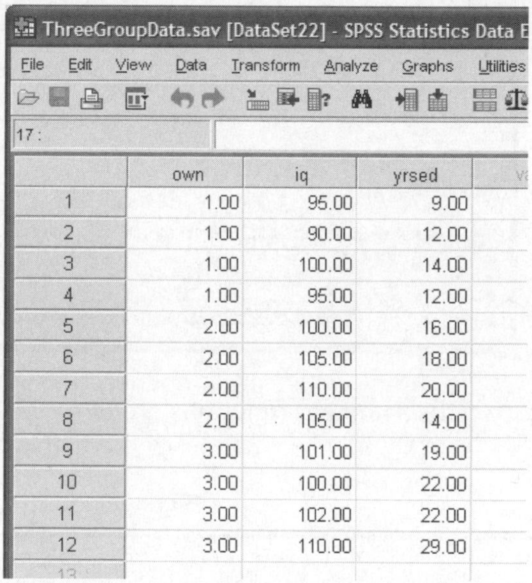

	own	iq	yrsed
1	1.00	95.00	9.00
2	1.00	90.00	12.00
3	1.00	100.00	14.00
4	1.00	95.00	12.00
5	2.00	100.00	16.00
6	2.00	105.00	18.00
7	2.00	110.00	20.00
8	2.00	105.00	14.00
9	3.00	101.00	19.00
10	3.00	100.00	22.00
11	3.00	102.00	22.00
12	3.00	110.00	29.00

The procedure used to request a discriminant analysis for these data is identical to that specified for the two-group case except that the range of values used to define the grouping variable (see step 5 in **Requesting the Analysis**) now is 1 to 3, as shown below:

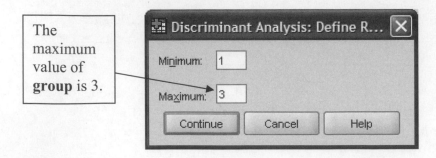

The maximum value of **group** is 3.

In addition, in the **Discriminant Analysis: Classification** window (see step 11) the **Combined-groups** plot is requested:

Select this plot.

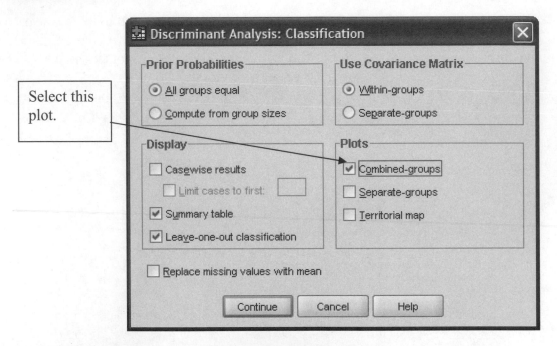

The output shows that two discriminant functions are derived:

These refer to the two functions.

Eigenvalues

Function	Eigenvalue	% of Variance	Cumulative %	Canonical Correlation
1	3.259[a]	74.6	74.6	.875
2	1.109[a]	25.4	100.0	.725

a. First 2 canonical discriminant functions were used in the analysis.

Function 2 is always less important (lower eigenvalue) than 1.

The significance test begins with analysis of both discriminant functions combined; then the function with the highest eigenvalue (function 1) is removed and the significance of the remaining function is evaluated.

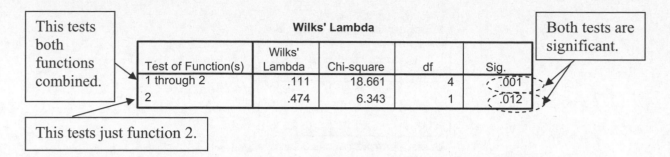

Wilks' Lambda

Test of Function(s)	Wilks' Lambda	Chi-square	df	Sig.
1 through 2	.111	18.661	4	.001
2	.474	6.343	1	.012

This tests both functions combined.

Both tests are significant.

This tests just function 2.

Because both tests shown above in the **Wilks' Lambda** table are significant, we can conclude that functions 1 and 2 are each individually significant.

Interpretation of the functions is made from the standardized and structure coefficients shown in the following two tables:

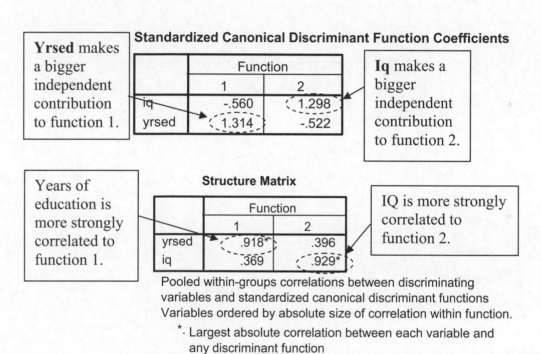

Standardized Canonical Discriminant Function Coefficients

	Function 1	Function 2
iq	-.560	1.298
yrsed	1.314	-.522

Yrsed makes a bigger independent contribution to function 1.

Iq makes a bigger independent contribution to function 2.

Structure Matrix

	Function 1	Function 2
yrsed	.918*	.396
iq	.369	.929*

Years of education is more strongly correlated to function 1.

IQ is more strongly correlated to function 2.

Pooled within-groups correlations between discriminating variables and standardized canonical discriminant functions
Variables ordered by absolute size of correlation within function.

*. Largest absolute correlation between each variable and any discriminant function

Because the value of the standardized coefficient for the predictor years of education is higher in function 1 than that corresponding to IQ, years of education makes a bigger independent contribution than does IQ to function 1. For function 2, IQ makes a relatively bigger independent contribution than does years of education. Thus, as supported by the structure coefficients, function 1 can be thought of as reflecting years of education and function 2 as IQ.

The table labeled **Functions at Group Centroids** shows the mean D value of each group in the 2-dimensional space defined by the discriminant functions. The function 1 values of -1.527 for group 1 and 2.148 for group 3 indicate that function 1, which primarily reflects years of education, is most effective in separating groups 1 and 3. Values of function 2 (which reflects IQ) best distinguishes group 2 from the others.

Functions at Group Centroids

own	Function	
	1	2
1.00	-1.527	-.933
2.00	-.622	1.238
3.00	2.148	-.305

Unstandardized canonical discriminant
functions evaluated at group means

The group centroids defined by the pairs of values shown in the preceding table are plotted below as solid squares. Included in the plot below (requested earlier as the **Combined-groups** option) is the location of each case in each group. Note that high values on function 1 correspond to more years of education and high values on function 2 correspond to lower IQ.

Canonical Discriminant Functions

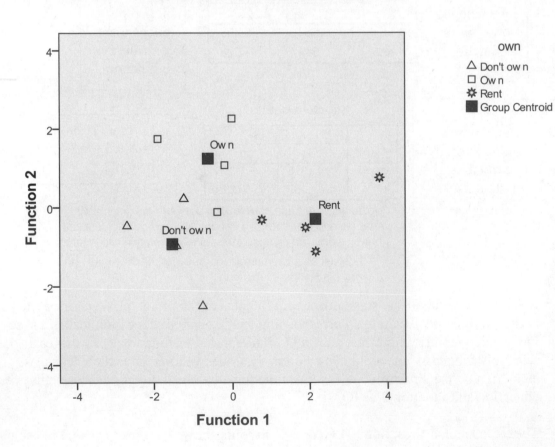

Exercises for Chapter 19

Exercise 19.1

Use the data for the three groups of computer owners shown in the section *Another Example* to perform a discriminant analysis. From the analysis, determine the following:
1. What are the Fisher discriminant functions that can be used to classify each case?
2. What is the overall success rate of classifying the cases in the sample?
3. Overall, how successful will the classifications based on the Fisher functions be on another sample, based on the leave-one-out procedure?
4. What is the predicted classification of each case shown below?

Case #	IQ	Years of Education
1	109	26
2	99	12

Exercise 19.2

The file *World95.sav* is located in the SPSS subdirectory of C:\Program Files. It contains a string variable **religion**. Use **Recode into Different Variables** to make a new numeric variable **RelCat** consisting of the values 0 through 3 that have the correspondence shown below in the second window.

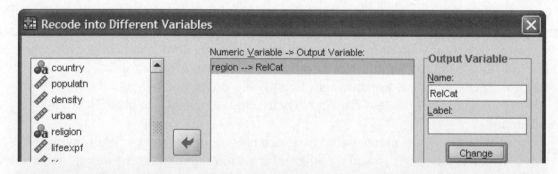

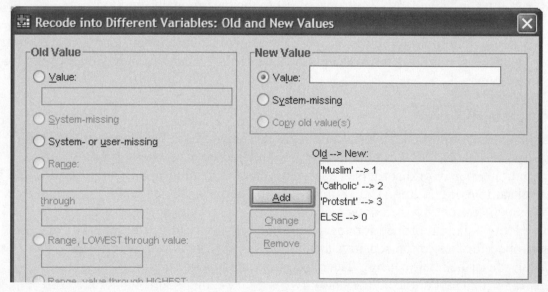

Perform a discriminant analysis to determine the dimensions that best allow religions 1-3 to be distinguished. The table below shows the variable names together with their labels that should be included as predictors in the analysis:

Variable Name	Variable Label
density	Population in thousands
pop_incr	Population increase (% per year))
babymort	Infant mortality (deaths per 1000 live births)
birth_rt	Birth rate per 1000 people
lit_male	Males who read (%)
lit_fema	Females who read (%)
gdp_cap	Gross domestic product / capita

Answer the following questions:
1. Based on the group centroids, which religions are best distinguished by each function?
2. Based on the structure coefficients, what labels might be suitable for describing each dimension?

Exercise 19.3

The file *BodyDimensions.sav*, described earlier in Exercise 11.4, contains measurements of various physical characteristics of healthy male and female adults. Use all the variables except **age** to determine how effectively cases can be classified according to their **gender** (0 = female, 1 = male). In performing the analysis, assume there is an equal proportion of males and females in the population. Report the following information:
1. Does the discriminant function significantly aid prediction of group membership?
2. What is the overall percent correct classification rate using the classification functions?
3. Using structure coefficients, what two variables correlate most strongly with the discriminant function? Based on other information included in the output, which two variables independently contribute most to the discriminant function?
4. Use just the variables obtained as answers to question 3 as predictors of gender. Based on the four predictors what are the answers to questions 1 and 2 above? What equations should be used to determine a person's gender based on values of the four variables?

Exercise 19.4

Data gathered by Patricia K. Kerig and Kurt K. Stellwagen at the University of North Carolina at Chapel Hill was obtained both from children diagnosed primarily with externalizing behavior disorders at a large psychiatric institution in North Carolina and a control sample of children. The 18-item questionnaire (Ayduk et al., 2000) included six questions that probed for anxious rejection sensitivity (see example question 1a in the table below), six that probed for angry rejection sensitivity (e.g., question 1b), and six that probed for a rejection sensitive attributional bias (e.g., question 1c). Perform the analyses described below using data in file *ConductdvsControl.sav*, available at the website for this text at the address http://www.pearsonhighered.com/stern2e. The data appear here by permission of Professors Kerig (now at Miami University) and Stellwagen (now at Eastern Washington University). Do three discriminant analyses. In the first, use the six questions that probed for anxious rejection sensitivity (variables **crsq1_a** – **crsq6_a**) to predict group membership (variable **Category** with values 0 = control, 1 = externalizing behavior disorder). In the second discriminant analysis, use the six questions that probed for angry rejection sensitivity (variables **crsq1_b** – **crsq6_b**) to predict group membership. In the third discriminant analysis, use the six questions that probed for rejection sensitive attributional bias (variables **crsq1_c** – **crsq6_c**) to predict group membership. In conducting the analyses, have the program compute prior probabilities based on group sizes. For each analysis, answer these questions:

1. Does the discriminant function significantly aid prediction of group membership?
2. What is the overall percent correct classification rate using the classification function?

Example Questions

Imagine you are the last to leave your classroom for lunch one day. As you're running down the stairs to get to the cafeteria, you hear some kids whispering on the stairs below you. You wonder if they are talking about YOU.

1a. How NERVOUS would you feel, RIGHT THEN, about whether or not those kids were badmouthing you?

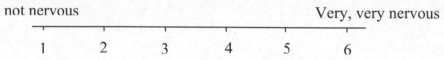

    not nervous   Very, very nervous

        1   2   3   4   5   6

1b. How MAD would you feel, RIGHT THEN, about whether or not those kids were badmouthing you?

    not mad   Very, very mad

        1   2   3   4   5   6

1c. Do you think they <u>were</u> saying bad things about you?

        Yes!!!   NO!!!

            1   2   3   4   5   6

Appendix *A*: Using the *Chart Editor* to Insert a Reference Line and Data Labels

When analyzing data for a regression analysis, it is often helpful to have a reference line at the zero point on the y-axis inserted in the scatterplot that shows standardized predicted values on the x-axis and standardized residual values on the y-axis. It may also be helpful to show labels for selected data points in a scatterplot. Here's how to do this:

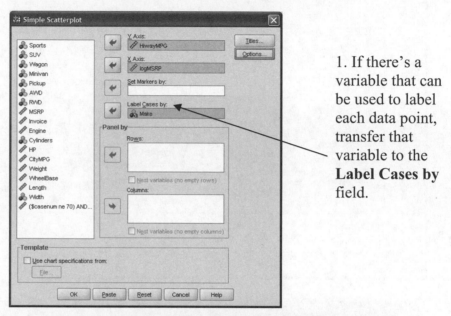

1. If there's a variable that can be used to label each data point, transfer that variable to the **Label Cases by** field.

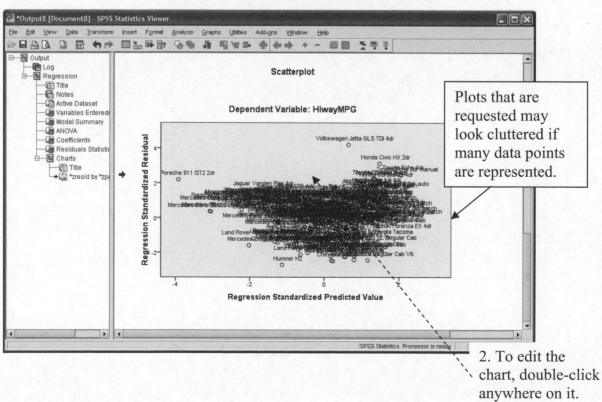

Plots that are requested may look cluttered if many data points are represented.

2. To edit the chart, double-click anywhere on it.

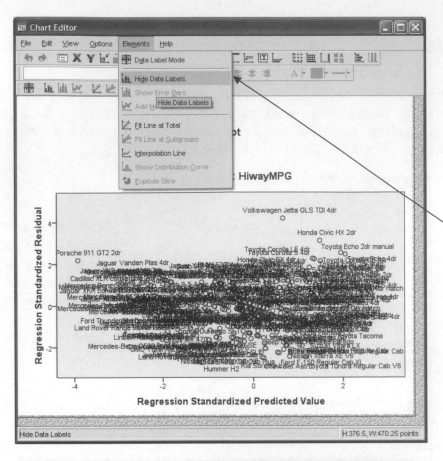

3. In the **Chart Editor** that appears, select **Hide Data Labels** from the **Elements** menu.

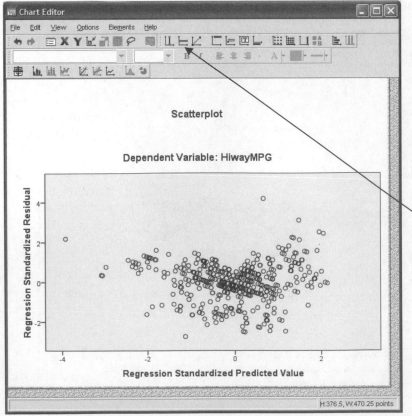

4. To add a reference line through the y-axis, click this button.

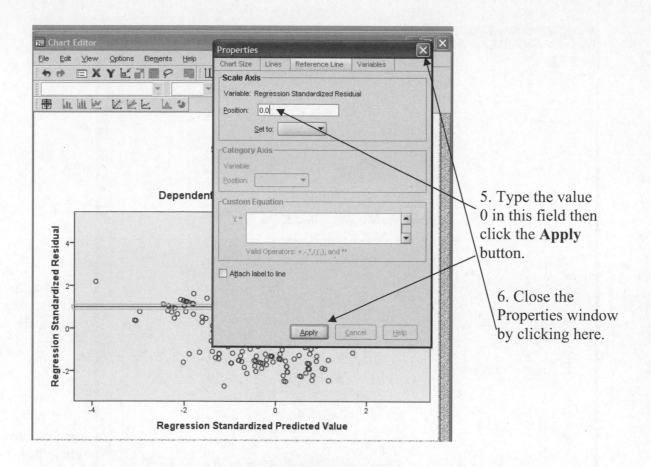

5. Type the value 0 in this field then click the **Apply** button.

6. Close the Properties window by clicking here.

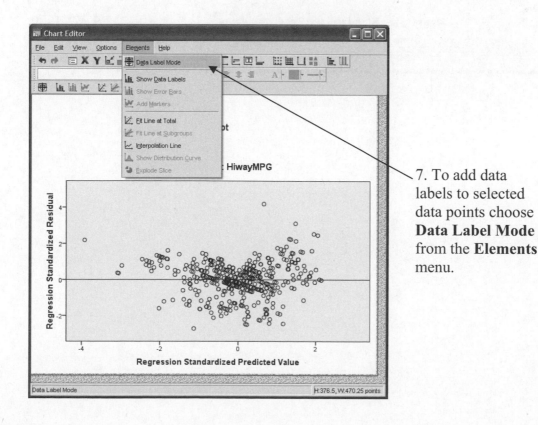

7. To add data labels to selected data points choose **Data Label Mode** from the **Elements** menu.

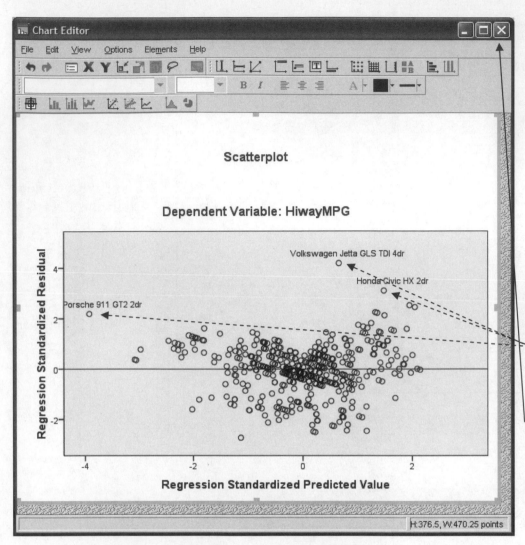

8. Using the data label pointer that appears, click on each point for which a label is desired then click the close box to exit the editor.

Appendix *B*: Using the *Chart Editor* to Add a Title to the X-Axis

An error bar chart that summarizes the data of separate variables will not have a title on the x-axis, as shown below. To add one, follow this procedure:

1. Double-click on the plot to edit it.

2. In the **Chart Editor** select **Text Box** from the **Options** menu.

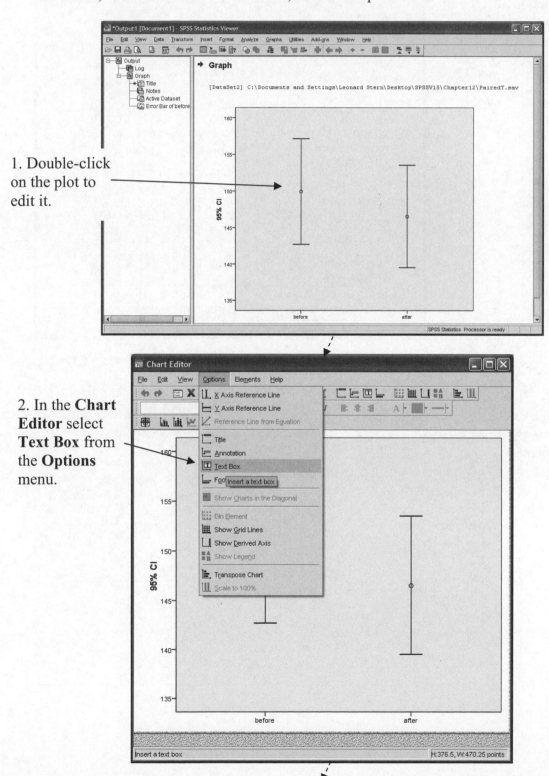

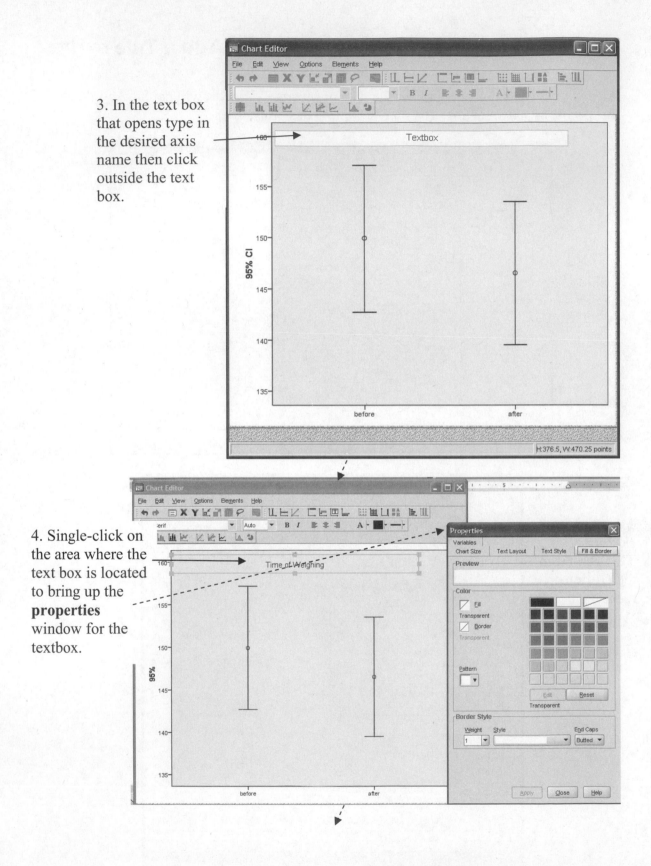

3. In the text box that opens type in the desired axis name then click outside the text box.

4. Single-click on the area where the text box is located to bring up the **properties** window for the textbox.

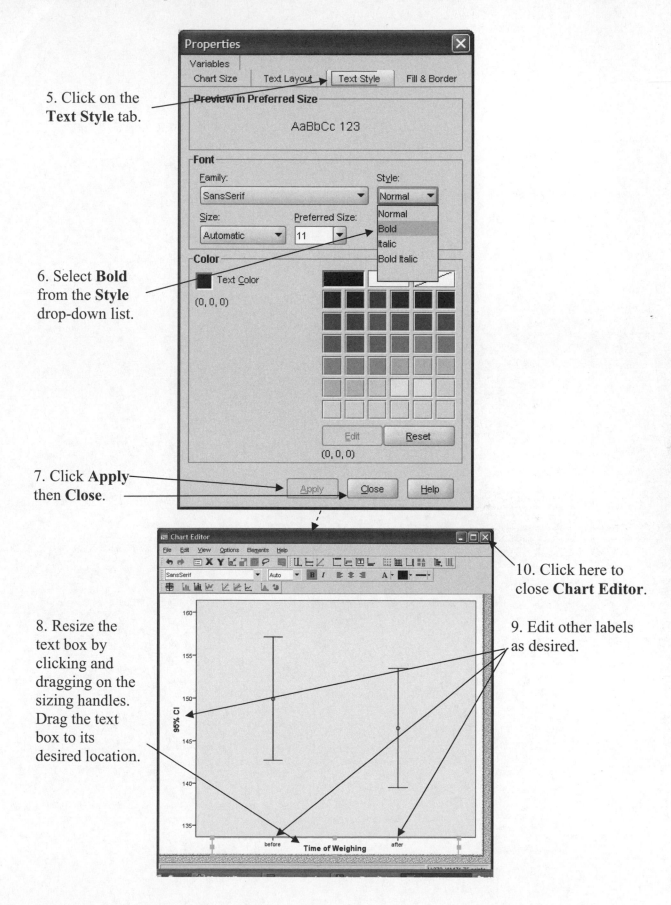

5. Click on the **Text Style** tab.

6. Select **Bold** from the **Style** drop-down list.

7. Click **Apply** then **Close**.

8. Resize the text box by clicking and dragging on the sizing handles. Drag the text box to its desired location.

10. Click here to close **Chart Editor**.

9. Edit other labels as desired.

Appendix *C*: Using *Codebook* to Obtain an Overview of the Variables in a Data File

When an *SPSS* data file has been prepared by someone else, the person inspecting the file may wish to obtain an overview of the variables in the data set, information such as the variable names, the labels given the variables, each variable's measurement scale, the value labels, if any, for each variable, etc. A quick way to do this, one which produces output that can be easily inspected and printed, is to use **Codebook**. Use of this procedure is illustrated for the data file *04cars.sav*.

1. With the data file of interest in the **Data Editor**, select **Reports** then **Codebook** from the **Analyze** menu.

2. Click to highlight the **Variables** tab if it's not already highlighted.

3. Select each variable of interest by clicking on it (use Ctrl-click to select noncontiguous variables) and click here to transfer each selected name

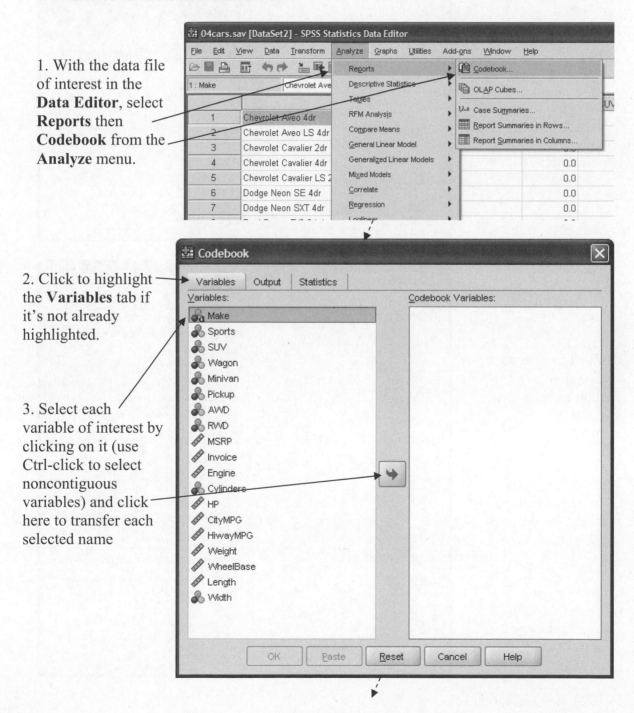

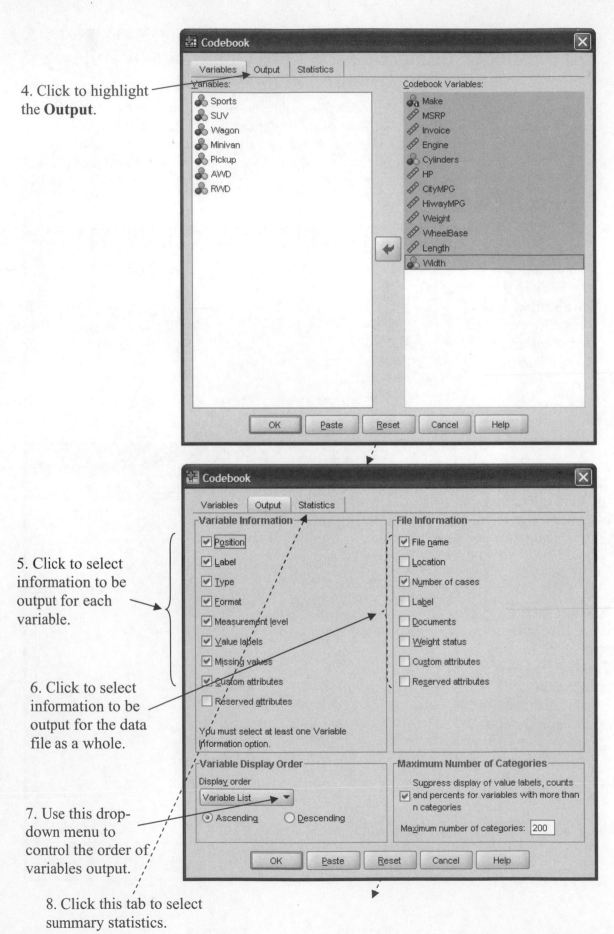

4. Click to highlight the **Output**.

5. Click to select information to be output for each variable.

6. Click to select information to be output for the data file as a whole.

7. Use this drop-down menu to control the order of variables output.

8. Click this tab to select summary statistics.

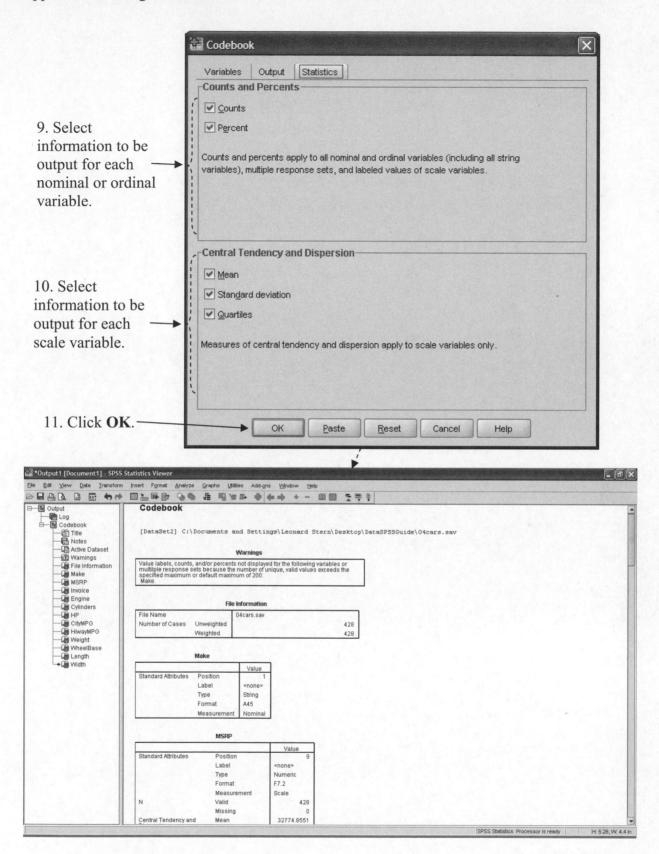

9. Select information to be output for each nominal or ordinal variable.

10. Select information to be output for each scale variable.

11. Click **OK**.

References

Ayduk, O., Mendoza-Denton, R., Mischel, W., Downey, G., Peake, P. K., & Rodriguez, M. (2000). Regulating the interpersonal self. Strategic self-regulation for coping with rejection sensitivity. *Journal of Personality and Social Psychology, 79,* 776-792.

Barber, T. X. (1969). *Hypnosis: A scientific approach.* New York: Van Nostrand Reinhold.

Bliss, C. I. (1967). *Statistics in biology.* Vol. 1. NY: McGraw Hill.

Bottlender, M., Preuss, U. W., & Soyka, M., (2006). Association of personality disorders with Type A and Type B alcoholics. *European Archives of Psychiatry Clinical Neuroscience,* 256, 55-61.

Bradley, J. V. (1968). *Distribution-free statistical tests.* Englewood Cliffs, NJ: Prentice-Hall.

Camilli, G., & Hopkins, G. D. (1978). Applicability of chi-square to 2 x 2 contingency tables with small expected cell frequencies. *Psychological Bulletin, 85,* 163-167.

Card, D., & Krueger, A. (1994). Minimum Wages and Employment: A Case Study of the Fast-Food Industry in New Jersey and Pennsylvania. *The American Economic Review 84,* 772-793.

Cochran, W. G. (1954). Some methods of strengthening the common χ^2 tests. *Biometrics, 10,* 417-451.

Cohen, J. (1988). *Statistical power analysis for the behavioral sciences.* Hillsdale, NJ: Lawrence Erlbaum.

Crick, N. R., & Grotpeter, J. K. (1995). Relational aggression, gender, and social psychological adjustment. *Child Development, 66,* 722.

Crocker, J., Niiya, Y, & Mischkowski, D. (2008). Why does writing about important values reduce defensiveness? Self-affirmation and the role of positive other-directed feelings. *Psychological Science, 19,* (740-747).

David, J. A., & Edwards, A. W. F. (2001). *Annotated readings in the history of statistics.* New York: Springer-Verlag.

DeCarlo, L. T. (1997). On the meaning and use of kurtosis. *Psychological Methods, 2,* 292-307.

Fabrigar, L. R., Wegener, D. T., MacCallum, R. C., & Strahan, E. J. (1999). Evaluating the use of exploratory factor analysis in psychological research. *Psychological Methods, 4,* 272-299.

Galinsky, A. D., Magee, J. C., Inesi, M. W., & Grunefeld, D. H. (2006). Power and perspectives not taken. *Psychological Science, 17,* 1068-1074.

Green, S. B. (1991). How many subjects does it take to do a regression analysis? *Multivariate Behavioral Research, 26,* 499-510.

Guadagnoli, E., & Velicer, W. F. (1988). Relation of sample size to the stability of component patterns. *Psychological Bulletin, 103,* 265-275.

Heinz, G., Peterson, L. J., Johnson, R. W., & Kerk, C. J. (2003). Exploring relationships in body dimensions. *Journal of Statistics Education*, *11*, http://www.amstat.org/publications/jse/v11n2/datasets.heinz.html.

Huberty, C. J. (1975). The stability of three indices of relative variable contribution in discriminant analysis. *Journal of Experimental Education, 4,* 59-64.

Huberty, C. J. (1984). Issues in the used and interpretation of discriminant analysis. *Psychological Bulletin, 95,* 156-171.

Huberty, C. J., & Hussein, M. H. (2003). Some problems in reporting use of discriminant analyses, *The Journal of Experimental Education, 71,* 177-191.

Keppel, G. (1991). *Design and analysis: A researcher's Handbook.* Upper Saddle River, NJ: Pearson-Prentice Hall.

Keppel, G., & Wickens, T. D. (2004). *Design and analysis: A researcher's Handbook.* Upper Saddle River, NJ: Pearson-Prentice Hall.

Klecka, W. R. (1980). *Discriminant analysis.* Beverly Hills: Sage Publications.

MacIntyre, P. D. (1990) Issues and recommendations in the use of factor analysis. *The Western Journal of Graduate Research, 2,* 59-73.

Olson, K. R., Banaji, M. R., Dweck, C. S., & Spelke, E. S. (2006). Children's biased evaluations of lucky versus unlucky people and their social groups. *Psychological Science, 17,* 845-846.

Ruxton, C. H. S., Reilly, J. J., & Kirk, T. R. (1999). Body composition of healthy 7- and 8-year-old children and a comparison with the `reference child'. *International Journal of Obesity, 23,* 1276-1281.

Shoemaker, A. L. (1996). What's normal?--Temperature, gender, and heart rate. *Journal of Statistics* [On-line], *4,* Available: www.amstat.org/publications/jse.

Siegel, S., & Castellan, N. J., (1988). *Nonparametric statistics for the behavioral sciences.* New York: McGraw-Hill.

Slatcher, R. B., & Pennebaker, J. W. (2006). How do I love thee? Let me count the words: The social effects of expressive writing. *Psychological Science, 17,* 660-664.

Tabachnick, B. G., & Fidell, L. S. (2007). *Using multivariate statistics.* Boston: Allyn & Bacon.

Tramo, M.J., Loftus, W.C., Green, R.L., Stukel, T.A., Weaver, J.B., and Gazzaniga, M.S. (1998). Brain size, head size, and IQ in monozygotic twins. *Neurology, 50,* 1246-1252.

Vargha, A., & Delaney, H. D. (2000). A Critique and Improvement of the "CL" Common Language Effect Size Statistics of McGraw and Wong. *Journal of Educational and Behavioral Statistics, 25,* 101-132.

Wickens, T. D. (1989). *Multiway contingency tables analysis for the social sciences.* Hillsdale, NJ: Lawrence Erlbaum.

Zwick, W. R., & Velicer, W. F. (1982). Factors influencing four rules in determining the number of components to retain. *Multivariate Behavioral Research, 17,* 253-269.

Index